ROMANCING THE l

Two hundred years ago the romantic movement precipitated a revolution in aesthetics, sensibility and thought. The neoclassical ethos of order, rectitude and rationality was replaced by an emphasis on creativity, innovation, individuality, spontaneity and imagination.

Marketing, as an academic discipline, is dominated by neoclassical ideals of dispassionate science, 'truth' and objectivity. The international contributors to this volume argue for a neo-romantic approach to Marketing scholarship which will invigorate, infuriate and illuminate the discipline. Subjects covered include:

- luxury, romanticism and consumer desire
- sex, shopping and subjectivity
- the romantic roots of postmodern advertising
- branding in an age of marketing romanticism
- falling in love with segmentation
- the mythopoetic subtext of relationship marketing
- the love affair between researchers and SMEs

Original, provocative and stimulating, *Romancing the Market* is a powerful challenge to the orthodoxies of Marketing.

Stephen Brown is Professor of Retailing at the University of Ulster. **Anne Marie Doherty** lectures in the School of Commerce and International Business Studies at the University of Ulster. **Bill Clarke** is Professor of Export Marketing at the University of Ulster.

ROUTLEDGE INTERPRETIVE MARKETING
RESEARCH SERIES
Edited by Stephen Brown, *University of Ulster, Northern Ireland*,
and Barbara B. Stern, *State University of New Jersey*

Recent years have witnessed an 'interpretive turn' in marketing and consumer research. Methodologies from the humanities are taking their place alongside those drawn from the traditional social sciences. Qualitative and literary modes of marketing discourse are growing in popularity. Art and aesthetics are increasingly firing the marketing imagination.

This series of scholarly monographs and edited volumes brings together the most innovative work in the burgeoning interpretative marketing research tradition. It ranges across the methodological spectrum from grounded theory to personal introspection, covers all aspects of the postmodern marketing 'mix', from advertising to product development, and embraces marketing's principal sub-disciplines.

REPRESENTING CONSUMERS
Voices, views and visions
Edited by Barbara B. Stern

ROMANCING THE MARKET
Edited by Stephen Brown, Anne Marie Doherty and Bill Clarke

ROMANCING
THE MARKET

*Stephen Brown, Anne Marie Doherty
and Bill Clarke*

London and New York

First published 1998
by Routledge
11 New Fetter Lane, London EC4P 4EE

Simultaneously published in the USA and Canada
by Routledge
29 West 35th Street, New York, NY 10001

Typeset in Bembo by
M Rules
Printed and bound in Great Britain by Redwood Books, Trowbridge, Wiltshire

British Library Cataloguing in Publication Data
A catalogue record for this book is available from the British Library

Library of Congress Cataloguing in Publication Data
Romancing the Market/edited by Stephen Brown, Anne Marie Doherty, and Bill Clarke.
p. cm. – (Interpretive marketing research series)
Includes bibliographical references and index.
1. Marketing–Congresses. 2. Romanticism–Congresses. I. Brown, Stephen.
II. Doherty, Anne Marie. III. Clarke, Bill. IV. Series.
HF5411.R66 1998   98-4028
658.8–dc21   CIP

ISBN 0-415-18417-7 (hbk)
ISBN 0-415-18418-5 (pbk)

The Crime of the Ancient Marketer

Journals, journals everywhere,
And not a board did shrink;
Journals, journals everywhere,
Nor any thought to think.

Down dropt the books, the books dropt down,
'Twas sad as sad could be;
And we did speak but could not break
The salience of the P!

The marketer, whose eye is dull,
Whose beard with age is hoar,
Is gone: and now the practitioner
Turned from the ivory tower.

He went like one that hath been stunned,
And is of course forlorn:
A smarter and a wiser man,
He chose the morrow morn.

CONTENTS

CONTENTS

ILLUSTRATIONS

Figures

Tables

CONTRIBUTORS

Eric J. Arnould is Associate Professor of Marketing at the University of South Florida, Tampa, Florida, despite the fact that he holds a PhD degree in social anthropology from the University of Arizona. He teaches courses in consumer behaviour, international marketing, and research employing qualitative data. The long-term themes of his research fall into the following categories: diffusion of innovations, channels structure and market organisation in West Africa, household organisation, consumption ritual, services marketing and economic development. To his enduring surprise, Dr Arnould's work appears in the three major US marketing journals, as well as other marketing and social science periodicals and books. Dr Arnould is an outdoor enthusiast, speaks French and Hausa, and enjoys being a parent.

Russell W. Belk is N. Eldon Tanner Professor of Marketing in the David Eccles School of Business at the University of Utah. He has taught there since 1979 and has had previous appointments at the University of Illinois, Temple University, the University of British Columbia, the University of Craiova, Romania, and Edith Cowan University, Perth, Australia. His PhD is from the University of Minnesota. He is Past President of the Association for Consumer Research, and a Fellow of the American Psychological Association, the Society for Consumer Psychology, and the Association for Consumer Research. He has written and edited fifteen books or monographs, and has published over 200 articles and papers. His research primarily involves the meanings of possessions and materialism and his methods have been increasingly qualitative and cross-cultural.

Stephen Brown. Not many marketing academics can claim to have wrestled a fully-grown lion, bungee jumped from the top of Sears Tower, raced in the Indie-Car 500, discovered a cure for the common cold and circled the earth in the Mir space station. Neither can Stephen Brown. A shy and retiring, yet immensely engaging, Irishman, Stephen is modest to a fault, adored by his wife and family, and full of the milk of human kindness. But only on blue moons. The rest of the time, he is a monstrously egotistical, foul-mouthed, ill-tempered misanthrope who harangues his spouse, terrorises the kids and maltreats assorted domestic livestock (anything smaller than himself, basically) if they so much as squeak when he's trying to write. No one knows why Stephen gets so agitated since he's never been published in the principal academic journals and his books remain resolutely unsold, though he has high hopes for *Romancing the Market*. Some people never learn.

Bill Clarke is Head of the School of Management at the University of Ulster. A romantic at heart, he empathises strongly with the captain of the *Titanic*, who he nevertheless believes should have done better, having had only one iceberg to deal with. Consumed with angst that this is an insufficient overall contribution, he further attempts to justify his salary by teaching International Marketing at both undergraduate and post-graduate level, even though as a result of his own research in this field he is currently deconstructing much of what he teaches. In true romantic style, he is content in his own contradictions, equally at home with Bach, Brahms and Brubeck. He would probably be much happier sending postcards from the edge of a wild and windswept beach in the West of Ireland, but his logically positive analysis of the likely future direction of marketing education makes him worry vaguely that he might end up doing just that rather sooner than originally planned.

Anne Marie Doherty is Lecturer in the School of Commerce and International Business Studies at the University of Ulster, Coleraine, Northern Ireland. Her research focuses on retailer internationalisation and retailer market entry mode strategy. Previously, she helped organise the Marketing Education Group Annual Conference (1994) and the Marketing Eschatology Retreat (1995), hosted by the University of Ulster. She is currently the Ireland Regional Chair of the Academy of Marketing (UK).

Benoît Heilbrunn teaches marketing and consumer behaviour at the Groupe ESC Lyons and at Université Paris III-Sorbonne. His areas of interest include philosophy, semiology, aesthetics and their possible infusion in marketing thought. He is an editor of *European Perspectives in Consumer Behaviour*, published by Prentice-Hall.

Morris B. Holbrook is the W.T. Dillard Professor of Marketing, Graduate School of Business, Columbia University, New York, where he teaches courses in communication and in consumer behaviour. Recent books include: *Daytime Television Game Shows and the Celebration of Merchandise: The Price is Right*; *The Semiotics of Consumption: Interpreting Symbolic Consumer Behavior in Popular Culture and Works of Art* (with Elizabeth C. Hirschman); *Postmodern Consumer Research: The Study of Consumption as Text* (with Elizabeth C. Hirschman); and *Consumer Research: Introspective Essays on the Study of Consumption*.

Christian Jantzen is Associate Professor at the Department of Communication, Aalborg University, Denmark, where he teaches media and cultural theory. He graduated from Rijksuniversiteit Utrecht and Odense University, Denmark, and obtained a PhD degree at Aalborg University in cultural analysis. His research is in the fields of market communication and cultural theory and analysis. His works are primarily in Danish, and he is currently working on a book on how to study cultural phenomena.

Pauline Maclaran is Senior Lecturer in Marketing at the School of Management, the Queen's University of Belfast. Prior to becoming an academic she worked in industry for many years, initially in marketing positions and then as a founder partner in her own business. Her main research interests are: feminist perspectives and gender issues in marketing and the theoretical and philosophical assumptions therein; and the utopian dimensions of contemporary consumption, as displayed in festival shopping malls.

Andrew McAuley completed his PhD on the attraction of new firms to the former Notts–Derbys Intermediate Area in 1985, before taking up an appointment as Research Assistant in the Department of Geography, University of Lancaster. He has since joined the Department of Marketing at Stirling University. His main academic interests are in small business and exporting. More importantly, he is a keen painter who takes inspiration from Van Gogh, standing stones and his own demons. Thus he follows a kind of artistic cycle of eating, drinking, painting, getting depressed, writing poetry, eating, drinking and being merry!

Per Østergaard is Associate Professor at the Department of Marketing, Odense University, Denmark. He holds degrees in social science and philosophy from Odense University, and a PhD in marketing from Odense University. His research interests include interpretive consumer research, qualitative methods, and philosophy of science.

Cele Otnes received her PhD from the University of Tennessee, her MA from the University of Texas at Austin, and her BA from Louisiana State University. Before joining the faculty at the University of Illinois, Otnes spent time as a freelance copywriter and producer. Her current research entails the discovery of how information sources are used within the context of consumers' participation in consumption rituals and understanding the necessary and desired elements of consumption rituals. She has published many papers in various journals including the *Journal of Advertising*, *Journal of Consumer Research*, *Journalism Educator*, *Journal of Popular Culture*, *Journal of Business Research* and *Journal of Ritual Studies*.

Paul Power, PhD student at Rutgers School of Communication, Information, and Library Studies, received his MBA from Rutgers Graduate School of Management in 1981. He has been a marketing professional for over twenty-five years, working in positions in publishing, consumer products, and telecommunications. For the past fifteen years he has been in television syndication and is currently Vice President, Research, with King World Productions.

Linda L. Price is Professor of Marketing at the University of South Florida. Prior to her present position, she was an associate professor of Marketing at the University of Colorado, and before that an assistant professor at the University of Pittsburgh. Dr Price has published over fifty research papers in areas of marketing and consumer behaviour. Her papers appear in major marketing and management journals such as *Journal of Marketing, Journal of Consumer Research* and *Organization Science*. Her research focuses on consumers as emotional, imaginative and creative agents and on the relational dimensions of consumers' behaviours. Linda is the mother of a 3-year-old girl, and enjoys running, hiking, skiing and other outdoor activities.

Barbara B. Stern is Professor of Marketing at Rutgers, the State University of New Jersey, Faculty of Management, Newark. She has published articles in the *Journal of Marketing, Journal of Consumer Research, Journal of Advertising, Journal of Consumer Marketing, Journal of Promotion Management, Journal of Current Research in Advertising*, and other publications. Her research has introduced principles of literary criticism into the study of marketing, consumer behaviour, and advertising. Additionally, she has focused on gender issues from the perspective of feminist literary criticism, using feminist deconstruction to analyse values encoded in advertising text.

Lorna Stevens is Lecturer in Marketing in the School of Commerce and International Business Studies at the University of Ulster, Magee. Prior to embarking on her academic career she worked for ten years as an editor in the book publishing industry in Dublin, Belfast and London. Her research interests lie in the area of feminist perspectives and gender issues in marketing and consumer behaviour, including postmodern perspectives on consumption and popular culture. She is currently undertaking a PhD on women's consumption of magazines.

Craig J. Thompson is Associate Professor of Marketing at the University of Wisconsin-Madison. He received his doctorate in marketing from the University of Tennessee in 1992. His research focuses on the use of hermeneutical methodologies in marketing, gender differences between consumers, media effects on consumer perceptions and body images, and the symbolic aspects of consumption. His articles have been published in the *Journal of Consumer Research, Journal of Marketing Research, Journal of Public*

Policy and Marketing, Culture, Markets, Consumption, Journal of Advertising, Psychology and Marketing, International Journal of Research in Marketing, European Journal of Marketing, and *Advances in Consumer Research.*

Robin Wensley is Professor of Strategic Management and Marketing at the Warwick Business School and was Chair of the School from 1989 to 1994. He is also currently Chair of the Faculty of Social Studies. He was previously with RHM Foods, Tube Investments and the London Business School and was visiting Professor twice at UCLA and the University of Florida. His research and consultancy interests include marketing strategy and planning, investment decision-making and the assessment of competitive advantage. In this regard he has published a number of books and articles in the *Harvard Business Review,* the *Journal of Marketing* and the *Strategic Management Journal* and worked closely with other academics and practitioners both in Europe and the USA. He is on the Editorial Board of the *International Journal of Research in Marketing* and has twice won the annual Alpha Kappa Psi award for the most influential article in the US *Journal of Marketing.*

BY WAY OF A PRELUDE

The charge of the light brigade

If Alfred, Lord Tennyson were with us today – and, God knows, he probably is, albeit as one of the past lives of a New Age town planner from Penge – he would doubtless be deeply moved by the contents of *Romancing the Market*. So much so, that I can just imagine him sitting down at his escritoire, setting aside that second-rate slab of homoerotic hackwork, *In Memoriam*, and dashing off the following immortal lines: Half a page, half a page,/Half a page onward,/Into the volume of dearth/Rode the six hundred. Critics to the right of them,/Critics to the left of them,/Into the valley of debt/Rode the six hundred. When can their credit limit fade?/O the wild charge card they made!/All the world wide web wonder'd./Barnes and Noble six hundred!

Well, okay, maybe not. As acts of valour go, this volume is hardly the academic equivalent of the heroic failure of Cardigan's finest at Balaclava (it's not even a marketing muff, an acrylic marketing muff). Nor, let's be honest, is it likely to be perused by more than six hundred scholars, however noble. (You're heard of the thin read line? That's us!) Our more conservative colleagues, what is more, are almost certain to come up with comments of the *C'est magnifique, mais ce n'est pas le marketing* variety. Come back, Marshal Bosquet, all is forgiven.

Still, it seems to me that we academics – the canon fodder of post-industrial society – have something to learn from the likes of Alfred, Lord Tennyson. In our fragmented, de-centred, hyper-real, ever-accelerating *fin de siècle* marketing milieu, where mechanistic, technocratic, pseudo-scientific models of analysis, planning, implementation and control no longer seem to 'work', a radically different approach to marketing understanding is urgently required. For many contemporary commentators, poets, novelists, creative artists and their copious late twentieth-century avatars – journalists, movie makers, television producers, stand-up comedians, etc. – can provide insights into the post-human condition that are as good as *if not better* than those derived from more established scholarly sources. And it is the contention of this book that marketing has as much to gain from William Blake's grain of sand as Isaac Newton's *Principia Mathematica*.

Such suggestions, of course, are not new. The case for humanities-led marketing research has already been made – and cogently made – by several of the contributors to *Romancing the Market*, although the message bears repeating. What's more, the notion that creative writers and artists are blessed with what Ernst Bloch terms 'anticipatory illumination', an ability to articulate the as-yet-inarticulate, to make the inchoate cohere, has been around for a very long time. Since the time of Tennyson, in point of fact. Although he is not normally classified as a romantic poet (albeit his early work was heavily influenced by Coleridge and Keats, his immediate predecessors), Tennyson was part of that profound nineteenth-century revolution in consciousness known as romanticism or the romantic movement. Romanticism has been defined in a host of ways, but a central component is the enormous emphasis it placed upon the imagination, the inspiration, the inner light of the creative writer and artist. The work of the romantics didn't so much passively reflect as actively illuminate that to which it referred. Illumination, as Abrams rightly observes, is the apotheosis of romanticism.

Illumination, to be sure, is a wonderful word. Apart from its connections to the romantic movement, it carries connotations of Arthur Rimbaud, secret societies, stained-glass windows, medieval scriptoria, illuminated manuscripts, Walter Benjamin and, Heaven help us, the recent comeback album by 1970s' rock band, Wishbone Ash. For many Britons, moreover, illumination is evocative of Blackpool, that vulgarian of urbanism, that *civitas* of the carnivalesque, that municipality of marketing. Blackpool, in many ways, is a perfect metaphor for marketing scholarship. It came to prominence approximately 100 years ago; it reached its peak in the late 1950s–early 1960s; and, according to some authorities, it is in terminal decline despite increasingly desperate attempts to add to its attractions ('roll up, roll up, Relationship Marketing, the biggest white elephant in the world'). Marketing practice, what is more, has long been characterised by the irreverent, bawdy, candy-flossed, end-of-the-pier, saucy picture postcard, dirty weekend spirit that is embodied, indeed epitomised, by Blackpool ('buy one get one free', 'I can't believe it's not butter', 'FCUK' and, naturally, 'Beaver España').

These associations, then, formed the basis of a Marketing Illuminations Spectacular, which was held – paradoxically enough – at St Clement's Retreat House in the hills overlooking Belfast, Northern Ireland. During a three-day period in September 1997, the light brigade of marketing scholarship (*c.* 60 rather than 600 in number) cantered into the valley of disciplinary death, impetuously charged the batteries of the field and, as this volume of essays testifies, lived to tell the tale in a suitably romantic fashion. Theirs not to make reply,/Theirs not to reason why,/Theirs but to do or die,/Rode the outnumbered.

Romanticised perhaps, eccentric undoubtedly, but these ballads of marketing's light brigade would not have been possible without the heroic endeavours of the contributors, who revised and returned their chapters in double quick time. The Marketing Illuminations Spectacular was brilliantly administered by my colleagues and co-editors, Anne Marie Doherty and Bill Clarke, for which

I am very grateful. I would also like to extend my heartfelt thanks to Stuart Hay and Craig Fowlie of Routledge, both for keeping an eye on us at the Spectacular and supporting this admittedly unconventional academic venture (though I prefer to consider it 'windswept and interesting'). Susan Dunsmore, copy-editor extraordinaire, kept me on the right side of the laws of grammar (and libel!); my esteemed colleagues Pat Ibbotson and Lorna Stevens helped with the difficult task of assembling the final manuscript and, as the MS deadline loomed, my ever-loving wife, Linda, wisely took herself off on a West End shopping spree. Thank you all (I can't believe I've just written that).

Love, so you see, is not dead and it is entirely fitting that I should be composing this hopelessly romantic preface (well, hopeless, certainly) about the romanticism of marketing on St Valentine's Day, of all days. Not only does St Valentine's Day epitomise the commercialisation of love – marketing the romance, so to speak – but the festival commemorates an early Christian priest, who was beheaded in 269CE for conducting the marriage ceremonies of covert lovers, though some say it was because he cured and converted the blind daughter of a Roman official. Yet others maintain that it was Valentine's voluminous outpouring of inflammatory letters and pamphlets during his incarceration – hence the tradition of sending cards – that precipitated the death penalty. Be that as it may, this combination of decapitation, deception and discourse, with just a *frisson* of Levittite astigmatism, cannot fail to send shivers down the spine of late twentieth-century marketing scholars. I'm not sure if this book will give its market a romantic textual tingle or whether it will be dismissed as light, all-too-light reading – the Mills and Boon of the marketing academy – but hopefully it will illuminate some of the intriguing connections between romanticism and marketing. Marketing, remember, is for lovers. Here endeth the prefatorial billet-doux.

Stephen Brown
Coleraine
14 February 1998

1

STONING THE ROMANCE

On marketing's mind-forg'd manacles

Stephen Brown, Anne Marie Doherty and Bill Clarke

> I wander thro' each charter'd street,
> Near where the charter'd Thames does flow,
> And mark in every face I meet
> Marks of weakness, marks of woe.
>
> In every cry of every Man,
> In every Infant's cry of fear,
> In every voice, in every ban,
> The mind-forg'd manacles I hear.
> William Blake, *Songs of Innocence and Experience*

Bliss was it

Two hundred years ago, a brace of young poets, William Wordsworth and Samuel Taylor Coleridge, scandalised polite society when they published the first edition of their poetic manifesto, *Lyrical Ballads* (Brett and Jones 1991). Inspired, in part, by the emancipatory euphoria that accompanied the unfurling of the French Revolution, and containing such never-to-be-forgotten (once-learnt-by-rote) classics as *Tintern Abbey* and *The Rime of the Ancient Mariner*, *Lyrical Ballads* ushered in a whole new era of Western culture, commonly known as romanticism or the romantic movement (Day 1996). True, Wordsworth and Coleridge didn't actually employ the term 'romantic' (Furst 1971). The word and its cognates, what is more, were in widespread use prior to 1798 (Sanders 1996). Indeed, the originality of *Lyrical Ballads* has also been called into question, as has the extent of the controversy surrounding its publication (Ashton 1996). Nevertheless, it is generally acknowledged that, thanks in no small part to Wordsworth and Coleridge, the dog days of the eighteenth century witnessed a revolution in aesthetics, in sensibility, in thought. Not only did this represent, as Berlin (1991: 209) rightly records, 'the largest shift in European consciousness since the Reformation', but romanticism is still with us in the shape of our own great '-ism', our -ism *in excelsis*, the *nulli secundus* of -isms, *postmodernism* (Elam 1992; Livingston 1997; Readings and Schaber 1993).

The basic problem with -isms, of course, is isn't (Brown 1995). That is to say, when it comes to -isms there isn't a single, satisfactory, all-encompassing, universally agreed definition, or even agreement on the fact that there isn't a single, satisfactory, all-encompassing, universally agreed definition of the -ism in question. Whether it be realism, relativism, conservatism, liberalism, idealism, empiricism, communism, capitalism, fascism, feminism, gnosticism, aestheticism, asceticism, athleticism, mysticism, mesmerism, masochism, modernism, marxism, malapropism or any other '-ism' that those mad for macaronicism, liable to lexiphanicism or smitten by sesquipedalianism are inclined to conjugate, the only thing that everyone knows for certain is that there is no certainty about the thing everyone 'knows'. The ism isn't.

The same is true of romanticism, a subject which has been subject to all manner of competing definitions ranging from Rousseau's 'return to nature', through Pater's 'the addition of strangeness to beauty', to Phelps's 'sentimental melancholy' (see Furst 1971). How, for that matter, can we possibly forget Goethe's contention that 'romanticism is disease' (young Werther has a lot to be sorrowful for), Ker's suggestion that it represents 'the fairy way of writing' (not in this neck of the woods, buster!), and Fairchild's cryptic confabulation that romanticism comprises 'a desire to find the infinite within the finite, to effect a synthesis of the real and the unreal, the expression in art of what in theology would be called pantheistic enthusiasm' (keep taking the tablets, sunshine, or the laudanum at least)?

Aptly described as 'bafflingly vague and used in an appallingly large number of different ways in different contexts' (Gray 1992: 251), romanticism is defined in *The Oxford Companion to English Literature* as:

> A literary movement, and profound shift in sensibility, which took place in Britain and throughout Europe . . . Intellectually it marked a violent reaction to the Enlightenment. Politically it was inspired by the revolutions in America and France . . . Emotionally it expressed an extreme assertion of the self and the value of individual experience together with the sense of the infinite and transcendental . . . The stylistic keynote of romanticism is intensity, and its watchword is 'imagination'.
>
> (Drabble 1995: 853)

Like many aesthetic movements, of course, romanticism only really makes sense in terms of what it is not. And the 'not' that romanticism is usually compared to is neoclassicism (albeit the case for 'realism' is probably stronger – see Travers 1998). As the term implies, neoclassicism essentially involved the excavation, establishment, elaboration and enactment of aesthetic ideas derived from ancient Greek and Roman arbiters like Aristotle, Horace, Quintilian and Longinus (Abrams 1993; Barzun 1962). These authorities were assumed to have attained unequalled excellence in their respective spheres of endeavour and thus their writings were regarded as models to which all great art should aspire. Neoclassicism, then, was characterised by conformity, traditionalism, distrust of radical

2

innovation and an overwhelming emphasis upon the tried and tested. Its leading eighteenth-century exponents, such as Swift, Dryden, Pope and Goldsmith, strove for elegance, grace, decorum, propriety and adherence to, or refinement of, the 'rules' of the relevant genre. Innovation, admittedly, was by no means depreciated but the primary challenge was to display wit, ease, suavity, sophistication, skill and polish within existing, highly restricted conventions (in drama, the three unities of time, place and action, the closed couplet in poetry, etc.).

As Furst (1969: 15) observes, the authoritarianism of the neoclassical period largely stemmed from an unqualified belief in the powers of the mind, the intellect and, above all, *reason*. The scientific achievements of the Enlightenment fostered an assumption that all things were knowable and that this knowledge was attainable by means of rational investigation. Just as Newton had shown this to be the case in the physical world, so too the milieux of morals, politics, ethics and art could be systematically examined and their universal 'truths' uncovered, extracted and disseminated. The adepts of neoclassicism thus attempted to establish the 'laws' of aesthetics, which if properly observed and carefully followed would result in a 'correct' composition, be it musical, literary, dramatic or whatever. 'The artist, like the scientist, was expected to operate by calculation, judgement and reason, for . . . the making of a book was considered a task like the making of a clock' (Furst 1969: 16).

The romantics, by contrast, championed innovation, creativity, iconoclasm, individuality and radical experimentation over traditionalism, refinement, rectitude and the seemly veneration of extant materials, forms, styles or genres (Butler 1981; Cranston 1994). They espoused spontaneity, informality, exuberance, elementalism, naturalism and aboriginal rusticity – as, for instance, in their use of vernacular language, their enthusiasm for 'lowly', 'impolite' or 'common' subjects, and, not least, their unqualified love of nature, landscape and the sheer *élan vital* of existence.[1] Conspicuously non-rational perspectives predicated upon visionary, mystical, supernatural, spiritual and otherworldly experiences came to prominence in the romantic period, as did a veritable catalogue of halt, lame and lonely wanderers, noble savages, innocent children, restless phantoms, pastoral panoramas, verdant vistas, sylvan glades, faery grottoes, crumbling ruins, gnarled oaks and, lest you think we've forgotten, golden daffodils. Although described with remarkable accuracy, compassion and power, it must be stressed that such 'external' phenomena primarily served to stimulate the inner feelings/reflections/emotions/introspections of the poet, author or creative artist. Much of romanticism's legacy therefore comprises meditations or reveries on the creator's inner Self, though, as these people were often social misfits, nonconformists or malcontents, it is dominated by melancholic, anxiety-stricken, self-pitying expressions of the inner emotional turmoil of imaginative outsiders. Imagination, in short, coupled with an apocalyptic sense of out-with-the-old-and-in-with-the-new, was the cynosure of the romantics (Barzun 1944; Bowra 1961; Day 1996; Shaffer 1995). Romanticism is nothing less than an 'apocalypse of the imagination' (Bloom 1970a: 19).

3

In that dawn

If 'imagination' is the abstract noun most commonly conjoined with romanticism, it is not the only one. The essence of the movement has been captured in a host of one-word descriptors including 'inspiration', 'intuition', 'creativity', 'originality', 'spontaneity', 'sentimentality', 'passion', 'natural', 'organic', 'orgiastic', 'visionary' and 'phantasmagorical', to name but a few (Furst 1969, 1971). Neoclassicism, similarly, has been summarised by terms like 'straightforward', 'unadorned', 'unemotional', 'economical', 'exact', 'proportioned', 'disciplined', 'correct', 'controlled', 'linear', 'literal' and, not least, the copious derivatives of 'reason' (reasoned, reasonable, reasoning, reasoner, etc.). Perhaps the most celebrated, and still the most cited, attempt to encapsulate the romantic–neoclassical dialectic dates from the early post-war period, when literary theorist M.H. Abrams (1953) made a metaphorical distinction between the *mirror* and the *lamp*. The neoclassical mindset, according to Abrams, was premised upon mimesis, an assumption that works of literature unambiguously imitated or reflected that to which they referred. In effect, 'a mirror held up to nature'. The romantic worldview, on the other hand, rested on the assumption that artistic artefacts emanated from the muse, the psyche, the genius, the wellsprings, the creativity, the imagination, the self-scrutiny of the artist him or herself. The romantic lamp thus shed light on the world rather than passively reflecting it. Illumination transcended imitation, projection eclipsed reflection, the lamp outshone the mirror. Or, in the rather more resonant words of Wordsworth's *Prelude*, 'An auxiliar light/Came from my mind which on the setting sun/Bestow'd new splendour'.

Convenient though it is to distinguish between neoclassicism, with its emphasis upon logical, reasoned intellectualisation, and romanticism, which valorises instinctive irrational emotionality – the head, in effect, versus the heart – it is important to acknowledge that the latter was far from monolithic. Nor, indeed, did the romantic propensity appear fully formed and fighting fit, as it were, in 1798 (Abrams 1971; Bloom 1970b). On the contrary, it was presaged by the so-called pre-romantics of the 'Age of Sensibility', a post-Puritan emotional outpouring exemplified by the Gothic novels of Richardson, Walpole and Beckford, the *Sturm und Drang* histrionics of Schiller, Herder and Goethe, and arch-jester James Macpherson's decidedly wild, hopelessly woolly, yet staggeringly influential, *Poems of Ossian*.[2] As the terminology implies, moreover, the roots of romanticism are deeply embedded in pre-Enlightenment tales of chivalry, adventure, love and courtly derring-do, such as *Sir Gawain and the Green Knight*, Malory's *Le Morte d'Arthur* and the twelfth-century poems of Chrétien de Troyes. Bloom (1970a), indeed, maintains that the defining feature of romanticism is the 'internalisation of the quest romance' (i.e. a psychospiritual quest for the grail of personal redemption and self-knowledge), albeit some rather more quixotic commentators have traced its origins back to Homer's *Odyssey* and the Garden of Eden, where it seems that 'the serpent was the first romantic' (Lovejoy 1966: 15).

Just as the roots of romanticism long pre-dated 1798, so too the romantic revolution was remarkably varied in space, time and domain. Striking differences, for example, are evident between (say) German, French and English romanticism, as well as within these contrasting national traditions (Porter and Teich 1988; Travers 1998). To put it *very* crudely, German romanticism was predominantly programmatic, idealistic and reactionary, the French variant predictably political, subversive and anarchistic, whereas England's 'warm intuitive muddle' (Furst 1969: 45) was primarily pragmatic, non-systematic and individualistic. Temporally, moreover, Schiller, Novalis and the Schlegels started the romantic ball rolling; Blake, Wordsworth and Coleridge swiftly followed suit; and, thanks to the Napoleonic hiatus, Hugo, Lamartine and Sainte-Beuve brought up the rear. A distinction is also occasionally made between first, second and third phase romantics (Germany's 'early', 'high' and 'late' romanticism; the 'Wordsworth' group of 1798–1806, the 'Scott' group of 1805-10, the 'Shelley' group of 1818–22, etc.) and it almost goes without saying that the movement was not confined to poetry and literature (Clay 1981). Music, art, dance, drama, opera, architecture and landscape gardening, to mention but a few areas of aesthetic endeavour, all experienced a romantic revolt of one kind or another, as did spheres as disparate as politics, philosophy, theology, history, ethics, economics and even the physical sciences (Hobsbawm 1973).

Despite the infinite variety of romanticism – or romanticisms, rather – the movement did possess an underlying unity in so far as it was an aesthetics-led reaction against the 'rationalist belief in a single coherent body of logically deduced conclusions, arrived at by universally valid principles of thought and founded upon carefully sifted data of observation or experiment' (Berlin 1981: 2). The central doctrine of the Enlightenment, 'that methods similar to those of Newtonian physics, which had achieved such triumphs in the realm of inanimate nature, could be applied with equal success to the fields of ethics, politics and human relationships' (Berlin 1981: 1), was contemptuously rejected by the romantics. Rational analysis distorted reality, dissection was akin to murder and God, for them, was a poet not a mathematician. As Barzun (1944: 83-4) brilliantly observed, at a time when romanticism was tarred with fascism and the neoclassical ethos of order, abstraction, propriety and reason, once again held sway:

> As against poetic diction and 'noble' words, the romanticists admitted all words, especially the neglected host of common words; as against the exclusive use of a selected Greco-Roman mythology, they took in the Celtic and the Germanic; as against the uniform setting and tone of classical tragedy, they studied and reproduced the real diversities known as 'local colour'. As against the antique objects and the set scale of pictorial merits prescribed by the Academy, they took in the whole world, seen and unseen, and the whole range of colours. As against the academic rules prohibiting the use of certain chords, tonalities and modulations, they sought to use and give shape to all manageable combinations of sound. As against the assumption that no civilisation had

existed since the fall of Rome, they rediscovered the Middle Ages and the sixteenth century, and made history their dominant avocation. As against the provincial belief that Paris and London were the sole centres of civilised life, they travelled to remote places such as America and the Near East, and earned the name of 'exotic' for their pains. As against the snobbish idea that the products of sophistication and refined living are the only topics worth treating, they began to treasure folk literature and folk music, and to draw the subject matter of their art from every class and condition of men. As against the materialist view that whatever is must be tangible, they made room in their notion of reality for the world of dreams, the mysterious in man and nature, and the supernatural.

To be alive

Strictly speaking, of course, romanticism should not be described in the past tense. Although this 'movement to end all movements' (Bann 1995: 3) officially ended in or around the mid-nineteenth century, when realism, naturalism and utilitarianism came increasingly to prominence, the romantic propensity has been very much alive and well in the intervening 150 years. And indeed it remains so (Bloom 1970b, 1970c; Cranston 1994; Simpson 1993). Albeit intermittent, this anti-Enlightenment, anti-establishment, anti-instrumentalist, anti-nomian impulse is identifiable in the anti-authoritarian endeavours of Schopenhauer, Nietzsche, Wagner, Ibsen, Joyce, Kafka, Beckett, Sartre, the Symbolists, Decadents, Surrealists and countless others besides (see Barzun 1944; Berlin 1991; Furst 1971; Tarnas 1991). For many commentators, however, romanticism's latest, possibly greatest, recrudescence trades under the less than incognito guise of *postmodernism*, our contemporary end of movements movement.

This is hardly the place to proffer a pseudo-scholarly treatise on perceived parallels between romanticism and postmodernism. That comes later. For our present purposes, it is sufficient to note that they are respectively associated with the nineteenth-century emergence and latter-day intensification of the consuming impulse, the urge to acquire, the buying desire, the marketing condition. Romanticism, admittedly, is usually portrayed as a poetics-propelled protest against the depredations of the Industrial Revolution, then in its 'take off' phase (Litvack 1996; Sanders 1996; Talmon 1979; Wu 1997). Closer inspection, however, reveals an intriguing relationship between romanticism and the marketplace. According to Rowland's (1996) recent analysis, the romantic period witnessed the emergence of the modern, 'free' market in artworks. The patronage of the aristocratic few was replaced, for the first time, by the capricious demands of a mass audience. Many of the literati, moreover, actually hailed from, or had close connections with, the trading classes. Blake, for example, was an engraver by profession, Southey the son of a draper, Keats came from a family of ostlers and Coleridge was sponsored by those celebrated protomarketers, the Wedgwoods. Indeed, it is only a slight exaggeration to state that the romantics, on the whole, were opposed to industry rather than commerce.

Opportune though it is to intimate that the romantics were more marketing-than production-orientated, the reality was much less straightforward. While some authors were comfortable with making a comfortable living – the staggering success of Byron and Scott testified to the potential size of the literary market at the start of the nineteenth century – many romantics were torn between 'giving the customers what they want' and remaining true to their calling, their inner light, their vision, their muse. The archetype of unappreciated artistic genius toiling without reward in an insalubrious garret dates from the romantic epoch, as does the elitist disdain felt towards those who prostitute their talent by pandering to the tastes of the petit bourgeois hordes. Yet, as the prefatorial 'advertisement' in the first edition of *Lyrical Ballads* perfectly illustrates, the romantics felt compelled to explain themselves, to justify their break with literary convention, to ask their readers for understanding and patience (Brett and Jones 1991). Whatever else they represent, these attempts to accommodate their customers are hardly the actions of devil may care, art for art's sake, production-orientated aesthetes.

The ambivalence of the relationship between romanticism and the marketplace is nowhere better illustrated than in Campbell's (1987) celebrated thesis that a 'romantic ethic' stimulated the spirit of modern consumption. Faced with the Weberian conundrum concerning the emergence of consumer society, at a time when the Puritan ethos of self-denial, dispassion, asceticism and the accumulation of capital was purportedly at its height, Campbell contended that Weber's Protestant ethic only really held sway until the end of the seventeenth century. Thereafter, thanks to the Neoplatonists' dilution of the austere Dissenting tradition, the emotional ecstasies that characterised the pre-romantic Age of Sensibility, and the romantics' self-absorbed emphasis upon contemplation, longing, unrequited love and the protean powers of the human imagination, a climate conducive to the advent of 'modern autonomous imaginative hedonism' was created (Campbell 1987). This desire for pleasure, as opposed to utilitarian need fulfilment, was driven by the disparity between idealised pre-experience expectations and the all too imperfect reality of the actual consumption experiences themselves. This dialectic of imaginative anticipation and disappointing outcome generated a self-perpetuating desire for consuming experiences, an insatiable appetite for different, for new, for more, and more exciting, consumer behaviours. Consumption, in short, became an end in itself, an end expedited, exacerbated and exonerated by the romantic ethic.

Pathbreaking though it is, Campbell's thesis is not without its critics. Holbrook (1993, 1996), for example, has challenged his representation of romanticism – claiming that it ignores key elements in the romantic movement, most notably its medieval and oriental inclinations – though the revolution was so disparate, and subject to *post hoc* reinterpretation, that de-emphasising certain strands seems unavoidable, especially in a work which does not claim to offer a comprehensive account of romanticism. More importantly perhaps, Campbell disregards (or, rather, considers but downplays) the pro-active part played by marketing-related institutions and developments – department stores, national brands, advertisements, magazines, gaslight, improved distribution networks – many of which date from the (late) romantic epoch (Fullerton 1985, 1988). Campbell's intimation that consumption experiences *always* prove disappointing is also questionable, because it is perfectly possible to exceed consumer expectations, as every exponent of services marketing knows. If satisfaction is permitted, however, Campbell's thesis breaks down, since it is predicated on the assumption that consumers' pre-experience experiences, which are rehearsed and anticipated through day-dreaming, reverie and suchlike, are unfailingly superior to the 'real thing'. It is this disjunction between perfect image and imperfect reality that drives the whole process and stimulates consumer desire for more (the object of which is once again eagerly anticipated and once again disappoints, thereby stimulating the desire for more . . .).

Disappointment is undeniably an integral aspect of the marketing offer (see Douglas 1997) and, while it may not explain everything, Campbell's romantic ethic helps us comprehend why consumers are consumed with consumption, take pleasure from pleasure, desire to desire and want to want. Thanks to the revolution in consciousness stimulated by romanticism and brought to fruition by the post-Fordist, late-capitalist, hyper-hedonist ethos that characterises postmodernity, a climate of consuming opinion now obtains, consumption is the done thing, it is the what-goes-without-saying of late twentieth-century society. I shop therefore I am. This impulse, it must be stressed, is not innate, since 'traditional' consumption is quite fixed, with only a finite number of needs to be filled. 'Today, of course, matters seem to be reversed – the modern consumer considers with alarm anyone who does not want to consume more and more, who does not seem interested in new wants and desires' (Corrigan 1997: 10). Indeed, almost every commentator on contemporary society stresses the overwhelming significance of consumption, the fact that people's identities are no longer defined by their occupations, social class, political affiliations, etc., but by their inventory of possessions, their repertoire of requisite brand names, their deck of credit cards, unshuffled or otherwise. It can, admittedly, be countered that this ostensible consuming mania is largely an artefact of the academic gaze. After ignoring consumption for decades, sociologists, anthropologists, cultural theorists and the like have finally acknowledged its place in the greater scheme of things, though some would say they're overcompensating (e.g. Gabriel and Lang 1995; Falk and Campbell 1997; Featherstone 1991; Mort 1996; Nava *et al.*. 1997). Nevertheless, it would be wrong to conclude that a latter-day consumer revolution hasn't occurred or that marketing phenomena aren't an integral part of our postmodern shift in sensibility. As Bocock (1993: 4) observes:

> Consumption has been seen as epitomising [the] move into postmodernity, for it implies a move away from productive work roles being central to people's lives, to their sense of identity, of who they are. In place of work roles, it is

8

roles in various kinds of family formations, in sexual partnerships of various kinds, in leisure-time pursuits, in consumption in general which have come to be seen as being more and more significant to people. These concerns have been reflected in sociology and social theory as a debate about whether or not western societies are moving towards becoming postmodern.

But to be a marketing man

So where does this leave marketing? Some might say pretty well placed. After all, it doesn't take a great deal of academic prestidigitation to demonstrate that marketing is, and always has been, inherently romantic in ethos. Like romanticism, it has consistently resisted definition, as have its conceptual components like 'loyalty', 'involvement', 'internationalisation', 'branding', 'impulse shopping', and so on (Baker 1987). Like romanticism, its identity largely derives from what it is not, namely the dreaded production wash-your-mouth-out-with-soap-and-water orientation (Desmond 1993). Like romanticism, it has successfully insinuated itself into all manner of propinquitous and non-propinquitous domains – not-for-profit marketing, social marketing, green marketing, macro-marketing, internal marketing, arts marketing, the marketing of places, people, ideas, activities, denominations and doubtless golden daffodils.[3] Like romanticism, it began as a laudable attempt to break down the barriers between high and low, as a bridge between the abstractions of ivory tower economists and the needs of practising managers (Jones 1995; Jones and Monieson 1990). Like romanticism, it is preoccupied with the organisational Self, in so far as marketing constantly strives to look inwards, to see organisations and their offerings as customers see them (Piercy 1997). And, as the 'mid-life crisis' literature indicates, contemporary marketing scholarship is suffused with a melancholic air of failure, uncertainty, disillusion and para-apocalyptic despair (Brady and Davis 1993; Brown et al. 1996; Doyle 1995; McDonald 1994).

Above all, marketing's romantic credentials are exemplified by its complete and unequivocal fetishisation of the consumer. Marketers are routinely exhorted to care for their customers, or potential customers, to bear their welfare in mind at all times, to really, really, *really* love them. In practice, of course, an element of ambivalence is apparent – not every consumer need can be met, profit is of paramount importance, it is only necessary to outdo the customer orientation of the competition, since it is impossible to be all things to all consumers, it is necessary to divide and conquer through segmentation, etc., etc., etc. Nevertheless, as the courtship/marriage metaphor that undergirds the burgeoning relationship marketing paradigm perfectly illustrates, practitioners and academics are expected to – wait for it – *romance the market*. In fact, if ever a discipline has completely 'internalised the quest romance', as Bloom accused the romantics of doing, then surely it is marketing. Apart from the latter-day advent of 'process-based' approaches to marketing, which emphasise Becoming rather than Being (Murray and O'Driscoll 1996, 1997; Piercy and Morgan 1997), the relentless pursuit of the grail of customer orientation is the *sine qua non* of marketing practice and philosophy. True, the fulfilment of this mission is impeded by the poisoned chalices of operations, the flame-breathing beasts in finance, the sirens of human resources, the goblins in R&D and the necromancers of strategic management, but a perfect paradisiacal state is waiting at the end of the marketing pilgrimage. It is a place containing:

> perfectly satisfied, not to say delighted customers, whose every conceivable want or need is anticipated, investigated and accommodated by perennially profitable companies, which are fully integrated around the marketing function and where careful analysis, planning, implementation and control are the orders of the day.
>
> (Brown and Maclaran 1996: 266)

Few would deny, furthermore, that marketing possesses many of the qualities of the romantic hero, anthropomorphised androcentrism notwithstanding. It is charismatic, dynamic, exciting, risk-taking, adventurous, outrageous, restless, roguish, swashbuckling, sexy. A bit Byronic perhaps, a tad Don Juanish and Manfred is manifestly its middle name (albeit most sensible consumers treat marketing's declarations of undying love with a healthy dose of scepticism whilst revelling in the flirtatiousness, the flattery, the flannel). Like Goethe's Werther, Chateaubriand's René and Musset's Octave, marketing constantly oscillates between profound, almost suicidal melancholy (e.g. the contemporary 'crisis' literature and the perennial complaint that no one takes the discipline seriously) and rampant, well-nigh certifiable megalomania (the broadening debate, periodic paroxysms of 'rediscovery', etc.). The romantic hero may be 'a multiple persona which drew upon images of the aristocrat, the dandy, the womaniser, the social and political outcast, and the rebel' (Travers 1998: 18), yet he is no less prone to 'lose a sense of perspective through constant self-observation, self-analysis and self-pity, so that he sinks deeper and deeper into the quagmire of his egocentricity' (Furst 1969: 98). Do they mean us?

Of course, highlighting the inherent romanticism of marketing hardly constitutes an original insight. Countless management gurus, consultants, proselytisers and soothsayers have stressed the imaginative, intuitive, inspirational, spontaneous, rambunctious, essentially Promethian side of marketing endeavour, and laughed all the way to an off-shore tax haven. One thinks, for example, of Ted Levitt's (1983) emphasis on the Marketing Imagination; Hugh Davidson's (1987, 1997) exhortations on 'offensive' and 'even more offensive' marketing; Peter Doyle's (1985, 1994) distinction between 'right-brained', marketing-orientated organisations and 'left-brained', finance-dominated companies; Simon Majaro's (1992) oft-repeated calls for marketing creativity, enthusiasm, passion, effervescence, etc.; and, then, of course there's the one and only Tom Peters. Well, what can one say about Tom Peters that isn't libellous? Regrets he's had too few but then again there are a few worth mentioning. (Oh, if only we could all concoct a management best-seller out of a single resonant word – excellence, liberation, chaos and the like. Mind you, 'romance' has a ring to it. Whatever you do, don't tell Tom!) Yet, in fairness to the under-read and over-paid brute (as has been alleged – but not by me, your honour!), Peters has always been an evangelist for evangelical marketing, for the crusade, revival, jihad, mission – call it what you will – of customer orientation.

Sadly, the scholarly inquisition does not see things in quite the same rose-tinted way. On the contrary, there seems to be an academic *auto-da-fé* on anything that smacks of romancing the market. The contents of our discipline's learned journals are almost entirely neoclassical in tenor. Reason, rationality, logic, propriety, exactitude, accuracy, consistency, replicability, respectability and precision are everywhere apparent. As indicated by the formal, quasi-ritualistic structure of most published papers – introduction, literature review, statement of hypotheses, methodology, results, discussion, conclusion – there is a 'proper', a 'correct', a 'right' way of doing things (Brown 1998). The marketing academy, similarly, has been absolutely single-minded in its pursuit of scientific status, its perceived passport to intellectual respectability, albeit the precise character of 'marketing science' has given rise to vigorous debate (Brown 1996, 1997). When all is said and done, however, our unending search for meaningful marketing generalisations is entirely neoclassical in ethos, as is our fondness for machine-cum-military precision metaphors, as is the unadorned utilitarianism of the 'marketing is exchange' credo, as is the fact that companies are encouraged, not to do their own thing, but to follow extant frameworks, models, guidelines, processes (and, should they fail, it is because they didn't embrace marketing wholeheartedly enough).

Now, this is not to suggest that the neoclassical approach to marketing scholarship is worthless or devoid of originality. On the contrary, many such publications and conceptualisations are elegant, graceful, refined, polished and admirable in their own terms, mind-bogglingly restrictive though these are. The distinction between marketing romanticism and neoclassicism is not clearcut, moreover. Many familiar marketing frameworks are touchingly romantic in tenor – the organicism of the PLC, the culinary creativity implied by the 4Ps, and so on – albeit these unfailingly rank amongst our most derided principles, the ones most in need of 'refinement', 'precision', 'rigour', careful specification and all-round stiffening up (as the recent backlash against relationship marketing demonstrates). Nor, for that matter, would anyone with an open mind gainsay the fact that our discipline's neoclassicism has, to put it politely, occasionally got the better of it. Reflect for a moment on Shostack's (1981) famous services marketing folly, his so-called 'molecular modelling approach'. Or what about Bettman's (1979) absurd blizzard of boxes and arrows in *An Information Processing Theory of Consumer Choice*? And then again there's Baker's (1995) bombastic claim, which he has been making for more than twenty years, that marketing is on the cusp of greatness akin to medical science before Harvey's discovery of the circulation of the blood (rush of blood to the head, some would say).

All things considered, nevertheless, it is not unreasonable to suggest that much of marketing scholarship is essentially neoclassical in spirit, whereas marketing practice is predominantly romantic in ethos. Positing practitioners as the keepers of marketing's romantic flame is, of course, itself an exercise in rose-tinted romanticism. As Carson (1993) shows, a case can and has been made for marketing managers' inherent neoclassicism and the much-recycled truism that marketers merely respond to or reflect consumer needs (mirror) rather than creating or inculcating them (lamp) is nothing if not neoclassical, though this may have more to do with political perspicacity (who's going to confess to fomenting frivolous expenditure?) or academic indoctrination (surely not!), than the 'real' mind set of marketing managers. Be that as it may, the neoclassical–romanticism dichotomy does at least help us comprehend why practitioners get so little from the academic journals and academics feel obliged to shackle practitioners' spontaneity, incarcerate ideographic approaches, hobble organisations with value chains, fetter managers with meaningless frameworks, torture all and sundry with thought-free theories, and generally stone the romance of marketing.

Was very heaven

If this were a work of romantic fiction, a chivalrous knight in shining scholarly armour would doubtless suddenly materialise, rescue our damsel in academic distress and slay the statistical sorcerers of neoclassicism. Laugh if you like, but such people actually exist. They are well endowed, if somewhat world-weary, intellectual mercenaries who wander from kingdom to kingdom, telling their tales, singing their songs and fighting the good fight. No one knows who these noble rovers in the groves Elysian are for sure, except that they hail from the house of PoMo, espouse aesthetics, imagination, magic and new literary forms, and – believe it or not – are currently passing through our field of academic dreams, the principality of the 4Ps, the empire of the brand, the kingdom of Kotler, the land of Levitt, the haunt of Hunt. It is rumoured that they find it an uninviting place, infertile, desiccated, aeolian, prosaic. However, in the belief that our domain is in sore need of academic aeration, we have managed – at no small cost to ourselves – to assemble a selection of their scholarly songs, cerebral chronicles, intellectual incantations and marketing *Märchen*.

The first of our selections, Chapter 2, sets out to untangle the intricately intertwined historical roots of romanticism and marketing. Starting from the famous *lettre du voyant* by that celebrated marketing man and sometime poet, Arthur Rimbaud, the author argues – after Abrams, via Van Morrison and with a token nod to Jacques Lacan – that 'illumination' is a central conceit of the romantic worldview. This worldview, what is more, not only pre-dates the 'lamp' of late eighteenth-century romanticism but is part and parcel of a magical, mystical, illuminist tradition that goes back to the very dawn of time.

Brown goes on to suggest that marketing is also deeply embedded in this school of thought, though its affiliation to 'the subterranean underside of western rationalism' has been systematically repressed by the gatekeepers of the academy. Taking his cue from three emblematic contributors to this pre-romantic illuminist tradition, all of whom have connections to marketing, the author contends that it is time to recover and rejoice in the magical side of marketing, the side symbolised by Arthur Rimbaud's incomparable *Illuminations*.

A near contemporary of Rimbaud, the Russian quasi-romantic-novelist, Nikolai Gogol, acts as the fulcrum of Chapter 3. For Belk, Gogol's morality tale, *The Overcoat*, is a 'micro-metonym' of macro-marketing in general and the marketising economies of Eastern Europe and the developing world in particular. Like the world in a grain of Blakean sand, it describes the character and unfortunate consequences of one consumer's overwhelming hunger for a luxurious overcoat and, in so doing, captures the pleasure, desire and yearning that inflame contemporary consumer society. Although consuming passion has traditionally been frowned upon in Judaeo-Christian cultures – associated as it is with frivolity, luxury, extravagance, unwarranted expenditure and wanton 'feminine' traits – the ubiquity, indeed necessity, of consumer desire is emphasised by Belk. It is a pan-human phenomenon and carries our hopes for something better, even though unscrupulous marketers may exploit it for their mendacious ends.

The exploitative side of marketing also looms large in Chapter 4, which again focuses on an artefact of popular culture. According to Thompson's witty, irreverent and minutely detailed deconstructive reading, the postmodern romantic movie *Jerry Maguire* not only exemplifies today's so-called 'crisis of masculinity' – epitomised by the Bly-by-night men's movement – but it illustrates the current 'mid-life crisis' of marketing masculinity. Marketing, he argues, has traditionally occupied an androgynous zone between the patriarchs of production and the matriarchs of consumption. Hence, it is riven with 'performance anxieties' (are we real men or mere mousetrap builders?) and prone to self-serving boasts about its overall importance, its conquest of many and varied domains, its irreplaceable place in the grand scheme of things and the size of its organisation. Lest we forget or fail to stand rigidly to attention at the very mention of it, the marketing concept has been and remains a force for the good, a universal verity, the be-all and end-all of management. Show me the hegemony.

Marginalised by necessity (and choice), postmodern marketing academics constitute a cadre of genre-blurring, gender-blending, agenda-bending romantics, for Thompson at least. In Chapter 5, Wensley takes a somewhat different stance with regard to segmentation and the wider issue of 'relevance'. A central plank of the Kotlerite paradigm – ladies and gentlemen, please put your hands together and give a very warm, postmodern welcome to those old marketing troopers, analysis, planning, implementation and control – STP has blinded marketing practitioners to the wider social and political implications of their actions ('but we only give the customers what they want, m'lord'), whilst permitting academics to indulge in unwarranted self-congratulatory approbation (segmentation works!). Both parties, Wensley maintains, have fallen in love with their own seductive myths about the nature of marketing and the functioning of the marketplace. In so doing they have overlooked some broader issues concerning the relationship between marketing scholarship, marketing management and the place of practical knowledge. A collective sense of insecurity prevails.

This call to address a serious scholarly shortcoming is echoed by Holbrook in Chapter 6. The shortcoming on this occasion, however, is predominantly methodological. Photographs have long been an integral part of the marketing and consumer research tool kit. They are used as sources of data, for eliciting information, presenting corroborative evidence or expressing introspective insights. Compelling though such applications undoubtedly are, they remain handicapped by the flatness, the two-dimensionality, the lack of depth of the pictorial images themselves. Faced with this insurmountable problem, Holbrook recommends stereoscopy and, in an exegesis that ranges across romanticism, illuminism, creativity and the viewing process, he makes a characteristically comprehensive case for stereoscopic photographs. It remains to be seen whether these will be employed as a matter of course in a discipline long dominated by the written word, but no one can accuse Holbrook of underselling stereoscopy's merits, not least the magical moment of revelation when the 3D image suddenly 'breaks camouflage' and erupts into view.

The idea of 'breaking camouflage' is no less applicable to a hitherto neglected aspect of consumer behaviour, described in Chapter 7. In the opinion of Jantzen and Østergaard, marketing's conception of the consumer is predicated upon notions of rationality and order derived from neoclassical economics and sociology. However, this emphasis upon utilitarian functionalism obscures the irrational – *the necessarily irrational* – side of human behaviour. Life is just as much about wasting time, squandering money, going crazy and generally doing nothing as it is about sensibility, achievement, rectitude, propriety and carefully planned, meticulously executed, earnest, all-too-earnest endeavour. Drawing upon the inter-war work of Georges Bataille, the authors suggest that disorder, derangement, deviation and desire are integral parts of existence, often the most important parts of everyday existence, romantic love being a paramount, mad passionate example of such 'irrational', 'antisocial', 'useless' behaviour.

The next chapter doesn't quite comprise the 'theory of love' that Jantzen and Østergaard consider necessary, but it does highlight the sheer carnality of routine shopping experiences. Based upon the introspective accounts of more than 100 undergraduate students, and written in an extravagant, 'show me the metonymy' manner, Brown demonstrates that 'the shops' are important 'talent spotting' arenas, liminoid locales for establishing, developing and fantasising about romantic liaisons. What's more, this lonely-hearts club conceit is no less applicable to the shopping expedition itself, where people fall head-over-heels in love with products, experience the para-orgasmic thrills of longing, possession and denial, or suffer the abject, heartbroken agonies of unrequited love when shopping encounters go unconsummated, as they often do in the retailing orgasmatron.

Retailing also features in Chapter 9 by Maclaran and Stevens, albeit in the form of a festival shopping mall. Festival malls, to be sure, are two a penny these days, as are analyses of their nature, structure, layout, location, tenant mix, sources of funding, and so forth (Brown 1992). Rather than indulge in such hackneyed modes of academic reportage, however, the authors give us a flight of romantic fantasy concerning their own, highly personal reactions to the festival mall experience. This phantasmagoric method, aptly termed stream-of-scholarly-consciousness, is coupled with the key theoretical constructs of Russian literary theorist, Mikhail Bakhtin, to provide a quasi-Coleridgean evocation of the inherent magic of the festival mall. Powerscourt shopping centre may not be a late twentieth-century equivalent of the stately pleasure dome that Kubla Khan decreed in Xanadu, but at least the authors' reveries weren't interrupted by a person on business from Porlock.

It is now well established, of course, that the reviled business person from Porlock didn't actually exist. Coleridge's *Kubla Khan*, unlike *Christabel*, is a complete work, not an opium-induced, sadly interrupted slice of the romantic sublime (Ashton 1996). Nevertheless, this phoney-Porlockian's pragmatic concerns are symptomatic of the disenchantment of the world, the decline of magic, the de-naturalisation of supernaturalism, that have purportedly accompanied the rise of modern, bureaucratic, mass re-production-orientated society. This 'loss of aura' is the theme of the tenth chapter, where Heilbrunn contends that the aura of the brand is in the process of being recaptured, reinscribed, rearticulated, re-illuminated. Thanks to the ingenious work of innovative product designers like Philippe Starck and Michael Graves, we live in an era of re-romanticisation, where everyday objects are being rescued from the abyss of utilitarian neoclassicism *noveau*. A kettle is no longer a kettle, nor a toothbrush a toothbrush, but an auratic object which questions its identity and function, thereby helping us 'break through' to a better world.

The romanticisation of the contemporary marketplace is not confined to product design or festival malls and, in Chapter 11, Power and Stern ruminate on an advertisement for a personal computer. Eschewing the hi-tech, hi-spec, product feature-led, predominantly prosaic mode of promotional discourse that traditionally prevails in such advertising treatments, this particular Sony PC commercial proffers a postmodern, para-romantic moment of inspiration, a veritable 'product epiphany'. The 'text' is then subject to a deconstructive reading in terms of five characteristically postmodern/romantic themes – hyperreality, fragmentation, decentred subjects, reversal of production/consumption and juxtaposition of opposites – which reveals a profound contradiction between the ad's factual information and fantastic imagery. Contradiction, of course, is yet another characteristic of our paradoxical postmodern times, leading the authors to conclude that contemporary advertising is an agonistic domain where romance and rationality clash – and clash creatively.

An analogous clash is apparent in the sub-discipline of international marketing, according to McAuley. In Chapter 12, he bemoans the methodological reductionism that sadly prevails in studies of small firm internationalisation. Little of the copious research conducted on SMEs is useful to the managers of small firms and most of it comprises minor variations on the same old methods (large-scale, cross-sectional questionnaire surveys), the same old models (FDI theory, networks, stages of internationalisation) and the same old recommendations (more research is necessary). Instead of continuing to tell the same old stories – 4,000 words maximum, top-ranked journal preferred – or throwing ever more elaborate algorithms and computer power at the problem, the author suggests we strive to break out of our current pseudo-scientific mind set, where presentations are determined by the parameters of PowerPoint, and endeavour to romance the market through poetry, plays, painting, parables . . .

Pocus, of the hocus variety, is yet another possibility and, appropriately enough, this is the focus of Chapter 13. Unlucky for some perhaps, but not those renowned prestidigitators of prose, Arnould, Price and Otnes, who take this thaumaturgic opportunity to enchant us with the magic of services marketing. Drawing upon their extensive ethnographic work on white water rafting and the extended service encounter, the authors steer a steady course through the shoals of sorcery, cataracts of conjuration and whirlpools of witchcraft. They argue that just as the romantic movement succeeded in reintroducing magical ideas and language into Western thought, so too the late twentieth century is witnessing the waning of scientific rationality and the rise of magical romance. This re-romanticisation may be mediated by, but it is not subordinate to, the marketing system. On the contrary, magic operates in a oxymoronic market-space where rational commercial enterprise evaporates and the primal vitality of the natural world re-emerges.

Now history does not repeat itself, though academics regrettably do. In the final chapter, Brown reappears to regale us, yet again, with eternal recurrence, his *idée fixe*. Starting with Kundera's recapitulation of Nietzsche's recapitulation of Vico's recapitulation of Zeno, the author ponderously ponders the parallels between romanticism and postmodernism, wonders what would happen if the marketing academy had the opportunity to do it all over again (apart of course from debarring ruminations on romanticism), and restates several of the issues raised in earlier chapters in a transparently obvious attempt to rewrite history, conform to the ironic authorial re-pose that characterised both romanticism and postmodernism, and impose retrospective coherence upon this disparate volume. Romance may not be dead and love may well be capable of conquering all, but only the most smitten of scholarly swains would fall for such a recycled tissue of flagrantly flirtatious falsehoods. Sweet nothings indeed.

O times, in which the meagre[4]

It remains to be seen whether these lays of the marketing minstrels will have any effect on the intellectual lineaments or organisation of our field, *le champs du marketing*. Doubtless our contributors will be dismissed as hopeless romantics in a hard-headed world, as quixotic tilters at academic windmills, as the troubadours of thought, out of place, out of time, as mere meistersingers of marketing. We have, to be sure, attempted to structure this volume in accordance with the schema of most mainstream textbooks – historical background, macro-environment, marketing concept, segmentation, research methods, consumer behaviour, components of the mix, marketing in context, kite-flying conclusion – thereby rendering it reasonably accessible. We firmly believe, what is more, that the romantic outpourings contained herein are *closer* to the concerns, the mind set, the ethos of many marketing practitioners than the neoclassical pabulum that prevails in most academic journals. True, in keeping with their code of honour, some of our Ivanhoes of academe, our Lochinvars of scholarship, our Chú Chúlainns of cerebration, refuse to have anything to do with the quondam world of marketing management. As with the romantic poets, indeed, several of them write in a manner that is less than immediately accessible to marketing's *hoi polloi*. But we maintain that this has less to do with the incomprehensibility of the ideas themselves than the ingrained, not to say ideological, character of extant modes of academic discourse. At this time of crisis, transition, change and purported marketing apocalypse, we feel it is necessary to release the rack of reason, outlaw the lash of logic, slip the stocks of science, abandon the gibbet of generalisation, get off the treadmill of theory, ban the ball and chain of boxes and arrows, forget the ferule of frameworks, unlock the cuffs of concepts, escape the iron maiden of matrices, dismantle the cross of Charter'd Institutes and, above all, break the mind-forg'd manacles of marketing.

Notes

1 Lest accusations of anachronism come winging our way, we are well aware of the fact that Bergson coined the term *élan vital* at the turn of the present century. Bergson, however, was closely associated with the Symbolists and Decadents, who were the true heirs and exponents of French romanticism (see Furst 1969).

2 Now almost forgotten, James Macpherson's *Tales of Ossian* caused a sensation when they were published in the 1760s. Supposedly an anthology of ancient Bardic legends, stories and myths, albeit largely concocted by Macpherson himself, they were regarded by many pre-romantics, Goethe included, as on a par with the works of

Shakespeare, and stimulated a spate of imitations – collections of folk tales, fairy stories, *Märchen* and suchlike.

3 The *reductio ad absurdum* is surely a book I once came across, *Marketing for Fish Farmers* (SB), though one of us used to teach marketing to construction workers (BC). You haven't lived 'til you've expatiated on the 4Ps of pre-stressed concrete!

4 Adapted with apologies from Wordsworth's *The Prelude*, a long autobiographical poem which was started around the time of *Lyrical Ballads*, constantly refined, considered a preliminary to his projected (but uncompleted) masterwork, *The Recluse*, and posthumously published in 1850.

References

Abrams, M.H. (1953), *The Mirror and the Lamp: Romantic Theory and the Critical Tradition*, Oxford: Oxford University Press.

Abrams, M.H. (1971), *Natural Supernaturalism: Tradition and Revolution in Romantic Literature*, New York: W.W. Norton.

Abrams, M.H. (1993), *A Glossary of Literary Terms*, sixth edition, Fort Worth: Harcourt Brace.

Ashton, R. (1996), *The Life of Samuel Taylor Coleridge*, Oxford: Blackwell.

Baker, M.J. (1987), 'One more time – what is marketing?', in M.J. Baker (ed.), *The Marketing Book*, London: Heinemann, 3–9.

Baker, M.J. (1995), 'Marketing – philosophy or function?', in M.J. Baker (ed.), *Companion Encyclopedia of Marketing*, London: Routledge, 3–22.

Bann, S. (1995), *Romanticism and the Rise of History*, New York: Twayne.

Barzun, J. (1944), *Romanticism and the Modern Ego*, Boston: Little Brown.

Barzun, J. (1962), *Classic, Romantic and Modern*, London: William Pickering.

Berlin, I. (1981), 'The counter-Enlightenment', in I. Berlin, *Against the Current: Essays in the History of Ideas*, Oxford: Clarendon, 1-24.

Berlin, I. (1991), 'The apotheosis of the romantic will: the revolt against the myth of an ideal world', in I. Berlin (ed.), *The Crooked Timber of Humanity: Chapters in the History of Ideas*, London: Collins, 207–37.

Bettman, J.R. (1979), *An Information Processing Theory of Consumer Choice*, Reading: Addison-Wesley.

Bloom, H. (1970a), 'The internalization of quest romance', in H. Bloom, *The Ringers in the Tower: Studies in Romantic Tradition*, Chicago: University of Chicago Press, 12–35.

Bloom, H. (1970b), 'Introduction: first and last romantics', in H. Bloom, *The Ringers in the Tower: Studies in Romantic Tradition*, Chicago: University of Chicago Press, 2–11.

Bloom, H. (1970c), *The Visionary Company: A Reading of English Romantic Poetry*, Ithaca: Cornell University Press.

Bocock, R. (1993), *Consumption*, London: Routledge.

Bowra, M. (1961), *The Romantic Imagination*, Oxford: Oxford University Press.

Brady, J. and Davis, I. (1993), 'Marketing's mid-life crisis', *McKinsey Quarterly*, 2, 17–28.

Brett, R.L. and Jones, A.R. (1991), 'Introduction', in W. Wordsworth and S.T. Coleridge, *Lyrical Ballads*, London: Routledge, xix–liv.

Brown, S. (1992), *Retail Location: A Micro-Scale Perspective*, Aldershot: Avebury.

Brown, S. (1995), *Postmodern Marketing*, London: Routledge.

Brown, S. (1996), 'Art or science?: fifty years of marketing debate', *Journal of Marketing Management*, 12(4), 243–67.

Brown, S. (1997), 'Marketing science in a postmodern world', *European Journal of Marketing*, 31(3/4), 167–82.

Brown, S. (1998), *Postmodern Marketing Two: Telling Tales*, London: ITBP.

Brown, S., Bell, J. and Carson, D.J. (1996), 'Apocaholics anonymous: looking back on the end of marketing', in S. Brown, J. Bell and D.J. Carson, *Marketing Apocalypse: Eschatology, Escapology and the Illusion of the End*, London: Routledge, 1–20.

Brown, S. and Maclaran, P. (1996), 'The future is past: marketing, apocalypse and the retreat from Utopia', in S. Brown, J. Bell and D.J. Carson, *Marketing Apocalypse: Eschatology, Escapology and the Illusion of the End*, London: Routledge, 260–77.

Butler, M. (1981), *Romantics, Rebels and Reactionaries: English Literature and its Background 1760–1830*, Oxford: Oxford University Press.

Campbell, C. (1987), *The Romantic Ethic and the Spirit of Modern Consumerism*, Oxford: Blackwell.

Carson, D.J. (1993), 'A philosophy for marketing education in small firms', *Journal of Marketing Management*, 9(2), 189–204.

Clay, J. (1981 [1980]), *Romanticism*, trans. D. Wheeler and C. Owen, Oxford: Phaidon.

Corrigan, P. (1997), *The Sociology of Consumption: An Introduction*, London: Sage.

Cranston, M. (1994), *The Romantic Movement*, Oxford: Blackwell.

Davidson, H. (1987), *Offensive Marketing: Or How To Make Your Competitors Followers*, second edition, Harmondsworth: Penguin.

Davidson, H. (1997), *Even More Offensive Marketing: An Exhilarating Action Guide to Winning in Business*, Harmondsworth: Penguin.

Day, A. (1996), *Romanticism*, London: Routledge.

Desmond, J. (1993), 'Marketing – the split subject', in D. Brownlie *et al.* (eds), *Rethinking Marketing*, Coventry: Warwick Business School Research Bureau, 259–69.

Douglas, M. (1997), *Thought Styles: Critical Essays on Good Taste*, London: Sage.

Doyle, P. (1985), 'Marketing and the competitive performance of British industry: areas for research', *Journal of Marketing Management*, 1(1), 87–98.

Doyle, P. (1994), *Marketing Management and Strategy*, Hemel Hempsted: Prentice Hall.

Doyle, P. (1995), 'Marketing in the new millennium', *European Journal of Marketing*, 29(13), 23–41.

Drabble, M. (ed.) (1995), *The Oxford Companion to English Literature*, Oxford: Oxford University Press.

Elam, D. (1992), *Romancing the Postmodern*, London: Routledge.

Falk, P. and Campbell, C. (eds) (1997), *The Shopping Experience*, London: Sage.

Featherstone, M. (1991), *Consumer Culture and Postmodernism*, London: Sage.

Fullerton, R. (1985), 'Was there a "production era" in marketing history? A multinational study', in S.C. Hollander and T. Nevett (eds), *Marketing in the Long Run*, East Lansing: Michigan State University, 388–400.

Fullerton, R. (1988), 'How modern is modern marketing? Marketing's evolution and the myth of the "production era"', *Journal of Marketing*, 52 (January), 108–25.

Furst, L.R. (1969), *Romanticism in Perspective: A Comparative Study of Aspects of the Romantic Movements in England, France and Germany*, Basingstoke: Macmillan.

Furst, L.R. (1971), *Romanticism*, London: Methuen.

Gabriel, Y. and Lang, T. (1995), *The Unmanageable Consumer: Contemporary Consumption and its Fragmentations*, London: Sage.

Gray, M. (1992), *A Dictionary of Literary Terms*, Harlow: Longman.

Hobsbawm, E. (1973), *The Age of Revolution: Europe 1789–1848*, London: Abacus.

Holbrook, M.B. (1993), 'Romanticism and sentimentality in consumer behavior: a literary approach to the joys and sorrows of consumption', in M.B. Holbrook and E.C. Hirschman (eds), *The Semiotics of Consumption: Interpreting Symbolic Consumer Behaviour in Popular Culture and Works of Art*, Berlin: Mouton de Gruyter, 151-228.

Holbrook, M.B. (1996), 'Romanticism, introspection and the roots of experiential consumption: Morris the Epicurean' in R.W. Belk, N. Dholakia and A. Venkatesh (eds), *Consumption and Marketing: Macro Dimensions*, Cincinnati: South-Western, 20–82.

Jones, D.G.B. (1995), 'Historical research in marketing', in M.J. Baker (ed.), *Companion Encyclopedia of Marketing*, London: Routledge, 23–43.

Jones, D.G.B. and Monieson, D.D. (1990), 'Early development of the philosophy of marketing thought', *Journal of Marketing*, 54 (January), 102–13.

Levitt, T. (1983), *The Marketing Imagination*, New York: Free Press.

Litvack, L. (1996), 'Romanticism', in R. Bradford (ed.), *Introducing Literary Studies*, Hemel Hempstead: Harvester Wheatsheaf , 231–64.

Livingston, I. (1997), *Arrow of Chaos: Romanticism and Postmodernity*, Minneapolis: University of Minnesota Press.

Lovejoy, A.O. (1966), 'On the discrimination of romanticisms', in A.K. Thorlby (ed.), *The Romantic Movement*, Harlow: Longmans, 14–19.

McDonald, M.H.B. (1994), 'Marketing – a mid-life crisis?', *Marketing Business*, 30 (May), 10–14.

Majaro, S. (1992), *Managing Ideas for Profit: The Creative Gap*, Maidenhead: McGraw-Hill.

Mort, F. (1996), *Cultures of Consumption: Masculinities and Social Space in the Late-Twentieth-Century Britain*, London: Routledge.

Murray, J.A. and O'Driscoll, A. (1996), *Strategy and Process in Marketing*, Hemel Hempstead: Prentice Hall.

Murray, J.A. and O'Driscoll, A. (1997), 'Messianic eschatology: some redemptive reflections on marketing and the benefits of a process approach', *European Journal of Marketing*, 31(9/10), 706-19.

Nava, M., Blake, A., MacRury, I. and Richards, B.(eds) (1997), *Buy This Book: Studies in Advertising and Consumption*, London: Routledge.

Piercy, N.F. (1997), *Market-led Strategic Change*, Oxford: Butterworth-Heinemann.

Piercy, N.F. and Morgan, N.A. (1997), 'The impact of lean thinking and the lean enterprise on marketing: threat or synergy?', *Journal of Marketing Management*, 13(7), 679–93.

Porter, R. and Teich, M. (eds) (1988), *Romanticism in National Context*, Cambridge: Cambridge University Press.

Readings, B. and Schaber, B. (eds) (1993), *Postmodernism Across the Ages: Essays for a Postmodernity That Wasn't Born Yesterday*, Syracuse: Syracuse University Press.

Rowland, W.G. (1996), *Literature and the Marketplace: Romantic Writers and Their Audiences in Great Britain and the United States*, Lincoln: University of Nebraska Press.

Sanders, A. (1996), *A Short Oxford History of English Literature*, Oxford: Oxford University Press.

Shaffer, E. (1995), 'Secular apocalypse: prophets and apocalyptics at the end of the eighteenth century', in M. Bull (ed.), *Apocalypse Theory and the Ends of the World*, Oxford: Blackwell, 137–58.

Shostack, G.L. (1981), 'How to design a service', in J.H. Donnelly and W.R. George (eds), *Marketing of Services*, Chicago: American Marketing Association, 221–9.

Simpson, D. (1993), *Romanticism, Nationalism and the Revolt Against Theory*, Chicago: University of Chicago Press.

Talmon, J.L. (1979), *Romanticism and Revolt: Europe 1815–1848*, Norton: New York.

Tarnas, R. (1991), *The Passion of the Western Mind*, London: Pimlico.

Travers, M. (1998), *An Introduction to Modern European Literature: From Romanticism to Postmodernism*, Basingstoke: Macmillan.

Wu, D. (1997), 'Introduction', in D. Wu (ed.), *Romanticism: An Anthology*, Oxford: Blackwell, xxx-xxxviii

2

TORE DOWN À LA RIMBAUD

Illuminating the marketing imaginary

Stephen Brown

*Les Voix reconstituées; l'éveil fraternel de toutes les énergies
chorales et orchestrales et leurs applications instantanées;
l'occasion, unique, de dégager nos sens!
À vendre les corps sans prix, hors de tout race, de tout monde, de
tout sexe, de tout descendance! Les richesses jaillissant à chaque
démarche! Solde de diamants sans contrôle!
À vendre l'anarchie pour les masses; la satisfaction irrépressible
pour les amateurs supérieurs; la morte atroce pour les fidèles et les amants!
À vendre les habitations et les migrations, sports, féeries et
conforts parfaits, et le bruit, le mouvement et l'avenir qu'ils font!
À vendre les applications de calcul et les sauts d'harmonie inouïs.
Les trouvailles et les termes non soupçonnés, possession immédiate.*[1]

Solde, from Rimbaud's *Les Illuminations*

Into the mystic

On 15 May 1871, an ambitious 16-year-old wrote a remarkable letter to Paul Démeny, a provincial schoolteacher tenuously connected to the leading lights of the Parisian literary establishment. This *lettre du voyant*, from the precocious and never less than immodest Arthur Rimbaud, set out the putative poet's personal manifesto. At a time when French poetry, thanks to the legacy of Racine, Lamartine, Musset and the Parnassian school, was characterised by extreme rigidity of structure, syntax and metre, the young Rimbaud famously announced that the time was ripe for a free-flowing, impressionistic, fragmented, allusive, vivid, dream-like, essentially mystical perspective. 'The poet,' as he so arrestingly put it, 'makes himself a *seer* by a long, prodigious and rational *disordering of all the senses* (*dérèglement* de *tous les sens*)'.

Like many would-be literary revolutionaries, Rimbaud found that his mesmeric compositions, his brilliantly evocative poetic collages and prose poems, were almost totally ignored at the time (Bernard 1986; Chadwick 1979). True, part of the disdain he endured was due to his somewhat scandalous lifestyle – the usual artistic cocktail of drink, drugs and rampant homosexuality (not forgetting the notorious shooting incident with his lover, Paul Verlaine, which led to the latter spending two years in a Belgian jail) – but such was the indifference and open hostility of the French literary establishment that Rimbaud completely renounced poetry at the tender age of 20 and became, believe it or not, a marketing man! He was a gun runner, slave trader and, aside from a short spell as an independent agent, spent the bulk of his career as principal buyer-cum-store manager for *Viannay, Mazeran, Bardey et Cie*, dealers in East African coffee and hides.

Although Rimbaud's primary claim to fame rests on the exceptionally rich poetic seam that he mined, refined and seemingly exhausted in four short years, it is noteworthy that he considered himself to be a marketer, first and foremost. Towards the end of his tragically short life, when his *œuvre* was discovered by the French Symbolists, widely re-published and hailed as veritable works of poetic genius, he refused to abandon the world of commerce, the only world where he truly felt at home (Nicholl,1997). So indifferent was Rimbaud to his belated literary celebrity that not only did he fail to collect the ample royalties that were his due but he omitted to shed light on the manifold mysteries that surrounded, and still surround, his work. Apart from copious 'missing' poems (which continued to turn up until the late 1930s) and the precise timing of *Une Saison en Enfer* (widely considered to be his 'farewell' to literature, though some scholars maintain that several later works were composed), there is the enigma of Rimbaud's finest literary hour, the forty-two prose poems that make up *Les Illuminations*. Not only is there no consensus over the content and sequencing of the collection, but it is not even known if the title itself was Rimbaud's preferred choice (Little 1983; Osmond 1976).

Arthur Rimbaud may have regarded marketing and poetry as two entirely separate spheres of his existence, as have most subsequent commentators, but surely they are less disconnected than is commonly supposed. A true romantic, Rimbaud never really found what he was looking for in the ethereal world of letters, literary salons and polite society. Yet by all accounts, his romantic, mystical, rebellious, poetic propensities were more than satisfied in the bantering, bartering, boasting and barking milieu of the Abyssinian marketplace. To be sure, he was not a very good marketing man. Rimbaud lost money on gun running and slave trading, was out-negotiated on numerous occasions (even by 'the natives') and, as his failure to collect outstanding royalties amply demonstrates, he simply wasn't cut out for the cut-and-thrust world of business. Nevertheless, the few surviving letters from his post-literary life suggest that this prodigiously gifted individual derived greater personal fulfilment from the poetics of the marketplace than the marketplace of poetics (Nicholl,1997).

Bright side of the road

Approximately one hundred years on from the late, great Arthur Rimbaud (he died on 10 December 1891, at the age of 37), the marketplace is still poetic, still mesmeric, still romantic, still beguiling, still mysterious, still fulfilling, still fantastic, still intriguing, still sensual, still carnal. One only has to witness the excited faces of children in the pre-Christmas period or cull the compendious published studies of consumer behaviour (if you must), to appreciate that, for all its faults, for all the false consciousness, for all the over-indulgence and materialism, for all the scams, rip-offs and aberrant activities, there is still something special, something incredible, something mysterious, something compelling, something supernatural, something extraordinary, something miraculous about markets and marketing.

Yet if Rimbaud were to be revived, resurrected or reconfigured today, it is doubtful whether he would be impressed by our prosaic attempts to capture the poetics of the marketplace. While there are any number of gifted thinkers and writers in the academic marketing community, and while the marketing literature is nothing if not voluminous, it has to be said that the essential enchantment of the marketplace still eludes us. Indeed, if Rimbaud *were* alive today, one suspects that he would once again turn his back on the world of marketing letters and seek *dérèglement de tous les sens* in the hyperreality of the 'reproduction African bazaar' at the nearest mega-regional shopping mall. Come to think of it, he might even pick up a few free gifts, air miles, cents-off coupons and Ronald McDonald decals for good measure.

Of course, condemning the state of contemporary marketing scholarship has become a popular academic pastime. In addition to the purported complaints of marketing practitioners, who apparently find nothing of relevance in the principal journals (Denison and McDonald 1995; Mowen and Leigh 1996), the vacuity of the model builders, relationship mongers, quants jocks, pseudo-scientists and their knuckle-dragging epigones is routinely ridiculed by the apocalyptics of the academy (Brown et al. 1996). *And rightly so.* One suspects, however, that until such times as these postmodern millenarians put forward a fully-fledged alternative to Kotlerite orthodoxy – premised as it is on the western scientific logos of rationality, objectivity, dispassion and truth – it will continue on its merry way, oblivious to the critiques of all comers, no matter how fashionable, colourful or precious their philosophical raiment.

This is hardly the place to present a formal replacement for the Venerable Phil's priceless paradigm, nor indeed do I have a replacement to offer. Nevertheless, if poets possess premonitional qualities, as romantics like Coleridge, Shelley and the Schlegels suggest (Brown 1998), then Arthur Rimbaud may serve as a suitably inspirational icon for the intractable task that awaits us in the impending post-Philip era. Just as he showed Van Morrison (1984) 'the light out of the tunnel/when there was darkness all around', so too the great Symbolist symbolises the inherent romance of the marketplace. Lest there is any misunderstanding, however, it must be stressed that Rimbaud's iconic function does not inhere in the fact that he was the original juvenile delinquent, who wrote in an anti-authoritarian, wilfully obscurantist, arrestingly beautiful manner. It resides, rather, in the *mysticism* that, as the title of his most famous collection testifies, informs, infuses and indeed suffuses his entire poetic *œuvre*. Thanks to the pioneering research of Enid Starkie (1961), we now know that Rimbaud was very deeply versed in the dark side of western culture – the occult, alchemy, kabbalah, gnosticism, neoplatonism, Rosicrucianism, Swedenborgianism, Carpocratianism, etc. – and his poems, especially the enigmatic *Sonnet des Voyelles*, reflect this fact (Bernard 1986; Osmond 1976).

Rimbaud, to be sure, was not alone in his illuminist inclinations. Mysticism was part of the intellectual armoury of innumerable romantic and post-romantic types from Blake and Balzac to Byron and, especially, W.B. Yeats. Starkie (1961) cogently observes that the works of celebrated occultists, most notably Eliphas Lévi, were as familiar to the pre-twentieth-century intelligentsia as those of Freud and Jung are today. As noted in Chapter 1, indeed, the entire romantic tradition is characterised by 'abrupt illumination in an arrest of time' (Abrams 1971: 419), by the metaphor of the lamp rather than the mirror of neoclassicism (Abrams 1953). There were, of course, many other distinctive features of romanticism but, as Abrams (1971) demonstrated in his masterwork, *Natural Supernaturalism*, the movement was built upon magical, mystical, illuminist foundations (see also Kroeber 1988; Prickett 1976; Taylor 1979). Although we twentieth-century sophisticates tend to associate 'illuminations' with Walter Benjamin, Ernst Bloch, Pierre Bourdieu and, above all, Blackpool, the illuminist tradition stretches back to the very dawn of time, if not before. As a visit to any New Age bookstore readily demonstrates, 'enlightenment' in general and 'luminescence' in particular are an integral part of many religious and spiritual traditions, both exoteric and esoteric (Faivre 1994; Godwin 1994).

Rimbaud's romantic outpourings,[2] his famous *lettre du voyant*, his desire to be a seer, and his incomparable *Illuminations* are thus premised upon a long-established illuminist worldview. The giving, receiving, absorption within, or exposure to light is found in Islam, Sufism, Buddhism, Hinduism and Zoroastrianism, as well as Judaism, Christianity and their manifold mystical offshoots (Roland 1995). In the limited space that is available, it is impossible to provide a full account of what Bruss (1982: 285) aptly describes as 'the subterranean underside of western rationalism'. For our present purposes, it is sufficient to draw attention to three emblematic figures who pre-dated the romantic revolution of 1798, who have some kind of connection to the marketing system, and from whom we marketing millenarians may derive a modicum of much-needed inspiration and possibly a moment or two of illumination.

Beautiful vision

Hildegard of Bingen (1098-1179) was one of the most remarkable women of her time, or indeed of any time. In an era when female subordination was absolute and their voices virtually silent, she was a poetess, composer, hymnist, playwright, public speaker, exorciser of demons, performer of miracles, political spin-doctor to princes and prelates, part-time clairvoyant-cum-apocalyptic, and a sort of spiritual agony aunt for abbots, archbishops and anchorites alike (Flanagan 1989; Newman 1990; Weeks 1993). What's more, she founded, nourished and sustained two separate nunneries, wrote three major theological and two encyclopaedic scientific treatises (as well as diverse 'Lives of the Saints') and invented an entire private language, plus accompanying alphabet. She was also endowed with a refreshingly affirmative attitude to human sexuality, aberrance excepted,[3] and famously furnished the first extant description of the female orgasm, complete with vaginal contractions. It is little wonder she was elevated to the sainthood in 1324 (Bobko *et al.* 1995; Bowie and Davies 1990).

Variously described as the 'Sibyl of the Rhine' (Bowie and Davies 1990: 10) and 'one of the most important early medieval theologians' (Newman 1990: 22), Hildegard of Bingen was by no means the earliest exponent of Christian mysticism. Direct encounters with the Godhead date from the Pentutrach, if not beforehand, and the seminal three-fold way of St Bonaventure, comprising *purgation, illumination* and *union*, was originally outlined by Dionysius the Aeropagite at the end of the fifth century CE. Nor, for that matter, was Hildegard the most mystical of female mystics in the history of Christendom. Vivid though they undoubtedly were, her visionary experiences seem somewhat tame – she didn't lose consciousness, for example, or fall into a trance – compared to the highly sensual, not to say erotically charged, spiritual encounters reported by later Christian mystics like Greta the Great (*c.* 1256–1302, principal work: *The Messenger of Divine Love*), Mechthild of Magdeburg (*c.* 1210–1290, principal work: *Flowing Light of the Godhead*) and members of the Beguine movement generally. (Renowned for their 'mysticism of love', the Beguines comprised lay communities of pious women who remained unattached to any convent (Bowie 1989; Davies 1989). The cult flourished in the first half of the fourteenth century but was deemed heretical and mercilessly put down along with its male equivalent, the Beghards.)

Understandably, then, there is considerable debate in theological circles over Hildegard's qualifications as a mystic (Grant 1983; McGinn 1992, 1994; Weeks 1993). Since mysticism normally involves some form of coming together or union with the Godhead, she is perhaps better described as a visionary or prophetess. Her visions, nevertheless, were extraordinarily graphic, incredibly powerful and, by all accounts, an almost permanent feature of her daily, illness-wracked existence. It has been hypothesised that she suffered from a rare form of migraine known as 'scintillating scotoma' (Sacks 1986), though the intermittent nature of this particular affliction is somewhat different from Hildegard's specific symptoms. Her visual field was filled at all times by a strange luminosity, which she termed 'the shadow of the living light' (*umbra viventis lucis*), albeit this background 'noise' – literally, since elements of synaesthesia were also involved – was periodically interrupted by dazzling shafts of the so-called 'living light' (*lux vivens*). Irrespective of the bio-chemical causes of her condition, the most monumental of Hildegard's hallucinations occurred in 1141, when 'a fiery light of exceeding brilliance flashed through my entire brain' (Bingen

1990: 59). This was accompanied by a revelation concerning the meaning of the scriptures as well as a divine command to disseminate the content of her celestial visitation. After enlisting the support of the major-domo of medieval mysticism, St Bernard of Clairvaux, who pressed her case with Pope Eugenius III, Hildegard's work was given the papal seal of approval in 1147.[4] The first volume of her theological trilogy, *Scivias* (an abbreviation of *Scito vias Domini*, 'Know the Ways of the Lord') was completed in 1151; the second, *Liber vitae meritorum* ('The Book of Life's Merits'), was written between 1158 and 1163; and the third, *De operatione Dei* ('On the Activity of God') brought to fruition in 1174, five years before her death.

Although the content of the Bigentine corpus is fairly conventional (the 'usual' ecclesiastical triad of creation, redemption and salvation), and her interpretation of Christian doctrine orthodox verging on reactionary (she repeatedly rails against the then commonplace practices of simony, priestly concubinage and Catharism), Hildegard's mode of literary exposition is virtually unique and her cosmology strikingly original (Newman 1990). Less than accessible though her language sometimes is, the component parts of Hildegard's trilogy follow the same basic format: a brief description of the relevant revelation, coupled with an extended expatiation on its meaning, allegorical properties and lessons thereby learned. She espouses a worldview, moreover, that is essentially holistic, balanced, optimistic, pragmatic, life-affirming and comprises what today would be described as an 'eco-friendly', or indeed 'feminine', stance. Hildegard's doctrinal position, admittedly, was not especially novel in itself, yet her essentially positive view of humankind, her basic sympathy for human faults and foibles, is not only unusual for a twelfth-century theologian but remarkably 'modern' in outlook. In light of this anthropocentric rather than Christocentric cosmology (where living, breathing, fallen humanity occupies a central position, as opposed to an idealised image of the Creator), it is perhaps not surprising that a Hildegardian 'cult' has emerged in recent years. Her books have been republished, music recorded, plays performed – a commemorative stamp was even issued by the German post office – and she has been raised to more than mere sainthood; she is now regarded as a proto-feminist (Newman 1987).

Despite her impressively progressive cosmological credentials, in one respect at least Hildegard was an ecclesiastic of her time, in word if not in deed. Her views on commerce, exchange, buying and selling – in short, the marketing system – were consistently hostile. Consumption, materialism, covetousness, avarice and all the analogous temptations associated with trading were not only roundly condemned but considered to be the most diabolical weapons in the Devil's nefarious armory. It is noteworthy that her principal vision concerning Satan's maleficent ways features a 'kind of marketplace', peopled with sinister merchants, and abundantly stocked with 'human wealth and worldly delights and various sorts of merchandise' (Bingen 1990: 293). In her explanatory gloss, Hildegard interprets this alluring consumer cornucopia as symptomatic of the Devil's malevolent machinations: 'pride and vainglory in corruptible riches, licentiousness and lust for transitory pleasures, and trafficking in all kinds of earthly desires' (Bingen 1990: 295). What's more, the accompanying illustration depicts the mendacious merchants – in the symbolically significant lower part of the panel – disporting the distinctive hats worn by medieval Jews.

Set against this, however, Hildegard's own behaviour reveals that she was nothing if not obsessed with worldly possessions and the good things of life. She battled tirelessly for the financial autonomy of, settlements on and rights accorded to her convents (e.g. the lucrative burial of well-endowed local worthies); encouraged her nuns to wear bright clothing and veils; contemptuously dismissed the carping of her more ascetically inclined contemporaries, who objected to the multi-coloured 'tiaras' and jewelry that adorned the backsliding Benedictines of Bingen; and, towards the end of her career, endured a papal interdict, which denied her flock the sacraments, rather than disinter the body of a wealthy excommunicant (Flanagan 1989). Indeed, her visions are absolutely replete with consumption-related imagery – perfumes, precious stones, expensive textiles and clothing (the last of these was a constantly recurring symbol of 'virtue') – and, in an astonishingly prescient account of the post-purchase depression suffered by compulsive shoppers, she attributed the vice of 'world sadness' to the after-effects of unrestrained avarice (Flanagan 1996). Of course, it is grossly unfair, not to say anachronistic, to try to take Hildegard to task for hypocritical covetousness. Being human, she was a sinner, subject to the temptations that all sinners suffer, and as someone from a wealthy background who spent most of her life toiling under the church's abstemious regime, she was perhaps more tempted than most. Nevertheless, when it comes to the marketing system, 'the first great woman theologian in Christian history' (McGinn 1994: 333) manifestly failed to practise what she preached.

Whenever God shines his light

Philippus Theophrastus Bombastus of Hohenheim (1493–1541) was not simply larger than life, he was larger than larger than life. Monstrously egotistical, carouser of legend and castrated in a childhood encounter with a wild boar, Bombastus was a fat, foul-mouthed, follicly challenged, unspeakably malodorous, incessantly argumentative, utterly incorrigible dipsomaniac, who died a penniless physical wreck – though some say he was poisoned – at the age of 47 (Aveni 1996). He was also the pre-eminent *magus* of the late medieval period. Like the primordial Magi, a tribe of pre-Zoroastrian shamans whose descendants practised 'everyday' magic and sold their spells, charms, amulets and occult concoctions on the peripheries of the ancient Athenian agora, Bombastus spent the bulk of his career as an itinerant apothecary, a huckster of herbs, cures, catholicons, precipitates, prescriptions and what we would today describe as homeopathic medicine (Roland 1995).

Theophrastus Bombastus, in other words, was the original snake-oil salesman, complete with personality, patter, persuasiveness and self-importance to the point of pomposity (hence 'bombast'). Granted, just as Hildegard of Bingen failed to practise what she preached, so too Bombastus was less than complimentary about his calling and hence something of a commercial casuist. Although he was a highly successful peripatetic physician, occasional metal dealer on the London exchange and not averse to issuing extravagant advertising fliers for his forthcoming literary endeavours, Theophrastus excoriated any kind of trading activity, abhorred its practitioners and, as a consequence of his involvement in the millenarian Peasant's Revolt of 1524 (unlike its charismatic leader, Thomas Müntzer, Bombastus narrowly escaped execution), championed the creation of a quasi-communistic state, where personal possessions were disavowed, international trade rigorously controlled, wealth equally divided and all manifestations of the marketing system eradicated (Pachter 1961).

Theophrastus, however, was much more than a trucker of tinctures, peddler of potions, metal-monger *manqué* and hypocritical hawker of utopian hallucinogens. He was a *magus* in the original sense of the word, someone 'wise' in the ways of the world and indeed the underworld. Amongst his manifold magical accomplishments, Bombastus specialised in alchemy and thaumaturgy, though his prodigious personal reputation led to the bestowal of several lucrative scholarly sinecures. Yet despite his phenomenal, albeit largely unpublished, academic output, these professorial appointments did not prosper. Anything but. His imperiousness was such that he took the name Paracelsus, meaning 'above Celsus' (the renowned Roman physician of the fifth century CE); organised a book-burning ceremony in Basle, where the works of Galen, Avicenna and Hippocrates were consigned to the flames by his students; and, blessed with a turn of phrase that puts even the most abusive of marketing apocalyptics to shame, Bombastus variously described his copious opponents in cerebration as 'learned fools', 'wormy lousy sophists', 'not worthy that a dog should lift his hind leg against them' and, of particular relevance to the academic marketing community, 'at universities you cannot learn as much as at the Frankfurt Fair' (Wilson 1995). What's more, when the rest of the Basle professoriate denounced him as a charlatan and exhibitionist, and moved to strike him from the university roster, Paracelsus announced a public lecture during which he promised to reveal his celebrated alchemical secrets. Needless to say, the event attracted the most illustrious scholars, thinkers and physicians of the day, though the eminence of the audience was eclipsed when Theophrastus entered, in full professorial garb, carrying a brimming tureen of steaming human ordure. As the learned scrambled for the exit, the great man regaled them with a reminder that all their erudition 'shed as much light as Spanish Fly in a dysentery stool' (Roland 1995).[5]

Above all, then, Paracelsus was a rebel, a revolutionary, a late medieval headbanger, someone who was not prepared to accept the accepted or toe the party line. This antinomian propensity, moreover, was as true of his medical practices as his inter-personal skills. He refused, for example, to treat war wounds by the then standard practice of cauterisation with boiling oil, preferring to employ his proprietary ointments, enchanted unguents and, not least, clean dressings. Shattered limbs, similarly, were sutured instead of being allowed to turn gangrenous prior to unanaesthetised amputation, the shock of which killed more patients than the affliction (Pachter 1961). On one notorious occasion, indeed, Paracelsus managed to combine his diagnostic convictions, social shortcomings and anti-marketing inclinations to disastrous effect, when he launched a vitriolic attack on the profiteering of the Fuggers, an enormously powerful banking dynasty that held the monopoly on guiac wood and mercury, the then recommended treatments for syphilis. Strangely enough, Theophrastus was unwelcome in Augsburg thereafter (Weeks 1997).

Bombastus's congenital, if less than politically astute, unwillingness to defer to the authority of the authorities was equally apparent in his theoretical-cum-philosophical-cum-theological work, which was not only written in vernacular German rather than the Latin of the academic elite, but characterised by a paradoxical – characteristically Paraclesian – form of anti-magical magic. Thus he denounced sorcery, superstition, miracles, legerdemain, conjuring tricks and the hocus-pocus of his less scrupulous necromantic brethren. Yet Bombastus was a firm believer in demons, ghosts, goblins, succubae, incubi, telepathy, telekinesis, mediumistic states, etc., as well as the innate healing properties of spells, stones, numbers and incantations. In effect, the entire apparatus of the so-called 'mantic arts' (Webster 1982).

In this respect, of course, Paracelsus was no different from the vast majority of his magic circle, but the key difference between him and them – the difference that ensured his place as 'the most revered alchemist of the Hermetic Age' (Aveni 1996: 107), as 'a man of unrivaled insight and imagination' (Roland 1995: 66) – was the fact that he tried to account for his success, to explain how nature worked, to understand the assumptions upon which his activities were based. For Paracelsus, it was not enough that these medical 'miracles' were made available through divine dispensation, what he called 'the Light of God'. The 'Light of Nature', he contended, could also be comprehended in its own, non-miraculous terms. Since the Light of God created the Light of Nature – and wished it to be understood by humankind – studying the latter was a way of glorifying the former. After all, as God made the world in his own image, and as his presence was everywhere manifest, knowledge of nature obviously equated to knowledge of the Lord (Weeks 1993, 1997).

This perceived parallelism between humanity and the deity, the microcosm in the macrocosm, comprises the essence of Paracelsian cosmology. Albeit of ancient provenance – Hildegard of Bingen was a major influence – his notion of *omnes in omnibus*, the idea that everything is in everything else, that the most profound metaphysical insights can be obtained by scrutinising the merest blade of grass,[6] provided the basis of Bombastus's celebrated concept of 'signatures'. Essentially a semiotic system of correspondences and the complete antithesis of Galenic orthodoxy, which treated diseases as manifestations of humoral imbalance ('contrary cures contrary'), Paracelsus's signatures were premised on a belief that 'like cures like'. A kidney-shaped plant, for instance, was regarded as efficacious in renal-related conditions, although the reasoning behind the correspondences is often much less straightforward. Thus, syphilis was treated with tincture of mercury because Mercury was the god of the marketplace and marketplaces were the haunts of women in general and diseased whores in particular (Pagel 1984).

Given these sentiments, it is highly unlikely that Paracelsus will ever be lionised as a proto-feminist. However, just as Hildegard, his mystical mentor, has latterly been catapulted to cult status, so too a bizarre Bombastian fad materialised in Germany during the 1930s and 1940s (Weeks 1997). Apart from the Basle book-burning episode, which unsurprisingly resonated with the National Socialists, Theophrastus was treated as a 'signature' of innate Teutonic superiority, the archetypal 'modern' man who emerged triumphant at the dawn of a new era (*dei Neuzeit*). Although there is no doubt that Paracelsus's emphasis on empirical, experimental, 'rational' approaches to the natural world represents a prescient precursor of the scientific method, it is important to appreciate that this ostensibly 'modern' element was predicated upon and an integral part of his occult, alchemical and theological belief system. As Weeks (1997) has recently observed, the two 'sides' of Paracelsus – paradoxical though this combination of sorcerer and scientist seems to us – were inextricably intertwined. Above all else, the-artist-formerly-known-as-Bombastus fervently believed that the power of the human imagination was capable of 'illuminating the eternal light of nature'.

Here comes the knight

Few would deny that Hildegard of Bingen and Theophrastus Bombastus are colourful characters, but compared to Guiseppe Balsamo (1743-1795) they are positively monochromatic. Magician, clairvoyant, conjurer, kabbalist, alchemist, pharmacist, petty thief, forger, extortionist, womaniser, mountebank and charlatan *non-pareil*, this charismatic scoundrel cut a swathe through the *ancien régime* of pre-Revolutionary France and the rest of continental Europe (Gervaso 1974; Wilson 1995). So much so, that he completely eclipsed his contemporaneous rivals in con-artistry-cum-concupiscence, Giovanni Casanova and Anton Mesmer. Born in Palermo, the only son of a costume jeweller, Balsamo's natural talents were soon on show when, as a novice monk, he was expelled from the Fatebenefratelli seminary for a sacrilegious act – reading the litanies aloud with the names of local prostitutes replacing those of the saints. Flight from Sicily swiftly followed as a consequence of another elaborate scam, whereby a credulous silversmith was led to believe that Guiseppe knew the whereabouts of a hidden hoard of treasure. Although it was guarded by (uncommonly worldly) demons, who could be bought off for the not unreasonable price of sixty silver pieces, Balsamo persuaded the apprehensive but avaricious shopkeeper to put up the stake for a share of the loot. However, in a remote field at midnight, as the silversmith was digging for victory whilst Guiseppe recounted the magic words, the twosome were set upon by several 'demons', who beat the patsy senseless, stole his stake and 'spirited' the treasure trove to a safer location. It was only some time later, when Balsamo boasted of the stunt, that the hapless shopkeeper realised he'd been had (Gervaso 1974).

Persona non-grata in Palermo, Balsamo took himself an alluring young bride, Lorenza Feliciani, and the devious duo set off on a lightning tour of Europe. This alacrity was prompted, as much as anything, by the need to get out of town quickly before the long arm of the law descended, or their chicanery was discovered by the dupes upon whom they preyed. Thanks to his innate pharmaceutical dexterity and a number of alchemical recipes picked up in the course of the couple's peregrinations, Balsamo produced, promoted and purveyed all manner of quack medicines, miracle cures, love potions, infertility alleviates, age retardants, impotency combatants, performance-enhancing embrocations and, naturally, the philosopher's stone itself. Unsurprisingly, the last of these proved particularly popular, though Balsamo and Co's principal sources of revenue remained those good old-fashioned standbys: prostitution, blackmail and, as often as not, a creative combination of both. Lorenza attracted the unwary to her boudoir, Guiseppe burst in at an indelicate moment, played the outraged cuckold and, faced with the prospect of ruined personal reputations, a veritable catalogue of counts, cardinals, curates and Calvinists paid up rather than have their peccadilloes exposed (Wilson 1995).

Successful as their prototype Ann Summers' party plan undoubtedly proved and lucrative though the trusty honey-trap turned out to be, the Balsamos only really hit their stride when Guiseppe found he had a remarkable facility for faith healing, prestidigitation and the manifold mantic arts beloved by Bombastus, his prodigious if less flamboyant predecessor. Known, in fact, as 'the New Paracelsus', Balsamo made copious predictions, performed numerous miracles, held countless seances and developed a nifty sideline in necromancy. So accurate were Guiseppe's guesses (his ability to pick winning lottery numbers became legendary); so stupendous his healing touch (death's door recoveries, a speciality); so illustrious the spirits he summoned (as ample first-hand reports testify); and so engaging his conversations with the always already interred (he once organised a dinner party for the dearly departed which attracted Voltaire, Diderot and Montesquieu amongst others) that he quickly became the toast of western Europe. Emperors, aristocrats, intellectuals, artists, theologians, socialites, well-to-dos, *hoi polloi* – in short, all and sundry – fell under the great man's spell. The fact that he spoke in a utterly incomprehensible heteroglot of several European languages only added to the attraction, as did the distinguished alias he quickly adopted. Commensurate with his status as sorcerer supreme and alchemist to kings, he transmuted the base metal of Balsamo into the 24 carat gold of Cagliostro – Count Alessandro Cagliostro.

Armed with this eloquent sobriquet, the Count and his equally exalted wife, Countess Serafina, Queen of Sheba, spent ten years or so in regal procession around the palaces and courts of Europe (Randi 1992). Kept in the lap of luxury by gullible admirers, lionised by the popular press, and everywhere mobbed by mendicants, well-wishers and individuals in need of medical attention, Cagliostro became the centre of a personality cult, the sheer scale of which almost defies description. The market was literally flooded with Cagliostro tie-in merchandise – busts, books, portraits, porcelain, trinkets, tinctures, amulets, magic wands, philosopher's stones, the lot! – and the Count's attempts to control the commercial frenzy, by denouncing the charlatans who exploited his name without permission, only added fuel to the flames, since they created a secondary market in 'officially sanctioned' Cagliostro merchandise, with prices to match (Gervaso 1974).

The bubble had to burst and it did so in the most dramatic fashion, when the Count became involved in the notorious 'Queen's Necklace' affair, an attempt to defraud a lovestruck French nobleman. Madly in love with Marie Antoinette and led to believe that the Queen's favours would be bestowed upon him if he acted as her guarantor for a priceless necklace, the infatuated Cardinal Louis Rohan foolishly agreed. Time passed, the jewellers duly asked for settlement – the necklace meanwhile had been appropriated, broken up and resold by the confidence tricksters – and the embarrassed Cardinal found himself unable to meet their demands. The exasperated jewellers then contacted Marie Antoinette personally and, since she knew absolutely nothing about the necklace, the Queen was more than a little irritated, as was Louis XVI. However, instead of hushing up the whole sordid business, the incandescent bluebloods instituted legal proceedings against everyone connected with the case including Cagliostro, a confidant of the Cardinal. The subsequent trial, plus accompanying publicity, ensured that a great deal of dirty linen was washed in public, to the detriment of defendants and plaintiffs alike (in the public eye it confirmed the corruption and immorality at Court). Although he was completely exonerated, Cagliostro suffered grievously as a result of the affair – tortured, betrayed by Lorenza and his chicanery laid bare – albeit not as much as Marie Antoinette and Louis XVI, whose already suspect reputations were completely and very publicly ruined. Be that as it may, Cagliostro's decline was rapid in the wake of the revelations and ridicule. Having unwisely decided to return to Italy, he was arrested in Rome, tried by the Papal Court for alleged heresy, sentenced to life imprisonment and died, a broken man, on 26 August 1795 (Aveni 1996; Trowbridge n.d.).

While there is more than a little irony in Balsamo's fall from grace – the trickster tricked – there is no denying that he was a marketer through and through: brilliant self-publicist; source of a merchandising bonanza that puts Batman, Cabbage Patch Dolls and the Teenage Mutant Ninja Turtles to shame; and, thanks to his best-selling range of beauty products, wrinkle-reducing libations and coitus uninterruptus elixirs, an exemplary itinerant purveyor of the 'hope' that Ted Levitt repeatedly extols. Count Alessandro Cagliostro, however, was much more than a pre-Revolutionary cross between Richard Branson and the

Avon Lady. His success was attributable in no small part to his position as one of the most prominent 'Illuminated Ones' of the period (Gervaso 1974). Widely read in neoplatonism, the kabbalah and the western mystical tradition, Balsamo was inducted into the Masonic Order at the age of 33, quickly rose to prominence as a result of his impeccable magical credentials and established a very close connection to the *Illuminati*, an elite offshoot of the Order, established by Adam Weishaupt in 1776 (Daraul 1989). Like all *Illuminati*, Cagliostro was committed to the establishment – by revolutionary means if necessary – of an utopian superstate. This necessitated the eschewal of political authority, private property, personal possessions and the iniquitous marketing system, thereby ensuring egalitarianism, peaceful co-existence, religious tolerance and the universal rights of man. Liberty, equality and fraternity, in other words. The connection to the French Revolution is not accidental, since the Masonic Order in general and the *Illuminati* in particular have frequently been accused of deliberately engineering the downfall of the Valois–Bourbon regime (Daraul 1989; Howard 1989). It is uncertain whether this grand conspiracy theory has any historical veracity but it has often been claimed that the Queen's Necklace affair was the *Illuminati*'s attempt to discredit the royal couple, albeit one of their own was caught up in the political crossfire. As a martyr for modernity, Cagliostro cuts a curious figure. As a marketing illuminatus, the 'all-time champion of humbugs' (Randi 1992: 27) is beyond compare.

Piper at the gates of dawn

Fascinating though the shenanigans of our pre-romantic romantics undoubtedly are, many might wonder about the extent of their relevance to contemporary marketing thought. While it is interesting to reflect on marketing phenomena of times past, and diverting to read about the strange people responsible, the scotopic visions of a twelfth-century virgin, the cosmology of a fifteenth-century occultist and the chicanery of an eighteenth-century confidence man have nothing to say to the sophisticates of marketing scholarship at the close of the twentieth century. As a new millennium beckons, surely it is time for marketers to look forward, not back, to advance the cause of marketing understanding, to break new ground, employ original methods, tackle fresh challenges, test null hypotheses, develop novel models, constructs, ideas . . .

Isn't it?

Well, it seems to me that if we are living in a postmodern world, as many maintain, if marketing is the quintessence of postmodernity, as copious commentators contend, and if postmodernists 'look forward by looking back at looking forward', as Weeks (1997: 19) wryly observes, then the illuminist tradition, symbolised by the inimitable Arthur Rimbaud, does contain some lessons for us, after all. The first of these concerns *magic*. Everyone knows that marketing is inherently magical. Advertisers routinely inform us of the miraculous properties of products, often by means of a cavalcade of otherworldly characters (talking dogs, cartoon camels, jolly green giants, etc.); people believe, or try to pretend they don't believe, in the transformational power of perfumes, cosmetics, cigarettes, clothing, household cleaners, motor cars, multi-vitamins, service encounters, and so on; the manifold magic kingdoms of hyperreal estate have held countless children (Disneyworld) and adults (Las Vegas) spellbound by their amazing disappearing-dollar tricks; and we are regularly treated to 'fantastic', 'incredible', 'extraordinary' and 'superhuman' price reductions, which simply have to be seen to be believed.

The marketing literature, furthermore, is replete with magic spells, incantations, mandalas, hocus-pocus and intellectual hey prestos. Thus we have four Ps, five forces, seven Ss and, Heaven help us, 30 Rs. We have matrices beyond measure, models beyond a joke and enough figures of pyramids, pentagrams and boxes and arrows to defoliate an entire forest of (kabbalistic) 'trees of life'. The principal journals are repositories of numerological rumination – the numbers and equations don't actually 'mean' anything, though they signify a great deal to other adepts of academic alchemy – and, of course, we all subscribe to the notion that the transmutational properties of the marketing concept only work when companies really, *really* believe in it, say the magic words ('customers', 'relationships', 'value-added', etc.) and, naturally, wish upon a star from the constellation Kotler, Webster or McDonald. Indeed, if they follow the sage advice of the keeper of the marketing philosopher's stone, Shelby D. Hunt, the transmigration of the sold from product to marketing orientation is virtually guaranteed.

Another, closely related, issue concerns *mysticism*. Marketing, again, is irredeemably mystical, albeit this propensity is less immediately apparent than the magical components of marketing practice and theory. The difficulty is compounded by the complete lack of academic consensus on 'the mystic' (Grant 1983; McGinn 1992). Nevertheless, just as mysticism involves some sort of coming together, union with or direct experience of the Godhead, so too marketing is predicated upon closeness to, oneness with or privileged insight into THE CUSTOMER. True, every technical advance in our ability to approach this immanent, transcendent, nothing if not reified being – segmentation, lifestyles, micro-marketing, one-on-one marketing, and so on – only involves its further displacement to a point just beyond reach (multiple 'selves', for example). But, everything about marketing, not least its attempts to lord it over other functional areas, such as the bean-counters of accounts, the head-hunters of HRM, the unmentionables of R&D and the sneak-thieves of strategy, is premised on this purported access to the One who must be obeyed.

In a similar vein, marketing relies entirely upon the fundamental mystical concept of the microcosm in the macrocosm, everything is in everything else, *as above so below*. This idea, first articulated by Hermes Trismegistos in the second century BCE, saturates our discipline all the way from case studies, key informants and representative samples (where one stands for many), through the presumption that the marketing concept is universally applicable (industries, organisations, places, people, etc.), to the very idea that there is a 'right' way of analysing, planning, implementing and controlling – in short, *doing* – marketing. Adumbrated in innumerable marketing management textbooks and used to browbeat generations of recalcitrant practitioners or prospective practitioners, the 'success' of the marketing microcosm (companies, organisations, and so on) is deemed to rest upon its ability to mirror, absorb, reproduce and *become* the macrocosm (we call it marketing 'orientated', but it means doing things the marketing *way*).

Of course, the problem with marketing, as it is presently constituted, is not the fact that it is magical or mystical. The problem is that it denies its inherent magic and mysticism, or at least its academic avatars do. Marketing purports to be rigorous, objective, rational, sensible and 'scientific' when it is nothing of the sort. The witchhunters of marketing scholarship may like to think they are engaged in the noble pursuit of Truth, Reason, Realism and what have you, but no one else in the academy believes they are, no manager with a modicum of common sense believes they are and, frankly, for all the Marketing Inquisition's huffing and puffing none of its adepts will ever produce a more resonant concept than the magisterial, the majestic, the magical 4Ps. The upshot of this absurd infatuation with dispassion, this nonsense about sensibility, this unscientific scientism, this objectification of objectivity, is that there is a growing disjunction between marketing theory and practice, between marketing teaching and doing, between marketing pure and applied.

Indeed, one doesn't need to be an expert in academic psychoanalysis (though, God knows, I'm quite partial to pretension, can babble *non-sequiturs* with the best of them and have even been known to employ ostentatious, foreign language epigraphs) to appreciate that this neoclassical emphasis upon reason, rationality and order is a fundamental *misrecognition* of marketing's true character. Like the developing child, marketing is trapped by an image outside itself, an image of scientific rectitude, with which it identifies, to which it aspires and from which it is hopelessly alienated (Leader and Groves 1995; Roudinesco 1997). However, rather than get caught up in a Lacanian limbo (do I mean the dance or the anteroom of Hell where unbaptised infants and the righteous irreligious reside? – you decide!) or even pause to record the fact that Lacan also hailed from a marketing background (his father was a sales rep.), it is sufficient to stress that the utopian world of marketing science is an illusion, it is unattainable, it is an internalisation of the romantic quest, it is the chimerical realm of the academic Imaginary, where subjects console themselves by identifying with chosen fragments of the world, by finding an imagined wholeness of the ego reflected in the seeming wholeness of that which is perceived. As Bowie (1991: 92) observes, 'the Imaginary is the scene of a desperate delusional attempt to be and remain "what one is" by gathering to oneself ever more instances of sameness, resemblance and self-replication'. Marketing, in short, is 'haunted by an Imaginary identification with a rational scientific imago' (Desmond 1993: 264).

There is, however, a tradition of thought, a complete worldview that is much longer established than western rationalism and better describes the incantations, abracadabras and, not least, *charms* of marketing than all the miracles of the Lisrel-ites, all the sorcery of SERQVAL and all the prestidigitation of Relationship it's-done-with-mirrors-you-know Marketing. It is the pre-romantic illuminist tradition represented herein by Hildegard of Bingen, Theophrastus Bombastus and the one and only Guiseppe Balsamo.[7] It is the tradition of malcontents, millenarianism, marginality, misappropriation, mutineers and madness. It is the tradition of marketing. It is the manner of marketing. It is the matter of marketing. It is the manna, the marinade, the mayonnaise, the – yes – manure of marketing. It is the manifest destiny of marketing.

Gloria

The enigmatic prose poems that make up *Les Illuminations* are generally regarded as Arthur Rimbaud's greatest literary achievement. Written at the end of his incandescent career – he truly was the Rambo of French Letters – they are understandably suffused with sadness, disillusionment and despair. The principal exception is the very last of *Les Illuminations*, which in light of his subsequent reinvention as a marketing man, is aptly entitled *Solde* (Clearance Sale). In it, Rimbaud reiterates his credo of disordering, of derangement, of *mixture*; calls for renewal, the freeing of our senses, the dissolution of established worldviews; and concludes with the inspirational, inadvertently appropriate words, *Les vendeurs ne sont pas à bout de solde! Les voyageurs n'ont pas à rendre leur commission de sitôt!* (The company is not at the end of its clearance sale! The marketing men won't have to turn in their accounts for a long time yet!) Gloria, G-L-O-R-I-A, Gloria . . .

Dweller on the threshold

1 Still pretentious after all these years! Translation (see Bernard 1986):

> The Voices reconstituted; the fraternal awakening of all choral and orchestral energies and their immediate application; the opportunity, unique, of freeing our senses!
>
> For sale bodies above price, not to be found in any race, world, sex, or line of descent! Riches spurting at every step! Unrationed sale of diamonds!
>
> For sale anarchy for the masses; irrepressible satisfaction for connoisseurs; frightful death for the faithful and for lovers!
>
> For sale dwelling places and migrations, sports, perfect magic and perfect comfort, and the noise, the movement, and the future they create!
>
> For sale unheard-of applications of reckoning and leaps of harmony. Lucky finds and terms unsuspected, with immediate possession.

2 Rimbaud is usually classified as a Symbolist, post-romantic poet. However, as the first generation of French 'romantics' drew their inspiration from the *pre-romantics* of

the *Sturm und Drang* tradition, 'the true heirs of the German romanticism of 1800–15 were the French Symbolist poets of the latter half of the nineteenth century. Baudelaire, Nerval, Mallarmé and Rimbaud subscribed to a new conception of art and the artist, which was closely akin to the theories of the German Jena romantic group: poetic experience was envisaged as essentially different from ordinary experience, a magic form of intuitive spiritual activity, a mysterious expansion into the transcendental in which the visionary poet adventured into a dream realm to explore the hidden sources and 'correspondences' of life' (Furst 1969: 49).

3 Thus Hildegard vigorously opposed homosexuality, lesbianism, bestiality and masturbation. For those so afflicted, she recommended a range of penitential remedies including lamentation, fasting, maceration of the flesh and heavy beatings (Flanagan 1989). In other respects, however, she was very progressive. Unlike many medieval ecclesiastics, Hildegard did not debar menstruating women from church attendance, though she drew the line at men who were experiencing 'nocturnal emissions'. For the latter ailment, she prescribed a balm made out of the entrails of sparrow-hawk. When smeared on the genitals for five days, it cleared up the condition within a month. You read it here first!

4 The significance of this endorsement cannot be overemphasised. Women, even exceptionally talented women like the infamous Héloïse – Hildegard's contemporary – were ordinarily denied this privilege.

5 No, I don't know what it means either, but it sounds great! In truth, his actions would have appeared much less dramatic at the time, since students were then advised not to throw stones or dung during lectures. Would someone please remind mine?!

6 If this reminds you of Blake's 'To see a World in a Grain of Sand/And a Heaven in a Wild Flower/Hold Infinity in the palm of your hand/And Eternity in an hour', it should do! William Blake was heavily influenced by the thought of Emmanuel Swedenborg (1688–1772), who was deeply indebted to Jacob Boehme (1575–1624), who was inspired in turn by Theophrastus Bombastus (Ackroyd 1995).

7 Elsewhere I have described this lot as 'the 4Bs of marketing illuminations' (Brown 1997). Yes, I know there's one missing, I'm not *completely* innumerate! Fear not, friends, the fourth B will materialise before this volume is out. Try to control yourselves!

Days like this

Abrams, M.H. (1953), *The Mirror and the Lamp:Romantic Theory and the Critical Tradition*, Oxford: Oxford University Press.

Abrams, M.H. (1971), *Natural Supernaturalism: Tradition and Revolution in Romantic Literature*, New York: Norton.

Ackroyd, P. (1995), *Blake: A Biography*, London: Sinclair-Stevenson.

Aveni, A. (1996), *Behind the Crystal Ball: Magic and Science from Antiquity to the New Age*, London: Newleaf.

Bernard, O. (1986), 'Introduction', in A. Rimbaud, *Collected Poems*, Harmondsworth: Penguin, xxiii–xxxii.

Bingen, H. von (1990 [1151]), *Scivias*, trans. Mtr. C. Hart and J. Bishop, New York: Paulist Press.

Bobko, J., Newman, B. and Fox, M. (1995), *Vision: The Life and Music of Hildegard of Bingen*, New York: Penguin.

Bowie, F. (1989), *Beguine Spirituality: An Anthology*, London: SPCK.

Bowie, F. and Davies, O. (1990), *Hildegard of Bingen: An Anthology*, London: SPCK.

Bowie, M. (1991), *Lacan*, London: Collins.

Brown, S. (1997), 'Tore down *à la* Rimbaud: the 4Bs of marketing illuminations', in S. Brown *et al.* (eds), *Proceedings of the Marketing Illuminations Spectacular*, Belfast: University of Ulster, 1-15.

Brown, S. (1998), *Postmodern Marketing Two: Telling Tales*, London: ITBP.

Brown, S., Bell, J. and Carson, D. (1996), 'Apocaholics anonymous: looking back on the end of marketing', in S. Brown *et al.* (eds), *Marketing Apocalypse: Eschatology, Escapology and the Illusion of the End*, London: Routledge, 1-20.

Bruss, E.W. (1982), *Beautiful Theories: The Spectacle of Discourse in Contemporary Criticism*, Baltimore: The Johns Hopkins University Press.

Chadwick, C. (1979), *Rimbaud*, London: Athlone.

Daraul, A. (1989), *A History of Secret Societies*, Secaucus: Citadel Press.

Davies, O. (1989), *The Rhineland Mystics: An Anthology*, London: SPCK.

Denison, T. and McDonald, M. (1995), 'The role of marketing: past, present and future', *Journal of Marketing Practice: Applied Marketing Science*, 1(1), 54–76.

Desmond, J. (1993), 'Marketing – the split subject', in D. Brownlie *et al.* (eds), *Rethinking Marketing: New Perspectives on the Discipline and Profession*, Coventry: Warwick University Research Bureau, 259–69.

Faivre, A. (1994), *Access to Western Mysticism*, Albany: State University of New York Press.

Flanagan, S. (1989), *Hildegard of Bingen, 1098–1179: A Visionary Life*, London: Routledge.

Flanagan, S. (1996), *Secrets of God: Writings of Hildegard of Bingen*, Boston: Shambala.

Furst, L.R. (1969), *Romanticism in Perspective: A Comparative Study of Aspects of the Romantic Movements in England, France and Germany*, Basingstoke: Macmillan.

Gervaso, R. (1974), *Cagliostro: A Biography*, London: Victor Gollancz.

Godwin, J. (1994), *The Theosophical Enlightenment*, Albany: State University of New York Press.

Grant, P. (1983), *Literature of Mysticism in Western Tradition*, Basingstoke: Macmillan.

Howard, M. (1989), *The Occult Conspiracy: Secret Societies – Their Influence and Power in World History*, Rochester: Destiny Books.

Kroeber, K. (1988), *Romantic Fantasy and Science Fiction*, New Haven: Yale University Press.

Leader, D. and Groves, J. (1995), *Lacan for Beginners*, Cambridge: Icon.

Little, R. (1983), *Rimbaud: Illuminations*, London: Grant & Cutler.

McGinn, B. (1992), *The Foundations of Mysticism*, New York: Crossroad.

McGinn, B. (1994), *The Growth of Mysticism*, New York: Crossroad.

Morrison, V. (1984), 'Tore down à la Rimbaud', from the album *A Sense of Wonder*, New York: Polygram Records.

Mowen, J.C. and Leigh, T.W. (1996), 'State of marketing thought and practice: a panel discussion', *Marketing Educator*, 15(1), 1–3.

Newman, B.J. (1987), *Sister of Wisdom: St. Hildegard's Theology of the Feminine*, Berkeley: University of California Press.

Newman, B.J. (1990), 'Introduction', in H. of Bingen, *Scivias*, trans. Mtr. C. Hart and J. Bishop, New York: Paulist Press, 9–53.

Nicholl, C. (1997), *Somebody Else: Arthur Rimband in Africa*, London: Jonathon Cape.

Osmond, N. (1976), *Rimbaud: Illuminations,* London: Athlone.

Pachter, H.M. (1961), *Paracelsus: Magic Into Science*, New York: Collier Books.

Pagel, W. (1984), *The Smiling Spleen: Paracelsianism in Storm and Stress*, Basle: Karger.

Prickett, S. (1976), *Romanticism and Religion: The Tradition of Coleridge and Wordsworth in the Victorian Church*, Cambridge: Cambridge University Press.

Randi, J. (1992), *Conjuring*, New York: St Martin's Press.

Roland, P. (1995), *Revelations: Wisdom of the Ages*, Berkeley: Ulysses Press.

Roudinesco, E. (1997 [1994]), *Jacques Lacan*, trans. B. Bray, Cambridge: Polity.

Sacks, O. (1986), *The Man who Mistook his Wife for a Hat*, New York: Summit Books.

Starkie, E. (1961), *Arthur Rimbaud*, New York: New Directions.

Taylor, A. (1979), *Magic and English Romanticism*, Athens: University of Georgia Press.

Trowbridge, W.H.R. (n.d.), *Cagliostro: Saint or Scoundrel? The True Role of This Splendid, Tragic Figure*, Hyde Park: University Books.

Webster, C. (1982), *From Paracelsus to Newton: Magic and the Making of Modern Science*, Cambridge: Cambridge University Press.

Weeks, A. (1993), *German Mysticism: From Hildegard of Bingen to Ludwig Wittgenstein*, Albany: State University of New York Press.

Weeks, A. (1997), *Paracelsus: Speculative Theory and the Crisis of the Early Reformation*, Albany: State University of New York Press.

Wilson, C. (1995), *The Occult: A History*, New York: Barnes & Noble.

Zaehner, R.C. (1970), *Concordant Discord*, Oxford: Clarendon.

3

IN THE ARMS OF THE OVERCOAT

On luxury, romanticism and consumer desire

Russell W. Belk

A primary preoccupation of the romantic writers was passionate desire. This preoccupation led both to celebrating such passion as the height of joy in human experience and to condemning such desire as something to be deplored, rationalised, sublimated, suppressed, or transcended. The battle between indulging and controlling or transforming desire continues today. Robinson (1991: 10) sees the relevance of romanticism to the present age as consisting of 'dramatizing in our culture the competing drives . . . toward the beautiful as transcendence and the beautiful as erotic pleasure and desire'.

While the romantic poets and writers were primarily concerned with erotic passion for another person, they also focused on passion for aesthetic objects, luxury objects, nature, and God. Whether the object is a person, a deity, an art-work, or a manufactured product, the tension between indulging and transcending these desires is the same one later discussed by Freud in considering whether we can move 'beyond the pleasure principle' (Trilling 1963). What is shared in the passion towards each of these objects, Bloom (1970) notes, is enchantment. Reason is the great disenchanter, while indulging libidinal passion as well as resisting such passion in favour of a greater self-transcendent pleasure, both embrace enchantment. Erotic passion, religious passion, and consumer passion all involve the domination of reason by the emotional state of enchantment and the attendant state of desire (Belk *et al.* 1996).

The essential romantic desire is a desire to give ourselves over to something greater than the self and to thereby become a part of the enchanted object. The enchanted, extended, engulfed self – becoming one with the object of desire – is the supreme goal. This is a goal that is greatly enlivened by anticipation and imagination. Campbell (1987) goes further and suggests that the pleasures of imagined fulfilment exceed those of fulfilment itself. Such states of longing are therefore sought after in much the same way that an often unobtainable loved one was sought after in courtly love. It is this questing spirit of romanticism that

Campbell effectively argues gave birth to contemporary consumer culture. Furthermore, he surmises that in the Puritan and Protestant emphasis on raising children to deny pleasures and delay gratifications (the ostensibly rationalising aspect of romantic desire), the actual result may be to foster the very daydreaming, fantasising, and imaginative passion that underwrite consumerism.

Nevertheless, as Campbell (1987) is also careful to point out, the contribution of the romantics to modern consumerism is ironic in light of their avowed disdain for the overt selfishness of pursuing pleasure through novel consumer goods. As Wordsworth (1806) complained, 'The world is too much with us: late and soon, Getting and spending, we lay waste our powers.' Holbrook (1996: 27) maintains, however, that 'romanticism pervades consumer behavior to its very core'. In Holbrook's view, romanticism stimulated a focus on experiential consumption, and passions arise as a consequence of such experience. By restricting experiential consumption to that which is involved in the 'acquiring, using, and disposing of products,' Holbrook (ibid.: 287) retains an emphasis on romantic passion, but eliminates Campbell's (1987) emphasis on anticipatory consumer desire as the key phenomenon in contemporary consumption. In Campbell's view, we derive more pleasure than pain from imagining ourselves in possession of the object of our desires (1987: 246). Even if the lack of the object becomes a kind of torment, we enjoy fantasising about a future or possible self that possesses the desired object. This enjoyment leads to what Lefebvre (1991: 394) called, 'a desire for desire'. This, I believe, is the greatest legacy of romanticism for consumption. Passionate desire has become an end in itself.

As Campbell (1987) also recognised, such imaginative passion is unlikely to attach to mundane objects and experiences. He specifies that it is most likely to instead focus on novel goods. I believe that the notion of luxury goods is a broader way to construe such objects of desire. It encompasses both those novel goods likely to newly capture our imaginations, and those musty, but rare or valuable, goods for which we may have long longed. I wish to consider here the lure of luxury by examining it among those to whom it might be thought to be least applicable – the less affluent have-nots of the world. I have focused elsewhere on the cases of consumer desire in the so-called Third World (Belk 1988; Ger and Belk 1996) and Fourth World (Groves and Belk 1995). Here I focus on the Second World of Russia and Eastern Europe, beginning in pre-communist days and ending in current post-communist days. I begin in the literature of romanticism and end in the everyday experiences of such consumers and the marketers who entice them with luxurious consumer goods.

Pre-communist luxury

Romanticism flourished in Eastern Europe as it did in Western Europe, even though the East has received far less attention (Nemoianu 1984). There are romantic poets and literary figures in Czech, Hungarian, Polish, and, especially, Russian and Romanian literatures. Prominent among the Russian romanticists is Nikolai Gogol. While detailed ethnographies of everyday luxury consumption in pre-communist Russia are lacking, there is a quintessential example of such consumption in Gogol's (1985) tale, 'The Overcoat'. Dostoevsky reputedly said of Russian literature, 'We all come out of Gogol's "Overcoat".' Although the story may mark the beginning of Gogol's slide towards realism, it nevertheless captures the romantic essence of pre-communist Russian consumer desire, if not the more basic essences of being Russian and of desiring consumer luxuries.

The central character in Gogol's story, the lowly clerk Akaky Akakievich, has a seemingly modest desire for a winter overcoat. He is treated rudely at work, lacks power, has no companion, and has only a threadbare coat that is certain not to last the coming winter. When the tailor tells him it can be patched no more and that he must spend the unthinkable sum of 150 rubles for a new one, Akaky becomes, in stages, alarmed, despondent, resigned and then hopefully committed to saving for the new coat. In Gogol's (1985) telling:

> Akaky Akakievich thought and thought and decided at last that he would have to diminish his ordinary expenses, at least for a year; give up burning candles in the evening, and if he had to do any work he must go into the landlady's room and work by her candle; that as he walked along the streets he must walk as lightly and carefully as possible, almost on tiptoe, on the cobbles and flagstones, so that his soles might last a little longer than usual.
>
> (p. 316)

Before these sacrifices are complete, his commitment becomes an erotic passion, 'a displacement of the libido' (Erlich 1969: 149). Gogol's phrases indeed suggest the enlivening effects of passionate love for another person, but directed in this case to the desired overcoat:

> To tell the truth, he found it at first rather difficult to get used to these privations, but after a while it became a habit and went smoothly enough – he even became quite accustomed to being hungry in the evening; on the other hand, he had spiritual nourishment, for he carried ever in his thoughts the idea of his future overcoat. His whole existence had in a sense become fuller, as though some other person were present with him, as though he were no longer alone but an agreeable companion had consented to walk the path of life hand in hand with him, and that companion was none other than the new overcoat with its thick padding and its strong, durable lining. He became, as it were, more alive, even more strong-willed, like a man who has set before himself a definite goal. . . . the most bold and audacious ideas flashed through his mind. Why not really have marten on the collar?
>
> (1985: 316–17)

When Akaky finally gets the coat (he settles for a cat collar rather than marten),

43

he is elated and others suddenly begin to treat him with greater respect. He is invited out to a party where he immensely enjoys the admiring looks of others. But when he is robbed of the coat in the streets on his way home, Akaky soon withers and dies. His obsession with the coat does not end after death and his ghost returns to haunt those in the city who have nice overcoats as well as the unsympathetic bureaucrats who refused to help him recover his beloved coat.

There are two possible, but quite different, interpretations of this tale of desire for luxury in pre-Bolshevik Russia. One view suggests that this is a tale of 'overinvestment in trivia' (Erlich 1969: 143). From this perspective, Akaky's desire for the overcoat is pitiful. Despite Gogol's words that Akaky found spiritual nourishment in his passion, Erlich suggests that his material desire is really a case of spiritual impoverishment. People and the life around him matter little to Akaky; only his precious coat is of any consequence. This interpretation of the story seems to accord with a passage from Gogol's (1942) *Dead Souls* written in the same year as 'The Overcoat':

> Acquisition is the root of all evil . . . Everything transforms itself quickly in man; before one has a chance to turn around there has already grown up within him a fearful cankerworm that has imperiously diverted all his life sap to itself. And more than once some passion – not merely some sweeping grand longing but a mean, sneaky yen for something insignificant – has developed in a man born for great deeds, making him forget great and significant obligations and see something great and sacred in insignificant gewgaws. As countless as the sands of the sea are the passions of man, and no one of them resembles another and all of them, the base and the splendidly beautiful, are in the beginning submissive to the will of man and only later on become fearful tyrants dominating him.
>
> (1942: 297)

The metaphor of sand here inverts William Blake's (1803) couplet 'To see a world in a grain of sand, And heaven in a wild flower.' Instead of contemplating heaven and earth in a single grain of sand, Gogol compares our desires to all the sands of the sea. Where Blake collapses all desire to the micro-metonym of a tiny piece of nature, Gogol explodes desire into the macro-metaphor of infiniteness. Where Blake denies the imperiousness of desires, Gogol affirms the economists' assumption of limitless wants. In both cases, however, a single insignificant thing – a grain of sand or an overcoat – becomes the total focus of concentration. But to Gogol, Erlich (1969) suggests, the result is tragically comic – the result of a dead soul, whereas to Blake such fixation is a triumph of the soul.

A quite different romantic reading suggests that this is a tale of 'the kindling of the human soul, its rebirth under the influence of love' (Chizhevsky 1974: 315). From this perspective, while the story remains a tragedy, Akaky's downfall is due to an ennobling love of something and his fervour and passion are self-transcending. His sacrifices for the coat are acts of love from this perspective and the thought of the coat gives him something to live for and strive for; it gives him hope. This is the transcendent side of the romantic ambivalence about indulging versus transcending desires. Before attempting to resolve these opposing interpretations of Gogol's story, we should examine subsequent and non-fictional cases of Eastern European consumer desire.

Communist luxury

The original conceptions of society and economy in the Soviet Union were unenchanted rational formulations that focused on efficient production and egalitarian distribution more than they did on consumption. But, as Gronow (1997) details, by the mid-1930s ideals of egalitarianism had begun to give way to greater recognition of industriousness, talent, and various desired skills. While income differences increased greatly in this era, many of the rewards came in special luxury consumption privileges such as summer homes, holiday travel, and in some cases even private cars and homes. Foreign goods such as Parker pens and imported cigarettes became status symbols, and the new middle class also began to adopt traditionally elite entertainments such as ballet and classical music (Stites 1992). In Bourdieu's (1984) terms, this might be thought of as appropriating and cultivating a broad-based cultural capital rather than absorbing it by more exclusive cultural inheritance. While increased class stratification may be seen in these Soviet patterns, the classical arts, like certain other luxury goods, were still officially regarded as part of 'the people's' culture'.

In the case of material consumption, there was a parallel concerted effort to produce democratised consumer luxury goods through which the masses could theoretically enjoy the finest luxuries in the world. Much of the model for such luxury consumption in this 'worker's paradise' was pre-Bolshevik European aristocratic life, or at least a semblance of it. Thus, the state geared up to produce cheap luxury goods: champagnes, cognacs, chocolates, perfumes, crystal, fur hats, caviar, and two types of cakes (Gronow 1997). Noting the irony of this 'let them eat cake' mentality that produced luxury goods which had little appeal to the proletariat, while at the same time failing to deliver enough necessities such as bread, Gronow (1997: 53) labels these out-dated and out of place luxury goods 'Soviet kitsch': cheap imitations of the finer goods of another time or place – goods that Gronow implies were pathetic. Boym (1994a) similarly labels such objects 'totalitarian kitsch,' but suggests that they may nevertheless have acted as symbols of hope and dreams of escape. In this sense they offered elements of romantic fantasy amid the otherwise stark socialist realism of the Soviet economy.

In 1959 US Vice-President Richard Nixon visited Moscow for the United States Trade and Cultural Fair in Sokolniki Park. There he and Soviet Premier Nikita Khrushchev engaged in 'the kitchen debates' about which nation had the most and best everyday consumer goods. This escalated into a new cold war race to produce more consumer goods in the Soviet Union. The pseudo-elite goods of prior decades continued to be produced, but starting in the 1950s and 1960s the Soviet Union began to produce new consumer goods for the masses, intending to demonstrate that communism could deliver a standard of living equal to or better than that of capitalism, and make it available to all. These new goods included radios, movies, televisions, refrigerators, stereos, affordable cars, high rise apartments, and more fashionable clothing. Although the apartments may have been cold and ugly (Boym 1994b), the cars may not have been comparable to the latest models elsewhere in the world, and the radios and television sets may have only been designed to pick up the one or two state channels, these further democratic luxuries sustained the hope that parity with the West was close at hand (Gronow 1997). In efforts to afford these new goods, and lacking any way to increase incomes, the sacrifices made were not unlike those of Akaky Akakievich in Gogol's story. In communist Romania, stories of people who ate only yogurt in order to save for luxuries like books and cars were common (Belk 1997b). Other luxuries worth such sacrifices included foreign rock music, cigarettes, sunglasses, souvenirs, perfume, and jeans. All implied modernity and contact with the West, and were especially coveted for this reason (Bar-Häim 1987, 1989; Willis 1985). For Eastern European consumers, the West emerged in this cold war era as a romanticised and fantasised consumption Xanadu, as fantastic as the one envisioned by Coleridge.

Eventually, as the actual lack of parity with the West became more glaringly evident due to a globe shrunk by electronic communications, Western media, and international tourism, consumer hope gave way to pessimism. It now seems clear that this pessimism was a major cause of the collapse of the Communist Bloc in 1989 and the Soviet Union in 1991-92 (e.g. Bauman 1990–91; Kozminski 1992). Kohak (1992) concludes that 'as former subjects of the Soviet empire dream it, the American dream has very little to do with liberty and justice for all and a great deal to do with soap operas and the Sears Catalogue' (p. 209).

While communism continued to satisfy basic needs, its lack of responsiveness to the rapidly changing luxury desires of a consumer culture could not be addressed without a market economy (Gronow 1997: 68). Berry (1994: 229) reaches a similar conclusion, but notes further that while capitalism is willing to accept consumer desires as true consumer preferences, communism assumes that such desires are self-deceptions and that needs are a better distributive principle for the good society. Stated differently, capitalism nourishes and indulges softheaded romantic fantasy, while communism adheres to the reason of a hard-headed realism. This is the political economic counterpart of Campbell's (1987) thesis that romanticism nourished consumer culture, at least in the capitalist West.

Post-communist luxury

The shift, whether wholesale or piecemeal, to a market economy, has had a strange effect on both the luxury goods available and the nature of consumer desires within Eastern Europe and the former Soviet Union. After the collapse of communism, foreign goods began to flood the markets of the cities. In Romania, having just come through the 1979–89 decade in which consumers were massively deprived as all available consumer goods were exported in order to repay foreign debt, consumers were hungry for goods. There were shortages of bread, flour, gasoline, sugar, meat, and many other basic consumer goods (Belk 1997a). But the foreign goods that began to flood the market were not these things at all. They were instead imported luxury goods such as candies, liquors, cameras, German cars, Turkish leather jackets, French, British, and American cigarettes, and Japanese electronics (see Belk and Ger 1994). Similar patterns occurred in Russia (Dixon and Polyakov 1997; Humphrey 1995); Albania (Dahab *et al.* 1997; Drakuli 1996), and elsewhere in the former communist empire.

Nevertheless, the Eastern European dream of instantly achieving a Western consumer lifestyle with all its luxuries and decencies has proven illusory for all but a small subset of consumers. Besides the high prices of the new, non-subsidised foreign goods, inflation and freer prices have made even local goods less affordable for most workers. Coupled with increased expectations due to the open window on the world and the flood of new luxury goods, the result is great disillusionment and frustration for many Romanian and other Eastern European consumers. As is most evident in the former Soviet Union, Czechoslovakia, and Yugoslavia, one result generally has been an increase in ethnic scapegoating, hatred, and violence (Belk and Paun 1995).

Sacrifices continue to be made for the newly available consumer goods, but the nature of these sacrifices has changed. Now besides eating less to afford luxuries, people take second jobs, become part-time entrepreneurs, or sell existing belongings if necessary (see Belk 1997a; Bonnell 1997; Dixon and Polyakov 1997; Drakuli 1996; Piirainen 1997). One 32-year-old Romanian woman described her additional work as involving a sacrifice of time with her 6-year-old daughter:

> Now that I have the opportunity to gain more money, above my current salary, I don't give up. Although I'm revolted when I realize I can't read a book, I can't take good care of my child because I want to earn more.

The notion of giving up former more cultural and idealistic pursuits in order to pursue more materialistic goals was also expressed by a 30-year-old Romanian man:

> Ask people how many books they've read since 1989. Personally, I love books, but I have no more time. I have to work more because now I want more things. To be culturally and spiritually satisfied [is not possible]. . . . Maybe we'll turn back to our cultural life when the balance between the new needs and achievements stabilizes.

A 31-year-old Romanian man described money as driving out art and poetry:

> I don't think there is anybody not interested in money. Maybe the son of a
> millionaire, who doesn't ask for money, he has that money all the time. The
> only things he wants is to paint, to write poems, to travel.

There is not only resigned disillusionment in such comments, but also an abandonment of a romantic hope for a richer life. Ironically, such romanticism was
better sustained under the former communist economy. Daily life may have
been dull, but just as delay of gratifications may nurture a richer fantasy life, so
apparently did the austerity of life under late communism with its perpetual
promises that a true workers' paradise was just around the corner.

In place of former fantasies, a new grim realism soon took over the lives of
those in the former communist empire. As one 32-year-old Romanian woman
expressed it:

> It is very easy to be a nice, decent, moral person when life has never forced
> you to be otherwise. You live there in your 'nest' and serve the truth. But
> when life challenges you, you can't be the same and [you] start to change,
> become mean, materialist, selfish.

Another woman said of her friends that:

> They were people living through and for their ideas, but now they had to
> adapt to the market economy. . . . There is no way back. The material side will
> gain more importance. It's like Communism – no way back. So you can't be
> once more idealist. Things changed; nobody will give you anything to eat only
> for your beautiful ideas:

The pursuit of wealth seemingly takes precedence over 'higher' more self-
transcendent pleasures like the pursuit of truth, ideas, and beauty. But perhaps
the ultimate sacrifice for some Romanians is the practice, outlawed for a time,
of having children in order to put them up for foreign adoption and thereby
obtain money for such consumer luxuries as video cassette recorders.

Besides electronics, nice winter coats have also been identified as an object of
fervent desire for many Romanians (Drazin 1994; Lascu *et al.* 1994). Twenty-
five-year-old Angela had recently bought such a coat, but reflected on her
feelings if she couldn't have afforded it: 'I wouldn't give up. I would be very
anxious. I would think about that coat night and day; that it would match with
other clothes I have – which meanwhile would become without any value.'
Surely shades of Akaky's desire for the overcoat can be heard in these lines. And
like Akaky, this woman reported that the coat made her very happy and that it
was, in fact, much better than having a boyfriend.

While to an outside observer such sacrifices for the sake of trivial luxuries
seem to reflect a perverse inversion of values, it is also possible to see Romanian

and other Eastern European consumers as striving for a life of decency and dignity. For example, Lempert reports of Russian homes that:

> Most Russians seemed to have one or two examples of 'state of the art' Soviet products or luxuries in their homes, though no more than that. There were Soviet televisions (widespread) and, more rarely, cameras and calculators. Several years before, gold spoons were sold for 5 rubles and 34 kopecks. I rarely saw more products than these in the typical home.
>
> (1996: 193)

Yet these few items, as well as the foreign novelties displayed by those fortunate enough to have been abroad, may be seen as luxuries symbolising hope and sophistication in an otherwise dreary life. More poignantly, Drakuli asks:

> what is the minimum you must have so you don't feel humiliated as a woman? It makes me understand a complaint I heard repeatedly from women in Warsaw, Budapest, Prague, Sofia, East Berlin: 'Look at us – we don't even look like women. There are no deodorants, perfumes, sometimes even no soap or toothpaste. There is no fine underwear, no pantyhose, no nice lingerie. Worst of all, there are no sanitary napkins. What can one say except that it is humiliating?'
>
> (1991: 31)

Or as a 25-year-old Romanian woman put it: 'You make love to a man. Your panties are broken or your underwear is old. You are ashamed to switch on the light. Afterward you would like to drink something good; not filthy water.' Seen from this perspective, the drive for modest luxury seems not only innocent and good, but an issue of human rights. This difference in perspectives on the pursuit of luxury brings us back to the ultimate questions of what constitutes luxury and whether or not its pursuit is good for us. It brings us back to the two ways of dealing with desire in romanticism and to the two conflicting interpretations of Gogol's tale.

The lap of luxury

The two preceding pleas for decent and dignified luxuries are notably by women, but otherwise echo the earnest passion of Akaky Akakievich for his beloved overcoat. His death without the coat suggests that he has been completely dominated and overpowered by his desire for this one luxurious object. Without it his life is not worth living and he may be viewed as dying of a broken heart. The metaphor of seduction and abandonment seems apt here. And, Akaky to the contrary, the seducers and abandoners are traditionally male, while those seduced and abandoned are traditionally female.

Berry (1994) demonstrates that luxury has long been criticised as effeminate.

For several thousand years in the West, we have been warned that those who pursue luxuries are weak, self-indulgent, and lacking in self-control. Reekie (1993) has similarly argued that the history of the department store is a history of commercial seduction of women by men. And Gronow (1997: 49) makes it a point to note that goods singled out to demonstrate democratic luxury in the Soviet Union were 'very feminine goods, welcome gifts for women' such as champagne, perfume, chocolates, cake, and caviar sandwiches. Feminine gendering might, as well, be attributed to the former Eastern European passions for the arts, literature, and poetry. These may also be seen as non-material feminine luxuries that were supplanted by material, but still feminine, luxuries as the latter became available.

The disparagement of luxury consumption as feminine may help in understanding why Gogol's story of 'The Overcoat' has been interpreted both as a pitiful 'overinvestment in trivia' (Erlich 1969) and, at the same time, as a 'kindling of the human soul, its rebirth under the influence of love' (Chizhevsky 1974). For love and caring, whether for other people or objects, are stereotypically female traits as well. Thus the weak clerk of Nikolai Gogol has been seduced by a very human passion. This is at once decried as a sign of feminine weakness and celebrated as a demonstration of masculine energising passion that makes life worth living and that initiates a noble quest. The fact that Akaky makes the inanimate coat the love interest of his life, can only be a cause for criticism from an elitist perspective that elevates one set of luxuries as being more legitimate than others. For example, as Trilling (1963) observes, Keats cast women as a luxury, and as Chizhevsky (1974) notes, Dostoevsky made it a point of redoing Gogol's tale as 'Poor Folk', but redeemed it by making a woman rather than an overcoat into the desired object. Thus a woman can be a 'luxury' worthy of any sacrifice and any quest, while an overcoat is judged by Dostoevsky to be a superfluous luxury worthy of little serious consideration. This distinction was the focus by which Dostoevsky chose to challenge the strong poet, Gogol, who preceded him.

That such judgements about worthy and unworthy luxuries are often made, does not make them defensible. It may nevertheless make the pursuit of certain luxuries more socially acceptable than others. In the long history of luxury, we have continuously constructed ever newer things to desire in life, and at the same time we have socially constructed new frameworks to justify our own indulgences while decrying those of others. We are refined; they are crude. We serve a higher purpose; they serve only themselves. We know what is good; they know only what they like. Ours are more enduring and enlightening pleasures; theirs are only momentary conflagrations of misplaced passion. Or more commonly, we are strong, stoic, striving, and masculine; they are weak, hedonistic, indulgent, and feminine. Thus, as Saisselin observes in nineteenth-century France, men were regarded as 'serious and creative' collectors of numerous objects, while female collectors of these same objects were disparaged as 'mere buyers of bibelots' (1984: 84).

It is especially ironic that women should receive the brunt of blame and criticism for indulging in and acceding to consumer desire (Belk 1994, 1995; Firat 1991). First, it is ironic that women, perhaps out of anxiety that they control as much as 80 per cent of buying (Nava 1992: 190), are singled out as having consumer desires, at the same time that they, perhaps out of anxiety about insatiable female sexual appetites (Fuery 1995; Irigaray 1985), are singled out as lacking sexual desires. Second, the feminisation of consumer desire is ironic because as Ross (1989) correctly insists, romanticism (from which contemporary consumer desire arguably sprung) is historically a masculine phenomenon. The adventurous romantic quest, the nobility of self-denial, the cultivation of the wild emotions of revolution, the retreat from the industrial revolution and into the Edenic bliss of nature, and the secular redemption of the fallen self are all part of a distinctly masculine pursuit of romanticism.

While it is facile to cast men as producers and women as consumers, with a narrow definition of production as paid employment, there is at least some historical precedent for this prejudice. But to cast women as creatures of desire and men as unemotional creatures of reason is without foundation. Desire, whether sexual, religious, or consumer, is increasingly recognised as ubiquitous (Jankowiak 1995). It heeds no boundaries of sex, class, region, religion, or ethnicity. Likewise luxury, for all its feminine historical attributions, appears to be a pan-human phenomenon. To the extent that luxury may be construed as involving a hope for something better, this should hardly be surprising. And this hope is, I think, the essence of consumer desire for luxuries. Or as Keats (1817), though speaking of desire for a woman, wrote:

> My restless spirit never could endure
> To brood so long upon one luxury,
> Unless it did, though fearfully, espy
> A hope beyond the shadow of a dream.

The role of the marketer

If there is little or nothing intrinsically wrong in the pursuit of luxury, if such pursuit may provide us with hope for greater happiness, and if criticisms of others' desires for luxuries are largely justifications for our own materialism, what then of the role of the marketer in the creation of desire? While the tailor in 'The Overcoat' did not need to seduce Akaky into wanting a luxurious coat, what of more sophisticated contemporary marketers who help to shape the nature of our desires? One case study that problematises this question is Timothy Burke's (1996) historical study of marketing of consumer toiletries in Rhodesia/Zimbabwe. When these toiletries began to be sold to blacks in Africa they were initially stamped 'For Natives Only', lest their appeal to whites declined. Burke (1996) finds that a consistent theme in the Zimbabwean marketing campaigns of cosmetics firms like Lever Brothers and Colgate was that these products would make black users more like the white colonial Europeans in their country. This appeal was well received and these soaps and cosmetics were apparently bought, like the foreign goods that entered after the collapse of Eastern European communism, as symbols of Western European modernity. Also a part of the appeal of European cosmetics in Zimbabwe was a particular type of 'enlightenment': skin lightening creams and soaps that promised extra 'strength' to help cleanse 'dirty' Africans. This racial 'cleansing' theme has been reported as a part of marketing campaigns elsewhere in colonial Africa as well and it was a part of imperialist advertising in England at the same time (McClintock 1994).

This example makes clear that the marketing of luxury goods and the stimulation of consumer desire are not necessarily innocent or good. Other examples of racist, sexist, ageist, or class-based marketing efforts are not difficult to come by. It is not that the marketing of luxury goods is inherently bad, that luxury is bad, or that such goods should only be made available to some groups and not others. But when the strategy used is to imply that some people are better than others and that those unfortunate enough to be in the 'others' category can hope to be like their 'betters' by owning or using a certain luxury product or service, then there is an acute ethical problem. By emphasising differences that these goods cannot really affect, dissatisfaction, discontent, and envy are all stimulated in the service of selling. Desire then becomes desire to alleviate the negative psychological states that have been evoked rather than simply desire for a more pleasurable state of luxury. To call this desire hope is quite misleading. For the hoped-for state is to be as happy as we might have been if we had not been encouraged to feel dissatisfied, discontent, and envious. And because the product or service being promoted cannot really bring about this state of happiness, the result is likely to be a general increase in our negative feelings about ourselves as well as our resentment of the 'others' who are presented as better-off models.

Of course this need not be the case. There are marketing campaigns that do not play on provoking unhappiness. Even if such marketing over-promises and the products and services do not bring fulfilment, we are not worse off, save the fruitless expenditure of money and resources, in these cases. And if we have been given cause for hope, even false hope, that alone may make us better off. Consider perfume. Even if the magical and romantic promises of the benefits of a particular perfume are chemically impossible, we may well be better off for believing them. Such belief is hope and may even create a self-deceiving placebo effect invigorating our self-confidence. This too is a result of marketing. It would be a dull and dreary world without such glittering promises.

In the long run, consumers in the former communist empire may find that they are better off in the world of such glittering promises. It may, beneath the glitter, still be a world of trivial overcoats, but their more attractive packaging makes it difficult not to hope. It is a world of better promises. If these better promises cause us to sacrifice more, work harder, or even engage in a romantic quest to obtain the products and services of the promise-makers, we may just find that the accomplishment of attaining these goods is its own reward. That is, as with travel, the process may be at least as fulfilling as the arrival at a destination. So long as we have not harmed others in the process of striving for luxury goods and so long as the promises made in marketing these goods do not provoke unhappiness, a fixation on desire for an overcoat may be as wonderful as imagining the world in a grain of sand and heaven in a wild flower.

References

Bar-Häim, G. (1987), 'The meaning of western commercial artifacts for Eastern European youth', *Journal of Contemporary Ethnography*, 16 (July), 205–26.

Bar-Häim, G. (1989), 'Actions and heroes: the meaning of western pop information for Eastern European youth', *British Journal of Sociology*, 40 (March), 22–45.

Bauman, Z. (1990–91), 'Communism: a post-mortem', *Praxis International*, 10(3–4), 185–92.

Belk, R.W. (1988), 'Third world consumer culture', in E. Kumcu and A.F. Firat (eds), *Marketing and Development: Toward Broader Dimensions*, Greenwich, CT: JAI Press, 103–27.

Belk, R.W. (1994), 'Battling worldliness in the new Zion: mercantilism versus homespun in 19th century Utah', *Journal of Macromarketing*, 14 (Spring), 9–22.

Belk, R.W. (1995), *Collecting in a Consumer Society*, London: Routledge.

Belk, R.W. (1997a), 'Everyday life for Eastern consumers', in D-N. Lascu, I. Cătoiu, N. Dholakia, and S. Grossbart (eds), *Marketing Challenges in Transition Economies*, Mangalia, Romania: International Society for Marketing and Development, 1–8.

Belk, R.W. (1997b), 'Romanian consumer desires and feelings of deservingness', in L. Stan (ed.), *Romania in Transition*, Dartmouth, Aldershot, 191–208.

Belk, R.W. (1997c), 'The goblin and the huckster: a story of consumer desire for sensual luxury,' in S. Brown, A.M. Doherty and B. Clarke (eds), *Proceedings of the Marketing Illuminations Spectacular*, Belfast: University of Ulster, 290–9.

Belk, R.W. and Ger, G. (1994), 'Problems of marketization in Romania and Turkey', in C.J. Shultz III, R.W. Belk, and G. Ger (eds), *Consumption in Marketizing Economies*, Greenwich, CT: JAI Press, 123–6.

Belk, R.W., Ger, G. and Askegaard, S. (1996), 'Metaphors of consumer desire,' in K.P. Corfman and J.G. Lynch (eds), *Advances in Consumer Research*, 23, Provo, UT: Association for Consumer Research, 368–73.

Belk, R.W. and Paun, M. (1995), 'Ethnicity and consumption in Romania', in J.A. Costa and G. Bamossy (eds), *Marketing, Consumption, and Ethnicity*, Thousand Oaks, CA: Sage, 180–208.

Berry, C.J. (1994), *The Idea of Luxury: A Conceptual and Historical Investigation*, Cambridge: Cambridge University Press.

Blake, W. (1803), 'Auguries of Innocence', electronic text version from *Library of the Future*, 3rd edn, Irvine, CA: World Library.

Bloom, H. (1970), 'The internalization of the quest-romance', in H. Bloom (ed.), *Romanticism and Consciousness: Essays in Criticism*, New York: W.W. Norton, 3–24.

Bonnell, V.E. (1997), 'Winners and losers in Russia's economic transition', in V.E. Bonnell (ed.), *Identities in Transition: Eastern Europe and Russia After the Collapse of*

Communism, Center for Slavic and East European Studies, Berkeley, CA: University of California, 13–28.

Bourdieu, P. (1984), *Distinction: A Social Critique of the Judgement of Taste*, London: Routledge and Kegan Paul.

Boym, S. (1994a), 'The archaeology of banality: the Soviet home', *Public Culture*, 6 (Winter), 263–92.

Boym, S. (1994b), *Common Places: Mythologies of Everyday Life in Russia*, Cambridge, MA: Harvard University Press.

Burke, T. (1996), *Lifebuoy Men, Lux Women: Commodification, Consumption, and Cleanliness in Modern Zimbabwe*, Durham, NC: Duke University Press.

Campbell, C. (1987), *The Romantic Ethic and the Spirit of Modern Consumerism*, Oxford: Basil Blackwell.

Chizhevsky, D. (1974), 'About Gogol's "Overcoat"', in R.A. Maguire (ed.), *Gogol from the Twentieth Century: Eleven Essays*, Princeton, NJ: Princeton University Press, 295–322.

Dahab, D.J., Su, W., Riolli, L. and Marquardt, R. (1997), 'Shopping Albanian markets: satisfaction with retail strategy', *International Journal of Commerce and Management*, 7(1), 29–56.

Dixon, D.F. and Polyakov, E. (1997), 'Physical quality-of-life indicators in post-Stalinist Russia', *Journal of Macromarketing*, 17 (Spring), 39–55.

Drakuli, S. (1991), *How We Survived Communism and Even Laughed*, New York: W.W. Norton.

Drakuli, S. (1996), *Cafe Europe: Life After Communism*. New York: W.W. Norton.

Drazin, A.M. (1994), 'Changing appearances in Romania', in C.J. Shultz III, R.W. Belk, and G. Ger (eds), *Consumption in Marketizing Economies*, Greenwich, CT: JAI Press, 57–88.

Erlich, V. (1969), *Gogol*, New Haven, CT: Yale University Press.

Firat, F. (1991), 'Consumption and gender: a common history', in J.A. Costa (ed), *Gender and Consumer Behavior Conference Proceedings*, Salt Lake City, UT: University of Utah Printing Service, 378–86.

Fuery, P. (1995), *Theories of Desire*, Melbourne: Melbourne University Press.

Ger, G. and Belk, R.W. (1996), 'I'd like to buy the world a Coke: consumptionscapes of the "less affluent world"', *Journal of Consumer Policy*, 19(3), 271–304.

Gogol, N. (1942), *Dead Souls*, trans. B.G. Guerney, New York: Holt, Rinehart and Winston.

Gogol, N. (1985 [1842]), 'The Overcoat', in L.J. Kent (ed.), C. Garnett (trans.), *The Complete Tales of Nikolai Gogol, Volume 2*, Chicago: University of Chicago Press, 304–34.

Gronow, J. (1997), *The Sociology of Taste*, London: Sage.

Groves, R. and Belk, R.W. (1995), 'The Odyssey Downunder: a qualitative study of Aboriginal consumers', in F.R. Kardes and M. Sujan (eds), *Advances in Consumer Research*, 22, Provo, UT: Association for Consumer Research, 303–5.

Holbrook, M.B. (1996), 'Romanticism, introspection and the roots of experiential consumption: Morris the Epicurean', in R.W. Belk, N. Dholakia, and A. Venkatesh (eds), *Consumption and Marketing: Macro Dimensions*, Cincinnati: South Western, 20–82.

Humphrey, C. (1995), 'Creating a culture of disillusionment: consumption in Moscow, a chronicle of changing times', in D. Miller (ed.), *Worlds Apart: Modernity Through the Prism of the Local*, London: Routledge, 43–68.

Irigaray, L. (1985), *This Sex Which is Not One*, trans. C. Porter and C. Burke, Ithaca, NY: Cornell University Press (original, *Sexe Qui n'en est pas Un*, Paris: Editions de Minuit, 1977).

Jankowiak, W. (ed.) (1995), *Romantic Passion: A Universal Experience?*, New York: Columbia University Press.

Keats, J. (1817), 'Endymion, A Poetic Romance', electronic text from *Library of the Future*, 3rd edn, Irvine, CA: World Library.

Kohak, E. (1992), 'Ashes, ashes . . . central Europe after forty years', *Daedalus*, 121 (Spring), 197–215.

Kozminski, A.K. (1992), 'Consumers in transition from the centrally planned economy to the market economy', *Journal of Consumer Policy*, 14(4), 351–69.

Lascu, D-N., Manrai, L.A. and Manrai, A.K. (1994), 'Status-concern and consumer purchase behavior in Romania', in C.J. Shultz III, R.W. Belk, and G. Ger (eds), *Consumption in Marketizing Economies*, Greenwich, CT: JAI Press, 89–122.

Lefebvre, H. (1991), *Critique of Everyday Life, 1*, London: Verso (original *Critique de la Vie Quotidienne I: Introduction*, Paris: L'Arche, 1958).

Lempert, D.H. (1996), *Daily Life in a Crumbling Empire: The Absorption of Russia into the World Economy*, Boulder, CO: East European Monographs.

McClintock, A. (1994), 'Soft-soaping Empire: commodity racism and imperial advertising', in G. Robertson, M. Mash, L. Tickner, J. Bird, B. Curtis and T. Putnam (eds), *Travellers' Tales: Narratives of Home and Displacement*, London: Routledge, 131–54.

Nava, M. (1992), *Changing Cultures: Feminism, Youth and Consumerism*, London: Sage.

Nemoianu, V. (1984), *The Taming of Romanticism: European Literature and the Age of Biedermeier*, Cambridge, MA: Harvard University Press.

Piirainen, T. (1997), *Towards a New Social Order in Russia: Transforming Structures and Everyday Life*, Dartmouth: Aldershot.

Reekie, G. (1993), *Temptations: Sex, Selling, and the Department Store*, St Leonards, New South Wales: Allen & Unwin.

Robinson, J.C. (1991), *The Current of Romantic Passion*, Madison: University of Wisconsin Press.

Ross, M.B. (1989), *The Contours of Masculine Desire: Romanticism and the Rise of Women's Poetry*, New York: Oxford University Press.

Saisselin, R. (1984), *Bricabracomania: The Bourgeois and the Bibelot*, New Brunswick, NJ: Rutgers University Press.

Stites, R. (1992), *Russian Popular Culture: Entertainment and Society Since 1900*, Cambridge: Cambridge University Press.

Trilling, L. (1963), 'The fate of pleasure: Wordsworth to Dostoevsky', in N. Frye (ed.), *Romanticism Reconsidered*, New York: Columbia University Press, 73–106.

Willis, D.K. (1985), *Klass: How Russians Really Live*, New York: St Martin's Press.

Wordsworth, W. (1806), 'The World is Too Much With Us', electronic text from *Library of the Future*, 3rd edn, Irvine, CA: World Library.

4

SHOW ME THE DEEP MASCULINITY

Jerry Maguire's postmodernised identity crisis
and the romantic revitalisation of patriarchy
(or the mythopoetic subtext of
relationship marketing)

Craig J. Thompson

Help me help you

In this deconstruction, I contend that the Hollywood blockbuster *Jerry Maguire* – hereafter "*JM*" – documents a pilgrimage towards "mature masculinity" (Bly 1990; Meade 1993) undertaken by an alienated and disenchanted organisation man (e.g. Whyte 1956). In the postmodern economy of signs and images, the organisation man is neither a meek-mannered bureaucrat nor a Willy Loman pathos. He is now an extroverted, attractive, status-wielding, career-climbing, marketing man. Like the organisation man of old, however, the postmodern marketing man is no longer a rugged individualist (e.g. the cultural ideal of authentic masculinity). While suffering from the false conceit that he controls his own fate, he lives in a subservient state; his actions serve the interests of his capitalist benefactors and his life, career, and pretensions to manhood are contingent on forces outside his control: he remains a replaceable commodity – albeit a well-dressed and well-remunerated one – in the capitalist production of hyperrealities.

JM assuages this nexus of 'gender troubles' by creating a new masculine archetype: a caring, empathetic, and domestically centred patriarch who claims heroic autonomy by subverting the dehumanising, disempowering, and disenchanting effects of the advanced capitalist economy. This uplifting, focus–group approved resolution to the crisis of masculinity turns on the ironic premise that Jerry Maguire – by refusing to place profit over principle or to define his self-identity in market terms – gains the distinctive competency needed to win the socio-economic derby of big-time sports agency. In so doing, this newly glamorised, sensitised, and moralised construction of the autonomous patriarch affirms all claims to masculine privilege and, thereby, erases the institutional forces of power and domination manifested in capitalism's gender (and racial) hierarchies.

Oh no, I have once again fallen into that irresistible PoMo trap of not being able to see the text for the subtexts. First and foremost, *JM* a is story about romance but not your everyday, run-of-the-mill, boy meets girl variety. No, this love story is one of those messy, polymorphic, alternative family structures, it's a 1990s' thing, so what's the big deal about Woody Allen? get-us-all-a-therapist-quick kind of romantic entanglements. And as detailed by *JM's* writer–director Cameron Crowe, *JM's* tangled intertextual web extends back to the legendary work of Billy Wilder:

> I love them all [Billy Wilder films] but the one that reached the most was 'The Apartment.' There was something about this biting yet touchingly hilarious portrait of a then contemporary working man and his bittersweet love affair with an elevator operator. It is my favorite film and the one that inspired me to begin writing my own portrait of the contemporary man, that faceless guy who puts on a suit and tie every day, Jerry Maguire.[1]
>
> (1996: 137)

Crowe envisioned his script to be a tribute to his cinematic idol and artistic father figure Billy Wilder. In his *Rolling Stone* memoir published during the PR hyping of *JM*, Crowe recounts his vain effort to cast Billy Wilder in the role of Dicky Fox, a deceased 'mature' patriarchal figure who exemplified the golden age of sports agency before it sold its (artisan soul) to the marketing devil. Wilder declined the offer but perhaps Crowe took solace in the hard fact that *JM* had a bigger box office draw than any film in Wilder's *œuvre*.

Culturally savvy readers will, of course, reject this unkind conjecture because it turns on such a clichéd Oedipally-infused, 'masculine' response to an iden- tity threat or challenge. It also shamelessly invokes the hackneyed Freud-by-way-of-Hollywood script about sons sublimating the inner rage they feel towards their larger, more potent fathers by tirelessly striving to eclipse the grand ole man's achievements. As the story goes, these prodigal sons can never feel accomplished in pursuit of this Oedipal project; no rebellious identity feels authentic and no conquest seems grandiose enough. OK, maybe you're right. Surely, this clichéd narrative couldn't generate a smash hit, critically acclaimed, Academy Award winning motion picture. Then again, Oedipus runs deep even in postmodern waters.

In an era where the audience for cinema is increasingly divided along gender lines (testosterone-infused, explosion-a-frame, Tom Clancy-fied action films for guys and empathy inducing, kleenex-a-frame, Jane Austin-fied relationship films for gals), *JM* managed to transcend this hormonal divide. *JM's* signature phrase of 'Show me the money' functioned as a powerful interpellation of the movie-going public who enriched Sony Pictures Inc. to the very catchy tune of over 270 million dollars in box office revenue (Masters 1997). The lucrative cross-gender appeal of *JM* lies in its creation of a seductive postmodern patriarchal archetype who juxtaposes an impossible combination of idealised masculine qualities: economic autonomy, competitive drive, social *savoir faire*, heroism, unrelenting determination in the face of seemingly insurmountable challenges, moral virtue, romantic passion, emotional sensitivity, and familial responsibility.

As targeted to male audiences, *JM* resolves the postmodern crises of masculinity by proclaiming the triumph of a new, 'new man' over the dysfunctional society wrought by the emasculating confluence of feminism and the crushingly violent, competitive ethos of technocratic capitalism. Jerry Maguire is postmodernity's Zarathustra, seamlessly blending the king, warrior, magician, and lover archetypes of Western patriarchy (Moore and Gillette 1990). As targeted to women audiences, *JM* presents an equally captivating image of an enlightened, caring form of patriarchy that offers the security and stability of the old patriarchal regime plus the added bonus of personal fulfilment through an intense emotional relationship with an expressive, nurturing, 'whole' man (and not even to mention that he is a bonafide hunk).

By analysing this remarkable syncretic archetype and its hegemonising effects, illumination can be shed on marketing's role in glamorising and popularising ideological discourses and images that serve the interests of the patriarchy and that insulate capitalism from institutional critiques: in essence, the problematic effects of capitalism are recognised and 'explained' as a failing of immature men lacking in moral vision and fortitude. Rather than challenging the hegemonic status of capitalism/patriarchy, these narratives call only for its therapeutic recovery. The system of discourse to which I refer is the so-called mythopoetic men's movement as exemplified in the works of Robert Bly (1990), Sam Keen (1991), and Michael Meade (1993). In the broader societal conversation on masculinity, mythopoetic discourse has been pushed to the cultural margins; reduced to televised images of pudgy, middle-aged men obsessing about their inner wounds and going off in the woods to beat drums, dance, and chant (see Kimmel 1996). *JM* interjects this mythopoetic discourse into the cultural centre by retextualising (in an aesthetically pleasing and emotionally engrossing manner) its diagnoses about the contemporary crisis of masculinity, its homosocial prescription for recovering an authentically empowering 'deep masculinity', and its utopian vision of patriarchy.

I further propose that deconstructing this intertextual (and mainstreaming) alliance between *JM* and the therapeutic ethos of the mythopoetic men's movement also sheds illumination upon the institutional matrix in which marketing pursues its identity-affirming quest to be acknowledged as an autonomous field around which the business world turns. These same conditions will also be shown to underlie the field's current infatuation with the notion of relationship marketing. Now, on with the show.

Brutal truth

American men have been searching for their lost manhood since the middle of the nineteenth century. Plagued by chronic anxiety that our masculinity is constantly being tested, American men have raided that cultural treasure chest for symbolic objects that might restore this lost manhood.

(Michael Kimmel, 1994: 7)

JM is first and foremost a story about *masculinity in crisis*. To be a man in Western consumer culture is to always be concerned if one is man enough or a real man. If manhood is by cultural definition a state of crisis, the chimeric ideal of 'authentic' masculinity has to be located in a mythologised past or a future utopia. As an example of the latter case, one might think of Arnold Schwarzenegger's portrayal of ideal masculinity in *Terminator II*. *JM* saves the movie-going public from yet another special effects extravaganza, by appealing instead to a halcyon golden age when men had honour, conviction, a higher sense of purpose, and most of all, control of their (and their communities') political and economic destinies. In this golden age, we are told that individuals enjoyed a perfect unity between their public and private lives and that their actions were motivated by a moral commitment to the civic good rather than utilitarian assessments of self-interest.

Contemporary critiques of postmodern culture typically cite the rise of a consumer aesthetic based on expressive individualism as the source of a great many social ills (Bellah et al 1985). The consumerist society is said to be a depthless society populated by 'empty selves' (Cushman 1990) for whom materialistic pursuits and superficial pleasures provide an (ultimately unsatisfying) substitute for deep, real, authentic, true-blue, uncommodified (you get the idea) emotional and spiritual commitments. The fact that the dire influences of consumer culture have historically been constructed as feminising ones (see Kimmel 1996; Sparke 1995) generally goes without saying except, of course, when mythopoetic writers scream this implication from the tops of their lungs.

The mythopoetic men's movement is closely identified with the works of Robert Bly and his seminally saturated work *Iron John*. However, a number of other writers carry this socio-political banner such as Michael Meade, Sam Keen, Shepherd Bliss, and James Hillman to name a few. Despite having a fairly substantial following among American and Canadian men (Messner 1997), mainstream media coverage has tended to ignore the mythopoetic men's movement altogether or to lampoon it via images of pudgy middle-aged white guys bonding through dreadful renditions of African and Native American chants and dances.

Despite this cultural marginalisation, the mythopoets' panegyric odes to a lost patriarchal utopia promote a romanticised conception of masculinity and a virtuous society that is perfectly attuned to the therapeutic ethos of contemporary consumer culture. The central concept in the mythopoetic narrative is the cycle of emasculation. Echoing a romantic theme canonised by Marx, the mythopoets locate the root of all societal ills in the rise of modern technocratic capitalism. Once men lose control of their labour, they become dehumanised, disempowered, commodified, and alienated from the natural order of society. Mythopoets further argue that men's isolation in this capitalist 'iron cage' has severed the primordial bond between fathers and sons. Men are no longer autonomous artisans who can model the ways of 'authentic masculinity' to their sons. Instead, they have been turned into enervated 'organisation men' who are emotionally and physically distanced from their sons' lives (see Bly 1990).

The demise of the self-directed artisan has disempowered men and robbed them of their sense of purpose and defiled the great patriarchal rituals of father-to-son succession. In this morally de-centred market-oriented world, men have been taken out of the home and, conversely, sons and daughters have been denied their fathers (Bly 1990; Keen 1991). These conditions create an imma-ture, 'toxic' masculinity that is destructively competitive, self-centred, and unable to fulfil the responsibilities of fatherhood. What of the daughters, you ask? Well, they grow up to be 'ideological feminists' and take revenge for the absence of a strong patriarch in their lives by symbolically castrating men: that is, by shaming them and making them feel guilty for inner masculine strength and power (Keen 1991).

Mythopoets argue that only men can heal the 'father wounds' suffered by other men. So, wounded men need to retreat into a therapeutic homosocial sphere where they can ritualistically recall the atavistic spirits of mature patriarchs and experience the company of men free from the shame, doubt, and fear they have learned to feel about their inner masculine strengths. Through a combina-tion of shamanism, story-telling, Norman Vincent Peale-styled positive thinking, and college-age fraternal bonding, the mythopoets promise that men can tap into an oppressed source of inner strength to unite their public and private lives.

Mythopoets have appropriated many feminist critiques of patriarchal oppres-sion to paradoxically argue for a colonising form of patriarchy that re-attains hegemony over both public and private spheres. Their hagiographic accounts of distant patriarchs and their therapeutic prescriptions ignore class, race and gender-based power relationships in favour of individuated practices of recov-ery and self-enlightenment. Men simply need to go on redemptive journeys that women either support or impede and women's actions should always be in response to men's initiatives.

As an ideological medium, *JM* aestheticises this mythopoetic synthesis and thereby shifts its prescriptions for an enlightened patriarchal order from the cul-tural margins to the cultural centre. The charming, endearingly insecure persona of Jerry Maguire perfectly embodies this mythopoetic narrative. In this character, we find a postmodern pastiche of masculine types whose inter-nal tensions and conflicts provide the engine for the mythopoetic machinations on masculinity. Now let us turn to the ideological structure of *JM*'s narrative and its mythopoetic representation of one prodigal son's pilgrimage towards mature masculinity.

Stronger than oak

Table 4.1 offers a summary of *JM*'s main characters. Only *JM*'s three primary characters are developed in depth: Jerry Maguire, his 'loyal' client Rod Tidwell (played by Cuba Gooding) – an undersized, underpaid, underappreciated, and self-aggrandising professional football player – and his 'loyal' woman supporter Dorothy Boyd (played by Renee Zellweger). *JM*'s other male and female characters are superficially rendered 'types'. This lack of characterological development ensures that these secondary roles will be read through the deeper gender archetypes that occupy the public mind of North American audiences.

Table 4.1 The cast of characters

Character	Type
Jerry Maguire	the 'Top Gun' of the sports agency field and a man in crisis
Dorothy Boyd	the supportive wife/mother stereotype
Rod Tidwell	Maguire's mirror image: the key player in the homosocial union needed for Maguire to become a mature patriarch
Avery Bishop	the castrating bitch/dominatrix/Amazonian archetype
Laurel Boyd	the emasculating but well-meaning matriarch
The 'divorcees'	the men-bashing, shame-inducing voice of feminism
Dicky Fox	the atavistic image of a mature patriarch
Bob Sugar	the vile embodiment of immature masculinity and its destructive force
Chad the Nanny	the endearingly sweet but hopelessly inept and impotent version of immature masculinity
Ray Boyd	the precocious image of masculinity in jeopardy

The masculine characters symbolise various archetypes of immature and/or damaged masculinity: the unscrupulous organisation man, the devious father (of a prize rookie football player Frank 'Cush' Cushman) and, finally, boys in dire need of mature father figures ('Cush' and Dorothy Boyd's prepubescent son, Ray, and Tidwell's son, Tyson). This collection of damaged men and boys in very proximate danger of receiving 'father wounds', is situated within the mythopoetic critique of capitalist production. Rather than overturning the capitalist system, however, the mythopoets want to revitalise it through therapeutic intervention. Hence, the moral salvation of society lies in men helping each other to heal their 'father wounds' and regain their masculine vitality. This mythopoetic narrative sets the stage for Jerry Maguire's redemptive pilgrimage.

A key element of mythopoetic therapy is ritual. Men must engage in rituals in order to draw spiritual inspiration from the ways of their forefathers and to forge a healing connection to the 'deep masculine principle' that reigned supreme in the (mythic) past when men were well, you know. In *JM*, this inspiration is provided through the plain-dressing, plain-speaking image of 'Dicky Fox': a dearly departed 'old world' sports agent who had been Jerry Maguire's mentor. Throughout the film, Jerry Maguire ritualistically recalls this 'man of integrity' and his virtuous philosophy of sports agency (and by implication business and life). Through this atavistic persona, *JM* draws a stark contrast between the depraved state of contemporary capitalism (and the dysfunctional actions undertaken by wounded marketing men) and a lost golden age steeped in the tradition of republican virtue; that is, a morally-centred patriarchal order of free-thinking artisans who placed the needs of their community over economic self-interest (Bellah et al 1985).

The secondary female characters reproduce the mythopoetic discourse on the emasculating wrath of feminism by deploying the standard Hollywood stereotypes: the castrating bitch and men-bashing divorcees. *JM* pulls for a mythopoetic reading of these stereotypes as 'failed women' who are suffering from their own 'father wounds'. These 'ideological feminists' (Keen 1991) take revenge for the absence of a mature patriarch in their lives by shaming men. In these women's emasculating presence, men are made to feel guilty about their vital masculine energy. Out of shame, they repress the very source of strength needed to heal their 'father wounds' and become caring and committed husbands and fathers (e.g. Bly 1990).

Only by escaping into a homosocial therapeutic space can men vanquish this disempowering alliance between technocratic capitalism and ideological feminism. *JM* represents this therapeutic context through the relationship between Jerry Maguire and Rod Tidwell. In the healing space of this homosocial union, these icons of 'everyman' can become postmodern, Nietzschean Supermen.

Becoming the man he almost is

JM's opening scene introduces the audience to the manic, glamorous world of professional sport agency. Initially, Jerry Maguire can only be read intertextually. He is the quintessential Tom Cruise character: clearly the 'Top Gun' in this fast-paced, celebrity-creating, wheeling-dealing spectacular of the marketplace. This Cruise archetype is a Peter Pan-like character who blends boyish charm, charisma, unabashed competitive drive, athleticised sexual virtuosity, untameable vitality, and histrionic skill.

But wait, Tom Cruise/Jerry Maguire is not quite himself. He suffers from self-doubt: he has a new-found concern for others; he feels an emerging moral sense and pangs of consciousness; he is haunted by a gnawing feeling that there must be more to life than just making more money and more women. At age 35, his self-confidence has given way to a pervasive existential angst. What the hell has happened?

Tom Cruise/Jerry Maguire has been re-inscribed in the 1990s therapeutic discourse on masculinity. His adolescent bravado, his repression of emotion (and all else associated with his feminine side), and his flight from interpersonal commitment are now retextualised as the desperate cries of a wounded masculinity. We 'read' his affluent, hyperkinetic lifestyle as having spun out of control; we know that he suffers from feelings of emotional isolation but lacks the inner strength to vanquish his deep-seated fear of interpersonal commitment. As per Robert Bly's (1990) *Iron John*, we can see that underneath Tom Cruise/Jerry Maguire's veneer of hard masculinity lies an insecure inner child who has yet to heal his 'father wounds'.

In *JM*, the moment of agon occurs when Jerry Maguire suffers a crisis of consciousness after one of his clients – an ageing hockey player named Steve Remo – has a serious head injury. As a symbol of capitalism's commodification and oppression of the worker, the injured athlete Steve Remo is anxious to return to the game (and risk permanent injury) so that he can fulfil a bonus clause in his contract. Steve's son Jesse appeals to Maguire to dissuade his father from pursuing this course. Maguire elides this plea by effecting his 'win friends and influence people' persona. This transparently insincere response is greeted with a resounding 'fuck you'. Suddenly, Maguire realises that he is just 'a shark-in-a-suit'. His steely man-on-the-make panache gives way to moral trepidation.

In a fervour of moral inspiration, Maguire writes a capitalist manifesto for the millennial age. He articulates a grand new vision of an intimate, caring, and emotionally rewarding way of doing business. His revolutionary vision is eloquently summarised by the principle 'fewer clients, less money'.[2] Jerry Maguire demurely refers to his manifesto as a 'mission statement'. This juxtaposition of a radical re-visioning of capitalism and traditional business lexicon indicates that Maguire has not yet fully realised that he can no longer function (nor does he have a place) in a system that demands 'more clients, more money'. Moreover, it signifies that Maguire has not yet fully committed – in the deep emotional way of a mature man – to this noble vision. Once again, Maguire's public image lacks inner substance.

Maguire's 'mission statement' is circulated to everyone at Sports Management International (SMI) – the cut-throat firm for whom Jerry Maguire 'labours' – and he loses his institutional credibility. Like any commodity in the capitalist system, he is easily replaced by a new model. Maguire is 'downsized' by his former mentoree and soon to be arch rival Bob Sugar (played by Jay Mohr): an unscrupulous, villainous organisation man devoid of integrity, charisma, and emotional appeal. This reviling embodiment of immature masculinity fires Maguire in a cowardly manner that symbolically equates to 'a shoot'em in the back' ambush.

Maguire suddenly realises that he is an alienated, exploited, and obsolete worker. He responds defensively by regressing to his hyper-macho posturing. 'The hell with fewer clients and less money,' he says (to paraphrase just a wee bit). In a brilliantly orchestrated scene, Maguire and Sugar rush back to their offices to vie for the hearts and minds of SMI's prize clients in a testosterone-infused battle of phone seduction. Sugar – undisturbed by matters of conscience or scruples – proves to be faster, smoother, and harder. Client after client, Jerry Maguire comes up short and his swaggering self-assurance withers. A more ruthless, more brazen, and, above all else, more potent 'Top Gun' has arisen. Things look very grim for Jerry Maguire.

Until that is, he makes a fate-transforming phone call to Rod Tidwell: an unpopular, journeyman football player who obviously had been at the bottom of Sugar's list, if it all. Maguire soon becomes ensnared in Tidwell's endless litany of complaints, demands, and boasts. This verbal foreplay establishes that 1) Tidwell suffers from his own 'father wounds' and 2) he will stand by his man, Jerry Maguire. Their arousing conservation closes with Maguire and Tidwell reaching a climatic epiphany in which they scream in shared ecstasy 'show me the money'. Their transformative homosocial bond has been consummated. In the interim, Sugar has won the battle for Maguire's remaining clients. Our battered protagonist has little choice but to pursue his moral vision of 'fewer clients, less money'.[3]

Before departing SMI's offices for good, Maguire makes one last attempt to reassert his charismatic power by recruiting staff members to join his new one-agent-one-client venture. He is once again ineffectual, seen by the staff as a discredited outcast. But wait, fate once again turns ever so slightly in his favour. Dorothy Boyd – an otherwise shy and retiring book keeper – makes a bold choice to follow Jerry Maguire and his prodigiously 'inspiring' mission statement. He may no longer be a high-profile organisation man but perhaps he is on his way to becoming a 'real man'.

The character of Dorothy Boyd represents a 1990s' version of the wife/mother stereotype. She is a 26-year-old widow struggling to raise a son on her own. The death of her husband Roger [yes, yes, of course this plot detail is a metaphor for the demise of masculinity in the capitalist economy] has left her in a precarious financial and emotional position.[4] Through these tragic circumstances, Dorothy is forced to assume the 'unnatural' position of being the family breadwinner and of mentoring her precocious young son (Ray) in the mysterious ways of manhood. Dorothy is assisted in this task by an introverted jazz-obsessed effete 'Nanny' named Chad (played by Todd Louiso), who futilely insists that he be referred to as an au pair. Chad represents the softer side of damaged masculinity. While portrayed as a concerned and caring friend, the text of *JM* leaves little doubt that Chad could never be a romantic partner for Dorothy or a genuine father to Ray.

One scene in particular sensitises the audience to the absence of a strong patriarch figure in Ray's life and the dire threat it poses to his own masculinity. In this scene, Jerry Maguire, Dorothy, and Ray had all coincidentally taken the same flight and are waiting for their luggage at an airport baggage claim terminal. The explicit narrative function of the scene is to portray the incipient relationship between Dorothy and Maguire. Their brief platonically flirtatious encounter exhibits that always ineffable, 'will they or won't they', chemistry that has been a staple of Hollywood romantic comedies since Hepburn and Tracy. The scene, however, also encodes Dorothy's loving but none the less emasculating maternalism. She loses sight of Ray and panics. Maguire 'rescues' Dorothy from her hysterical anxieties by pointing to Ray who is gleefully playing on the airport transom. Dorothy admonishes Ray's precocious display of masculine bravado and exploration, warning him, 'you scared me, don't you ever do that again, ever, ever, ever.' Although I cannot prove it, I am convinced that the words 'Castration Anxiety' subliminally flashed across the screen at this precise moment.

Dorothy and her now-clearly-in-need-of-a-father-figure-to-save-him-from-the-clutches-of-an-overprotective-mother son reside in the house of her older divorced sister, Laurel (played by Bonnie Hunt). Laurel functions as Dorothy's maternal figure. She repeatedly cautions Dorothy about becoming involved with Jerry Maguire and instead urges her to find a practical 'man'. Though well intended, Laurel's maternalistic advice would have led Dorothy back into the arms of another damaged man whose inner strength and essential masculine 'wildness' had been shamed and tamed beyond redemption.

Despite Laurel's jaded view of men and the man-bashing pronouncements of the divorcee support group that regularly convenes at her house, Dorothy expresses an unflagging optimism that men have redeeming virtues: some day her (and Ray's) prince will surely come. If there was ever a woman who can offer Jerry Maguire the unconditional positive regard needed to repair his damaged masculinity, Dorothy Boyd is it. Will Jerry Maguire come to this realisation in time?

From here, *JM*'s plot unfolds through parallel stories of recovery and redemption. The tale of recovery concerns Jerry Maguire's multi-faceted quest to overcome his fear of commitment, to heal his emotional scars, and to fulfil the masculinity-affirming responsibilities of being a husband and father. The tale of redemption concerns Jerry Maguire's efforts to re-establish his masculine potency in the competitive sphere. Here, he must transform his noble vision into a successful enterprise. These parallel narratives encode the mythopoetic view that mature masculinity necessitates an integration of the public and the private spheres. Can he become a whole man who exudes a vital masculinity in both his private and public life? Can he recover the repressed and oppressed power of his 'deep masculinity' (e.g. Bly 1990)?

As these parallel plot lines develop, we learn considerably more about Jerry Maguire's 'inner' crisis. He is a man who can't bear to be alone and yet paradoxically remains emotionally isolated when among his vast network of 'friends'. His romantic life is little more than an aerobics work-out. The relationship between Maguire and his fiancée Avery Bishop (played by Kelly

Preston) is devoid of deep feeling; their (childless) union is a simulacrum of a true heterosexual relationship. They form an attractive public image whose lives are linked only by their athleticised sexual encounters and the cultural capital they offer to each in the public realm.

Avery is a very high-powered PR agent for the NFL and her masculine name reflects her status as an unnaturally masculinised woman who is the better athlete and the more ruthless competitor than Jerry Maguire. This She-devil is portrayed as feminism's great revenge upon patriarchy. She is a seething cauldron of ego-threatening Amazonian sexuality. She is devoid of nurturing qualities and revels in dominating, shaming, and symbolically castrating men, as epitomised by her mantra for sustaining an open relationship: 'brutal truth'. When Maguire finally garners the courage to end their 'relationship', Avery punches him out, declares herself as too strong for him, and makes the final cut by brutally branding him a 'loser'. The scene leaves Jerry Maguire lying on the floor, a bloodied and broken marketing man. Strangely enough, Jerry Maguire has taken a major step towards recovering his masculinity.

At this juncture, *JM* affirms the mythopoetic view that men must remove themselves from the world of women to accomplish their transformative pilgrimage. For the mythopoets, a 'mature masculinity' can only be attained within the confines of a homosocial enclave. In these masculine spaces, men help men to recognise, acknowledge, and overcome their father wounds. Jerry Maguire gradually enters into this therapeutic homosocial realm by first breaking free from the clutches of the She-devil and later by separating from Dorothy soon after their ill-timed marriage.

By presenting obvious signs of stress and emotional detachment, *JM* leaves little doubt that Jerry Maguire married his most 'loyal' supporter Dorothy Boyd well before he was prepared for the responsibilities of being a husband and father. In marrying Dorothy, he once again sought refuge in the world of women (and hence once again capitulated to his wounded inner child who cannot bear to be alone).

Here, the difference between Dorothy (as the good mother/wife archetype) and Maguire's ex-dominatrix is made even more apparent. The She-devil sought to sustain their dysfunctional relationship and, hence, prevent Maguire from beginning his homosocial journey towards mature masculinity. In dramatic contrast, Dorothy supports Jerry Maguire in his journey by forcing him to leave this domesticated haven (at great emotional cost to her and her son). Dorothy says she loves Jerry Maguire 'for the man he almost is'. Can Jerry Maguire complete his journey and make Dorothy Boyd love him for the man he really is?

The answer to this question lies in the transformative, homosocial bond between Jerry Maguire and Rod Tidwell. Were it not for the socio-historic legacy of racial hierarchy and privilege institutionalised in mainstream Hollywood productions (see hooks 1992) – an institutional condition that the plot of *JM* tries so desperately to erase – this film could have easily been entitled *Rod Tidwell* or better yet *Tidwell and Maguire*. However, *JM* encodes the dominant position of the white male as well as capitalism's classist ideology: the audience is asked to identify and interpret events from the bourgeois position of the sports agent – who works in collusion with the owners that control the means of production – rather than the hyperreal working-class hero of the postmodern consumer economy: the professional athlete. *JM* is the story of Jerry Maguire's heroic journey and Rod Tidwell joins the Hollywood pantheon of ethnic side-kicks. Hi, yo silver![5]

JM portrays Maguire and Tidwell as the mirror images of each other. Maguire loves the public stage and easily exudes charisma and charm. He is a gregarious extrovert who can command a room just by flashing his winning smile. While Maguire is a PR virtuoso, his private life is quite another matter. Maguire attempts to fill his many emotional voids and buttress his always threatened sense of self through athleticised sexual encounters, a dog-eat-dog climb up the corporate ladder, symbols of status and material affluence, and the constant adrenalin rush afforded by capitalism's 'art of the deal'. Since *JM* is a mythopoetic allegory of masculine (and moral) redemption, everyone in the audience 'knows' immediately that these accoutrements of the capitalist system are poor substitutes for the 'real' thing: a mutually satisfying, deeply emotional heterosexual relationship.

In diametric contrast, Rod Tidwell is a caring and committed father-husband: a man who feels real deep passion; a man who can share his vulnerability with his supportive wife and gain strength from her counsel; a man who is securely anchored in his identity as husband and father. In the public sphere, however, Tidwell acts like the wounded child from hell. The ostensible public goal that Tidwell seeks is a 'big-time' contract with his team the Arizona Cardinals and a lucrative endorsement deal with a major athletic company. Tidwell's real goal, however, is the far more elusive and ephemeral state of 'Kwan': Tidwell's term for a nirvana-like state of completeness in which he has it 'all'; respect, community, and not incidentally, financial riches.

Kwan envy aside, Tidwell's damaged masculinity inspires actions that consistently preclude his attainment of Kwan/phallus. In the public sphere, his masculine virtues are hidden beneath a bellicose facade. He is labelled as an insecure man with a big chip on his shoulder; a braggart who talks a better game than he plays; a 'money' player in the most negative sense of the term; a brooding athlete unable to connect with the fans or media; a Napoleonic figure haunted by his lack of size. Most troublesome of all, Tidwell's 'play' lacks the spirited exuberance of a star player. However, *JM*'s plot line hints that, within Rod Tidwell's undersized body, lies a 'big-time' athlete with the heart of a lion. Can Rod Tidwell overcome his feelings of inadequacy and realise his inner potential? Can he make the sporting public love him for the man he really is? Can he get his Kwan/phallus?

Anyone who has seen *JM*, or is remotely familiar with the conventions of Hollywood film making, knows the answers to these questions. Tidwell's moment of self-revelation comes in the proverbial 'big' game: a season-ending, spectacular broadcast worldwide on ABC's *Monday Night Football* (and of course narrated by the Greek chorus of Frank Gifford, Al Michaels, and Dan Dierdorf). The opponent is the Dallas Cowboys who provide an instantly recognised icon of capitalism's venal influence upon sport. If Tidwell's David-like team, the Arizona Cardinals, can defeat this corporate Goliath of the grid-iron, they win a play-off bearth and, more importantly to the plot of *JM*, he can finally 'prove' himself to (who else?) himself: Napoleon can become Zarathustra.

We know from previous scenes that Tidwell had gambled his future on winning a big contract in the upcoming free-agency market: one injury and his family's economic security would be lost. In this game, however, Tidwell is playing with abandon and passion, like a 'money player' in the best sense of the word. He puts his heart, soul, and body on the line and makes 'punishing' catch after catch. The ABC broadcast team and the 'fans' are all taking notice. With the game's outcome hanging in the balance, Tidwell makes a gravity-defying touchdown catch. The victory and a play-off bearth have been secured. But wait, a crushing blow leaves Tidwell unconscious and unmoving. The fans' elation turns to dread: has their newly crowned hero been fallen?

When Jerry Maguire sees his client, friend, *alter ego,* and fellow traveller on the road to masculinity lying incapacitated, he rushes to the field, cellular phone in hand. This totemic symbol of the wheeling-dealing marketing tribe is now put to a much different use. Maguire calls – in a genuine display of concern and empathy – Tidwell's wife (Marcee) to console her in this time of emotional crisis. He empathetically connects with her in the 'deep' way of a mature man. All the while, Jerry Maguire, Marcee Tidwell, the fans, Frank, Al, Dan, everyone really, hold their breath and anxiously watch for some sign of life. The movie audience is on pins and needles too. Has this movie been focus-group tested upon a collection of sado-masochists who demanded that Tidwell be crippled for life? Will *JM* end on this horrifically tragic note and forfeit hundreds of millions of dollars in box office revenue, video rental receipts, and merchandise tie-ins?

Not to fear. Tidwell regains consciousness unscathed. The cheering of the fans swells in his ears. Their outpouring of adulation is almost palpable. Yes, they really love him! Tidwell has finally integrated his private passion and his public profession. The fans and, indeed the entire institutional matrix of professional football, now embrace a whole man, a paragon of 'deep' masculine strength. Tidwell returns this shower of affection by dancing and prancing in an epiphanic release of repressed emotion. Communitas is reached.

Soon after, Tidwell earns the big money contract, and like any self-respecting new age patriarch, he freely expresses his feelings, confesses to his past failings, and tearfully acknowledges all those who have helped him reach this pinnacle while appearing on a television show. All the world can see that his 'father wounds' are healed; the big chip on Tidwell's shoulder has been cast aside. His mature masculine stature now towers over his more physically endowed rivals. Eat your heart out Jerry Rice.

Maguire's journey is nearing completion as well. By 'winning' Tidwell the big contract (so much for the Marxian subtext), Maguire has regained his 'Top Gun' status in the world of sports agency. This time around, though, Maguire is no longer an organisational man – a 'shark-in-a-suit' who puts a pretty face on capitalism's exploitive and emasculating business practices. No, the 'game' is played on his terms and for motivations untainted by greed, false machismo, or Machiavellianism. Maguire's arch rival Bob Sugar is shown to be a callous, calculating, charlatan. The radical prescription of 'fewer clients, less money' iron-ically proves to be the perfect antidote for the ills of the capitalist marketplace: a gentler, kinder form of capitalism is actually the way to make *more* money.

Maguire's father wounds are now healed and his masculinity reclaimed. He is fully prepared for the final passage in his pilgrimage towards wholeness. Maguire triumphantly returns to Dorothy and Ray. When he appears in their doorway, the weekly meeting of men-bashing divorcees just happens to be in full swing. Not the least bit intimidated, Maguire wins Dorothy over and melts 'the cold, cold hearts' of these shaming-inducing proto-feminists with an impassioned, soul-baring soliloquy. Dorothy immediately realises that Maguire has become 'the man he almost is'. She welcomes home her caring patriarch. Her emotional void is filled and Ray has a real father to guide him in his own journey towards mature manhood. Jerry Maguire is truly whole: the spirit of Dicky Fox lives on.

In this revitalised patriarchal order, women are yet again naturalised in the domestic sphere. Only this time, the new patriarch wields moral authority over both the private and public spheres. In this way, *JM* articulates the ideological instructions for creating a more encompassing patriarchal order. As Sparke notes (1995), the domestic sphere has long been a source of women's power in a patriarchal society. The old patriarchal order sacralised the home and women's resulting claim to moral authority provided the cultural capital through which they mounted political resistance to masculine domination of the social and economic spheres. In the mythopoetic vision, men 'reclaim' this site of moral authority and, in so doing, colonise this domesticated space of resistance. No wonder Jerry Maguire looked so smug in all the promotional posters.

Everybody loves you

The key to this business is personal relationships.
(Dicky Fox', professing in *JM*)

JM is a postmodern self-referential film nonpareil. This mass-marketed, highly commercialised artistic good details the alienating and disenchanting effects that commercialisation and mass marketing have on those who 'labour' in the cultural circuit of commodification. In *JM*'s nostalgic framing, production (as in craft) is good while marketing is a corrupting and venal force on society. So it is an ironic turn that Jerry Maguire is a marketing man. He is an image maker of hyper-realities in the spectacle of sport and a cultural intermediary who helps to formulate the public image of these postmodern working-class heroes. His crisis of identity which drives the plot of *JM* parallels the liminoid status of the field of marketing; we are betwixt and between the masculine position of production and the feminised domain of consumption. Do marketers serve needs or do we create needs? Are we really hard, potent scientists who can predict and control or effete artists who rely on intuitive sensibilities? Are we as essential to business practice as R&D, engineering, and even logistics? At least they get to play with trucks and trains. Thus, Jerry Maguire's quest to regain this lost sense of man-hood is also a discourse on business practice and the redemption of marketing.

When Rod Tidwell delivered his 'show me the money' rap, he was really saying 'show me the respect due a real man'. The all too obvious irony is that Tidwell could never earn the 'money' (here a metaphor for the attainment of mature masculinity) while giving everyone this 'attitude'. *JM* encourages the audience to read Tidwell's 'show me the money' bravado as the defensive cry of a wounded masculinity lacking in true potency and unable to command the respect that would be given to a mature, potent patriarch. The sign that Tidwell (and Maguire) had overcome their father wounds was that they no longer needed to engage in defensive macho posturing, nor did they need the exter-nal validation offered by the capitalist system. Rather than working for the 'money', each pursued his craft out of intrinsic joy and the satisfaction of homosocial camaraderie. By escaping the disempowering forces of capitalism, they paradoxically gained power over the market. Perhaps *JM* is the story that Karl Marx would have written had he graduated from a Dale Carnegie seminar. In any event, it is now time to draw the critical linkage between *JM*'s mytho-poetic subtext and another domain that, like masculinity, is in perpetual crisis: marketing (see Brown 1998).

A number of distinct symbolic parallels can be seen between marketing's crisis of confidence and *JM*'s mythopoetic representation of masculinity. Like Jerry Maguire, our profession is one that does not control its own destiny. Rather, it is at the beck and call of the captains of industry and the fickle tastes of con-sumers. In the 1980s, however, a flurry of academic work proclaimed that an intensive focus on the customer (and hence marketing) must assume the strate-gic centre stage in the post-Fordist economy (e.g. McKenna 1991; Webster 1988). In other words, marketing stood up and yelled 'show me the money'.

Marketing's performance anxieties have deep historical roots. It has never been a masculinised field like production and engineering. Despite adopting the 'hard' veneer of quantitative precision, marketing is a touchy-feely profession that aims to make consumers feel warm, fuzzy, and cared for. Marketing activ-ities are also too closely aligned with the feminine domains of fashionability, shopping, and consumption to be a true 'manly' profession. Men produce, women consume, and marketers mediate the exchanges: a liminoid cultural position that almost ensures a perpetual crisis of identity. Much like Jerry

Maguire prior to his personal 'paradigm shift' (e.g. fewer clients, less money), marketing had sought to buttress its challenged sense of masculinity through the defensive bravado of repeated sexual conquest (we always had to be penetrating new markets), overt displays of power (e.g. dominating competitors, power retailing, and that S&M favourite, market segmentation), and phallologocentric status competition (i.e. my field's quantitative tools are bigger than your field's quantitative tools). But, marketing has seen the light and now proclaims its maturity and autonomy. No longer will this profession be the meek servant of capitalist production or the self-dominating, self-emasculating (ouch!) purveyor of commodity fetishism.

Marketers now proudly declare the 'marketing concept' as the fulcrum of the business world (see Brown 1995 for an extensive deconstruction of this megalomaniacal posturing; in fact just see Brown for just about everything addressed in this section). Invoking the ethos of Jerry Maguire's 'mission statement', marketers now espouse a doctrine of deep, lasting, empathetic customer relationships. Unlike Jerry Maguire, however, we fully 'understand' (and indeed preach) that genuine commitment to customer relationships will increase profitability, generate new heights of customer satisfaction, and loyalty, and, just in general, make the world a better place: Republican virtue meets Clinton-esque win-win pragmatism.

In a near perfect symbolic parallel to *JM*'s mythopoetic view of revitalised patriarchy, marketing's 'caring, kinder, gentler form of capitalism' is actually a prescription for greater control and domination over all sites of consumer resistance: we want to colonise consumers' private spaces and subjective lives; we demand to know customers deeply; to understand their inner motivation; to plumb their most secret desires and longings. In the face of increasingly resistant and sceptical consumers ('Mrs Consumer' is no longer a women, she has become a feminist!), we want to assuage their doubts, heal their wounds, and 'fulfil' their lives with a magical repertoire of products/services/images so perfectly tailored to their inner psyches that they will joyously and repeatedly 'show us the money'.

Moreover, marketing understands that, in the post-industrial age, socio-economic power lies not in the control of labour but rather in the control of consumption (Lash and Urry 1994). In this new world economic order, no longer can men be ignored as a consumer market. But no Machiavellian impulse is to be found here. Marketers want to use their power/knowledge to help men get in touch with their repressed feminine side and satisfy their deep emotional needs through therapeutic acts of consumption. In essence, marketers now position themselves as the mature masculine figure who will guide Mr 'no-longer-a-disenchanted-organisation-man-but-a-soon-to-be-liberated-consumer' in his pilgrimage towards 'deep masculinity'. Oh, damaged men just 'confess' your deepest desires to us and we will provide the requisite therapeutic goods, satisfaction guaranteed.

Whither postmodern marketing scholarship in this remarkable Foucauldian apparatus? I believe that we are the 'Ellen' of the field: a marginalised voice that has come out of the modernist closet and refuses to be silent. Postmodern marketers constitute a resistant community of genre-blurring aesthetes who take pleasure in subverting the field's patriarchal, mythopoetic pretensions through the use of irony, critique, and deconstructive readings. We destabilise naturalised gender divisions; we problematise therapeutic constructions of consumption; we deconstruct late capitalism's hegemonic narratives; we demystify advertising's mythical appeals to a golden age; and, by necessity, we remain a voice speaking from the margins.

Notes

1 Crowe has updated this Wilder narrative to fit the postmodern condition. In the hyperreal world of *JM*, the 'faceless guy' is embodied by the Hollywood handsome and captivatingly packaged but emotionally depthless Tom Cruise icon. Rather than the crisis of the dull, conformist organisation man we have the crisis of the dynamic, image wielding, marketing man.

2 In a perfect postmodern twist, Jerry Maguire's new-found revelatory life philosophy is but a slight variant upon Miller Lite's 'taste great, less filling' advertising slogan.

3 Alright, Maguire does have one prospective client left, a guaranteed first-round NFL draft choice Frank 'Cush' Cushman. Due to space limitations, I can only provide an abbreviated account of 'Cush's' symbolic function in *JM*'s plotline. After being fired from SMI, Maguire believes that he has won the right to represent this star athlete after striking a verbal agreement with Cush's father, Matt, who solemnly states that his 'word is stronger than oak'. This plot twist signifies that Maguire has still not fully embraced his vision of 'fewer clients, less money'. By representing Cush, Maguire is hedging on his commitment to Tidwell and he is still pursuing the disempowering project of beating SMI at their own game. Maguire's conceit is shattered when he discovers that Cush (at the behest of his father) has signed a contract with Bob Sugar. Matt Cushman is revealed to be a racist scoundrel. Maguire must now be totally committed to Tidwell and more resolute in his moral vision.

4 At one point in *JM*, Dorothy states that her husband 'had been popular, charming and not very nice to me'. Through this comment and other subtle passing references, *JM* established that Dorothy's deceased husband had been suffering from his own father wounds and that Dorothy had weathered a very troubled relationship. Her personal history further valorises her faith in Jerry Maguire (and the promise of mature masculinity) and reinforces her characterological contrast to the other men-bashing feminist types represented in *JM*.

5 Throughout *JM*, the prospect that the owners and management of the Arizona Cardinals franchise may be exploiting Tidwell is consistently invoked and then soundly rejected. While Tidwell continuously protests his treatment by the owner and the broader institution of professional football, his cries of exploitation are marginalised and indeed mocked. The narrative of *JM* makes it clear that Tidwell's failure to gain public adulation and a big money contract are circumstances solely of his own making and, conversely, solely within his province to change. His inappropriate public demeanour (which paradoxically is largely due to his 'false' sense of being exploited) and his failure to play the game 'with heart' are authoritatively inscribed as the true impediments to his success. In a classic ideological turn, institutional processes are reduced to psychological inadequacies and, hence, the victim of economic oppression is portrayed as being responsible for his own plight.

References

Bellah, R.N., Madsen, R., Sullivan, W., Swidler, A. and Tipton, S.M. (1985), *Habits of the Heart: Individualism and Commitment in American Life*, Berkeley, CA: University of California Press.

Bly, R. (1990), *Iron John: A Book About Men*, Reading, MA: Addison-Wesley.

Brown, S. (1995), *Postmodern Marketing*, London: Routledge.

Brown, S. (1998), *Postmodern Marketing Two: Telling Tales,* London: ITBP.

Crowe, C. (1996), 'The Jerry Maguire Journal', *Rolling Stone*, 750/751, 137–42.

Cushman, P. (1990), 'Why the self is empty: towards a historically situated psychology', *American Psychologist*, 45 (May), 599–611.

hooks, b. (1992), *Black Looks: Race and Representation*, Boston, MA: South End Press.

Keen, S. (1991), *Fire in the Belly: On Being a Man*, New York: Bantam Books.

Kimmel, M.S. (1994), 'Consuming manhood: the feminization of American culture and the recreation of the American male body, 1832–1920', *Michigan Quarterly Review*, XXXIII (Winter), 7–36.

Kimmel, M.S. (1996), *Manhood in America*, New York: The Free Press.

Kimmel, M.S. and Kauffman, M. (1995), 'Weekend warriors: the new men's movement', in M.S. Kimmel (ed.), *The Politics of Manhood*, Philadelphia, PA: Temple University Press, 15–43.

Lash, S. and Urry, J. (1994), *Economies of Signs and Space*, London: Sage.

Lears, T.J.J. (1981), *No Place of Grace: Anti-modernism and the Transformation of American Culture, 1880–1920*, Chicago, Ill: University of Chicago Press.

McKenna, R. (1991), *Relationship Marketing*, New York: Addison-Wesley.

Masters, K. (1997), 'Sony's blockbuster sequel', *Time*, 150(21), 62–4.

Meade, M. (1993), *Men and the Water of Life: Initiation and the Tempering of Men*, San Francisco: HarperCollins.

Messner, M.A. (1997), *Politics of Masculinities: Men in Movements*, Thousand Oaks, CA: Sage.

Moore, R. and Gillette, D. (1990), *King, Warrior, Magician, Lover: Rediscovering the Archetypes of the Mature Masculine*, San Francisco: Harper.

Silverman, K. (1992), *Masculinity at the Margins*, New York: Routledge.

Sparke, P. (1995), *As Long As It's Pink: The Sexual Politics of Taste*, San Francisco: Pandora.

Webster, F. (1988), 'Rediscovering the marketing concept', *Business Horizons*, 31(3), 29–39.

Whyte, W.H. (1956), *The Organization Man*, New York: Simon & Schuster.

5

FALLING IN LOVE WITH A MARKETING MYTH

The story of segmentation and the
issue of relevance

Robin Wensley

Although any attempt to describe a clear chronology in the development of a particular subject is itself a debatable question, it is difficult not to conclude that the early to mid-1960s in the United States proved to be a key period in the development of marketing theory and practice. Up to this period, marketing texts had mainly consisted of a considerable amount of largely descriptive material relating to the detail of individual market structures, with particular reference to agricultural products and also to a lesser extent the mid-West of the United States. There was to follow a much greater emphasis on analytical approaches and the issue of managerial relevance.

Hunt and Goolsby (1988) argued that much of the cause of the managerial emphasis can be traced to the twin pressures of scientification and relevance that the study of marketing, particularly in the USA, was subjected to in the early 1960s. Rightly or wrongly, the response to much of this pressure was to focus attention on what we might now term the operational details of marketing such as the development of marketing mix response models which moved the interest and attention further away from the broader context. One particular area in which these developments resulted in a wide range of work, which had a very significant impact, was the field of market segmentation.

This can be seen as closely linked to the whole marketing management paradigm through the central concept enunciated by Kotler and others with their emphasis on the process of segmentation, targeting and positioning. This chapter considers a central paradox in the developments of both practice and research in this critical domain of marketing management: specifically, that in the name of relevance, research has tended more and more to focus on marginal effects whilst practice has been able to claim that increased sophistication is directly benefiting customers with products and offerings more and more closely geared to their individual needs. This is not to suggest that the competitive process

74

might not have resulted anyway in greater degrees of both specialisation and fragmentation but that the social implications of such developments have been confused by a poor understanding of the underlying dynamics of consumer and competitive behaviour. Additionally, the failure to confront these realities has meant that practitioners in marketing have become ill-equipped to deal with the wider social and political implications of their marketing actions whilst the academics have found themselves asserting even more vigorously that not only are their more sophisticated models technically better but they also work in practice as well.

I would wish to suggest that in so doing both parties have in a sense 'fallen in love' with their own seductive myths about the nature of the marketplace. Having done so, they resort to various methods to deny alternative explanations of the world around them.

The old and the new debate: progress or cycle?

Debates about the nature of market segmentation have a long history. For instance, about twenty-five years ago, Collins (1971) raised questions about the empirical evidence:

> This is not to deny that segmentation does exist in terms of consumer require-ments within a product field, but only to say that if it exists it fails to lead to any similar patterning of behaviour in respect of brand-choice. It seems rea-sonable to suppose that different consumers, at some point in time, do have different requirements. The problem is to reconcile this with the regular pat-terning of brand-duplication.
>
> (Collins 1971:15)

This compared with established rationale for segmentation represented by, for instance:

> If you can divide a larger market into smaller segments with different prefer-ences and subsequently adjust your product (or service) to the preferences in the different segments, then you reduce the overall distance between what you are offering to the market and what the market requires. By doing so the mar-keter improves his competitive position.
>
> (Hansen 1972)

Much more recently, Wensley (1995) and Saunders (1995) have returned to debate very much the same issue. For instance:

> Much of the managerial approach to segmentation has assumed that not only can the individual consumer through time be recognised as a major source of variability in a consistent way across various different dimensions but that we can aggregate those consumers that show similar patterns in ways which will

then be correlated with other descriptors such as socio-demographics. Neither of these crucial assumptions seems to stand empirical testing except at the very gross level such as more affluent people buy more expensive cars. We can neither assume consistent behaviour in terms of response to marketing actions such as price or advertising nor with respect to previous behaviour except again in the very broad sense that, in general, heavy buyers in a particular category tend to remain heavy buyers.

(Wensley 1995)

compared with:

Although panel data does show segments it is easy to see why it has difficulty in finding them. It tracks the purchasers of buyers and, until recently, much of the data gathered depended upon buyers' diligence, honesty and memory. Some enthusiasts of panel data keep repeating this approach by looking for segments in a way that does not . . . try using cross-sectional data, it works! There is also a split between panel data researchers. While British researchers have failed to find segments, American researchers not only find segments but track them.

(Wensley 1995)

and:

occasionally it is worth throwing away obscure references and esoteric statistical methods and observing. If it is clear that the managerial model of segmentation fails . . . let us advertise the Amex Gold Card in job centres, the Milky Bar Kid to seven year olds, Barry Manilow to ravers, the Tory party to university lecturers and the *Journal of Marketing Research* to practitioners.

(Saunders 1995)

To start with we need to recognise that in any heterogeneous market, the original Hansen quotation above must *ceterus paribus* be true but also tautological. Most managerial treatments of segmentation place additional emphasis on the notion of both segmentation bases and segment descriptors: it is the essence of the long-running debate about the empirical evidence for segmentation that it is about the validity of such additional stages rather than the indisputable nature of heterogeneity itself. This confusion, as to what is the nature of the dispute, bedevils much argument of which the Wensley–Saunders exchange is but a recent example: so we must first consider whether segmentation is merely an issue of heterogeneity.

Most advanced but 'traditional' treatments for market segmentation (cf. for instance, Hooley and Saunders 1993) start by recognising both the commonly accepted criteria for managerial applicability in any segmentation schema (measurability, accessibility, and substantiality). Then, often with the assumption that individual purchases can basically be considered within the benefit/use framework[1] (originally developed by Stefflre 1979, and elaborated in more detail particularly by Day *et al.* 1979), they lead on to the identification of, first, bases for segmentation which distinguish between groups in terms of their purchase behaviour, and then to operational segment descriptors which correlate well with the bases.

The advocates of market segmentation and, in particular, the managerial relevance of such segmentation schemata often tend to confuse empirical evidence of heterogeneity with evidence of segmentation itself. The problem in this sense is that there is little agreement on the nature of an appropriate empirical test for segmentation. At one extreme amongst the advocates, there is a presumption that the mere existence of some form of cross-sectional variability establishes evidence for segmentation either based on qualitative argument, often associated with attitude data:

> Cross-sectional data analysis finds segments because it focuses on individual consumers, their behaviour and what drives them. After finding segments, marketers target one or more of them or, as is often the case, just ignore some unattractive segments. Targeting is done by positioning products so that they appeal to the target customer, and by selling it when and where the target customer buys. Panel data has problems in finding these segments because it only contains a trickle of information about purchases rather than the wealth of information used to form segments and positioning strategies. It is as likely to find segments as is any unidimensional way of examining people's behaviour.
> (Saunders 1995)

or, in the case of purchase data, by assuming that statistical procedures that are designed to estimate heterogeneity using a parsimonious estimation of the underlying distributions based on so-called mass points can be unproblematically interpreted as evidence of specific segments.[2]

Elasticity and purchase behaviour models of segmentation

Much further confusion in the debates about segmentation is caused by the extent to which we are considering approaches based on purchase behaviour patterns themselves, or cross-elasticity with respect to other competitive offerings, or elasticities with respect to, say, differing marketing mix elements. It is useful therefore to return to reconsider the underlying logic of the various approaches. Whilst it would seem that the most common discussion about the general issue of segmentation, like this chapter itself, starts from an assumption that segmentation implies a differential individual purchase pattern based on the benefit/use framework, we often cannot go too far without encountering the issue of elasticity. The central importance of elasticities is that they allow us to infer the nature of the so-called market structure from purchase patterns through time[3] rather than perceptual space based on attitude statements from a sample of customers.

Hence instead of using an analysis based on what might be unreliable responses to hypothetical questions such as, at the simplest, 'what would you buy if the brand you intended to buy was not available?', we actually estimate response from purchase data.[4] However, as with much econometric analysis we are left with numerous interpretational problems. The most obvious one in the context of segmentation is that, at the first stage, any elasticity estimation is inevitably based on the average response of the total sample: in this sense we treat the offerings as differentiated but the customers as unsegmented.

Much confusion is also caused by variable semantics. Those who have done empirical work in this area have generally tended to use the term 'market segmentation' to refer to a strict customer-behaviour based phenomenon and the term 'market structure' to incorporate the impact of competitive reactions, but still at the customer level. In the strategic marketing area, however, market segmentation tends to refer more closely to a combination of customer and competitive impacts. Kamakura and Russell (1989) set out to try and clarify this issue by using the terms 'consumer segmentation' and 'elasticity structure' but then tend to substitute 'market' for 'consumer' segmentation.

We might suggest that, from a marketing perspective, the following terms be used:

- *product differentiation*: this represents the fact that the various products or offerings are differentiated by the customers as a whole.
- *customer segmentation*: the extent to which groupings of customers based on operational descriptor variables respond differentially to the choices of both offerings and the way they are marketed.
- *market structure*: which is what Kamakura and Russell refer to as the elasticity structure and reflects the revealed nature of competition between offerings in the market as a whole.[5]
- *market organisation*: following on from Boxer and Wensley (1988, 1990), this refers to the overall relationships between firms and customers in the context of the previous levels of analysis and includes the nature of 'the network of inter-relationships between manufacturers, suppliers, other intermediaries and retailers' and customers themselves.

As we have suggested above, this set of concepts means that to establish empirically genuine *customer segmentation* in a particular context requires a well-designed experiment or analysis. It is also important to recognise that weaker tests of customer segmentation, which conflate the phenomenon with either or both *product differentiation* or *market structure*, do not justify the managerial assertion that more sophisticated analysis of customer research data is required as a means of refining the overall marketing programme. On the other hand, it is worth recognising that, as Ehrenberg and Uncles (1995) indicate, even with an assumption that segmentation, particularly at the brand level, is distinctly unusual, we can still identify an important role for market research and analysis in the brand marketing activity:

> Yet a steady repertoire of several such probabilistic habits still gives most consumers the freedom to exercise some choice. And occasionally a consumer tries out a new brand or drops an existing brand, as departures from the Dirichlet steady state. But *why* consumers have such steady portfolios, *why* the steady probabilities are what they are, and *how* they occasionally change (or come to be changed) is again outside the model as such – and not at all well understood in marketing.
>
> (1995: 13)

Institutionalising the link between practical knowledge and marketing praxis

As we have noted, besides the continued debates about the empirical evidence for market segmentation there is also a strong assertion that in the final analysis such debates should anyway be dominated by the 'fact' that in practice it clearly works. In an area such as marketing this is an important assertion: after all the inter-relationship of theory and practice is a central issue in a field which must justify its existence primarily on the basis of its role as a key business activity.

In fact, particularly if we look in more general terms at this relationship in the history of marketing institutions in both the USA and the UK, we find it has been somewhat problematic.[6] In reviewing the history of the *Journal of Marketing* in this context, Kerin notes that:

> Approximately 42% of published articles were written by business people during the first 16 years of *JM's* existence . . . for the period of 1960 to 1981, 22% of authors were marketing practitioners. Since 1982, and following *JM's* transformation into a scholarly-professional journal, practitioner authorship dwindled to less than 1% of the articles published. *Journal of Marketing* editorial board membership evidenced a similar trend. Marketing practitioner board membership has declined from its peak in the early 1960s when approximately 60% of the board were practitioners. This percentage decreased in each succeeding decade until practitioners constituted less than 5% of the *JM* board by the mid-1990s.
>
> [in the 1970s] concerns about limited progress in knowledge development were raised. Paradoxically though *JM* had attempted to become more topical, readable and practical in content, it, like much of the marketing literature in the previous two decades was judged as having only a modest impact on practice-improvement. A change in editorial policy ensued in 1979, with an emphasis on publishing only scholarly articles and the announced AMA view that *JM* would serve as a 'bridge between the scholarly and practical . . . for the thoughtful marketing practitioner and academician'. This action in turn led to the deletion of the 'Applied Marketing' section in 1979.
>
> (Kerin 1996: 3–6)

In the context of the impact on managerial practice, Hunt (1994) also points to an important paradox. In the name of managerial interest and the dominance of the managerial rather than functional view of marketing, he observes that marketing academe appears to have had relatively little impact at least at the strategic level:

> Why has our discipline made so few original contributions to the strategy dialogue? Why have we focused on dysfunctional rather than functional relationships, i.e. on unsuccessful rather than successful marketing practice? Why do qualitative studies lack acceptance in marketing?
>
> (1994: 13)

In Britain, both the institutional structure and the position with respect to key journals have been more confused. An informal meeting led to the formation of the Sales Managers' Association in 1911, and the first national conference of the Institute of Sales Management was held in Buxton in 1925. In 1931 ISMA changed the name of its own journal from *Sales Promotion* to *Marketing* but it was not until after an extended debate following the war that the name of the institution itself was changed to the 'Institute of Marketing and Sales Management' and finally in 1968 to the 'Institute of Marketing' and in 1989 came the granting of a Royal Charter. On the academic side, the Marketing Educators Group met first in 1967 and the Institute of Marketing sponsored the first UK chair in Marketing at Lancaster. However, the relationship over the years between the Marketing Educators Group and the Institute of Marketing has always appeared to be rather more problematic than in the USA and it was only in 1996 that the MEG both changed its name (to the Academy of Marketing) and voted to become formally incorporated within the, by now, Chartered Institute of Marketing. Similarly, in the field of marketing journals, there was much greater confusion. *The Quarterly Review of Marketing*, which had acted as the 'bridge' between practice and teaching in marketing, was discontinued by the Institute of Marketing in the 1980s and replaced by a much more arm's length relationship with the *Journal of Marketing Management*. Indeed, compared with the relative hegemony of the American Marketing Association with respect to key US academic journals in the field, the situation in the UK remains remarkably confused. *The International Journal of Research in Marketing* has strong links with the European Marketing Academy, whilst the *Journal of Marketing Management* retains primary links with Professor Michael Baker and both his current and erstwhile colleagues at Strathclyde, and the *European Journal of Marketing* is one of the core journals produced by MCB publications. In the middle of this, the Academy of Marketing is itself considering whether it should launch a new marketing journal!

Equally, a body with a broader remit, somewhat analogous to that of the US Marketing Science Institute, in the field of marketing, the Marketing Council, was only formed under the sponsorship of a number of large organisations in

1995.[7] Even in this case the Council seems to define its primary remit as to enhance the profile of marketing as a whole in that its first aim is 'to define and promote standards of best practice and customer service to achieve customer satisfaction and retention', and indeed has interpreted such an objective much more in terms of teaching and the development of case studies, or even, perhaps more accurately, case histories, rather than the encouragement of research.

The collective insecurity of marketing: the issue of practical knowledge

The institutional history therefore both in the USA and the UK seems to reflect a continual attempt to create institutional structures which integrate the practical and the theoretical, yet underneath such structures the integration seems very partial and tentative. Why do we go on doing it? To explain our own behaviour as marketing academics, we need to be reflective about our own positions and in particular the issue of practical knowledge. As far back as Aristotle, there was recognition that the domain of practical knowledge was different from that of scientific knowledge:

> Now it is thought to be a mark of a man of practical wisdom to be able to deliberate well about what is good and expedient for himself, not in some particular respect, but about what sorts of things are conducive to the good life in general.
>
> (1980: 142)

Interestingly, this skill or capability was seen by him as very closely related to what we would now describe as a generic management skill:

> It is for this reason that we think that . . . men like him have practical wisdom viz. because they can see what is good for themselves and what is good for men in general: we consider that those can do this who are good at managing households[8] or states.
>
> (ibid.: 143)

However, not surprisingly, the Aristotelian distinctions themselves are less helpful on the specific issue of validation of such wisdom. As Aristotle would put it, there is no possibility of what he called 'demonstration', which relates to scientific knowledge, in the case of practical wisdom. If we turn to the much more recent distinction developed by Habermas, we note a clear threefold taxonomy into empirical, interpretative and critical. Habermas has linked this distinction to a much clearer set of issues both in terms of the nature of knowledge and the wider impacts on the nature of society, and others in the management field have both applied his approach directly to such issues in management (see Mingers 1992) and questioned his emancipatory perspective on the impact of critical knowledge (see Burrell 1994). However, these developments do not particularly help in refining our notion of validation in the context of so-called practical knowledge. In his own analysis of the legitimation crisis of modern capitalist societies, Habermas (1976) does address such issues more directly even if still in the wider context of social norms and their legitimation. In particular he argues that:

> practical questions can be treated discursively and (it) is possible for social-scientific analysis to take the relation of norm systems to truth methodically into consideration. It is an open question whether in complex societies motive formation is actually still tied to norms that require justification, or whether norm systems have lost their relation to truth.
>
> (1976: 117)

Carr (1997), in commenting on somewhat analogous issues in the field of education research, suggests another three-way distinction:

> In many ways, the categories of action research which I have adopted (technical, practical, critical) may be seen as a crude attempt to employ the classical Aristotelian distinctions between the 'productive', 'practical' and 'theoretical' sciences . . . It would, however, be more accurate to say that the categories are intended to reflect Habermas' view that there are three general forms that the human and social sciences can take (empirical, interpretative, critical) each based on a different interpretation of the nature of human action (instrumental, communicative, reflective) and each incorporating different views about the sort of relationship to practice that social scientific knowledge can take.
>
> (1997: 4)

Carr goes on to note that in education these different views of social sciences compete with each other, in particular, for 'the allegiance of educational policy makers, teacher educators and others involved in the professional development of teachers'. It is perhaps clear that at least at the moment in the field of education the technical approach is in the ascendancy and that this creates the context in which academic enquiry is resourced and supported. In the world of marketing, partly perhaps because we face a much less monolithic institutional structure in terms of practitioners, the situation provides us with more scope to define the nature of our research. Only up to a point . . .

Maintaining the relationship between marketing academe and practice

The idea of marriage maintenance is anathema to those who hold a romantic view of it. It sounds far too prosaic and far too like keeping the engine tuned or one's body beautiful. But for those who see marriage as more of a working partnership, the idea of its having to be maintained is not so strange.

(Bailey 1984: 213)

Our marketing practitioner colleagues will collude with us, since they too share our insecurities about the nature of our subject and expertise, as long as we do not stretch their credulity too far. Additionally as Caroline Bailey discusses, in the context of marriage, in *A Loving Conspiracy*, most of us need to go beyond the romantic myths that might initially sustain a relationship. We need to be willing to operate on the interface between the practical and the critical and the most obvious way in which we will do this is by recognising both the practical dilemmas of marketing management and being critical about the nature of marketing in a wider social context. This also means recognising that the relevance construct is itself too problematic and indeed ambiguous to resolve the issue on its own. Relevance inevitably raises questions of: to whom? And for what? We might do well to recognise the very technical notion of relevance adopted by some psychologists who would see it as describing merely the nature of the encoding–communication–decoding process between one individual and another: what is relevant is solely what is decoded by the receiver.

If we are to engage in such a more meaningful discourse as marketing academics, however, we must not only be able to bring to the surface in a constructive fashion some of the underlying issues of interests and institutional structures but also be able to resolve, at least to some extent, our own insecurities!

Notes

1 Whilst we will accept in this chapter, the benefit/use assumption without question, it is important to recognise that it only really makes good sense if we accept a very functional view of benefits and a highly cognitive view of human action (for critique see a number of papers cited in Brown (1995)).

2 A more systematic critique of some of the empirical and statistical work used to support claims of market segmentation is to be found in Wensley (1996a).

3 Strictly speaking, of course, the analysis that is undertaken is still comparative static rather than dynamic.

4 Saunders (1995) argues rather controversially that because attitude data provide a richer description of purchase motivations they also provide a more effective means of conducting a segmentation procedure. Whilst outside the remit of this chapter it is important to recognise that this assertion raises important issues of research method particularly with respect to questions of interpretation and validity.

5 This is directly analogous to what Grover and Srinivasan (1987) termed previously as the nature of *competitive* market structure but it would seem that the notion of 'competitive' is itself tautological in the definition:

> Determining competitive market structures is a more recent thrust in marketing. The idea is to group a pre-specified set of brands in a product class on the basis of interbrand competition so that brands within a group 'compete more heavily with each other' than brands belonging to different groups. The determination of competitive market structure is carried out within a pre-specified product-market boundary. The delineation of a product-market boundary . . . can be pre-specified on the basis of managerial objectives (e.g. tactical vs. strategic).
>
> (Grover and Srinivasan 1987: 139)

6 The historical background to this issue is covered in more detail in Wensley (1997).
7 However, as discussed in more detail in Wensley (1997), part of the reason for this delay might well be the much more active part played in supporting research in marketing by the ESRC (previously SSRC) in the UK compared with the NSF in the USA.
8 Wensley (1996b) has argued about the degree to which principles of good household management can form an excellent basis for current more general principles of management.

References

Aristotle (1980), *The Nicomachean Ethics*, trans. D. Ross, Oxford: Oxford University Press.

Bailey, C. (1984), *A Loving Conspiracy*, London: Quartet Books.

Boxer, P. and Wensley, R. (1988), 'Niches and networks: prospects for strategic analysis', third IMP Conference, Manchester, September.

Boxer, P. and Wensley, R. (1990), 'Strategic market analysis in a chaotic world: towards a representation of inefficient markets', Marketing Science Conference, Champaign, Illinois, March.

Brown, S. (1995), 'Trinitarianism, the Eternal Evangel and the three eras schema', *Proceedings of the Marketing Eschatology Retreat*, St Clement's, Belfast, September, 298–314.

Burrell, G. (1994), 'Modernism, postmodernism and organizational analysis 4: the contribution of Jürgen Habermas', *Organizational Studies*, 15(1), 1–45.

Carr, W. (1997), 'Educational action research, professional development and the social sciences', paper presented at the ESRC Tavistock Institute Seminar 'Is action research real research?', London, July.

Collins, M. (1971), 'Market segmentation – the realities of buyer behaviour', *Journal of the Market Research Society*, 13(3), 3–15.

Day, G.S., Shocker, A.D. and Srivastava, R.K. (1979), 'Customer-oriented approaches to identifying product-markets', *Journal of Marketing*, 43, Fall, 8–19.

Ehrenberg, A.S.C. and Uncles, M. (1995), 'Dirichlet-type markets: a review', Working Paper, November, London: South Bank University.

Grover, R. and Srinivasan, V. (1987), 'A simultaneous approach to market segmentation and market structuring', *Journal of Marketing Research*, 24 (May), 139–53.

Habermas, J. (1976), *Legitimation Crisis*, London: Heinemann.

Hansen, F. (1972), 'Backwards segmentation using hierarchical clustering and Q factor analysis', ESOMAR seminar, May, London.

Hooley, G. and Saunders, J. (1993), *Competitive Positioning: The Key to Marketing Strategy*, Hemel Hempstead: Prentice Hall.

Hunt, S.D. (1994), 'On rethinking marketing, our discipline, our practice, our methods', *European Journal of Marketing*, 28(3), 13–25.

Hunt, S.D. and Goolsby, J. (1988), 'The rise and fall of the functional approach to marketing: a paradigm displacement perspective', in T. Nevett and R.A. Fullerton, *Historical Perspectives in Marketing*, Lexington: Lexington Books, 35–51.

Kamakura, W. and Russell, G.J. (1989), 'A probabilistic choice model for market segmentation', *Journal of Marketing Research*, 26 (Nov), 379–90.

Kerin, R.A. (1996), 'In pursuit of an ideal: the editorial and literary history of the Journal of Marketing', *Journal of Marketing*, 60(1), 1–13.

Mingers, J. (1992), 'Technical, practical and critical OR – past, present and future?', in M. Alvesson and H. Wilmott (eds), *Critical Management Studies,* London: Sage, 90–112.

Saunders, J. (1995), 'Market segmentation: invited comment on "a critical review of research in marketing"', *British Journal of Management,* 6 (Special Edition), S89–S91.

Steffire, V. (1979), 'New products: organizational and technical problems and opportunities' in A.D. Shocker, (ed.), *Analytical Approaches to Product and Market Planning,* Cambridge MA: MSI, April Report 79–104, 415–80.

Wensley, R. (1995), 'A critical review of research in marketing', *British Journal of Management,* 6 (Special Edition), S63–S82.

Wensley, R. (1996a), 'Forms of segmentation: definitions and empirical evidence', *MEG Conference Proceedings* (CD version) Session G Track 8, Department of Marketing, University of Strathclyde, 9–12 July, 1–11.

Wensley, R. (1996b), 'Isabella Beeton: management as everything in its place', *Business Strategy Review,* 7(1), 37–46.

Wensley, R. (1997), 'Two marketing cultures in search of the chimera of relevance', Keynote address at joint AMA and AM seminar 'Marketing Without Borders', Manchester, 7 July.

6

ILLUMINATIONS, IMPRESSIONS, AND RUMINATIONS ON ROMANTICISM

Some magical concepts and mystical comments from Morris the catoptric on the superiority of stereoscopy in visual representations of marketing and consumer research

Morris B. Holbrook

Introduction: (en)light(en)ing up

Romancing the stoned

Romanticism means many different things to many different commentators (Holbrook 1995b, 1997d), but the conceptualisation that I personally prefer (Holbrook 1987b, 1991, 1995a; Holbrook and Hirschman 1993) comes from Wordsworth by way of Abrams (1971) and emphasises the importance of a dialectic involving departure and return, dissolution and reunion, loss and recovery, dissonance and resolution, . . . opposition and reconciliation. Specifically, in a fragment from 'The Recluse', Wordsworth spoke of our Fall from Paradise and looked towards the recovery of this lost Bliss in the World of Everyday Consumption or, as he called it, 'this great consummation':

> For the discerning intellect of Man,
> When wedded to this goodly universe
> In love and holy passion, shall find these
> A simple produce of the common day.

Abrams (1971) takes these lines as his touchstone for romanticism, placing special emphasis on the theme of reconciliation and its links to the magic, mystical, or otherwise miraculous:

> The vision is that of the awesome depths and height of the human mind, and

of the power of that mind as in itself adequate, by consummating a holy marriage with the external universe, to create out of the world of all of us, in a quotidian and recurrent miracle, a new world which is the equivalent of paradise.

(1971: 28)

Clearly, this 'vision' entails the reconciliation of opposites or the fusion of contrarieties – the secular and the spiritual, the human and divine, the outer and inner, the earthly and heavenly, the mundane and miraculous, intellect and passion, sorrow and joy, multiplicity and (re)union. Thus, though his most famous poem 'Kubla Khan' was composed during a drug-induced stupor, at more level-headed moments Coleridge expressed a similar thought when he traced the mainsprings of creativity and artistic expression to a holistic emphasis on the criterion of 'multeity in unity' (Abrams 1971: 179) via 'a great circle from the One back to the One by way of the many' (ibid.: 272) in which 'this terminus of all the poet's journeyings is not only home and paradise, but also a recovered unity and wholeness which he had experienced nowhere else' (ibid.: 290). Awash in a kind of giddy paradox, this achievement of restorative experiential unity provides the sense in which 'the justification for the ordeal of human experience is located in experience itself' (ibid.: 187; see also Holbrook and Hirschman 1993: 153–8).

Comparable views of aesthetic appreciation have descended to this day, as in the work of Monroe Beardsley (1981) and his emphasis on the concept of Unity-In-Variety. Similarly, contemporary students of creativity have almost always stressed the importance of holistic Gestalts (Arnheim 1951), bisociation (Koestler 1964), structure–deviation–resolution (Meyer 1956, 1967), tension arousal and reduction (Berlyne 1971), and combining opposites to achieve complexity (Csikszentmihalyi 1996). Numerous thinkers have explicitly drawn the analogy with jazz improvisation (DePree 1992; Goldblum 1993; Kao 1996; Oldfather and West 1994). And all this has provided me personally with an endless excuse to ramble on and on about the dialectic as a foundation for both artistic creativity and aesthetic appreciation (Holbrook 1980, 1984, 1995a, 1997a, 1997b; Holbrook and Zirlin 1985).

Get thee to a nunnery

The reader will be relieved to learn that I do not plan to blabber further on this favourite romantic theme in the present chapter. Rather, I wish to dwell on a subcomponent of romanticism that inspired a recent conference held at St Clement's Retreat in Belfast; host(ess)ed by our estimable colleagues Doherty, Clarke, and Brown; and entitled *Marketing Illuminations Spectacular*. In his convocation on 'The 4Bs of Marketing Illuminations', Brown (1997a) makes the neglected but valuable point that illumination in our discipline often involves elements of magic and aspects of mysticism. And illumination, of course, is what we want and need in our profession because it offers us those moments of insight, enlightenment, revelation, and epiphany so prized by the romantics and their tradition (Abrams 1971) as well as by marketing managers and their minion researchers. So, on a roll with 'M' words, Stephen reels off a list of alliterative links that tie the Illuminist Tradition to the Magic and Mysticism of Marketing:

> It is the tradition of malcontents, millenarianism, marginality, misappropriation, mutineers, and madness. It is the tradition of marketing. It is the manner of marketing. It is the matter of marketing. It is the manna, the marinade, the mayonnaise, the – yes – manure of marketing.
>
> (Brown 1997a: 12)

I myself felt that Stephen was getting on the right track and just hitting his stride when he got to the part about the 'manure' – which might have led effortlessly to:

> maceration, Machiavellianism, machicolation, machinations, maculations, maelstrom, magniloquence, malaise, malarkey, malediction, malpractice, mammonism, mania, masochism, masturbation, materialism, mathematics, mayhem, megalomania, megrim, melodrama, menagerie, mendacity, mendicancy, menses, merchandising, merde, mesmerism, methodology, miasma, Mickey Mouse, micturition, middleman, mildew, military, mirage, misappropriation, miscreant, misfortune, misrepresentation, missionary position, mistrust, monger, monster, mons Veneris, mortification, muck, mucus, mumbo jumbo, murder, musk, or multivariate statistics – not to mention macabre, maladroit, malevolent, malicious, malign, malodorous, manipulative, maudlin, mawkish, meager, mealymouthed, mechanistic, mediocre, menial, mercenary, meretricious, meshuga, messy, misanthropic, mischievous, miserable, mouldy, monotonous, morbid, mordant, moronic, morose, mucilaginous, muddy, murky, musty, or mutant.

And, once we have opened the door to 'mayonnaise', how can we resist 'marmalade', 'marshmallows', 'marzipan', 'matzo balls', 'meat loaf', 'milk', 'molasses', 'mung beans', 'mushrooms', and 'mustard'? Indeed, a guy like me cannot help but wonder – to paraphrase another of the romantic poets – if eighteen M-words in four lines come, can 'Morris' be far behind?

Spectacular speculations through Bloom-coloured spectacles

As conveyed by the *Proceedings* from the aforementioned conference, the rest of the story emerges a mere 300 pages later when Brown (1997b) honours the titular promise to offer something 'Spectacular'. Here, he draws on the work of Harold Bloom to cast marketing literature into the framework of an implicit contest between a Father Figure (e.g. Ted Levitt) and an aspiring neophyte (e.g.

Morris B. Holbrook). Stephen emphasises an aspect of the Levitt–Holbrook relationship as precursor and ephebe that bears special relevance to the theme of illumination because it involves an analogy with eyesight in general and draws on the metaphor of eyeglasses or spectacles in particular:

> The final stages of the process . . . are found in Holbrook's . . . current pre-occupation with stereoscopic photographs. . . . Not only does this employ, exceed and eclipse Levitt's seemingly unsurpassable metaphor of marketing *myopia*, but Holbrook's stereoscopic images appear most vivid to those who suffer from short-sightedness. Thus, the precursor's single most significant contribution has been taken, transformed and transcended by the triumphant ephebe . . . Morris the Catoptric.
>
> (Brown 1997b: 322)

Looking up 'catoptric' in my dictionary and finding that it means 'of or relating to a mirror or reflected light', I see that Stephen's amazing play on words has tied the ethos of 'Morris the Cat' to the theme of 'Illuminations'. This connection is evinced by my claims (1) that stereopsis serves as a potent metaphor to depict the mainsprings of revelatory insights in our discipline (Holbrook 1997b), and (2) that three-dimensional stereographic displays work towards enhancing the impact of our visual representations (as developed more fully in this chapter).

(1) Syncretic thinking

The first of the points just made relates to the mechanism whereby stereopsis forms three-dimensional visual impressions and harks back to the aforementioned essence of romanticism. Specifically, in stereoptical perception, two different images observed by the right and left eyes and characterised by binocular disparity are fused into an overall impression of three-dimensional depth. The resulting 3-D experience has the character of a profound insight and suggests a metaphor for how we should think about the multidisciplinary nature of our field of study. Specifically, as argued by Hirschman and Holbrook (1992), we should welcome a pluralistic orientation in our willingness to embrace a variety of approaches in hopes of achieving an integration or synthesis that will permit us to understand various market-related phenomena in depth (Holbrook 1997b).

(2) Tools of the trade: the nitty gritty how and why

The second point concerns a more practical side of the stereoptical trope, one that bears directly on the theme of illumination. Specifically, I contend that three-dimensional stereography offers an approach that can enhance the vividness, clarity, realism, and depth of our visual displays in ways that might improve the ability of marketing researchers to visualise data and to communicate their findings to interested readers (Holbrook 1997e); that might suggest applications to the design of marketing strategy (Holbrook 1998c); that might enrich our photographic documentation of ethnographic results (Holbrook 1997c; Holbrook and Kuwahara 1997) or of mock-ethnographic materials (Holbrook 1998b); that might facilitate the self-expression of subjective personal intro-spections (Holbrook 1996a, 1996b); and that might even help to push consumer research to the edge of its boundaries (Holbrook 1997f). Some of this work uses stereo 3-D photos in ways that shed light on the nature of the consumption experience. Yet, in all this research, I have yet to provide a compelling defence of stereo 3-D photography as a route towards deepening our insights into the visual world of consumers. In other words, I believe I have previously provided plentiful examples to illustrate *that* stereography enriches our understanding of visual displays. But I have yet to demonstrate *how* and *why* this happens. This latter theme provides the main focus for the present chapter.

Do you believe in magic?

Back in the 1950s when I was only a lad of about 10 years old, I walked into our living room one evening to find my parents taking turns at peering intently into a black box while holding down a red button on its top. I soon learned that my Dad had recently bought a David White Stereo Realist camera; that he and my Mom were gazing in fascination at his first batch of stereo 3-D slides; and that the black box was the stereo slide viewer for magnifying and illuminating these images.

Illumination, indeed!

When invited to look at my Dad's stereo 3-D pictures, I experienced the proverbial moment of revelatory insight – the 'Eureka' phenomenon – in response to a sense of vividness, clarity, realism, and three-dimensional depth unlike anything I had ever seen in any sort of mechanical reproduction. To this day, when I revisit these old stereo photos, I still get the same mystical sensa-tion – a veritable *frisson* with near-magical qualities.

I am not the first to notice the magic and mystical power of three-dimen-sional stereography. Queen Victoria was transfixed by her first glimpse of the then-new technology at the World Exhibition in London in 1851. Only a few years earlier, even before the dawn of photography itself, Wheatstone had introduced the first stereoscope – whose magic, quite literally, depended on the use of mirrors directing two different images to the two different eyes. Today, we still associate stereography with magic, mysticism, and illumination. For example, N.E. Thing Enterprises (1993) has successfully marketed its fantasti-cally popular line of *Magic Eyes* books featuring extensive collections of stereograms. In his title, Johnstone (1995) refers explicitly to *Magic 3D*, while van Keulen (1990) relishes the play on words in his titular *3D Imagics . . . and . . . Magic Images.* Other telling titles of works featuring stereography include *Visual Magic* (Thomson 1991); *Magic Insight* (Brentwood Home Video

1994); and *3D Wonderland* (Saburi 1993). ImageTech produces a widely dis-
tributed line of disposable '3D Magic' and reusable '3D Wizard' cameras. And
drawing on the theme of enlightenment, tourist sites in North America have
recently begun to sell travelogue filmstrips and viewers under the name
'3Discover'. Clearly, those who buy and sell stereographic images believe that
there is something rather marvellous and even miraculous involved. Anyone
interested in the role of magic, mysticism, and illumination in the world of marketing might do well to pay attention.

Plain old photography

Millenary magic

As one of our culture's favourite aphorisms has it, 'A picture is worth a thousand words'. Indeed, this venerable saying captures an experience that we have
all shared when comparing the relatively cumbersome baggage of most verbal
discourse with the vivid impressions aroused by the best visual representations.
Most spectacularly – in the cinema or on television – films or videotapes convey
the nuances of dynamic action with an immediacy that almost approaches a
feeling of 'being there'. In print media, even still photographs convey a sense of
realism not matched by any other format available to fill an equivalent amount
of space. This role of photographs in revealing key information manifests itself
regularly in such journals as *Visual Sociology* or *Visual Anthropology*. Recently, it
has also appeared increasingly in the literature on marketing and consumer
research (Heisley and Levy 1991).

Plain old photography in the social sciences

Realising this power of photography to convey important truths, social scientists have long made use of visual representations captured on film. Thus,
psychologists have studied such images for clues to the essence of interpersonal
interactions (Ziller 1990). Sociologists have relied on photos to enrich their
accounts of various societal phenomena (Becker 1986, 1995; Chaplin 1994;
Wagner 1979). And anthropologists have viewed the camera as a key tool for the
ethnographic investigation of other cultures (Ball and Smith 1992; Bateson and
Mead 1942; Collier and Collier 1986). In general, such uses of photography in
the social sciences fall into at least four partially overlapping categories (cf.
Harper 1988; van der Does *et al.* 1992).

Photographs as data

First, many social scientists – especially historians – view photographs as a source
of primary data. For example, much of what we know about (say) Victorian
society or the American Civil War comes from the work of contemporaneous

91

photojournalists (Margolis 1994; Taft 1938; Trachtenberg 1989). As already noted, visual representation via photographs serves as a key research tool in ethnographic studies (Ball and Smith 1992; Bateson and Mead 1942). Further, a review of the photographic record left by a particular epoch can suggest insights into the ethos of its popular culture (Appel 1983) or commercial communication (Goffman 1979; Williamson 1978). And photos can provide raw data to facilitate comparisons of one era with another in the same locale (Cohen 1992; Watson 1976); of lifestyles in separate geographical areas (Gold 1995); or of material possessions in entirely different cultures (Menzel 1994).

Photographs as stimuli

Second, photographs may serve as stimuli helpful in prompting informants to recall information sought in depth interviews (Collier and Collier 1986; Harper 1989). For example, sociologists have applied this photo-elicitation technique to studies of the work environment (Harper 1987) and of Asian refugees (Gold 1991). Sometimes the informants themselves are invited to help take pictures and then to discuss them with the interviewer (van der Does et al. 1992).

Photographs as evidence

Even where they are not used to elicit insights from informants, photographs may play a key role in documenting the observations of social scientists (Chaplin 1994). In this case, they serve as a form of corroborative evidence to support general assertions about a (sub)culture and its milieu (Maio 1991; Suchar 1988) or to authenticate particular details about individuals and their groups (Neumann 1992; Steiger 1995).

Photographs as expression

Finally, social scientists may use photographic images to express thoughts or feelings otherwise accessible only to introspection (Grady 1991; Nordström 1994). Thus, one sociologist has presented photos to supplement poetic meditations on his midwestern homeland (Quinney 1995). Similarly, others have drawn on photographs to enhance their philosophical speculations concerning the impact of the sea coast (Stilgoe 1994; Winton 1993).

Plain old photography in marketing and consumer research

Along similar lines, marketing and consumer researchers have occasionally deployed cameras in an effort to enrich their accounts by means of visual representations. The honour of first emphasising the potential application of photography to marketing and consumer research probably belongs to Levy,

Rook, Wallendorf, and Heisley – who were all conversant with the influential work by Becker (1986) in visual sociology and who organised a conference session on this topic in 1985, but who did not themselves publish their own photographic images until somewhat later (Belk *et al.* 1988; Heisley and Levy 1991; Rook 1991). Meanwhile, others have followed their lead in four directions that parallel those of the social sciences.

Photographs as data

One of the first such publications of photographs appeared in the report on a naturalistic inquiry conducted at a swap meet (Belk *et al.* 1988). Meanwhile, three ethnographic researchers had used photographs as data in their study of a farmer's market (Heisley *et al.* 1991). Subsequently, consumer researchers have been invited to examine about 4,000 quasi-ethnographic photos (as well as plentiful videotapes) deposited in the archives of the Marketing Science Institute by the various members of the Consumer-Behavior Odyssey itself (Belk 1991). A second way of using photographs as data arises when consumer researchers perform critical analyses of advertisements or other pictorial records to draw inferences concerning the cultural meanings or historical development of key commercial themes (Lears 1994). One example appears in the application of categories from literary criticism to print ads interpreted as exhibiting different types of mythic narratives (Stern 1995).

Photographs as stimuli

One frequent and important use of photographs in marketing and consumer research employs the aforementioned technique of photo elicitation – often under the heading of 'autodriving'. For example, one such study compared the meal consumption styles of three families living in the same suburban neighbourhood (Heisley and Levy 1991). Another used five photograph-dominated print ads as the basis for a phenomenologically oriented probing of ad-generated experiences (Mick and Buhl 1992). Still another programme of research has asked informants to provide pictures and then to make electronically produced collages that serve as the basis for guided conversations about metaphorical product meanings (Zaltman 1997).

Photographs as evidence

Perhaps most commonly, marketing and consumer researchers have frequently presented pictorial images as corroborative support for their findings. Relevant themes documented by photographs have included a jazz-record collection (Holbrook 1987a); artistic household objects (Holbrook 1988); homelessness (Hill and Stamey 1990); a farmer's market (Heisley *et al.* 1991); a Barry Manilow fan club (O'Guinn 1991); the consumption-related acculturation of

Mexican immigrants (Peñaloza 1994); advertisements as text (Scott 1994); radio soap operas (Lavin 1995); and a subculture of motorcyclists (Schouten and McAlexander 1995).

Photographs as expression

Occasionally, a marketing or consumer researcher has shared subjective personal introspections by means of photographic images. One example concerns a researcher's self-reflections on being autodriven via photographs of possessions in his own home (Rook 1991). Another describes the phenomenon of consumption *by* (as opposed to 'of') pets in which an author fondly recalls the companionship offered by his recently deceased cat (Holbrook 1997a).

Expanding horizons: from Kilo- to Mega- to Giga-Vision

Obviously, if a thousand words is good (Kilo-Vision), a million is even better (Mega-Vision) and evokes hopes of someday reaching a billion (Giga-Vision), the sooner the better. In other words, powerful though the uses of plain old photography in our research might be, such applications have thus far confined themselves to the presentation of two-dimensional images (Kilo-Vision) that remain trapped in the inherent flatness of the printed page (Riemschneider 1994; Tufte 1990). True, such two-dimensional pictures do represent the third spatial dimension by means of more or less good perspective – including the effects of monocular depth cues provided by relative size, brightness, texture gradients, occlusion, shadows, convergence towards the horizon, and so forth (Frisby 1980; Gregory 1990; Marr 1982; McAllister 1993). But such spatial effects fall far short of the vivid sense of three-dimensional depth and accompanying feelings of vividness, clarity, and realism provided by the sort of 3-D experience that can only result from true stereoptical viewing. That is, true stereopsis – in which two binocularly disparate images presented to the left and right eyes separately are fused by the brain into one coherent 3-D experience – evokes a compelling sense of depth and enriches visual representation in ways not available to the standard monocular 2-D pictures found in most print media and in virtually all examples of photographs heretofore included in the literature from the social sciences and marketing or consumer research.

In what follows, I shall argue that 3-D representations in general and stereoscopy in particular offer a hitherto untapped opportunity for capturing the visual world in a manner guaranteed to enhance the power of pictorial images to shed light on the social sciences, to encourage insights in marketing, and to illuminate our understanding of consumption experiences. Though numerous possible applications of stereoscopy to print media exist (Darrah 1977; Girling 1990; Lorenz 1987; Sales 1994; Zone 1991), I shall emphasise those with a direct bearing on the use of printed photographs captured on film (as opposed to images drawn by hand, plotted by computer, or mapped in some other way). Here, I wish to argue that 3-D pictures presented in the form of stereographic photo pairs hold considerable promise for increasing the vividness, clarity, realism, and depth of the visual representations found in marketing and consumer research. This takes us to the level of Mega-Vision. By contrast, Giga-Vision – which will someday involve not only stereoscopy but also the animation and dynamic movement thereof – must await further developments in the next millennium.

I shall begin by describing stereography in general as an approach that figuratively breaks camouflage and that literally enhances the viewer's ability to identify objects in confusing, cluttered, crowded, and complex visual materials. I shall then review the basics of stereography as a method suitable to the presentation of pictorial images on the printed pages of scholarly journals or books. Finally, I shall offer several illustrations of how stereography can break camouflage to reveal insights by enhancing the vividness, clarity, realism, and depth of otherwise confusing, cluttered, crowded, or complex visual representations.

Stereography: old bottle, new wine

History: royal beginnings, territorial conquests, troubled times, recent abdications

The history of stereoptical displays extends back to 1838 when Wheatstone reported his development of a mirror-based stereoscope for viewing binocular drawings; with the advent of photography a year later, the extension of this new medium to stereographic applications followed immediately (Brown 1903; Burder and Whitehouse 1992; Darrah 1977; Ferwerda 1990; Girling 1990; Gregory 1970; Rheingold 1994; Taft 1938; Trachtenberg 1989; van Keulen 1986, 1990; Waack 1987; Waldsmith 1991; Zone 1991). By the end of the next decade, Brewster had perfected a greatly improved lens-based stereoviewer. Then, in 1851, stereographs attracted considerable attention at the World Exhibition held in London's Crystal Palace – greatly impressing Queen Victoria, among others. And, by 1860 in America, Holmes had produced a stereoscope that was easy to handle, inexpensive to produce, and destined for great popularity.

Holmes-type stereoscopes swept through every corner of polite society until virtually no European or American parlour lacked a viewer plus an assortment of stereo photos at which to gaze. Thus, stereographs became the first true international mass medium for the dissemination of visual information. During the last half of the nineteenth century and well into the twentieth, the horrors of war, the adventures of travel, and the glories of politicians all impressed themselves on the popular consciousness via exposure to pictures observed stereoscopically (Darrah 1977; Dyckman 1994; Norton 1994; Trachtenberg 1989; van Keulen 1986, 1990; Waldsmith 1991).

Further advances in stereo imaging occurred during the 1930s via the Tru-Vue film strips devoted mostly to travelogues (Dennis 1980); during the 1940s via the advent of child-oriented View-Master reels specialising in cartoon characters or educational scenes (Dennis 1984; Sell and Sell 1994a; van Keulen 1986; Waldsmith 1991); and during the 1950s via the cameras and stereoviewers offered by David White (the Stereo Realist), Kodak, Revere, and others (Burder and Whitehouse 1992; Tydings 1951; van Keulen 1986; Waack 1987). But as television gained ever greater ascendancy – amidst efforts by movie producers to recapture audiences by means of such gimmicks as poor-quality 3-D films like *Bwana Devil* or *House of Wax* (Halliwell 1989) – the popularity of stereo photography began to wane until, by the 1970s, virtually all the manufacturers of 3-D equipment had ceased production. The ill-fated Nimslo company tried unsuccessfully to revive the 3-D medium in the late 1970s with a multi-lensed camera that produced lenticular prints – a format that still exists today in the form of ImageTech's disposable 3D Magic or reusable 3D Wizard cameras (Image Technology International, Inc., 5172-G Brook Hollow Parkway, Norcross, GA 30071, 404-416-8848).

Currently – with the exception of View-Master, ImageTech, and some other highly specialised operations (mentioned later) – stereo photography as a commercial venture with widespread popular appeal has, in effect, abdicated its pre-eminence to such two-dimensional media as the point-and-shoot camera and the video camcorder. However, the underground work of stereography continues via the cultlike efforts of dedicated amateurs who subscribe to publications such as *Stereo World* (US), the *Journal of 3-D Imaging* (UK), *3D-Magazin* (Germany), or *Stereoscopy* (worldwide); who belong to associations like the National Stereoscopic Association (US), the Stereoscopic Society (UK), or the International Stereoscopic Union (Global); and who take stereo photos by every means available (discussed later). These stereographers pursue a flourishing interest in 3-D photography; conduct an extremely active news group on the Internet (Photo-3D accessible via the command 'subscribe photo-3d name@your.e-mail.address' sent to listserv@bobcat.etsu.edu); and evince a profound technical knowledge of the medium that they gladly (almost evangelically) share with others (me, for instance).

Psychophysics of stereopsis: some nuts and bolts

The experience of true three-dimensional perception depends on the phenomenon of stereopsis wherein the brain fuses slightly disparate images from the left and right eyes to produce a sense of depth. This impression of depth results from the fact that – because the two eyes regard the world from separate viewpoints (located about 2.5 inches apart) – each eye receives a somewhat different visual signal. This binocular disparity or parallax shift conveys information about the relative distances of objects from the viewer. Hence, when synthesised by the brain, the left–right discrepancy clarifies the spatial relationships among objects from near to far (Ferwerda 1990; Frisby 1980; Girling 1990; Gregory 1970, 1990; Julesz 1971, 1995; Marr 1982).

Breaking camouflage: the master metaphor

The point just made concerning stereopsis has been demonstrated conclusively by the Random Dot Stereogram or RDS. Developed during the 1960s by Bela Julesz (1971, 1995), the RDS presents a completely random pattern of small elements to each eye. Either image viewed separately conveys the visual analogue of white noise and, taken by itself, is completely meaningless. But one image contains a horizontal displacement of selected random material such that, when viewed stereoptically, this binocular disparity creates the impression of one or more surfaces seen in a true three-dimensional representation. Hence, when viewing an RDS correctly, one observes an object in depth – as if a hidden 3-D image had emerged, ghostlike and almost magically, from an otherwise meaningless void (Boyer 1990; Frisby 1980; Kinsman 1992; Marr 1982; Richardson 1994; Sakane 1994; Schwenker 1991). In the words of Julesz (1995: 19), 'these images, when viewed monocularly, are only aggregates of random dots': 'However, when binocularly fused, the correlated areas segregate in vivid depth.' The crucial significance of this phenomenon is that stereopsis *precedes* and, therefore, potentially *aids* object recognition:

> The first important conclusion which Julesz drew from his research into random-dot stereograms was that stereopsis can be computed by the visual system without need of a prior stage of object recognition. We cannot see any 'object' within either stereo half . . . viewed alone, but this does not prevent us fusing the two halves to achieve vivid stereopsis. Indeed, it is only *after* stereopsis has been computed that we can say 'Ah! There is a square' and thereby succeed in the business of object recognition.
>
> (Frisby 1980: 147)

In developing the RDS, Julesz (1971, 1995) drew inspiration from his work as a radar engineer familiar with the principles of aerial reconnaissance. Such surveillance from the air depends on taking two pictures of the ground from positions located at some distance apart. Typically, when viewed separately, each picture reveals relatively little information. But when viewed stereoptically, hidden topographical details emerge:

> As a former radar engineer, I knew that . . . in order to break camouflage in aerial reconnaissance, one would view aerial images (taken from two different positions, called *parallax*) through a stereoscope, and the camouflaged target would jump out in vivid depth.
>
> (Julesz 1995: 18)

Thus, a weapon covered by leaves may take shape and stand out against its background; a concealed tank may loom into clear view; a disguised military installation may reveal itself to the stereoscopic gaze (Girling 1990: 61; Richardson 1994: 26).

Julesz regards this phenomenon of *breaking camouflage* as the hallmark of stereopsis, proclaiming repeatedly that *no camouflage is possible in three dimensions* (1995: xxi, 20). Just as aerial surveillance benefits from such techniques in warfare, ordinary people enjoy the same advantages as part of their daily existence (Grossman and Cooper 1995). We spot a tiger lurking in the branches (danger) or a rabbit hiding in the snow (food) by virtue of the power of stereopsis to break camouflage: 'Since in 3-D there is no camouflage, stereopsis probably evolved in our insectivore primate predecessors . . . in order to counteract the freeze response of insects, which would blend into the foliage at the sign of danger' (Julesz 1995: 63). In short, this power of breaking camouflage stereoptically confers survival value and, perhaps as a result, produces a strongly gratifying sense of perceptual acuity – feeling good, we suspect, because it enhances our capacity to survive:

> Perhaps the initial evolutionary advantage of having two eyes was as a solution to the problem of decoding camouflage. Perhaps two-eyed vision really came into its own when it provided a means of grouping together stripe features belonging to the tiger (or other predator, or desirable but hidden prey), and separating them from stripe features produced by the branches, twigs and leaves of the tree in which he was hiding, ready to pounce. This speculation is certainly in keeping with the discovery of random-dot stereograms, because they show just how superb a camouflage-breaking system stereopsis is: only after their binocular fusion can any object whatsoever be seen.
>
> (Frisby 1980: 155)

When achieving this sort of perceptual integration via stereopsis, the resulting 3-D image conveys a sense of depth – immediacy, transparency, spatial perspective, inhabitability – that produces a level of involvement or insight comparable to the epiphanies associated with the proverbial 'Eureka' experience. One feels as if one has entered a well-defined surrounding space whose details have been frozen in time. These details emerge with a compelling degree of sharpness, palpability, richness, and inter-relatedness possible only in a truly three-dimensional perspective. The effect may resemble that of a magic trick or even a mystical encounter.

The 3-D experience: A Magical Mystery Tour

It strikes me as far from coincidental that – when the Rolling Stones created their satiric revision of the High-Pop consciousness expressed by the Beatles in such works as *Sgt Pepper* and *Magical Mystery Tour* – they included a stereographic three-dimensional lenticular print on the cover of *Their Satanic Majesties Request*. The fact is that, like the Stones, many seers throughout the last two centuries have regarded the 3-D experience as an almost miraculous or even supernatural form of magic and have described it as a nearly mystical or ecstatic sort of rapturous encounter with the vividness, clarity, realism, and depth of the visual world.

Thus, Brewster bragged about his newly invented stereoviewer that 'no portrait ever painted, and no statue ever carved, approximates in the slightest to the living reality now before us' (Ferwerda 1990: 56). Soon Holmes claimed that, via stereoscopy, 'the mind feels its way into the very depths of the picture' to observe 'a leaf torn from the book of God's recording angel' (Trachtenberg 1989: 17–18; Taft 1938: 169). By the beginning of the present century, Brown (1903) could state with authority that 'the stereoscope . . . opens a gate to . . . otherwise unapproachable . . . new discoveries' ('Introduction').

More recent commentators agree on the striking enhancement of vividness, clarity, realism, and depth contributed by stereography. Thus, Taft (1938: 167) credits stereo photography with conveying 'a sense of reality that no other form of picture can remotely equal'. Waack (1987: 40) notes that a stereograph 'invokes better insights [in which] physical . . . relationships become clearer'. Lorenz (1987: 5) adds that 'stereoscopic viewing makes evaluation easier in [various] fields of investigation', a boon that Trachtenberg (1989: 16) attributes to 'the extraordinary reality produced by these instruments'. Ferwerda (1990: 119) concurs that 'a stereo photo gives the impression of representing reality exactly'. And Tufte (1990: 17), an acknowledged guru of visual representation, makes a similar point and illustrates it with a stereoscopic pair of photos that vividly portrays the terrain of a river bed from the viewpoint of an airplane or helicopter flying overhead.

When commercially produced stereographic cameras and viewers appeared during the 1950s, proponents spoke about their merits with boundless enthusiasm. For example, Tydings (1951: 103) remarked, 'Many people have made the statement that anything that single-lens photography can do, stereo can do better': 'Stereo . . . can produce, through life-like depth, a momentary reality that is unmatched anywhere in the whole realm of the arts and sciences'. Kodak (1955: 5) agreed that 'the stereo effect . . . makes a good picture come alive [and] gives your pictures the extra zip, extra reality that makes them seem to live again'. Reviewing the century during which stereography first attained mass popularity, van Keulen (1986: 5) comments on the strong '"true-to-life" impression . . . evoked by the use of 3-D' and argues that the relevant images 'would not be nearly so fascinating and informative if they were simply two-dimensional'. On the same theme, according to Waldsmith (1991: 1), 'Looking into a stereoscope at a scene captured in detail and depth creates a special magic . . . as though you were there'. Similarly, Cadence (1994a: 36) describes this almost mystical feeling of participatory involvement as:

> a heightened sense of reality, of actually being there . . . The entire image

seems much brighter and sharper through stereoscopic vision, which makes us conscious of details we didn't even notice before, revealing the power hidden within a seemingly ordinary image and making for a truly extraordinary experience.

As stereographic techniques have made a bit of a comeback via the widespread popularity of autostereograms (discussed later), recent proponents have if anything commented even more enthusiastically on the magic power and mystical force of the 3-D experience. Such viewing produces a feeling described by Sakane (1994: 74) as a 'pure sense of joy':

> As our eyes find the correct focal point, vivid, three-dimensional images lurch out of the white noise of the two-dimensional image and into view. The experience is an eerie one, yet so compelling precisely because it is so real.

As co-inventor of the autostereogram remarking on what he calls this 'Oh, wow' reaction, Tyler (1994: 85) agrees that 'there are few experiences as visually exciting as . . . a really clear 3-D image'. And the latest technological wizards tout the wonders of three-dimensional Virtual Reality as 'just much more compelling'; by analogy, we appreciate stereoscopy 'the same as we like talking films more than silent ones and color films more than black-and-white' (Linden Rhoads, President of Virtual i-O, quoted by Coy and Hof 1995: 76).

Stereography: light! (illumination); cameras! (magic); reaction! (insight)

By virtue of the 3-D experience just described, the phenomenon of stereopsis promises to derive insights from images presented stereographically in ways not accessible to ordinary monocular viewing of two-dimensional pictures. Thus, stereographs convey an increased *vividness* in identifying features and perceiving details; greater *clarity* of shapes and juxtaposed surfaces; a heightened feeling of *realism* in portraying the subtleties of visual information; and an expanded sense of *depth* in capturing the spatial relationships among objects. Here, figuratively, an analogy with the metaphor of breaking camouflage becomes quite transparent. Specifically, when presented in ordinary two-dimensional displays, pictorial information found on the flat printed page may appear excessively confusing, cluttered, crowded, complex, or – in short – camouflaged. Important hidden meanings, buried insights, disguised essences, and obscured inter-relationships may lie concealed just below the surface but fail to appear to the viewer confined to a monocular two-dimensionally flat perspective. By contrast, the potentially revelatory stereo 3-D experience illuminates hitherto undetected identities, details, patterns, and even epiphanies with enhanced vividness, clarity, realism, and depth.

Earlier, we established that marketing and consumer researchers increasingly use photographs for purposes of data collection, information elicitation, evidentiary documentation, and personal expression. These aspects of Kilo-Vision have added greatly to our toolkit of available techniques. Nevertheless, moving in the direction of Mega-Vision, I take it as given that anything which aids our ability to *see* these photographs will thereby help to enhance our *understanding* of the relevant consumption experiences portrayed in marketing and consumer research based on photographic materials. Clearly, then, this potential for the use of stereography in marketing and consumer research deserves our careful consideration. In what follows, I propose a general method for the realisation of visual 3-D representations before providing some illustrative demonstrations of the benefits attainable via such applications of stereoscopy.

Method

Focus

Excellent coaching on the techniques of stereoscopy appears in a number of helpful treatises on this subject (Brown 1903; Burder and Whitehouse 1992; Ferwerda 1990; van Keulen 1986, 1990; Waack 1987). Further, numerous applications of 3-D imaging exist in a wide variety of alternative formats (reviewed by Holbrook 1997e, 1998c). Here, consistent with the theme of the present chapter, I shall focus primarily on aspects of stereoscopy that lend themselves to applications via the use of cameras intended to capture pictorial images for display in conventional print media.

Stereo pairs

By far the most straightforward format in which to present stereographic images in print media involves the use of stereo pairs (Burder and Whitehouse 1992; Cadence 1994a, 1994b; Ferwerda 1990; Johnstone 1995; Waack 1987). In this approach, the right and left visual images appear side-by-side on the printed page, displayed in such a way that they can be viewed separately by the two eyes. Such images may be produced by a double-lensed camera (e.g. a used Kodak or Stereo Realist) or by the outer two lenses of a multi-lensed camera (e.g. a Nimslo or ImageTech); by a single-lensed camera with a mirrored beam-splitter either built in (e.g. the Loreo camera) or added on (e.g. the Frankena attachment); by an ordinary rangefinder or single lens reflex (SLR) camera shifted from one position to another (during an interval of time in which nothing moves in the scene to be photographed); or by two cameras mounted side-by-side and fired together via either manual synchronisation (by pushing the shutters as close to simultaneously as possible) or mechanical triggering (by means of some device such as dual cable releases or electronic signals). As examples, I have at various times used a David White two-lensed Stereo Realist; ImageTech 3D Magics and 3D Wizards with the two outermost shots retained for the stereo pair; a double-mirror Loreo; a beam-splitting Frankena attachment mounted on a 35 mm Mamiya SLR; the same Mamiya or a Canonet QL17 rangefinder moved horizontally from one location to another; two Kodak or Fuji disposables taped together side-by-side and synchronised manually; two Olympus Stylus automatics connected in tandem and triggered via a home-made bracket; and two Yashica FX-3 manual SLRs mounted on a machine-tooled base and fired simultaneously by means of dual-cable shutter releases. In practice, I have obtained some excellent results (but also some disappointing failures) using all these various rigs.

One common distance between the two photographic exposures mimics the human eyes by being spread about 2.5 inches apart. Generally, however, the optimum ratio for a convincing 3-D effect is about 1:30 for the separation between exposures as a fraction of the distance to the nearest object (Ferwerda 1990; Waack 1987). Hence, a 2.5-inch separation implies that the nearest object should be about 6 feet away. By contrast, for an object at a distance of (say) 300 feet (such as a boat floating on the other side of a lake), one might wish to shoot a 'hyper stereo' by moving the camera positions to a distance of about 10 feet apart. Conversely, for very small objects at close range, one would move the exposures nearer together so as to shoot in 'macro stereo'. Unless the object is absolutely stationary, careful attention must be paid to synchronising the two shutters. Further, lighting should come from just one source so as to avoid the danger of having two different patterns of shadows in the two images. Any departures from these guidelines may produce anomalous 3-D images when the photos are fused stereoscopically.

The rules for taking good pictures change somewhat when one moves from monocular photos to stereography (Burder and Whitehouse 1992; Ferwerda 1990; Waack 1987). For example, in stereography, one should *not* follow the conventional photojournalistic practice of shooting at wide lens openings and focusing selectively on objects of interest with the background or foreground out of focus so as to direct the viewer's gaze to the appropriate material. Though effective in two-dimensional viewing, such fuzziness plays havoc with the process of stereopsis. Hence, in stereography, one should employ the smallest possible lens opening to achieve maximum depth of field, thereby permitting the viewer to fuse the two images into a fully realised 3-D experience.

The two images created in the ways just described must be carefully cropped and mounted in a manner that achieves accurate vertical alignment (to avoid eye strain and to facilitate a clear fusion of the left and right pictures); that maintains equivalent horizontal positioning of the object(s) closest to the viewer (to protect the integrity of the stereo window so as to avoid visual confusion at the edges of the display); and that preserves a width compatible with the viewing technique to be used by the targeted reader (with a combined width of 5 inches per pair imposing an upper limit on the size that can be comfortably viewed without the aid of some special optical device) (Burder and Whitehouse 1992; Ferwerda 1990; Waack 1987).

Stereo pairs photographed and displayed in the manner just described appear widely in the 3-D publications mentioned earlier (*Stereo World, Stereoscopy*, etc.), but only occasionally find their way into longer works. Examples of the latter that demonstrate the power of stereo pairs to evoke a nearly magic or even mystical 3-D experience include a collection featuring famous Hollywood celebrities taken by the actor Harold Lloyd (Hayes 1992); a travelogue containing scenic stereoviews of Paris (Setlak trans. 1994); a *tour de force* of exotic and bizarre spectacles captured in 3-D depth (Johnstone 1995); an account of the settling of California (Crain 1994); a history of the Russo-Japanese War (Blum 1987); and a tastefully composed portfolio of stereographic nudes (Schwartzman 1981). Any sceptical readers owe it to themselves to investigate these or other exemplars of stereography raised to its highest level.

Free-viewing

If confined to an overall width not greater than 5 inches, the aforementioned stereo pairs can be presented and viewed without the assistance of any sorts of optical aids or other devices whatsoever. I recommend such *free-viewing* as the preferred approach for two major reasons. First, as a practical matter, it seems unlikely that most readers will come equipped with the appropriate optical gadgets to aid their viewing or that publishers will feel inclined to supply the devices in question. Second, I believe that the 3-D experience attains its most compelling power when stereopsis is achieved directly without the intervention of mechanical assistance.

Tutorials on the art of free-viewing have appeared in a number of helpful sources (Alderson 1988; Best 1979; Brown 1903; Ferwerda 1990; Girling 1990; Grossman and Cooper 1995; Johnstone 1995; Norton 1994; Richardson 1994; Waack 1987; Waldsmith 1991). Basically, the task involves looking through or past the two members of a stereo pair with the eyes oriented straight ahead in a manner that causes the left and right pictures to float together and ultimately to fuse in one central three-dimensional image (flanked by a monocular picture on each side, which should be ignored in so far as possible). The free-viewer relaxes the eyes – sometimes described as letting them 'go soft' – so that each eye sees its intended picture in clear focus. Toward this end, it may help to start with the page as close to the face as possible, to slowly pull the page away from the eyes while continuing to look straight ahead, and to wait for the two pictures to come into focus and to float together so as to fuse into one stereo 3-D image.

The art of free-viewing is a skill that requires patience, practice, and perseverance to attain adequate mastery. The reason is that normally our eyes have the habit of converging (turning inward) and accommodating (focusing) at the same time. Usually, as an object moves closer, we look more cross-eyed while simultaneously adjusting for its proximity. By contrast, in free-viewing, we must learn to *decouple* the responses of convergence and accommodation

103

(Alderson 1988; Ferwerda 1990; Frisby 1980; Kinsman 1992; Richardson 1994). Specifically, the eyes must accommodate (focus) *without* converging (turning inward). Thus, we must look straight ahead while simultaneously focusing on the two separate pictures – something that we do not normally do and that therefore imposes the need to break old habits.

Though learning to accomplish this decoupling requires some effort, it lies within the capabilities of all but about 2 per cent of the population (Julesz 1971, 1995). Hence, the motivated reader should be persistent and keep trying. Assurance that success will eventually reward such efforts may be gleaned from the enormous popularity enjoyed by the line of *Magic Eyes* books of auto-stereograms offered by N.E. Thing Enterprises (1993), which have spent many weeks at the top of the *New York Times* best-seller list (Adolph 1994), as well as by fine publications from other comparable sources (Cadence 1994a, 1994b; Dyckman 1994; Riemschneider 1994; Saburi 1993; 21st Century 1994). If such a vast audience exists for these immensely popular books – all of which rely on the technique of free-viewing just described – we have every reason to assume that the necessary free-viewing skills also fall within the capacity of those who read the marketing- and consumer-research literature.

Viewing assistance

Nevertheless, I realise that some readers will wish to supplement their free-viewing capabilities with the help of various potential types of viewing assistance. Toward this end, perhaps the simplest viewing aid involves using a piece of cardboard cut to fit between the nose and the printed page so as to form a divider that prevents each eye from seeing the picture intended for the other eye and thereby eliminates the potentially distracting secondary and ter-tiary monocular pictures to the left and right of the central 3-D image (Alderson 1988; Burder and Whitehouse 1992; Johnstone 1995). Further, if two large magnifying glasses are held over the two images in a stereo pair and then slowly pulled apart to the right and left, respectively, the prismatic effect of their inside edges will cause the images to move together visually until they fuse (Dyckman 1994; Ferwerda 1990; Girling 1990; van Keulen 1990). Finally, the most effective aid to easier viewing of stereo pairs comes in the form of a pris-matic lorgnette viewer – that is, a hand-held pair of lenses, resembling spectacles with a handle, whose prismatic effect helps the two images to merge visually. Such viewers can be ordered for a cost of about £2 from the original manu-facturer (The Added Dimension, P.O. Box 15325, Clearwater, FL 34629, 813-446-9106); from Reel 3-D Enterprises (P.O. Box 2368, Culver City, CA 90231, 310-837-2368); from Cygnus Graphic (P.O. Box 32461, Phoenix, AZ 85064, 602-277-9253); from the Stereoscopic Society (c/o Eric Silk, 221 Arbury Road, Cambridge, CB4 2JJ, UK); or from Bode Verlag GmbH (Postfach 405, D-45716 Haltern, Germany).

Preview

The illustrations that follow cover a variety of visual materials that might interest those wishing to collect or to present pictorial images showing various aspects of the consumption experience (defined broadly as including a variety of goods, services, events, or ideas ranging from zoo attendance to foreign travel to transportation to retailing to home decor). For the most part, I have emphasised informational content over artistic merit; indeed, it sometimes happens that the need to crop photos to a size small enough for free-viewing reduces the aesthetic quality of what might otherwise be a more visually attractive composition. In general, by means of the following illustrations, I hope to demonstrate how stereography can enhance the vividness, clarity, realism, and depth of pictorial images so as to break camouflage due to confusion, clutter, crowding, or complexity in visual representations of consumption experiences in marketing or consumer research.

Illustrations: I've looked at life from both sides now

Confusion, clutter, crowding, and complexity as types of camouflage

The following illustrations reflect at least four inter-related types of pictorial camouflage wherein the details of images tend to be lost, hidden, submerged, or otherwise obscured – like mysteries waiting to be solved or spirits longing to break free. I shall refer to these as *confusion, clutter, crowding*, or *complexity*.

Confusion

Confusion refers to the sort of situation found when similar visual features, colours, textures, or patterns overlap so that the identities of focal objects tend to get lost against their backgrounds or in the context of neighbouring objects with a comparable appearance. Frisby shows several convincing pictorial examples in two dimensions – including a mottled bird whose markings blend into its woodland habitat, a dalmatian disappearing against a field of spots, a soldier disguised to look like a tree standing in a forest, and an airplane painted to resemble the scenery below (1980: 20, 116). In such cases, stereography can bring the hidden or ambiguous object into bold relief so as to reveal its identity and facilitate recognition. For example, in the picture of Mormon workers included by Darrah (1977: 89), a hut made from branches tends to blend into the trees shown in the background when viewed with either eye alone, but springs to life when seen stereoscopically. Similarly, Burder and Whitehouse (1992: 2) present stereo views of a turtle's green head against its green shell and of a yellow bumble bee against the yellow centre of a flower to demonstrate the point that 'subjects which appear confused and difficult to identify in flat photography stand out sharp and clear when viewed in 3-D'. Another vivid illustration appears when Graves (1989: 39) represents the corner of a log cabin; in three dimensions as opposed to two, each log stands out clearly as a separate entity; thus, 'stereo photography is a usually overlooked means of documentation which can richly record details missed by non-stereo photography' (ibid.: 38). Again, both Milligan (1995) and Dennis (1995) reproduce the same striking picture of a fish that, when seen in two dimensions, appears almost indistinguishable from the surrounding sea coral in order to show that 'a Hexagon Grouper's camouflage markings fail to hide it when viewed in stereo' (Dennis 1995: 21).

Clutter

Clutter arises in cases where there is so much visual information competing for our attention within a relatively small pictorial image that the relevant details tend to vanish in the resulting jumble. An obvious case in point would occur when a complex still life composed of numerous ordinary objects tends to swallow up the details of its constituent parts – as in the examples shown by Darrah (1977: 17) or by van Keulen (1990: 15). Such an example appears vividly in a photograph of Carl Sandburg in what Lewis (1993: 23) describes as 'the poet's cluttered office'; here, what looks like a hopeless mess in two dimensions reveals a wealth of detail that clearly suggests a 'method in the madness' when seen in 3-D. Indeed, this power of stereography to cut through visual clutter inspires Johnstone (1995: 13) to promise that 'you will see new things and discover details that you would never notice in a flat photograph' and to demonstrate this point via a picture that shows the bewildering array of controls on the instrument panel of a Boeing 737 in which 'we can see the fantastic detail of 3D' where, by contrast, 'in a mono picture much of the mass of knobs and switches would remain invisible or unnoticed' (ibid.: 29); the accuracy of this claim extends to the level of the plastic cup filled with orange juice and ice that sits next to the pilot.

Crowding

Crowding combines aspects of confusion and clutter in the sense that we often find multiple objects with similar characteristics crammed into the same picture with their common features repeated in a manner that makes them difficult to distinguish clearly. For example, such a phenomenon tends to occur when photographing large groups of people whose individual faces, until clarified by stereography, tend to disappear into the throng. Vivid instances appear in crowd scenes presented by Blum (1987: 22, 29, 38, 71), by Hayes (1992: 92), and by McShane (1993: 101). Similarly, the crowding effect can of course apply to non-human objects as well as to people. One clear example arises in a prizewinning photo by Trynoski entitled 'Aspens' that presents a plethora of vertical shapes in a visually crowded array; only when viewed three-dimensionally does the stereo pair reveal the individual identities of the trees that extend into the distance (Patterson 1994: 22).

Complexity

Complexity occurs when different images from different depth planes are over-lapped or juxtaposed in such a way that their distinct layers or spatial relationships are obscured. Such visual complexity tends to appear when photographing objects seen behind some sort of visual screen, reflections in mirrors, the partially transparent but also reflective surface of water or bubbles, and things or images viewed through or in a glass window. Again, stereography can greatly facilitate the eyes' ability to decipher such otherwise uninterpretably complex multi-layered, spatially inter-related visual material. For example, the use of mirrors frequently aids the stereographer in exploring spatial relationships ranging over multiple layers of depth, as in the striking photographs of nudes collected by Nazarieff (1993: 20, 48, 52, 132, 150). Another vivid case of pictorial complexity occurs when some part of a person's body is close to the camera and therefore suffers from foreshortening when seen in two dimensions; as shown by Ferwerda (1990: 80), the exaggerated size of a man's feet stretched out towards the viewer seems distorted in 2-D but makes perfect visual sense when viewed three-dimensionally. Finally, a spectacular example of the ability of stereography to clarify complex spatial relationships appears in the case of the 'impossible triangle' that presents a famous optical illusion when viewed two dimensionally (Frisby 1980: 24; Gregory 1970: 55) but that clearly reveals the contrasting spatial orientations of its two vertical legs when seen stereoptically (Gregory 1970: 56; Sell and Sell 1994b: 32).

Consumption experiences in 3-D

The power of stereography to break the four partially overlapping types of camouflage just described is illustrated by Figures 6.1, 6.2, 6.3 and 6.4, intended to cover the cases of confusion, clutter, crowding, and complexity in the context of pictorial images that address various aspects of consumption experiences. In each case, the relevant figure is intended to indicate how stereography – when applied to photographic representations of consumption experiences (at the zoo, during recreational travel, on wheels, at the retailer, in the home) – can clarify visual confusion, can cut through pictorial clutter, can crystallize objects in a crowded image, or can capture spatial complexity in the photos of interest to marketing and consumer researchers.

Confusion

Figure 6.1 features aspects of confusion that tend to cause the identities of individual objects to get lost against their backgrounds. Stereo Pair 6.1A comes

A

B

Figure 6.1 Confusion

about as close as the author gets to aerial reconnaissance – in this case a downward-looking photograph of the beach at Naples, Florida. A casual monocular glance might suggest that this picture portrays a seagull posing on sand whose uniform colour tends to give it a homogeneous appearance. However, much in the same way that binocular inspection of stereographs from the air can reveal hidden military installations, the 3-D experience clearly shows the bird to be standing next to a large sand castle whose turrets and ramparts emerge with clarity when seen stereoscopically. Pair 6.1B shows that such confusions can increase when neighbouring objects are similar not only in colour but also in texture. Here, in a photo of the surf breaking against the rocky shore at Bondi Beach near Sydney, the bottom half of the picture looks like one expansive rock ledge along the coast line until we fuse the stereo pair with both eyes and discover, perhaps with a start, that a precipitous drop plunges from the immediate foreground to the flat shelf of rock below.

Clutter

In Figure 6.2, we find examples of photographs containing so many consumption-related objects that the separate identities of these things – while clearly distinguishable on an individual basis – tend to get lost below the cluttered surface when viewed with just one eye. In each case, stereoscopy breaks through the photographic clutter to reveal the underlying details of the relevant consumption experiences. Thus, Stereo Pair 6.2A shows a group of motorcycles parked in front of a bike shop on a sidewalk in Melbourne, Australia. A monocular glance fails to distinguish the different vehicles or their component parts. By contrast, the stereoscopic gaze reveals details as subtle as a reflection in the rear-view mirror of the closest bike or the partially obscured brand names of three nearby cycles (Honda, Honda, Yamaha). Similar clutter characterises the magazines on display at a New York news stand in Pair 6.2B. Monocularly, we just see a rather intimidating profusion of reading material on sale. Stereographically, however, we easily pick out each individual publication – Allure, People, Essence on the left; comics in the centre; newspapers on the bottom; PC World, Adweek, Self on the right, and so forth. If one is inclined, one can 'browse' through this site stereoscopically and amuse oneself by searching for various magazines (Buzz?, Mad?, Playboy?).

Crowding

As noted earlier, crowding combines the characteristics of confusion and clutter in the sense that it involves numerous visually similar objects crammed into a small pictorial space. In Figure 6.3, Pair 6.3A shows a conventional picture that travellers might bring back from their trip to Western Australia, just south of Perth, where in autumn the trees drop their bark instead of their leaves. In two dimensions – to reverse the familiar aphorism – one can barely find the

A

B

Figure 6.3 Crowding

trees for the forest. The one-eyed visual impression is so crowded as to provide little information. When experienced stereoptically, however, each tree appears to stand apart as a separate entity. One feels capable of peering deep into the woods beyond, as if to visit its interior and to explore its mysteries. Something similar happens in the picture of a New York fruit-and-vegetable market in Pair 6.3B. The two-dimensional view looks like a formidably crowded collection of homogeneous fresh produce. By contrast, in the 3-D experience, one clearly sees each tomato, each lemon, each orange, each pear, and each grape in each bunch. Each piece of fruit attains a palpable individuality of its own. And the scales for weighing one's purchases hang in mid-air before our eyes.

Complexity

All the foregoing illustrations entail complexity in the broadest sense of this concept. However, as shown in Figure 6.4, another important aspect of complexity occurs when we observe key aspects of a scene through or in some sort of transparent or reflective surface so that important information appears on this surface as well as possibly behind it or reflected in it from behind the viewer. Stereo Pair 6.4A illustrates the sort of mind-boggling complexity that appears in almost any shop window on a sunny day, especially if one closes one eye while peering inside. Here, in two dimensions, we see a complexity of photographic material that virtually defies visual analysis. By contrast, stereopsis sorts out the various spatial relationships into the relevant visual planes. Thus, at the surface of the window glass for this laundromat in Adelaide, Australia, we see the words 'Cleaning' and 'Shoe Repairs'. Reflected in the glass and therefore behind us, we see a nearby car parked next to a sign that says 'Open Laundry Matt' (backwards, of course) and signs for a 'Bar' or 'Cafe' across the street (behind some umbrellas and another parked car). And through the window, inside the laundromat, we see a row of washing machines running from the front towards the back of the establishment. This spatial complexity is typical of the visual impressions that I have frequently encountered when photographing store windows. It greatly enhances the pictorial meaningfulness of retailing-related stereography. Pair 6.4B shows another store window, this time at a frame shop in New York City. Even in two dimensions, one can spot certain key consumption-related details, such as the twin-camera rig I used to take some of the pictures shown earlier. As usual, however, stereopsis emphasises various important additional aspects of the scene otherwise camouflaged in the two-dimensional visual image. Thus, consumption-related reflections in the window glass do appear in this photograph (e.g. the bicycle and the apartment building on the right-hand side). Of greater interest, perhaps, the mirror at the bottom of the picture provides a clear impression (vertically) of higher-floor living quarters in the building located behind me while its gilt frame extends (horizontally) towards the viewer. This interplay of vertical reflection and horizontal surface eludes the two-dimensional glance but adds a compelling sense of depth to the stereoscopic gaze.

Figure 6.4 Complexity

113

Discussion: the catoptrics of Morris the Cat's photo-opp tricks

The stereo 3-D pair just shown returns us full circle to Brown's (1997b) preoccupation with Stereographic Enlightenment in general and with the orientation of Morris the Catoptric in particular. Featuring reflections and mirrors, as it does, Pair 6.4B is the ultimate exercise in catoptric stereoptics. More importantly, it sheds light on how three-dimensional stereography reveals insights into images that would otherwise be difficult to interpret.

This chapter began from the vantage point of social scientists and marketing or consumer researchers wishing to bring the revelatory power of photography to bear on the role of visual representations in the research literature. The problem with conventional photos in our traditional journals or books is that, even when this level of Kilo-Vision conveys good perspectival effects to depict three-dimensional reality, these depthless two-dimensional pictures imprison the viewer in the flat surface of the printed page. By contrast, stereography offers a hitherto neglected potential to create a true 3-D experience within our typical print media so as to enhance the vividness, clarity, realism, and depth with which we visually represent consumption-based events in the lives of consumers.

In the preceding sections, I have described methods that any marketing or consumer researcher can follow to produce high-quality stereographic images suitable for free-viewing or aided viewing by virtually any reader. Though the 3-D experience itself might sometimes seem magic or even mystical, the truth is that – unlike sawing a woman in half or summoning long-departed spirits from the past to a seance – three-dimensional stereography is not some sort of esoteric technique that only a small number of highly trained initiates can employ. Rather, stereo 3-D approaches readily lend themselves to widespread use in our discipline and to dissemination via our common publications. As an example, on three separate occasions, I have equipped collaborators with dual disposable cameras and have persuaded them to take pictures of various consumption-related phenomena. The resulting 3-D images were not just good; they were often superb. Otherwise flat or lifeless representations of goods, services, scenes, or events appeared to come alive in ways that revealed a wealth of detail and an abundance of depth. I have illustrated comparable phenomena earlier in the present chapter. Here, my point is simply that all marketing or consumer researchers with an interest in visual representations owe it to themselves to try these stereographic approaches.

Some readers might wonder what proportion of the marketing- and consumer-research audience could successfully view stereo pairs of the type shown in the present chapter and/or what impact such stereoptical viewing might have on their interpretations of the relevant visual images. I would suggest that, in large measure, the answers to such questions come from the evidence of our own eyes in viewing the stereo pairs shown earlier. That is, many readers will find the claims for stereoscopy persuasive by virtue of their own visual experience with stereo pairs like the ones shown here. However, I gladly concede that such questions clearly deserve further empirical investigation in future studies of stereoptical viewing in marketing and consumer research. And though I do not claim to provide definitive answers in the present chapter, I have conducted two informal studies that seem to bolster the case that I have already made by means of conceptual arguments and illustrative demonstrations.

First, as noted earlier, Julesz (1971, 1995) has reported that all but about 2 per cent of the population are functionally capable of achieving stereopsis on the type of paired stimuli used here. However, this potential capability does not necessarily mean that 98 per cent of the marketing- and consumer-research audience would be motivated to spend the time and effort needed to learn the technique of free-viewing. One might therefore ask what percentage can attain stereopsis without the benefit of special training or practice. To address this question, in one informal study I asked 55 graduate students from my marketing classes to free-view a stereographic pair similar to those found in the present chapter and also to view four additional stereo pairs with the aid of viewers comparable or identical to the prismatic lorgnette recommended earlier. Without any prior instruction or practice, only 20.0 per cent could successfully free-view the relevant stereo pair. However, even without training of any kind, 58.2 per cent succeeded immediately in aided viewing of all four images; 83.6 per cent succeeded with at least three images; 92.7 per cent succeeded with at least two; and 96.4 per cent with at least one. Further, both of the two remaining respondents who were unable to achieve stereopsis in aided viewing reported that they suffered from ophthalmological problems (self-described as a 'lazy eye'). Hence, this result accords with the optimistic assessment suggested by Julesz (1971, 1995).

None the less, one might still also wonder whether the successful stereopsis just demonstrated is generally accompanied – in the sort of magic or mystical way claimed earlier – by the enhanced vividness, clarity, realism, and depth promised as a key premise for the present chapter. To explore this remaining question, in a second informal study I asked 30 graduate students from the same marketing classes just mentioned to examine four stereo pairs similar to those shown earlier. In free-viewing, again without the help of any mechanical assistance and without the benefit of special training or practice, 15 respondents (50.0 per cent) achieved successful stereopsis on at least one of the stereo pairs, with 8 respondents (26.7 per cent) successfully free-viewing two or more of the pairs. In aided viewing with the help of the prismatic lorgnette recommended earlier but again without special instruction, 19 respondents (63.3 per cent) achieved stereopsis with all four stereo 3-D pairs; 27 respondents (90.0 per cent) with at least three pairs; and 28 respondents (93.3 per cent) with at least two. Again, the two remaining respondents indicated that ophthalmological problems prevented them from achieving stereoptical vision. Respondents were also asked the following question concerning their overall stereoptical 3-D viewing experience:

'In *general*, when comparing the two-dimensional images given by just one member of the various pairs with the 3-D stereo images achieved when fusing the two members into one 3-D stereo view of the various pairs, what types of things do you tend to see in three dimensions that you do *not* tend to see in two dimensions?' In response, three respondents explicitly mentioned *vividness* [a sense of 'movement'; image seems to 'come alive'; ability to 'go into' the picture]. Ten respondents referred to enhanced clarity or one of its synonyms [clear(ness); distinct(ness); texture(d); focus(ed) attention]. Thirteen respondents observed a greater realism provided by an increased amount of *detail* [can see every object; certain image(s) stand(s) out; things are seen in relief; I notice more; some things become more obvious]. And twelve respondents emphasised the enhanced sense of *depth* or some synonym for the perception of spatial relationships [feeling of space; layers; relative positions; distances among objects].

Finally, consider the stereo pair shown in Figure 6.5. This stereograph covers the classic case of animal camouflage – as exhibited by a python at the zoo in Sydney, Australia. Notice how, when viewed monocularly in either half of the stereo pair, the markings on the head and body of this snake resemble those of the surrounding leaves, causing the creature to blend inconspicuously or even undetectably into the background. By contrast, stereopsis helps to break through this camouflage to reveal the ugly serpent in all its slithery charm. In

Figure 6.5 Python

the classroom exercise just described, the 30 respondents were asked whether they were able to see this particular 3-D image stereoscopically and, if so, 'then *what* (if anything) do you see in the 3-D stereo image that you do *not* see so clearly in a single two-dimensional member of the pair?' Of the 23 respondents who successfully achieved stereopsis with this particular stereo pair, 19 or 82.6 per cent correctly said that they saw the snake. In other words, stereoscopic viewing revealed to them something rather important that they would not otherwise have seen.

To summarise, though these various findings come from informal studies rather than from rigorously controlled experiments, I take them to indicate rather forcefully that when viewing stereo 3-D pairs of visual images in the pages of our literature, readers of the relevant books or journals can be expected to experience the enhanced vividness, clarity, realism, and depth claimed as key benefits in the present chapter.

I should emphasise that the sorts of stereographic phenomena illustrated by the stereographs presented here are in no way atypical of the three-dimensional effects that I routinely encounter in taking stereo pairs of images related to various consumption experiences. Indeed, in selecting the stereo pairs for this chapter, I was forced to omit countless equally good examples that would have demonstrated each of the points made earlier just as forcefully. Actually, it would be difficult to find a decent-quality stereo pair that fails to improve dramatically upon the monocular version. A photograph of a two-dimensional painting on a flat wall or a scenic panorama taken from a great distance might provide an exception to this generalization. But clearly, this would serve as the proverbial exception that proves the rule. And the rule is that – when compared with two-dimensional monocular photographs – the greater vividness, clarity, realism, and depth contributed by three-dimensional binocular stereography via its ability to cope with confusion, clutter, crowding, and complexity will enhance the meaningfulness, interpretability, impact, and understanding of most visual images used to represent consumption experiences in marketing and consumer research. One might say that stereo 3-D images contribute to our enlightenment by illuminating our visual world in a way that characterises the magical, the mystical, and the other good things in life.

This view of the potential role for stereoscopy is rather new, a little controversial, plenty entrancing, and way romantic. It is the sort of thing that Morris the Catoptric would come up with when he looks at the visual side of our discipline. It promises to move Kilo-Vision to the level of Mega-Vision and maybe someday to the exalted heights of Giga-Vision. It seeks enlightenment in the illumination provided by stereoptical techniques that – when appreciated as part of the 3-D experience – may evoke epiphanies or revelations that seem magical or even mystical. It offers images of the consumption experience that are vivid, clear, real, and profoundly deep. To paraphrase another great romantic poet, they are beautiful. And they are true. And that is all we need to know.

Acknowledgement

The author gratefully acknowledges the support of the Columbia Business School's Faculty Research Fund.

References

Abrams, M.H. (1971), *Natural Supernaturalism*, New York: W.W. Norton & Company.

Adolph, J. (1994), 'Seeing is believing', *New Age Journal*, (Sept./Oct.), 84–9.

Alderson, T. (1988), 'Everyone's guide to freevision', *Stereo World*, 15 (November/December), 12–17.

Appel, A., Jr. (1983), *Signs of Life*, New York: Alfred A. Knopf.

Arnheim, R. (1951), 'Gestalt psychology and artistic form', in L.L.Whyte (ed.), *Aspects of Form*, Bloomington, IN: Indiana University Press, 196–208.

Ball, M.S. and Gregory, W.H.S. (1992), *Analyzing Visual Data*, Newbury Park, CA: Sage Publications.

Ball, M.S. and Smith, G.W.W. (1992), *Analyzing Visual Data*, Newbury Park, CA: Sage Publications.

Bateson, G. and Mead, M. (1942), *Balinese Character: A Photographic Analysis*, New York: New York Academy of Sciences.

Beardsley, M.C. (1981), *Aesthetics: Problems in the Philosophy of Criticism*, Indianapolis, IN: Hackett Publishing Company.

Becker, H.S. (1986), 'Photography and sociology', in H.S. Becker (ed.), *Doing Things Together: Selected Papers*, Evanston, IL: Northwestern University Press, 221–72.

Becker, H.S. (1995), 'Visual sociology, documentary photography, and photojournalism: it's (almost) all a matter of context', *Visual Sociology*, 10 (Spring/Fall), 5–14.

Belk, R.W. (ed.) (1991), *Highways and Buyways: Naturalistic Research From the Consumer Behavior Odyssey*, Provo, UT: Association for Consumer Research.

Belk, R.W., Sherry, J.F., Jr. and Wallendorf, M. (1988), 'A naturalistic inquiry into buyer and seller behavior at a swap meet', *Journal of Consumer Research*, 14 (March), 449–70.

Berlyne, D.E. (1971), *Aesthetics and Psychobiology*, New York: Appleton-Century-Crofts.

Best, S.R. (1979), 'Free vision', *Stereo World*, 6 (November/December), 8–10.

Blum, R. (1987), *The Siege at Port Arthur: The Russo-Japanese War Through the Stereoscope*, Adelaide: Lutheran Publishing House.

Boyer, P.S. (1990), 'Random-dot stereograms', *Stereo World*, 17 (March/April), 30–3.

Brentwood Home Video (1994), *Magic Insight: 3D Animated Stereograms*, Westlake Village, CA: Brentwood Home Video.

Brown, S. (1997a), 'Tore down à la Rimbaud: the 4 Bs of marketing illumination', in S. Brown, A.M. Doherty and B. Clarke (eds), *Proceedings of the Marketing Illuminations Spectacular*, Belfast: University of Ulster, 1–15.

Brown, S. (1997b), 'The unbearable lightness of marketing: revisionism, antithetical criticism and the anxiety of academic influence', in S. Brown, A. M. Doherty and B. Clarke (eds), *Proceedings of the Marketing Illuminations Spectacular*, Belfast: University of Ulster, 315–26.

Brown, T. (1903, ed. 1994), *Stereoscopic Phenomena of Light and Sight*, Culver City, CA: Reel 3-D Enterprises, Inc.

Burder, D. and Whitehouse, P. (1992), *Photographing in 3-D*, 3rd edn, Surrey: The Stereoscopic Society.

Cadence Books (1994a), *Stereogram*, San Francisco: Cadence Books.

Cadence Books (1994b), *Super Stereogram*, San Francisco: Cadence Books.

Caulfield, J. (1991), 'The work of knowledge in the age of mechanical reproduction', *Visual Sociology*, 6 (Fall), 5–8.

Chaplin, E. (1994), *Sociology and Visual Representation*, London: Routledge.

Cohen, D. (ed.) (1992), *America Then and Now*, San Francisco: HarperCollins.

Collier, J., Jr. and Collier, M. (1986), *Visual Anthropology: Photography as a Research Method* (revised and expanded edition), Albuquerque, NM: University of New Mexico Press.

Coy, P. and Hof, R.D. (1995), '3-D computing', *Business Week*, (4 Sept.), 70–7.

Crain, J. (1994), *California in Depth: A Stereoscopic History*, San Francisco: Chronicle Books.

Csikszentmihalyi, M. (1996), *Creativity: Flow and the Psychology of Discovery and Invention*, New York: HarperCollins.

Darrah, W.C. (1977), *The World of Stereographs*, Gettysburg, PA: W. C. Darrah.

Dennis, J. (1980), 'TRU-VUE: stereo's missing link', *Stereo World*, 7 (July/Aug.), 4–14.

Dennis, J. (1984), 'Seven billion windows on the world – view-master then and now', *Stereo World*, 11 (March/April), 4–16.

Dennis, J. (1995), 'Underwater stereo with class', *Stereo World*, 21 (Jan./Feb.), 21–3.

DePree, M. (1992), Leadership Jazz, New York: Currency/Doubleday.

Dyckman, D. (1994), *Hidden Dimensions*, New York: Harmony Books.

Ferwerda, J.G. (1990), *The World of 3-D: A Practical Guide to Stereo Photography*, 2nd edn, Borger, The Netherlands: 3-D Book Productions.

Frisby, J.P. (1980), *Seeing: Illusion, Brain and Mind*, Oxford: Oxford University Press.

Girling, A.N. (1990), *Stereoscopic Drawing: A Theory of 3-D Vision and Its Application to Stereoscopic Drawing*, London: Arthur N. Girling.

Goffman, E. (1979), *Gender Advertisements*, London: Macmillan.

Golblum, R. (1993), 'Airborne: the uncanny resemblances of jazz and sports', *Jazziz*, 10 (May), 20–6.

Gold, S.J. (1991), 'Ethnic boundaries and ethnic entrepreneurship: a photo-elicitation study', *Visual Sociology*, 6 (Fall), 9–22.

Gold, S.J. (1995), 'New York/LA: a visual comparison of public life in two cities', *Visual Sociology*, 10 (Spring/Fall), 85–105.

Grady, J. (1991), 'The visual essay and sociology', *Visual Sociology*, 6 (Fall), 23–38.

Graves, T.E. (1989), 'Stereo documentation of folklife', *Stereo World*, 16 (May/June), 38–9.

Gregory, R.L. (1970), *The Intelligent Eye*, New York: McGraw-Hill.

Gregory, R.L. (1990), *Eye and Brain: The Psychology of Seeing*, 4th edn, Princeton, NJ: Princeton University Press.

Grossman, M. and Cooper, R. (1995), *Magic Eye: How To See 3D – The 3D Guide, A Training Manual by N.E. Thing Enterprises*, Kansas City: Andrews and McMeel.

Halliwell, L. (1989), *Halliwell's Film Guide*, 7th edn, New York: Harper & Row.

Harper, D. (1987), *Working Knowledge: Skill and Community in a Small Shop*, Chicago: University of Chicago Press.

Harper, D. (1988), 'Visual sociology: expanding sociological vision', *The American Sociologist*, 19 (Spring), 54–70.

Harper, D. (1989), 'Interpretive ethnography: from "authentic voice" to "interpretive eye"', in R.B. Flaes (ed.), *Eyes Across the Water: The Amsterdam Conference on Visual Anthropology and Sociology*, Amsterdam: Het Spinhuis, 33–42.

Hayes, S.L. (ed.) (1992), *3-D Hollywood: Photographs by Harold Lloyd*, New York: Simon & Schuster.

Heisley, D.D. and Levy, S.J. (1991), 'Autodriving: a photoelicitation technique', *Journal of Consumer Research*, 18 (December), 257–72.

Heisley, D.D., McGrath, M.A. and Sherry, J.F., Jr. (1991), '"To everything there is a season": A photoessay of a farmer's market', in R.W. Belk (ed.), *Highways and Buyways*, Provo, UT: Association for Consumer Research, 141–66.

Hill, R.P. and Stamey, M. (1990), 'The homeless in America: an examination of possessions and consumption behaviors', *Journal of Consumer Research*, 17 (December), 303–21.

Hirschman, E.C. and Holbrook, M.B. (1992), *Postmodern Consumer Research: The Study of Consumption as Text*, Newbury Park, CA: Sage Publications.

Holbrook, M.B. (1980), 'Some preliminary notes on research in consumer esthetics', in J.C. Olson (ed.), *Advances in Consumer Research*, vol. 7, Ann Arbor, MI: Association for Consumer Research, 104–8.

Holbrook, M.B. (1984), 'Theory development is a jazz solo: bird lives', in P.F. Anderson and M.J. Ryan (eds), *Proceedings, Winter Educators' Conference*, Chicago, IL: American Marketing Association, 48–52.

Holbrook, M.B. (1987a), 'An audiovisual inventory of some fanatic consumer behavior: the 25-cent tour of a jazz collector's home', in M.R. Wallendorf and P.F. Anderson (eds), *Advances in Consumer Research*, Provo, UT: Association for Consumer Research, 144–9.

Holbrook, M.B. (1987b), 'What is consumer research?', *Journal of Consumer Research*, 14 (June), 128–32.

Holbrook, M.B. (1988), 'Steps toward a psychoanalytic interpretation of consumption: a meta-meta-meta-analysis of some issues raised by the Consumer Behavior Odyssey', in M.J. Houston (ed.), *Advances in Consumer Research*, Vol. 15, Provo, UT: Association for Consumer Research, 537–42.

Holbrook, M.B. (1991), 'Romanticism and sentimentality in consumer behavior: a literary approach to the joys and sorrows of consumption', *Research in Consumer Behavior*, 5, 105–80

Holbrook, M.B. (1995a), *Consumer Research: Introspective Essays on the Study of Consumption*, Thousand Oaks, CA: Sage Publications.

Holbrook, M.B. (1995b), 'Romanticism, introspection, and the roots of experiential consumption: Morris the Epicurean', in R.W. Belk, N. Dholakia and A. Venkatesh (eds), *Consumption and Marketing: Macro Dimensions*, Cincinnati: South-Western College Publishing, 20–82.

Holbrook, M.B. (1996a), 'On eschatology, onanist scatology, or honest catology? Cats swinging, scat singing, and cat slinging as riffs, rifts, and writs in a catalytic catechism for the cataclysm', in S. Brown, J. Bell and D. Carson (eds), *Marketing Apocalypse: Eschatology, Escapology and the Illusion of the End*, London: Routledge, 237–59.

Holbrook, M.B. (1996b), 'Reflections on Rocky', *Society & Animals: Social Scientific Studies of the Human Experience of Other Animals*, 4(2), 147–68.

Holbrook, M.B. (1997a), 'Feline consumption: ethography, felologies, and unobtrusive participation in the life of a cat', *European Journal of Marketing*, 31(3/4), 214–33.

Holbrook, M.B. (1997b), 'Marketing across or beyond, without or among, and at or on the borders: some literal, littoral, and literary ideas whose times definitely have, probably have not, and maybe might have come', in *Marketing Without Borders*, Proceedings of the 31st Annual Conference, Manchester Metropolitan University, Manchester: Academy of Marketing, 811–49.

Holbrook, M.B. (1997c), 'The potential for 3-D stereo photographs in visual sociology: pedestrian icons on the Upper West Side', Working Paper, Graduate School of Business, Columbia University.

Holbrook, M.B. (1997d), 'Romanticism, introspection, and the roots of experiential consumption: Morris the Epicurean', *Consumption, Markets and Culture*, 1(2), 97–163.

Holbrook, M.B. (1997e), 'Stereographic visual displays and the three-dimensional communication of findings in marketing research', *Journal of Marketing Research*, 34 (November), 526–36.

Holbrook, M.B. (1997f), 'Walking on the edge: a stereographic photo essay on the verge of consumer research', in S. Brown and D. Turley (eds), *Consumer Research: postcards from the edge*, London: Routledge, 46–78.

Holbrook, M.B. (1998a), 'Borders, creativity, and the state of the art at the leading edge', Working Paper, Graduate School of Business, Columbia University.

Holbrook, M.B. (1998b), 'Journey To Kroywen: an ethnoscopic stereographic auto-auto-auto-driven photo essay' in B. Stern (ed.), *Representing Consumers: Voices, Views, and Visions*, London: Routledge.

Holbrook, M.B. (1998c), 'Marketing applications of three-dimensional stereography', *Marketing Letters*, 9(1), 51–64.

Holbrook, M.B. and Hirschman, E.C. (1982), 'The experiential aspects of consumption: consumer fantasies, feelings, and fun', *Journal of Consumer Research*, 9 (September), 132–40.

Holbrook, M.B. and Hirschman, E.C. (1993), *The Semiotics of Consumption: Interpreting Symbolic Consumer Behavior in Popular Culture and Works of Art*, Berlin: Mouton de Gruyter.

Holbrook, M.B. and Kuwahara, T. (1997), 'Probing a consumption experience in depth: a collective stereographic photo essay on "what New York means to me"', Working Paper, Graduate School of Business, Columbia University.

Holbrook, M.B. and Zirlin, R.B. (1985), 'Artistic creation, artworks, and aesthetic appreciation: some philosophical contributions to nonprofit marketing', *Advances in Nonprofit Marketing*, 1, 1–54.

Johnstone, T. (1995), *Magic 3D: Discover the Revolutionary World of Photographic Free-viewing*, London: Stanley Paul.

Julesz, B. (1971), *Foundations of Cyclopean Perception*, Chicago: University of Chicago Press.

Julesz, B. (1995), *Dialogues On Perception*, Cambridge, MA: MIT Press.

Kao, J. (1996), *Jamming*, New York: HarperBusiness.

Kinsman, A. (1992), *Random Dot Stereograms*, Rochester, NY: Kinsman Physics.

Kodak (1955), *Picture it in Stereo*, Publication No. C-7, Rochester, NY: Eastman Kodak.

Koestler, A. (1964), *The Act of Creation*, New York: Dell.

Lavin, M. (1995), 'Creating consumers in the 1930s: Irma Phillips and the radio soap opera', *Journal of Consumer Research*, 22 (June), 75–89.

Lears, J. (1994), *Fables of Abundance: A Cultural History of Advertising in America*, New York: Basic Books.

Lewis, W. (1993), 'George Lewis: Keystone's last stereographer', *Stereo World*, 20 (November/December), 4–25.

Lorenz, D. (1987), *The Stereo Image in Science and Technology: A Three-Dimensional Picture Book*, 2nd edn, Cologne: German Aerospace Research Establishment.

McAllister, D.F. (ed.) (1993), *Stereo Computer Graphics and Other True 3D Technologies*, Princeton, NJ: Princeton University Press.

McShane, L. (1993), *'When I Wanted the Sun to Shine': Kilburn and Other Littleton, New Hampshire Stereographers*, Littleton, NH: Sherwin Dodge.

Maio, M. (1991), 'Buffalo's old first ward: a photographic study', *Visual Sociology*, 6 (Fall), 53–77.

Margolis, E. (1994), 'Images in struggle: photographs of Colorado coal camps', *Visual Sociology*, 9 (Spring), 4–26.

Marr, D. (1982), *Vision: A Computational Investigation into the Human Representation and Processing of Visual Information*, New York: W.H. Freeman.

Menzel, P. (1994), *Material World: A Global Family Portrait*, San Francisco: Sierra Club Books.

Meyer, L.B. (1956), *Emotion and Meaning in Music*, Chicago: University of Chicago Press.

Meyer, L.B. (1967), *Music, the Arts, and Ideas*, Chicago: University of Chicago Press.

Mick, D.G. and Buhl, C. (1992), 'A meaning-based model of advertising experiences', *Journal of Consumer Research*, 19 (December), 317–38.

Milligan, P. (1995), *'Under Water – A 3-D Wonderland* by Johannes Hinterkircher', *Stereoscopy*, Series 2 (March), 27.

Montage Publications (1994), *Ultra 3-D*, San Diego: Front Line Art Publishing.

Nazarieff, S. (1993), *The Stereoscopic Nude: 1850–1930*, Cologne: Benedikt Taschen.

N.E. Thing Enterprises (1993), *Magic Eye: A New Way of Looking at the World*, Kansas City, MO: Andrews and McMeel.

Neumann, M. (1992), 'The traveling eye: photography, tourism and ethnography', *Visual Sociology*, 7 (Fall), 22–38.

Nordström, A.D. (1994), 'Photographies of art and science', *Visual Sociology*, 9 (Fall), 97–101.

Norton, R. (1994), *Stereoviews Illustrated – Volume I: Fifty Early American*, New Haven, CT: Stereoviews Illustrated Press.

O'Guinn, T.C. (1991), 'Touching greatness: the central midwest Barry Manilow fan club', in R.W. Belk (ed.), *Highways and Buyways*, Provo, UT: Association for Consumer Research, 102–11.

Oldfather, P. and West, J. (1994), 'Qualitative research and jazz', *Educational Researcher*, 23 (November), 22–6.

Patterson, N.B. (1994), 'Stereo and the future of film', *Stereo World*, 21 (May/June), 22–3.

Peñaloza, L. (1994), *'Altravesando fronteras*/border crossings: a critical ethnographic exploration of the consumer acculturation of Mexican immigrants', *Journal of Consumer Research*, 21, 32–54.

Quinney, R. (1995), 'A sense sublime: visual sociology as a fine art', *Visual Sociology*, 10 (Spring/Fall), 61–84.

Rheingold, H. (1994), 'Foreword', in *Stereogram*, San Francisco: Cadence Books, 6–9.

Richardson, D. (1994), *Create Stereograms on Your PC: Discover the World of 3D Illusion*, Corte Madera, CA: Waite Group Press.

RUMINATIONS ON ROMANTICISM

Riemschneider, B. (1994), *Interactive Pictures*, trans. K. Williams, Cologne: Benedikt Taschen.

Rook, D.W. (1991), 'I was observed (*in absentia*) and autodriven by the Consumer Behavior Odyssey', in R.W. Belk (ed.), *Highways and Buyways*, Provo, UT: Association for Consumer Research, 48–58.

Saburi, E.H. (ed.) (1993), *3D Wonderland*, Bellevue, WA: Tokuma Shoten Publishing Co.

Sakane, I. (1994), 'The random-dot stereogram and its contemporary significance: new directions in perceptual art', in *Stereogram*, San Francisco: Cadence Books, 73–82.

Sales, J.H. (1994), *Constructing Anaglyph Images*, West Covina, CA: J.H. Sales.

Schouten, J.W. and McAlexander, J.H. (1995), 'Subcultures of consumption: an ethnography of the new bikers', *Journal of Consumer Research*, 22 (June), 43–61.

Schwartzman, S. (1981), *Bodies of Light: Infrared Stereo Nudes*, Austin, TX: SunShine.

Schwenker, J.E. (1991), 'Stereo pairs on a computer', *Stereo World*, 17 (January/February), 19–21.

Scott, L.M. (1994), 'The bridge from text to mind: adapting reader-response theory to consumer research', *Journal of Consumer Research*, 21 (December), 461–80.

Sell, M.A. and Sell, W. (1994a), *View-Master Viewers: An Illustrated History*, Borger, The Netherlands: 3-D Book Productions.

Sell, W. and Sell, M.A. (1994b), 'Museum 3-D', *Stereo World*, 21 (March/April), 32–3, 47.

Setlak, J.-P. (trans. 1994), *Paris in 3-D*, Phoenix, AZ: Cygnus Graphic.

Steiger, R. (1995), 'First children and family dynamics', *Visual Sociology*, 10 (Spring/Fall), 28–49.

Stern, B.B. (1995), 'Consumer myths: Frye's taxonomy and the structural analysis of consumption text', *Journal of Consumer Research*, 22 (September), 165–85.

Stilgoe, J.R. (1994), *Alongshore*, New Haven, CT: Yale University Press.

Suchar, C.S. (1988), 'Photographing the changing material culture of a gentrified community', *Visual Sociology Review*, 3 (Fall), 17–21.

Taft, R. (1938, ed. 1989), *Photography and the American Scene*, New York: Dover Publications.

Thomson, D. (1991), *Visual Magic*, New York: Dial Books.

Trachtenberg, A. (1989), *Reading American Photographs: Images as History – Matthew Brady to Walker Evans*, New York: Hill and Wang.

Tufte, E.R. (1990), *Envisioning Information*, Cheshire, CT: Graphics Press.

21st Century Publishing (1994), *Another Dimension*, Los Angeles: 21st Century Publishing.

Tydings, K.S. (1951), *The Stereo-Realist Guide: Stereo Made Easy for Everyone*, New York: Greenberg.

Tyler, C.W. (1994), 'The birth of computer stereograms for unaided stereovision including a guide to creating random-dot stereograms', in *Stereogram*, San Francisco: Cadence Books, 83–9.

van der Does, P., Edelaar, S., Gooskens, I., Liefting, M. and van Mierlo, M. (1992), 'Reading images: a study of a Dutch neighborhood', *Visual Sociology*, 7 (Spring), 4–67.

van Keulen, W. (1986), *3-D Past and Present*, Borger, The Netherlands: 3-D Book Productions.

van Keulen, W. (1990), *3D Imagics: A Stereoscopic Guide to the 3D Past and its Magic Images, 1938–1900*, Borger, The Netherlands: 3-D Book Productions.

Waack, F.G. (1987), *Stereo Photography: An Introduction to Stereo Photo Technology and Practical Suggestions for Stereo Photography*, trans. L. Huelsbergen, Berlin: F.G. Waack.

Wagner, J. (ed.) (1979), *Images of Information: Still Photography in the Social Sciences*, Beverly Hills, CA: Sage Publications.

Waldsmith, J.S. (1991), *Stereo Views: An Illustrated History and Price Guide*, Radnor, PA: Wallace-Homestead Book Company.

Watson, E.B. (1976), *New York Then and Now: 83 Manhattan Sites Photographed in the Past and in the Present*, New York: Dover Publications, Inc.

Williamson, J. (1978), *Decoding Advertisements: Ideology and Meaning in Advertising*, London: Marion Boyars.

Winton, T. (1993), *Land's Edge*, Sydney: Pan Macmillan.

Zaltman, G. (1997), 'Rethinking market research: putting people back in', *Journal of Marketing Research*, 34 (November), 424–37.

Ziller, R.C. (1990), *Photographing THE SELF: Methods for Observing Personal Orientations*, Newbury Park, CA: Sage Publications.

Zone, R. (1991), *The Deep Image: 3-D in Art and Science*, Los Angeles: The 3-D Zone.

7

THE RATIONALITY OF 'IRRATIONAL' BEHAVIOUR

Georges Bataille on consuming extremities

Christian Jantzen and Per Østergaard

Though this be madness, yet there is method in't.
(Polonius, *Hamlet*)

Meaning beyond utility

(Post)modern life has been depicted negatively in such contradictory terms as having fallen prey to turmoil, upheaval, multiplication of oughts and wants, dissociation and fragmentation on the one hand, and on the other hand as characterised by security, social welfare, and regulations, i.e. by surveillance, boredom and indifference. Life is either all too rational or, on the contrary, lacks any basic sense of order. Underlying these assumptions, however, are notions of rationality and order derived from classical economics and sociology. These notions stress normative aspects of decision-making: of how behaviour ought to be functional and should serve useful purposes. Or the emphasis is on the uses and purposes of local disorder for the strengthening and emulation of a higher social order. Thus the lack of disorder – of disputes, disruptions and social involvement – is viewed as a symptom of 'anomie' (Durkheim 1951) which is critical for the long-term survival of any social bond, just as indeterminacy, on the other hand, is viewed as critical to individual decision-making in the long term. These types of diagnosis are in some way or another utilitarian. Either they stress the conscious goal-attainment and satisfaction-maximising behaviour of autonomous individuals, or they focus on the (often impeded) functionality of the social organism, thus adhering to the 'social utilitarianism' of Durkheimean sociology (see Sahlins 1976).

This scheme of thought is more or less unwittingly and uncritically reproduced by many consumer researchers and marketing theorists. Utilitarianism is for instance central to the 'marketing concept' and the 'societal marketing concept' as defined by Kotler (1988): the task of marketers is to determine the 'needs' and 'wants' of consumers, to provide a maximum of 'satisfaction', and to preserve the 'well-being' of society which is thus described in anthropomorphic terms. We do not want to dismiss this inherent utilitarianism in marketing theory as altogether misconceived, but we would assert that this foundation with its emphasis on purposes and utility obscures some important aspects of consumption. This is due to a too restricted conception of rationality, order, and 'well-being'. The rationality of economic life and of market behaviour is fundamentally regarded as a planned and structured activity, and discussed in terms of uses (or usefulness), calculation, productivity and meanings.

Life itself, though, is not quite that way. Living is also – and to a very substantial degree – a matter of wasting time, spending money without clear-cut aims, indulging in apparently meaningless actions, or simply doing nothing. This 'nothing' is neither just a symptom of quotidian life's boredom, nor solely a necessary (i.e. useful) element in the reproduction of the productive labour force. 'Nothingness' is also something individuals actively strive to accomplish. As a matter of fact, 'becoming nothing' by forgetting the self or by transgressing the boundaries of ordinary experience may in some cultures be regarded as the only true path to illumination and insight, e.g. in the 'satori' of a Zen archery or swordsmanship, where bow and arrow, sword and Zen have the same goal, that is, 'to slay the ego' (Herrigel 1948). Meditation is thus a process in which the self and its ordinary concerns and calculations are forgotten or reduced to nothing. The self is annihilated as a well-defined 'something', in order to reach a state of 'deeper and inner truth'. Many people regard this process as intrinsically meaningful, although in comparison to the symbolic meanings of ordinary social it life is an 'empty', minimal meaning, difficult or even impossible to communicate to others. It is personally gratifying, but socially without meaning. Much the same goes for quite the opposite of going 'into' your mind: the state of going 'out' of your mind. In running berserk, an old time favourite Viking pastime, the individual experiences moments of grandiosity and magnified force: the feeling of becoming 'everything' and being everywhere, all over the place. This is an extension of the self and, as such, another form of annihilating the self's socially defined boundaries. In fact, this process is often one of violence, destruction, abuse and waste, and exceeds the concept of utility and productivity. It is socially damaging, but may very often be experienced as temporary gratifying behaviour.

From a utilitarian perspective these two types of forgetting or losing the self have to be viewed as irrational phenomena, because they do not fit into the proper way of thinking. They may even be regarded as insane or at least as untypical behaviour that either does not have to be accounted for in any substantial way (meditation) or must be treated as a pathological, not as an economic issue (berserk fury). This, however, is a highly reductive point of view. It might even prove fatal to an illuminated understanding of market behaviour and to consumer research, because so much of the consumers' time and energy are spent (or wasted) in displaying and participating in these kinds of activity. Disorder, waste, and destruction are part of existence. They are not mere deviations from the normal way of life or marginal to everyday existence.

On the contrary, they often seem to be the most important part of existence, especially when life is evaluated in terms of intensity and involvement. Exuberant spending and extravaganza (e.g. fashion), expensive and time-consuming hobbies, excessive behaviour (drinking, eating, carnivals), transgressions of ordinary life (perversions, addictions, shoplifting), high-risk sports like mountaineering, etc., are certainly not rational in the strict (or restricted) sense of the term. None the less, all these phenomena are able to attract otherwise quite rational consumers, because they seem to convey a more profound or abysmal meaning of life that cannot easily be grasped by utilitarian notions of 'needs, wants, satisfaction and well-being'. Such activities, however irrational they might appear to be from a utilitarian point of view, or however meaningless and 'antisocial' from a symbolic one, spring from motivations, which have to be accounted for, when dealing with human (and especially consumer) behaviour.

'A theory of love'

'Love', which makes people go out of as well as into their minds, is the paramount example of 'antisocial', 'irrational' and 'useless' behaviour. It disrupts the sociability of ordinary life, makes people engage in haphazard and potentially (physically or mentally) dangerous activities for the sake of clichéd ideas or some kilos of bones, lumps of flesh, hair and blood vessels, which have become an adoring object, which people long for and are sometimes even willing to die for. Love – of another person, but also of pets, of values and ideas (one's own country, for example), of material objects, etc. – is an obsession, even 'madness', but is there not also some method in it? If the answer is affirmative, if 'love' is recognised as one of the crucial preoccupations in existence, and if the amount of time spent on 'love' – on loving, being in or out of love, etc. – is taken into consideration, then it becomes clear that marketing theory and consumer research desperately need a 'theory of love', i.e. a theory of the implications of 'falling' in (and out of) love, of the thrills of 'making' (and the unmaking of) love, of people's loving of love (their lust), of caring (the ways in which people try to be 'everything' to somebody), and of sacrifice (of giving their life away in order to preserve their personal idea(l) of holiness), etc.

The importance of love as one of the core emotions in life has been, with only few exceptions (Belk and Coon 1993), largely ignored by consumer researchers. This despite the fact that precisely this theme might give researchers a more complete understanding of their topic, because 'love' is not only something to be consumed and enjoyed by the self as an enrichment of life. It is dangerous and frightening too: a consuming force which – like the Sirens in Homer's *Odyssey* – might very well attract, lure, haunt, captivate and crush the self. It is at once illuminating and obscuring, real and illusive, an invaluable possession but also a possessive power, both infinitely meaningful and meaningless, productive as well as destructive. A 'theory of love', therefore, could illuminate the 'other' side of consumption and possession. Whereas seminal research has stressed the importance of possessions for the social construction of the self (Belk 1988), consumption is also about being possessed by emotions or long-ings, by other persons, ideas or objects, with the possible implication – one feared or/and yearned for – of not extending but of exhausting or losing the self.

What are the thrills and attractions of fear, debasement and violence? What are the pleasures of waste, disorder and risk? Which meaning does the mean-ingless have? What is the reason for 'irrational' behaviour like excess, expenditure and extravagance? Why does experience of inner harmony some-times count for more than social acceptance does? These and similar questions are not about calculable needs and wants, but about consuming passions like love and rage, i.e. about the other side of consumption. On the following pages we want to introduce a theory, which might illustrate some of the con-sumers' desires and appetites for objects and experiences beyond utility.

The general economy

Like Mikhail Bakhtin, Walter Benjamin, Ernst Bloch and Elias Canetti, Georges Bataille (1897-1962) was one of those writers from the inter-war period, who were marginal to the intellectual climate of the 1930s, but have had an enor-mous impact on the humanities since their 'rediscovery' in the 1960s. In Bataille's case, this marginality was for a large part self-inflicted, because of his opposition to the dominant thinkers and theories of intellectual life in France. In the late 1920s, he broke with the surrealist movement after a political dispute with its leader, André Breton. In the late 1940s, his writings were denounced as 'reactionary' by Jean Paul Sartre who was central to the fashion of the day, existentialism. Bataille's way to more lasting fame, therefore, first started after his death with the new poststructuralist movement of the 1960s, when his writings were recognised as seminal to the development of poststructuralism (Foucault 1962; Derrida 1978). In the 1970s his theory was embraced by the germinat-ing postmodernism (e.g. Baudrillard 1993; Perniola 1977).

Bataille was not a scholar by education, or at least not a university-trained scholar. As a lapsed seminarist, he became a librarian, and was in many ways an autodidact who none the less acquired a vast body of knowledge in philosophy (especially Hegel, Nietzsche), Marxism, psychoanalysis, religion, mysticism (gnosticism), sociology (Durkheim) and anthropology (Mauss, Granet). These disparate sources were combined in a highly original manner in his writings, that consist of articles often published in journals he himself founded and edited (the most famous of them is the renowned and still existing review *Critique*), larger theoretical expositions in bookform (e.g. the unfinished *Somme athéologique*, 3 vols), but also pornographic novels (e.g. Bataille 1977, 1979, 1989). Themes like sexuality, death, transgression, and excess persist through-out all of his works, the most important being the books on eroticism (Bataille

1962), on modern mysticism (Bataille 1988b) and on 'general economy' (Bataille 1988a, the first volume of *Somme athéologique*). This last book is of special interest to us, because of its attempt to ground a theory of exchange and consumption beyond the concept of utility in classical economics. The principles of this theory were sketched early by Bataille in an article in the 1932 issue of his journal *La Critique Sociale*, 'La Notion de dépense' (Bataille 1985a). This article draws heavily on the French anthropologist Marcel Mauss's reinterpretation of the German/American ethnographer Franz Boas's data on gift giving among the Kwakiutl Indians of the Northwest (Mauss 1954). According to Mauss, the exchange of gifts among Indian chiefs is not the result of friendly alliances among tribes, but derives from challenge and battle. Power and force are symbolised by the chief's ability to give gifts, the most powerful chief being the one who can give the largest gifts. This process of gift giving rests on three obligations: first, the obligation to give a gift; second, the obligation to receive a gift; and third, the obligation to return a (larger) gift in response to received gifts. The reciprocity of obligations makes gift giving a logic of expenditure, where chiefs and tribes exhaust and spill their wealth in order to defeat and seize on their counterparts. Thus, wealth is not a goal in itself, but merely acquired and accumulated in order to be wasted in these gift-giving duels, also called 'potlatch' by the Kwakiutls, in which the life and honour of the participants are at stake.

Bataille has generalised this logic of gift-giving into a universal logic of exchange. Thus, the meaning of life or the reason for living, according to Bataille, lies in expenditure even at the risk of dying. In fact, the very possibility of death by means of sacrifice, ecstasy or excessive behaviour gives magnitude to life: 'The danger of death is not avoided; it is the object of a strong unconscious attraction' (Bataille 1985a: 119). This attraction is interpreted by Bataille as an expression of an innate religious drive in humankind. In this respect, his writings should be understood as an attempt to elucidate how an urge for holiness is a core motivation in all human endeavour, and how this urge has been corrupted and perverted by modern bourgeois civilization for the sake of petty profits: 'The hatred of expenditure is the *raison d'être* of and the justification for the bourgeoisie' (ibid.: 124). His theory, especially in the 1930s, therefore proclaims the necessity and inevitability of an imminent bloody revolution by the working classes against their masters 'who have worked to lose *human nature*' (ibid.: 128). This analysis has, as so many other forecasts of things to come, proved totally wrong. Moreover it is written in a religious, messianic vocabulary typical of radical political ideologies, but unacceptable from an academic point of view (see Löwith 1949).

None the less, his assumptions on religion and on the logic of productivity, consumption and waste are illuminating, and certainly deserve attention from consumer researchers. As pointed out by sociologists of religion (e.g. Eliade 1957) the concept of 'God' as a transcendental principle has lost much of its traditional meaning. This is in part due to the fact that religious explanations no longer match the scientific models of modernity which in effect make them unfit to give a univocal answer to the question of 'Why do we exist?'. However, religion has also lost its role of collective consciousness in the Durkheimean sense, because the mere concept of transcendentality is of little appeal to modern man, i.e. the idea that there is something more real and essential behind the surface of everyday life, a 'something' we moreover must unconditionally obey and always fear, because it is larger and higher than our own existence. Such a premodern and servile concept is at odds with the modern concept of the autonomous and self-conscious individual which turns mankind – not the deity – into the 'creator' of society. This ideology is of course just as metaphysical as the old one. It has only replaced one metaphysical content ('God') with another ('the individual').

For Bataille, however, religion is not a matter of content, but of form: more exactly *an experience*. So although the influence of religion on the whole gamut of life has weakened considerably, this does not make holiness or religious experience irrelevant to modern man. The drive for this kind of experience is expressed in transgressions of ordinary life and in subversions of the profane sphere of work and productivity. These relations between religion and transgression or subversion are in no way new: mental states of ecstasy and excess (literally: of 'going out of your mind') and of mystic meditation are inherent in all religions. What is new about modernity is, on the contrary, the paramount dominance of the profane over the sacred and, by consequence, the reduction of the whole range of emotions and motivations – of life in its versatility – to calculation, accumulation and productivity. The different forms of unproductive expenditure, which are prerequisite to religious experience, are banned – if not from public life, then from public acceptance and spontaneous collective celebration.

This reduction of exchange to the profane sphere of production is, according to Bataille, due to 'the restricted economy', in which the sacred sphere merely fulfils a symbolic function. Expenses are thus assessed in terms of necessary investments for the growth of productivity, and consumption can only be appreciated as useful reproduction that serves as a means to production (see also Weber 1930). This is not only an impoverishing of life. In turning genuine religious experience away from collective life, excess and transgression come to haunt humanity in non-public forms. Addiction, perversions, obsessions are pitiful and 'personal' remnants of former expressions of joy and grandiosity. They now have to be hidden from society, and conducted in privacy or secrecy with a very limited degree of gratification. Shoplifting, overdrafts, compulsive buying, for example, are symptoms of obsessive, but abortive and shameful behaviour in the marketplace. Or otherwise excess returns to collective life in the completely perverted forms typical to the twentieth century with its numerous types of truly irrational destruction, e.g. the mass destruction of enemies that have replaced the honourable duel, the killing fields and planned massacres of anonymous civilians as a transformation of public and festive sacrifice, and pollution as a concealed form of waste.

Bataille criticises modernity not so much for the fact that the rationality of production annihilates the joyous and festive sides of life, but especially for its misconception of the role of productivity in life which turns the unproductive aspects of existence into destructive forces, dangerous to individuals as well as to society at large. His aim, therefore, is to restore the consciousness of the importance of waste, transgression and expenditure – of religious experience – by showing how productivity and accumulation of wealth serve the purpose of useless consumption. Like in the Kwakiutl 'potlatch', expenditure is primary to conservation and production. This is a reversal of the utility concept of classical economics, in that increase of wealth is regarded as the means of an economy of spending and loss, not as the goal of productivity. The 'restricted economy' of modernity is thus embedded in the larger exchange of a 'general economy' (Bataille 1988a), in which useless expenditure creates the surplus of energy for the production/consumption-circuit, but also for renewed expenditure. This larger circuit, according to Bataille universal to all cultures even to all organic life, could be sketched as shown in Figure 7.1

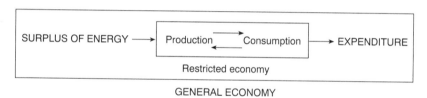

Figure 7.1 Consuming sacredness

Consuming sacredness

One way of characterising modernity is to describe it as a long stretched-out process of secularisation, starting with the Enlightenment in the eighteenth century or perhaps even earlier with the sixteenth-century Renaissance and Reformation. In this process traditional superstition has been overcome, while the institutional authority of the Church has crumbled. Nevertheless, this does not mean that the need for 'religious' explanation is waning. The emergence of new forms of superstition (various therapies, New Age) and the rise of fundamentalism (not only Islamic, but of all major denominations) are two striking examples of an opposite orientation towards holiness. This re-sacralisation is in one important aspect part and parcel of modernity: it depends on the individual consumer's choice of personal belief, and is thus a symptom of 'religious individualism' (Bellah *et al.* 1985: 233; Heelas 1994). Transcendentalism is no longer culturally inherited, but an effect of individuals' yearning for something 'higher' that might give existence a profound personal meaning. This of course turns 'religion' into a marketable good, where meaning (salvation, consolation, explanation) is offered for 'sale'.

Nonetheless, the sheer fact that the urge for religious experience has survived is an important case in point for Bataille's 'general economy'. The profane world of capitalism and the secular doctrines of modernity may have been successful in marginalising or even repressing religion from public life. Apparently this does not diminish the grip of religious yearnings on private life. Time and again these yearnings, just like 'the return of the repressed' in psychoanalyses, even lead to violent public outbursts that are difficult to forecast and control by politicians, educators or marketers. Such outbursts (e.g. riots, revolution, election victories to fundamentalists) may temporarily or more permanently upset the meticulously calculated order in the profane sphere of society. Although this sphere dominates modern societies, it can in such events become 'possessed' by those very 'useless' (i.e. destructive) forces it otherwise tries to repress. In this crisis, its ordinary sense of 'self' is lost: its orientation and coherence.

All this goes for individuals as well. There is one significant difference, however, namely that this crisis or loss can be something actively longed for, and therefore provoked by individuals in order to transgress the secure, but also trivial and impassionate normality of everyday life. It is a longing for something apart from ordinary existence, for something beyond the profane sphere of 'the restricted economy', for something 'higher' (sublime, serene and awe-inspiring) or 'larger' (more intense, dangerous and fascinating) than quotidian routines that make people indulge in this quest for 'Otherness' beyond the limits of the self. A quest both gratifying and destructive, because this 'Otherness' gives a transcendent meaning to existence, but cannot be assimilated to or integrated with ordinary experiences. It is a total 'Otherness' and thus heterogeneous in comparison to the homogeneity of the profane sphere: its attributes are a destructive as well as rescuing omnipotence, an uncanny (German: *unheimlich*) as well as a familiar appearance (see Otto 1952; Caillois 1939). Sacredness evokes both fear and veneration.

Inspired by gnosticism, Bataille elaborates this duality of sacredness further. Just as the restricted economy of useful production is embedded in the general economy of useless expenditure, the profane sphere of homogeneity (i.e. of productive society, where money serves as the common denominator, measuring the value of all useful activities) is surrounded by the heterogeneity of sacredness. Because of its duality, sacredness is on both sides of profanity. The 'other' side of life – heterogeneity – is, in other words, split into two realms: a pure and 'celestial' sacredness, and an impure and abysmal one, with profanity of productive life in between (Bataille 1985b: 144), see Figure 7.2.

This duality of sacredness is in accordance with the original meaning of sacred (Latin: *sacer* as 'holy' but also as consecrated to the gods of the underworld, therefore damned or cursed) as something beyond the ordinary and profane: something either much 'higher' – and thus unreachable – or much 'lower' – and thus untouchable – than everyday existence. Consequently, the sacred forms belong either to the exalted realm of devotion or to the excremental one of taboo. So this dualism gives rise to a whole set of oppositions between types of

Figure 7.2 The duality of sacredness

sacredness: pure vs. impure, high vs. low, rich vs. impoverished, unreachable vs. untouchable, devotion vs. taboo, adored (or worshipped) vs. accursed, honoured vs. disgusted, glorified vs. dejected, beauty vs. ugliness, eternity vs. corruption (or decay), immortality vs. death, 'brighter than bright' vs. 'darker than dark', exalted vs. excremental, etc. The important point is not so much these oppositions, but the varying quality of the affective reactions to them. Both sides can be attractive, both repulsive. As Bataille states: 'There is sometimes attraction, sometimes repulsion, and in certain circumstances, any object of repulsion can become an object of attraction and vice versa' (Bataille 1985b: 142). Death – not only heroic and glorious death, but the 'little death' of intercourse and the dark death of addiction too – can be as luring as immortality, and sublime beauty as terrifying as ugliness. Moreover, impure sacredness (e.g. the impoverished or the untouchables) can be exalted as the mark of truth, whereas pureness (the rich, adorable and beautiful) can be scorned for its meanness (essential impurity) or superficiality (profanity). What characterises sacred objects, regardless whether they are considered pure or impure, is thus the intensity of the affective reactions to them; a reaction, whose strength goes way beyond the calculus of wants and needs. These objects are not merely desired and selected. They are fiercely rejected (other people's hair, nails, odours, etc.), accursed (exotic products like garlic) or shamefully hidden (pornography, menstruation blood), or on the contrary madly desired (unobtainable luxury), unconditionally worshipped (e.g. unique art objects), and carefully looked after and nursed as a sacrament, a sign of the individual's most inner truth (family treasures). Or perhaps they are simultaneously adored and accursed, at the same time repulsive and attractive: attractive because they are so repulsive (e.g. slasher-movies), and repulsive because they are so attractive (e.g. obsessive misogyny). Sacredness is not an immanent quality of the objects themselves. It is a culturally ascribed quality that makes them stand out as 'special' – as elevated or vile – compared to 'ordinary' objects.

Some features may promote the sacredness of objects. Waste is one of them, excessive behaviour in connection to the acquisition and use, or in the dejection and dissociation from them is another. 'Poetry makes nothing happen', Auden once wrote: poetry has sacred qualities, precisely because the writing and reading of it are useless, a waste of time. Waste, however, comes in different forms: either the objects themselves are considered waste (garbage, especially other people's trash), or the making and/or consumption of it are a waste of time and money and, as such, a useless expenditure (art, luxury, hobbies), or otherwise this use of the object is dangerous: it can waste your life or may destroy your body (this makes a drug like ecstasy attractive or smoking cigarettes exciting). Other people's waste is often despicable and downright disgusting, while other forms of waste may be viewed as imputed with a 'higher' meaning (*l'art pour l'art*) that can lead you deeper into your mind, or, quite opposite, may be attractive because waste is an entrance to the darker side of life: to fantasies of death and decay, or to experiences of immense fear, rage, joy, and perhaps even insight (see Castanada 1968).

In passing this threshold, the individual transgresses the boundaries of everyday life and enters a realm, illuminated by a black sun – either for a short while (ecstasy, delirium) or more lasting (madness). At any rate, the consumption of sacred objects is a matter of intense yearning and strong passions, which show in the excessive behaviour connected to this consumption: in the enormous amounts of money and time spent on these objects, in the repetitive structure of deviations from normality (compulsive buying, shoplifting), but particularly in the violence, inherent in much excessive behaviour. This violence can be directed towards other persons in order to annihilate their unacceptable preferences for 'Otherness' or in aggression over their waste. Its aim can be to protect one's own privately worshipped 'Otherness' from others' offences and intrusions. It is often, though, a violence directed against homogeneity itself: against the conformity of mundane existence, against boredom in society, or against the indifference of routine actions (including producing, selling, buying, and consuming standardised goods) – in the end it is a violence against the self as a societal strait-jacket that only partially redeems the longings and ambitions of individuals. Sacred objects are thus consumed at the very possible risk of being absorbed by them: this loss of self, or at least of self-awareness, might even be their deepest attraction. As objects of consumption, they are also consuming objects.

Bataille in the marketplace

The motives for shopping, consumption and consumers' marketplace behaviour are complex. Of course, people prefer goods in expectation of some inherent utility. Undoubtably, product symbolism is also crucial to many buying decisions. Since the interpretive turn (Sherry 1991) in the beginning of the 1980s, symbolic meaning in the marketplace has been the object of substantial research. Still, remarkably, the underlying assumption of most of these contributions is still the utilitarian paradigm: products are bought and used because consumption of them is socially useful to the consumers. The meaning of products is the expected gain in social acceptance. So, according to this assumption, people shop and buy, wanting to be recognised and accepted by their peers. This supposition has recently been criticised by Douglas (1996) for being out of touch with what people really know and want, while they shop: 'The questions have been about why people want what they buy. Whereas, most shoppers will agree, people do not know what they want, but they are very clear about what they do not want' (Douglas 1996: 83). Instead, Douglas proposes 'a theory of hostility', that should be able to trace 'standardised hates' as a major motive in the marketplace.

Douglas's provocative statement is surely worth further considerations. All the same, we would assert that it is about time to make an even more drastic reversal of the common stock of knowledge in the field. However illuminating the famous dictum by Levy (1959) still is, consumer researchers should also consider the following statement: 'People not only buy goods for what they mean, but also for what they can do.' This 'doing' should not be understood in terms of the practical goals that products serve, but as the active role products have in consumers' play with or transgression of their social identities: the intense feelings they are able to invoke, the way products alter the consumers' perception of reality and his or her own position in it, the product's capacity to establish contact with more 'authentic' layers of self or, on the contrary, help individuals to get lost in 'antimonial' doings, etc. The study of consumption, that is, should to a higher degree focus on the sacred qualities of objects. Sacred, in the sense outlined by Bataille, and with the strong affective reactions of attraction and repulsion, of yearning, mourning, loving, but also of violence, terror and fear, all implied in the consumption of these objects.

For this purpose, a reconsideration of concepts like waste, loss, excess, inutility, and expenditure is required. These phenomena are not solely critical of the rationality in the marketplace or of consumers' and societies' well-being. They are not just something to be worried about, something mankind ought to be spared or saved from. They are not only hard to avoid. Often they are actively desired, even by quite rational and otherwise normal people. So they may appear irrational, but none the less seem to serve some innate longing in human beings. In this respect, this whole sphere of sacredness could be characterised as rational and meaningful on another level. Anyway, that is what love is all about – and quite a substantial part of the rest of life too.

References

Bataille, G. (1962 [1957]), *Eroticism*, London: Calder & Boyars.
Bataille, G. (1977 [1928]), *The Story of the Eye*, New York: Urizen Books.
Bataille, G. (1979 [1957]), *Blue of Noon*, London: Marion Boyars.
Bataille, G. (1985a [1932]), 'The notion of expenditure', in A. Stoekl (ed.), *Visions of Excess: Selected Writings 1927–1939*, Minneapolis: University of Minnesota Press, 116–29.
Bataille, G. (1985b [1933–4]), 'The psychological structure of fascism', in A. Stoekl (ed.), *Visions of Excess: Selected Writings 1927–1939*, Minneapolis: University of Minnesota Press, 137–60.
Bataille, G. (1988a [1949]), *The Accursed Share*, New York: Zone Books.

Bataille, G. (1988b [1942]), *Inner Experience*, Albany: State University of New York Press.

Bataille, G. (1989 [1956, 1966, 1967]), *My Mother, Madame Edwarda, The Dead Man*, London: Marion Boyars.

Baudrillard, J. (1993 [1976]), *Symbolic Exchange and Death*, London: Sage Publications.

Belk, R.W. (1988), 'Possessions and the extended self', *Journal of Consumer Research*, 15 (September), 139–68.

Belk, R.W. and Coon, G.S. (1993), 'Gift giving as agapic love: an alternative to the exchange paradigm based on dating experiences', *Journal of Consumer Research*, 20 (December), 393–417.

Bellah, R.N. *et al.* (1985), *Habits of the Heart: Individualism and Commitment in American Life*, Berkeley, CA: University of California Press.

Caillois, R. (1939), *L'Homme et le sacré*, Paris: E. Leroux.

Castanada, C. (1968), *The Teachings of Don Juan: A Yaqui Way of Knowledge*, Berkeley, CA: University of California Press.

Derrida, J. (1978 [1967]), 'From restricted to general economy: a Hegelianism without reservation', *Writing and Difference*, Chicago: University of Chicago Press.

Douglas, M. (1996), *Thought Styles*, London: Sage Publications.

Durkheim, E. (1951 [1897]), *Suicide: A Study in Sociology*, New York: The Free Press.

Eliade, M. (1957), *Das Heilige und das Profane*, Reinbek bei Hamburg: Rowohlt.

Foucault, M. (1962), 'Préface à la transgression', *Critique*, 19(195–6), 751–69.

Heelas, P. (1994), 'The limits of consumption and the post-modern "religion" of the New Age', in R. Keat *et al.* (eds), *The Authority of the Consumer*, London: Routledge.

Herrigel, E. (a.k.a. Bungaku Hakushi) (1948), *Zen in der Kunst des Bogenschiessens*, Frankfurt am Main: Fischer.

Kotler, P. (1988), *Marketing Management*, 6th edn, Englewood Cliffs, NJ: Prentice-Hall.

Levy, S. J. (1959), 'Symbols for sale', *Harvard Business Review*, 37 (July), 117–29.

Löwith, K. (1949), *Meaning in History*, Chicago: University of Chicago Press.

Mauss, M. (1954 [1923–4]), *The Gift*, London: Cohen & West.

Otto, R. (1952 [1917]), *The Idea of the Holy: An Inquiry into the Non-rational Factor in the Idea of the Divine and Its Relation to the Rational*, 2nd edn, London: Oxford University Press.

Perniola, M. (1977), *Georges Bataille e il negativo*, Milano: Feltrinelli.

Sahlins, M. (1976), *Culture and Practical Reason*, Chicago: University of Chicago Press.

Sherry, J.F., Jr. (1991), 'Postmodern alternatives: the interpretive turn in consumer research', in H. Kassarjian and T. Robertson (eds), *Handbook of Consumer Research*, Englewood Cliffs, NJ: Prentice-Hall, 548–91.

Weber, M. (1930 [1904-5]), *The Protestant Ethic and the Spirit of Capitalism*, London: Allen & Unwin.

8

WHAT'S LOVE GOT TO DO WITH IT?

Sex, shopping and subjective personal introspection

Stephen Brown

Let me ask you a question, boys and girls. What is your favourite research technique? Yes, you heard me correctly, your favourite methodology. Your all time, fave rave, numero uno, hot rockin', in with a bullet, double platinum, posters on the bedroom wall, the kids are dancin' in the streets, the line is stretching for four blocks and the scalpers are making a fortune, favourite research technique?

But, Stephen, I hear you say, what do you mean *favourite* research techniques? We don't have favourites! We modern marketing scientists eschew methodological preferences. They are just 'there', aren't they? They comprise an array, a library, a veritable home improvement depot of tools and techniques, the most apt of which is selected as the research occasion demands. It's not a question of favourites, merely a matter of those that are deemed appropriate to the task in hand, the job to be done, the particular issues, problems or – *gasp!* – hypotheses that the study seeks to address or test.

Tell me something, folks, do you really believe that I'm-an-objective-marketing-scientist-and-I-have-no-favourites hogwash? You do? More fool you. Take it from me, just as we have favourite books, albums, movies, restaurants, places, poems and sexual partners (I've always been very partial to ripe watermelons and dead metaphors, myself – that's right, I'm a melonomanicial necrotropophiliac, if you want to get technical about it), so too most marketing scholars have soft spots for certain methodological perspectives and procedures.

Some consumer researchers, for example, are besotted by the big-survey, big-libido, more-power, MMX-hard-drive, my-other-car's-a-Porsche, no-that's-not-a-defective-penile-implant-it-just-hangs-that-way style of research. Others prefer to eschew the macho, notch-on-the-scholarly-bedpost approach of the my-representative-sample's-bigger-than-yours fraternity, for the in-dwelling, lovey-dovey, soft-spoken, sympathetic-ear, heart-to-heart, all-sisters-together, great-earth-mother, do-you-mind-if-I-tape-record-our-conversation? of the in-depth, qualitative confessional.

Yet others, social maladjustees in the main, avoid human contact completely by foraging in the dusty archives and dank cellars, or doing the Peeping Tom, sad bastard thing popularly known as unobtrusive observation. And yet others, illiterates to a man, woman and, as often as not, bisexual, disdain the 'tyranny' of the written word for photographic, videotronic or cybernetic modes of research and representation (anything basically that involves lots of expensive equipment, 'cos they've got this big research grant and have to spend it somehow).

There is, of course, another type. Well, there are probably dozens of other types but we don't want to get ourselves into a typology of consumer researchers situation, now do we? The other type I have in mind is a particularly loathsome, short-sighted, stone deaf, hairy-palmed, grubby-raincoat wearing individual, or rather group of individuals, who can perhaps best be described as the onanists of marketing scholarship. I refer, needless to say, to the introspectionists and, as a merry member of that member-fixated fellowship, I'm speaking here with some authority, with my hands full, one tied behind my back, as it were, so to speak, on the whole, if you catch my drift . . .

Indeed, when you think about it, as introspectors invariably do, introspection may seem somewhat sad, decidedly selfish or simply sick, (from a scholarly research perspective, I hasten to add). Reflecting on one's own behaviour, reflecting on one's reflections on one's behaviour, reflecting on one's reflections on one's reflections on one's behaviour, etc., must come across as a particularly peculiar, some might say pathetic, way to spend one's waking hours (yes, the penultimate word is spelt correctly).

Yes, I know, it's a dirty job but, hey, someone's gotta do the 'it's a dirty job but someone's gotta do it' cliché. Someone has to be the, er, whipping boy for the rest of the marketing academy. Somebody has to be the butt of scholarly cracks and jibes, otherwise the hot-shot model-builders wouldn't be able to feel superior; the love-me-love-my-transcripts sorority might be forced to reflect on their own preferred procedure's shortcomings; the unspeakable mob of is-this-manuscript-in-Hebrew-or-did-I-spill-my-Dr-Pepper? inadequates might be required to communicate with the rest of us rather than commune with the dear departed; or indeed the I'm-a-respectable-social-scientist-officer-these-night-vision-binoculars-are-standard-equipment slimeballs might be put away for good. And not before time.

Now, you might have got the impression that exponents of introspection are not held in particularly high esteem by the marketing and consumer research community, and regrettably this seems to be the case. Apart from being constantly told to 'get a grip on ourselves' – which is part of the problem rather than the solution, believe me – and having our manuscripts rejected on receipt, it is no exaggeration to state that subjective personal introspectors are the Other, the untouchables, the unclean, the auto-eroticists of marketing discourse.

It was not always thus, however. Introspection was once the procedural *primus inter pares* of psychology. I kid you not. Espoused by such intellectual luminaries as Franz Bretano and William James, and honed into a rigorous methodological instrument by the indefatigable Wilhelm Wundt, introspection was widely regarded, at the start of the present century, as the royal road to self-knowledge. The basis upon which a fully-fledged science of psychology could be constructed, no less (Lyons 1986). Granted, introspection was not without its attendant difficulties. For example, the problem of divided attention, the brain's apparent inability to cope with two tasks at once, was perceived by some to be a potentially fatal flaw, albeit if you are one of the lucky few who can walk and chew gum at the same time, you'll probably disagree.

Be that as it may, introspectionism soon rapidly fell from grace, possibly on account of Wundt's excesses (his experiments involved displaying 10,000 green blocks, again and again, to luckless subjects), and the citadel of psychology was rapidly over-run by Watson, Tolman, Lashley and ensuing behaviourist hordes. For all I know, Wundt's catatonic volunteers may have led the charge of the behaviourist zombies. Certainly, compared to them, Skinner's electrocuted rodents were reasonably well treated and, in the circumstances, it is hardly surprising that the hapless introspectionees deserted the sinking psychological ship to make room for the rats.

Classical behaviourism, of course, all but abandoned consideration of mental processes in its pursuit of psychological science and the ensuing cognitive revolutionaries didn't have much time for introspection either. Stigmatised, marginalised and effectively consigned to the equivalent of the 'production-orientated' stage in the pseudo-history of psychology – as today's introductory textbooks continue to testify – introspection is widely regarded as psychology's youthful indiscretion, an intellectual error of judgement, a cerebral brainstorm, if I can put it like that.

Although, to switch metaphors for a moment, self-reflection may have been deserted by the regiments of psychological science, or at least its elite corps, it remains something of an intellectual mercenary. Some of the most interesting latter-day developments, in fact, indicate that it is now fighting for the other side. I refer, suffice it to say, to the humanities. Introspection, remember, has long been and remains a staple of artistic endeavour. To some extent at least, artists, poets, musicians, novelists and so on examine the inner self, evaluate these investigations and express the outcome of their deliberations in a creative fashion. Indeed, if ever a research technique warrants the description 'romantic', then surely it is subjective personal introspection. As Furst (1969) observes, the romantics were nothing if not obsessed with self-observation, self-analysis and, as often as not, self-pity.[1]

Artists and writers, admittedly, are a disreputable bunch on the whole and their personal hygiene often leaves a lot to be desired (I speak as a one shower per month Irishman – but only if I really need it). When it comes to diseases, filthy habits, offensive language and outrageous behaviour, be it Baudelaire's encomium to hallucinogens, Hemingway's hooch-fuelled bullfights, Keith Moon's fondness for blowing up portable toilets or Alice Cooper's love of, er, golf, you can rest assured that the artistic avant-garde will have got there before the rest of us. And, God knows, they're welcome to it.

For many marketing scholars, I grant you, the liberal arts and humanities comprise a wasteland of laid-back, long-haired, left-leaning, lotus eaters – smokers possibly – who lounge about in libraries and spend most of their time complaining about overpaid business school professors, while the latter are out selflessly helping companies cope with today's cut-and-thrust world of global competition (pausing only to count their selflessly sizeable consultancy fees). Worse, the languorous loafers of the liberal arts are so dissolute and degenerate that they don't even believe in themselves any more, what with their decon-structive, post-structuralised, solipsistic, Goddamn relativist talk. They are the conscientious objectors of the academy, intellectual draft dodgers, scholarly yellow-bellies, the white feather wearers of cerebration. They probably inhaled and, as for the pants around the ankles allegation, my lips are sealed.

Granted, it is not my place to defend the sometimes dirty, often delinquent and invariably dipsomaniac denizens of the liberal arts. Most of the ones in our place make William Burroughs look like a particularly well-scrubbed, clean-living Amish, with Calvinistic inclinations and a Jesuitical streak. A friend of the Society of Friends, so to speak. What's more, none of them has said so much as a kind word about marketing, unless you consider 'capitalist price-gouger' a compliment (though compared to some of the things I've been called, it is!). So, why the hell should we do the noble, community-of-scholars, live-and-let-live thing? Turning the other cheek on literary theorists is not recommended, if you catch my drift. Let's be honest, the humungoids of the humanities are perfectly capable of looking after themselves. Most of them have artistic ambitions, after all, and plan to quit academic life once their screenplay-in-progress gets green-lighted.

Some chance.

Like most stereotypes, marketing's view of the liberal artisans has some basis in fact. They *are* a grisly crew of malingering malcontents in the main, most definitely not the type of people you want to bring home to mother. Anthony Perkins excepted. Their arrogance, furthermore, is so breathtakingly boundless that even economists seem shy, retiring and modest by comparison. And econ-omists have much to be modest about, I'm sure you agree. This stereotype is mistaken, however, in so far as the liberal arts in general and literary criticism in particular are no longer the domain of the so-called boa-deconstructors. Possibly as a counter-reaction against the abstruse, author-excising afflatus of the post-structuralists, contemporary literary theory is suspiciously reader-friendly. Fiendishly complex exegeses of the paradoxes, aphorias and literary *non-sequiturs* of canonical texts have been superseded, to some extent at least, by a veritable slew of personal reminiscences, anecdotal remarks, candid soul-barings and endearingly conversational modes of address. Known as 'autobiographical criticism', this essentially comprises acts of academic introspection; that is, scholars reflecting on their individual, lived experiences with specific works of literature and writing a revelatory account of these highly private, sometimes deeply moving, textual encounters. So common, in fact, has it become that Simpson (1995: 24) claims, 'the award of tenure now seems to bring with it a contract for one's autobiography' and another has recently gone so far as to suggest that autobiographical criticism has taken over from deconstruction as the lit-crit orthodoxy (Veeser 1996).

Like me, you may be wondering why anyone in their right mind would want to read the so-called 'confessions of the critics'. Like you, I would rather be impaled on a rusty spike than peruse any of their revolting revelations, even heavily expurgated versions thereof. However, in the different strokes, *de gustibus*, no rules, whatever turns you on, post-postmodern spirit, I think we should permit them to tell their noisome tales, ideally well out of school. That said, I feel I should warn you that this textually transmitted disease is heading in our direction, having been spotted in sociology, philosophy, political science, anthropology, geography and, Heaven help us, organisation studies (Brown 1998a).

Vaccination, as you are no doubt aware, involves injecting a minute dose of the disease in order to increase resistance to the full-blown version. It follows that if we are to protect ourselves from the ebola virus of 'autoethnography', as it is sometimes called, it is necessary to introduce a diluted version of the stuff. To this end a few devoted, not to say self-abnegating, members of the marketing and consumer research community have been busy on the introspective front, writing first-person, first-hand, first-class, first past the postmodern marketing accounts of their own consumption experiences. Although introspective exercises remain comparatively rare, the range of consuming passions essayed thus far include skydiving, weight lifting, long-distance running, sexual sustenance, near death experiences and obsessive collecting behaviour. Basically, the sorts of things that most ordinary shoppers do on a Saturday morning (Brown and Reid 1997).

Sadly, the selfless actions of the consumer introspectionists have not been universally acclaimed, their self-effacing endeavours remain unappreciated, their willing self-sacrifices go unrewarded. Indeed, it pains me deeply to report the almost incomprehensible fact that not only are these consumer compositions uncompensated, but their authors' academic altruism, intellectual largesse and all-round marketing magnanimity have been roundly condemned. Although a number of voices have been raised in opposition, the principal critics of introspection are Wallendorf and Brucks. In a wide-ranging assessment, they distinguish between several different types of introspection and contend that 'researcher introspection' suffers from very severe shortcomings. These methodological inadequacies are so profound that the technique has little to recommend it, except as a means of accomplishing other, non-scholarly, essentially narcissistic, lamentably exhibitionist ends. Such studies, they conclude, 'make for fun reading but may mislead readers if not based on sound, carefully thought-out and articulated methods' (Wallendorf and Brucks 1993: 356).

I'm sure you agree, this is hardly the way to treat those who give of themselves so that the rest of us can sleep easy in our beds, safe in the knowledge that the mad dogs of the liberal arts are being kept firmly at bay. In fact, the introspector in chief, Steve Gould, paid the ultimate academic price – denial of tenure. As with so many other seers, visionaries and innovators, it seems that the autoethnographers are little more than a laughing stock who, to put it at its most charitable, add a dash of local colour and provide a modicum of light relief from the *real* research work being done by the mining engineers, the bridge builders, the dam busters, the rocket scientists, the moon walkers, the build-a-better-mousetraps of the marketing academy. Even those who are otherwise open-minded and supportive towards intellectual unorthodoxy have distanced themselves from introspection, a communicable disease that is doubtless debilitating, certainly contagious and probably terminal (Sherry 1996).

As peace-loving, self-effacing, shy and retiring humanitarians, the consumer introspectionists are understandably reluctant to indulge in epistemological fisticuffs. After all, it's hardly a fair fight since the weight difference is such that it makes David and Goliath look like Goliath's dad versus David's kid brother. Nevertheless, the bashful counter-punchers of introspection have developed a marketing equivalent of the old one–two. The left, thrown by Morris 'hitman' Holbrook and his erstwhile sparring partner Stephen J. no-I'm-not-the-Harvard-biologist-but-I-wish-I-had-his-royalties Gould, comprises an attempt to justify the technique in broadly 'scientific' terms. Drawing upon an impressive body of supporting literature, ranging from rhetoric and romanticism to neo-pragmatist philosophy, the dynamic duo posit that introspection is nothing less than the ultimate form of participant observation (Gould 1995; Holbrook 1996). In a familiar defensive feint, moreover, they aver that ruling the procedure out of court is both premature and unnecessarily restrictive (yes friends, the classic 'advancement of science, who knows what the future will hold' side-step, one routinely employed by the heavyweight champions of the hard sciences).

The right, lately swung by Sidney 'haymaker' Levy (1996), is yet another old knock-em-dead favourite. Indeed, it is the veritable horseshoe-in-the-glove, the below-the-belt-eye-waterer, the look-out-your-shoelace-is-undone, the sorry-ref-was-that-his-ear?-I-thought-it-was-a-cauliflower of academic discourse. That's right, the timeless *tu quoque*, you-do-it-too uppercut. Introspection, according to El-Sid, is an integral part of the research process, everyone does it, it cannot be avoided and to deny the utility of introspection is to deny the utility of research itself. The gossip round the gym, I'm told, is that a certain lightweight Irishman has accused those celebrated sluggers, Wallendorf and Brucks, of employing introspection in their much-vaunted critique of introspection. Disgraceful, I know, but they obviously don't fight by the Marquis of Queensbury rules over there. Barbarians, the lot of them.

Trusty as the old one–two undoubtedly is, and many an opponent though the left jab, right cross combination has efficiently felled, boxing remains a very dangerous cerebral sport. Goodness, there must be hundreds of brain-damaged, punch-drunk has-beens knocking around the marketing academy. You know the type, shuffling along, mumbling to themselves about truth, realism, model building, general theories, relationships and networks, and the like. Whatever you do, don't waste your sympathy on them. They had everything and threw it all away. They've no one to blame but themselves. They coulda been contenders and ended up in Palukaville. Nobody up here likes them.

Boxing, then, is a very risky pastime and an alternative approach, articulated by Stephen I'm-a-writer-not-a-fighter Brown (1998b), is to argue that the boxing analogy is singularly inappropriate. (Yes, friends, it's amazing what the 'fragmented authorial self' lets you get away with.) However, his basic point, as I understand it, is that the introspectors are playing a completely different sport, a non-contact sport, a non-sport sport. In short, that introspective essays are not, never were and should not be considered 'scientific', as such. They are works of art, which resonate, reverberate, dazzle and evoke an epiphanic 'A-ha, that rings true, *that's* the way it is' reaction in the reader. What I'm trying to say, I suppose, is that introspective essays do not – and simply cannot – conform to the standard scientific criteria of reliability, objectivity, trustworthiness and suchlike. They are not scientific in any conventional sense, but that does not mean they are uninsightful or that marketing and consumer research has nothing to learn from them. Or, rather, from well-written introspective essays.

Now you know and I know what's coming next. This is the point in our relationship where I ask if you want to come back to my place for cerebral coffee, to examine my academic etchings, see my collection of introspective essays (some of them are *this* big). While you're making up your mind – is that a protocol in your pocket or are you just pleased to see my transcripts? – let me just say a few choice, if not exactly well-chosen, words about intellectual life generally. Academics, as I'm sure you're aware, are a pretty rum bunch. Hypocrites to a man and duplicitous bastards to everyone else, they rabbit on about the so-called 'community of scholars' whilst stabbing each other in the back at every available opportunity (albeit the real opprobrium is reserved for those who break silence on the incessant intellectual back-stabbing). They gambol sycophantically at the feet of the movers and shakers of their field, lord it over those one rung lower on the ladder of cerebration and unremittingly disparage, as 'unacceptable', 'substandard' or 'woefully inadequate' the research endeavours of their peers. Happily, there's always something about a rival's research that can be condemned from the comfortable cabalistic cocoon of the senior common room or over a hard-earned libation on Friday evening – lack of background reading, poor problem formulation, flawed survey design, statistical sleight of hand, terribly badly written or, if all else fails, a blatant put-up job by the journal, whose editor is a friend, a very close 'friend' (nod, nod, wink, wink), of the author.

Perhaps the favourite focus of academic nit-picking, however, is the sampling process. The inherently aleatory character of sample surveys is sufficient to ensure endless opportunities for belittling one's competitors. Thus samples are inevitably too small, too restricted, too diffuse, too parochial, too unbalanced, too aberrant and, above all, too studenty. Personally, I have never understood academics' unremitting antipathy to student-only samples. Granted, they are a loathsome crew of malingerers and malcontents in the main (so are students, come to think of it), but compared to 'real' consumers, who are invariably cantankerous, all too easily distracted and often need to be slapped about a bit before they take the research project sufficiently seriously, students are veritable paragons of virtue. After all, they are ready, willing and able to answer most of our fatuous questions, otherwise course credit will be denied them or their exam performances are prone to prove inexplicably disappointing. Students, what is more, are not only a large and high spending market in themselves, but they are often in the throes of a significant life transition, where their so-called 'personalities', possible 'selves' and indeed consuming 'habits' are being actively shaped (*translation*, the buggers refuse to make up their minds). Hence, it is incumbent upon us to understand this repellent rabble, inarticulate, insolent, indolent, intimidating and downright ignorant though they indubitably are. Researchers who concentrate upon 'real' consumers, whatever that means, are reneging on their responsibilities, quite frankly, and ought to be ejected forthwith from the marketing academy.

Fortunately, one or two redoubtable researchers are ever ready to enter the undergraduate lair in order to examine the consuming passions of its hirsute *habitués*. In a moment of madness, I instructed a fetid pride of final year marketing students to write introspective essays about their shopping behaviour. True, it required liberal use of the whip and, with only a rickety professorial chair for protection, I consider myself lucky to be alive. Placing my head between the halitotic jaws of a final honours class is not the smartest move I've ever made, but never let it be said I'm unwilling to suffer for my art.

Anyway, there were more than one hundred of the brutes and, cowed into submission by my natural air of authority (maybe it was my manic stare or possibly my promise to fail them all if they failed to comply – yeah, you're right, it was the racking sobs and heartfelt pleas for help that swung it), they all managed to produce surprisingly coherent accounts of their personal shopping experiences. Introspection, admittedly, may come easily to young people on the cusp of adulthood, when self-preoccupation and 'person' prefixes-cum-suffixes seem to assume particular importance (personality, personal appearance, interpersonal skills, personability, etc.), yet their compositions averaged an astonishing 2,000 words. More astonishing still was the remarkable fact that many of these words were multisyllabic and some were even in the right order. No, I'm not making this up, their introspective essays were really quite superb and, as shall shortly become apparent, uncommonly insightful.

Without doubt, the most noteworthy aspect of the essayists' shopping behaviour is the fact that sex rears its ugly head again and again. Jeez, I thought I was going to have to break out the bromide at one stage. However, before you jump to the wrong conclusion or make some derogatory remark about my slap-happy research procedures – what's wrong with happy slappers, I say – let me just point out that the students were asked to write about shopping in general. Amatorial experiences were *not* solicited. They weren't, I tell you! Do you really think I'm the sort of sad, middle-aged, onanist who'd ask his students to write about sex under the guise of scholarship? Do you think I'm the kind of para-pervert that gets his kicks from pouring over undergraduates' erotic fantasies? Do you think I'll get away with it? It may be gross moral turpitude to you, Vice-chancellor, but it's solid empirical research to me, though I appreciate that the university's Rustication Committee may disagree . . .

Believe me or believe me not, boys and girls, it's entirely up to you. But libidinous anecdotes were not encouraged. Honest. (Not that I'd tell *you* if they were.) That said, I suspect my sample was slightly more tumescent than most. After all, it contained quite a few people with an agricultural background, and you know what they say about farmers and their flocks. I said flocks! What's more, it included a large number of post-adolescent males and you know what it's like at that age, when sex looms large in the psyche, as indeed does largeness. The sample, come to think of it, was almost entirely composed of single people and you don't need me to tell you that there's nothing quite like marriage to put passion in its place. Finally, and lest you've forgotten the most pertinent point of all, our informants were made up of *undergraduate students*. What more need be said? – except that they really ought to be hosed down, forced to wear chastity attire at all times or unceremoniously gelded without anaesthetic.

So, what did I discover on sifting through my students' sex 'n' shopping fan-tasies, apart from the fact that I've obviously led a very sheltered life? Well, this may come as a surprise to you, but it transpires that going shopping provides an opportunity to ogle members of the opposite sex. All except the most miserly, miserable and cantankerous consumers – do they mean me? – get something out of shopping, even if it's only a titillating glimpse of an attractive, semi-clad stranger.

> Another thing I can't help noticing is the amount of beautiful females walk-ing around town. This is probably the greatest pleasure which I gain from my shopping experience, and it usually fills most of my conversation – and which I shall not go into for obvious reasons of common decency.
>
> (male, 22)

> Once inside I go off on my own, 'blinkered' like a horse, straight to River Island. Typically, the first thing I look for is the 'talent' working in the shop. Sexist or what? Then I take a quick glance around the store in the hope of seeing my penultimate goal – clothes.
>
> (male, 21)

People keep saying that good customer service makes them always want to go back to certain stores. Friendly staff, after sales service and credit being several of the many attributes which make up this phenomenon. I don't know about anybody else but these factors don't really appeal to me when I choose which store to go into. It is not friendly staff I look for, it is nice-looking, young, tanned female staff, staff with long legs, nice eyes, cute behinds and big, big, big pairs of . . . earrings! Finding staff in shops like this are like hen's teeth, but when I find one or two who match some of the criteria set, you can bet your last pound that I will visit these certain shops more than once, not to buy something every time, just mainly to look at the merchandise, some for sale and, unfortunately, some not for sale.

(male, 21)

Indeed, some of our – how can I put this? – less prepossessing essayists actually seem to be slightly more successful in the shopping mall of lurve than better established pulling places (sorry, venues of social interaction), like discos, parties and pubs. Not so much pressure on them, you see; they don't look quite so desperate; standing at the side of the shopping centre dance-floor doing wallflower impressions is not permitted, after all.

Opposite the Virgin Megastore is the Perfume Shop which I always manage to pass a couple of times to catch a glimpse of a girl I used to know very well at secondary school. At school I never really noticed her much but she has turned into a cracker, so I always try to think of an excuse to go in and speak to her but those words of wisdom have otherwise evaded me.

(male, 20)

As it was a busy Friday afternoon, it came as no surprise and no less of an annoyance that each checkout had lengthy queues. All were generally the same, so I joined the nearest one (well, actually the one with a good-looking girl at the till) . . . The EPOS appears to be fairly sophisticated and Joanne, the checkout assistant, seems very efficient. If only her name-tag gave out phone numbers.

(male, 21)

Although men are more inclined to check out the checkout girls, as it were – or, rather, are more prepared to confess to it – women are no less aware of the amorousness of the agora. So much so, that shopping for merchandise and shopping for men are often one and the same.

There I stood, in the 'heart' of Belfast with strange faces passing me by the hundreds. My eyes were often caught by the sight of male specimens, which to me looked rather tasty. A real benefit of a shopping experience to me is stalking out the talent as well as buying something that I'm actually happy with, particularly when I return home and still like it. Already I was well satisfied with the products that were human and near at hand, but had definite signs of 'look but don't touch'.

(female, 21)

There were a number of people in the shop and as I turned the corner of a stand I bumped into what can only be described as sex on legs. Woah, what a body and those eyes. I stepped aside to let him past and of course he went the same way. Taking an absolute redner, I muttered a quick sorry and brushed past him. Shit, shit, shit, I thought as I clutched my burning face. Why does that always happen to me? I managed to take a glance around only to see my Mr Right leaving the shop hand-in-hand with what must have been his girl-friend. Ah well, you can but dream.

(female, 20)

The first thing to catch the eye of this student, who is meant to focus on shop design and atmospherics, is the guy behind the counter. He's just something else. Mum has started looking for ties for my brothers. I do not mind spend-ing time in this shop, looking at the staff I hasten to say. In fact the whole day spent browsing round would have satisfied all my desires, not just the shop-ping!! But all good things come to an end and we are leaving. Continuing down the shopping mall, to my surprise the place is full of these excellent looking guys. It must be something in their water supply because the men at home certainly are not a touch on these.

(female, 26)

Certainly, many women seem to take the opportunity to get dressed up, or try to look their best, when consumption calls, just in case they meet the man of their dreams, even if it is only a cardboard cut-out.

Well, I jumped out of bed, although already ten minutes late I don't worry too much, as Kerrie knows to give me at least half-an-hour's grace. I had decided what to wear last night. After all, although I am buying new clothes I still have to look my best. Who knows who I am going to meet?

(female, 21)

I drag myself out of bed and crawl into the shower to waken myself up. Which shower gel shall I use today, then? I know, Radox 'revitalising', that should do the trick. Oh fuck, the water is freezing. Ah well, it was a cold shower I needed anyway after that hot night of passion. 'I wish . . .' Oh yes, that reminds me, I might see my fancy man today in Belfast. I wouldn't mind unwrapping him as my Christmas present. Shopping today might not be as bad as I think. Oh no, Elaine, you're doing it again, fantasising. It's shopping you're going to do, not shagging. Wake up and smell the coffee.

(female, 22)

As I caught a glimpse of a 4ft x 8ft graphic, I never knew the effect a piece of laminated cardboard could do to a girl's hormones, or rather the vision super-imposed on it. He was a Sex God. A stunning build of a man, longish brown/fair hair loosely swept back off his chiselled cheekbones, piercing blue eyes, lips so smooth and voluptuous, all set against a canvas of lightly tanned skin. Pity he wasn't for sale. I'd have sold my granny for him. He wore a white round-neck cotton T-shirt under a ribbed V-neck sweater. It was navy with a broad lime and white stripe across the chest, and the trousers, a pair of navy and cream pinstripe. I had to have it, to try to mould my boyfriend into what I had just realised was my ideal man.

(female, 20)

There is more to the carnality of consumption, however, than look-don't-touch. On the contrary, shopping is a social event where conversations are struck up, chat-up lines are aired, assignations are negotiated, conquests are reconnoitred or, on occasion, claimed. Such boasts, of course, comprise little more than crude, post-adolescent sexual braggadocio – not that I'm jealous or anything – though it is clear that many consumers respond positively, shall we say, to physically attractive shop assistants, irrespective of gender.

> Paying for it with cash, I left the shop with a smile, relieved to have my shopping escapade over. On returning to the car, I met my ex-girlfriend, who persuaded me back to her house. But that's not shopping experience!
>
> (male, 22)

> But while I was waiting, I met a girl I've known for years and what a beautiful blonde I-want-you-to-have-my-babies type of woman she is. The very first thing she said to me was, 'Are you waiting for your girlfriend, Kelvin?' A beauty who was also psychic and on her own in town. I should have walked off with the dame, but no, a tap on the shoulder brought me down from the cloud I was sharing with this honey on our way to dreamland. Yes, it was Paula looking as if she had been dragged backwards through a bush by a herd of wild cavemen.
>
> (male, 23)

> Joining the stampede into the new store, one hand takes a store-plan leaflet while the other grabs for a shopping basket. Once on the sales floor, I'm asked by a pretty, oh what the hell I'll say it, sexy babe who wants me to sign up for the store's Reward Card. What a pleasure! I'm almost tempted to ask her out there and then, but decide to play it cool, trying out the best of my favourite chat-up lines. Believe me, they were so good that I ended up chatting to her long after she'd obtained my details and, just in case you're interested, yes I did get her phone number!
>
> (male, 21)

Several of our introspectors, moreover, openly acknowledge that they lose their powers of discrimination when dealing with an alluring sales clerk and freely admit that they not only patronise certain retail establishments because of the winsomeness, to put it politely, of its employees. What's more, they (rightly) suspect that this is a deliberate 'merchandising' ploy on the part of astute retail organisations, most notably River Island, Top Shop and Next.

My eyes wander everywhere when I shop and I tend to want to go into every shop to look around, listen to the music, try on things and the odd occasion goggle at the staff, who are always dressed to my perfect specifications. Nice looks and a smile can make me buy anything, I've been told by a certain mother.

(male, 21)

My attention was drawn towards this absolutely beautiful woman. Her hair, shape and posture, everything about this woman appealed to me. Being hypnotised by her presence I drifted over towards her, explaining with my tongue tied round my tonsils that I would like to see some suits. She gently pointed upstairs, indicating that it was not her department. Still fantasising about this woman, I was promptly brought back to reality by a '45 stone' woman, carrying what must have been a month's shopping, as she was forced to thrust herself against me.

(male, 22)

A quick thought crossed my mind. Did Next have an unwritten requirement when selecting staff that you had to rank at least 8/10 on the orgasmic scale? He was gorgeous. 'Hi there, I was just wondering if you had any of those jumpers left, up there on the wall?', I asked slightly flirtatiously. Only too pleased to assist, he escorted me to where they had been merchandised.

(female, 20)

Pleasurable as philandering with pulchritudinous sales personnel undoubtedly is – as is discussing the physical merits of those under scrutiny – by far the most steamy encounter takes place between the consumer and him or herself. Aside from the confidence-boosting effects of observing other people who are less beautiful, youthful, well endowed or whatever than ourselves (in all modesty of course), the endlessly reflective surfaces of retailing environments – windows, mirrors, glass panels, etc. – afford ample opportunities for secret acts of self-adoration (albeit there are few more embarrassing shopping experiences than being observed observing one's fetching reflection).

I had decided that the safest bet was to buy her perfume, so I made my way to the cosmetics section in Debenhams. On my way I noticed that the whole area surrounding the perfume section was carpeted and the fixtures and fittings were all gold and silver plated. Also there was an abundance of mirrors, so that all the poseurs could stop and check themselves out. I only had a quick glance.

(male, 22)

Next stop is the men's fashion store, Topman. As I enter, I ask myself what clothes am I really looking for? As I walked around the store, I keep admiring myself in the mirrors, while making sure nobody sees me doing this. I ask myself, is this normal or am I just a vain person?

(male, 23)

Whilst looking for a potentially adequate store, I found myself within a Morgan store with my girl-friend, Ann-Marie. I was not at all upset by this girl's store, as Oasis was playing in the background, and I was surrounded by some amazing female specimens. Sadly, the surrounding elements were forgotten in my relentless urge to see how I was looking in the many mirrors, of course without being noticed. Finally falling into a fixating stare, somewhere between two mirrors – for several minutes – I was rescued by a summons from a somewhat delirious girlfriend.

(male, 21)

In addition to the sheer eroticism of exchange, where the babe or hunk of one's wildest sexual fantasies may suddenly materialise and make their intentions known, it seems that the goods and services purchased, and the brand names displayed on our bodily billboards, act as a bridge to a sexier self. When wearing that little black dress, Levi's 501s, Benetton jumper, Ralph Lauren polo shirt, Gucci loafers or Safari eau de cologne we become more beautiful, more desirable, more captivating to members of the opposite sex, at least in the disco inferno of our febrile imaginations.

A label of which I am particularly fond, GoiGoi seemingly means 'peace' in Thailand and the clothing they produce is loaded with 'street cred'. I've just got to buy one! I spot a really nice shirt and try it on. This time I need no reassurance, probably because of the label, however I've just got to buy it. I can imagine the satisfaction I will get as friends comment on how nice it is, and on the extremely steep price of £75.

(male, 22)

I wake up and decide, 'I have to go shopping!' The Christmas dinner is next week and I don't have a sexy number in my wardrobe (even though there are about 20 dresses, some of which I have only worn once). I have a goal in mind – to get a dress which makes me look as good as Cindy Crawford. Tough goal but here goes!

(female, 21)

Presently I am wearing Dunnes Stores underwear, but I know if my financial situation was reversed I would not hesitate to pop out to the shops and slip on a pair of Calvin Klein undies, feeling like James Dean, and that would give the girlfriend something to smile about.

(male, 21)

Just one more item to get now, shoes. I may as well try here, I've done pretty well so far. There's two pairs of cream shoes, one pair of high ones and one pair of low ones. Yeah the high ones have about a three-inch heel and I'm 5ft 6 in. already. Ahh well, I'll look like I have legs up to my armpits.

(female, 20)

More meaningful perhaps than the transformative character of consumer goods – the (visitor's) passport they seemingly provide to an ideal self – consumer goods themselves possess sex appeal. Again and again and again our essayists employ libidinous language to describe the object of their consuming passion, their heart's desire. Potential acquisitions are unfailingly described as 'beautiful', 'gorgeous', 'stunning', 'ravishing', 'lovely', 'pretty', 'attractive', 'alluring', and so on. Falling head over heels in love with something, be it a computer game or bar of chocolate, is the norm rather than the exception; items are imbued with hypnotic-cum-magnetic power or are bathed in numinous buy-me light, or literally shout out for the customer's attention.

> Left turn for frozen fish and then ice-cream, trying to resist the boxes of three Galaxy Doves, that are calling out my name.
>
> (female, 21)

> I felt like the sandals were screaming 'buy me, buy me'. The assistant knew how delighted I was and handed the sandals to me.
>
> (female, 20)

> Next we went into Next, a shop which I have a passion for. After walking into the store I feel somewhat important and imagine myself buying all my clothes there when I finally graduate and get a good job. We walked around gazing at the clothes and of course the dreaded price labels. A jumper caught my eye and it was absolutely drop-dead gorgeous, and my friend agreed.
>
> (female, 22)

> The previous day, a new selection of bright shirts had arrived: lime green, midnight blue, canary yellow and violet, to name but a few. There it was, almost as if a light from Heaven was shining on it, my lime green shirt. Sizing wasn't a problem, they had everything. I immediately spotted a size 16 inch collar, this was what service was all about, meeting the demands of the consumer.
>
> (female, 20)

A sick and sorry bunch, I hear you say, and who am I to disagree? I mean, falling hopelessly in love with a Ferrari is one thing, getting hot to trot about a tube of Smarties is quite another. However, if we take these true confessions at face value, then it's clear that consumer concupiscence operates at several different levels. It is directed towards shopping in general (love to shop), specific retail stores (River Island is a particular favourite) and all manner of individual products from T-shirts to teapots. The essential point, as far as I can make out, is that utilitarian considerations are utterly irrelevant in many cases. If anything, the student introspectors espouse a 'love at first sight' credo of consumption. Purchases are expected to 'catch the eye', to stop shoppers in their tracks, to whet their appetites, to arouse a tumescent response. True, people often don't know what they want – love is indescribable, after all – but they know it when they see it, even if it isn't what they set out to buy.

Then I saw it. In that split second everything else in the world seemed to go out of focus. All I could see was that dress. Before I knew what was happening, I had unconsciously walked towards it. It was as if it contained a magnet. It was a rich chocolate brown colour with a luxurious velvet texture. I just knew that it would be perfect on. My heart stopped as I frantically scrambled inside for the price tag. It was meant for me.

(female, 20)

First port of call was River Island. No particular reason, it just happened to be one of the first clothes shops that I passed. A surprise then that I found exactly what I was looking for. Well, not exactly. To be honest, it wasn't even close. But it was too late. I was in love.

(male, 22)

I had not ruled on my final judgement, so knowing the owner of the shop I was permitted to take it home for a night . . . With a ripple of excitement in my heart, deep down I knew I was falling in love with the suit.

(male, 22)

I was feeling very happy with my day's shopping, just then, a lovely white cardigan in a window stopped me in my tracks. It was gorgeous and would go so well with my jeans for tonight. I had to have it, but I had already spent too much money, and this would be extravagance. On closer inspection, I discovered the shop was Dorothy Perkins, I grabbed my wallet and saw my plastic friend smiling back at me, the perfect solution, get now, worry later . . . Whoever said money can't buy you happiness hadn't discovered the art form of credit. Without a doubt shopping is the best medicine and I loved it.

(female, 21)

Indeed, it is no exaggeration to state that some of these episodes of overwhelming consuming passion border on the orgasmic. Fake orgasmic possibly – did the earth move for you, or The Body Shop at least? – but orgasmic all the same.

So I went inside and it was very warm, so I unzipped my coat and opened up my cardigan, the heat was very uncomfortable to be in. I walked around the shop and then I spotted THEEE dress. I held it up against me, and oh, how long it was. It was made of satin at the top and the rest of the dress was made of polyester. It was the colour red, it had a split at the back and it was fitted. It was just perfect in my eyes. I tried it on and it looked really nice on me, it fitted me perfectly, this was a dress I wanted. I wanted it so badly I purchased it without my mum, so I knew from that that this dress was the one.

(female, 21)

Dutifully, I browsed around to the clothes section and then my 'sensible' head started to grow weak as the most amazing jacket drew me like a magnet, like a fish to bait. My hands were trembling and knees weak as I made my way over to the object of my desire. It was mine! I had to have it! How did shopping for a birthday present eventually lead to this paralysing moment? It was versatile and could be co-ordinated with almost anything. Oh yes, I want it and God help anyone who stands in my way! Yes! I took deep breaths to conquer hyper-ventilating and quickly searched for my size. They better have it! A size 10 red jacket soon replaced the worn-out black one on my back. My heart pounding (why did shopping always have this ridiculous effect on me?), I whisked the jacket to the counter and just like that, all in a turn of a card, my shopping trip was complete.

(female, 21)

Obviously this is a metaphorical association (it is, isn't it?; please tell me it is; am I the only eunuch of exchange around here?), albeit some overexcited academic authorities assert that physical arousal can and does take place in the retailing orgasmatron. Metaphors, to be sure, are extremely powerful. They shape how we see, interpret and experience the world. Hence, very great care must be taken when anthropomorphising product attributes, portraying shopping centres as love nests *manqué* and generally shopping 'til you drop them. Never forget, friends, we're dealing with the love that dare not speak its brand name, but if this description isn't suggestive I don't know what is.

The minute that I walked into that shop I was lost. I wandered around the shop in a daze, just glancing at everything because I knew that I couldn't afford to do anything else. Then I saw it. I walked over to it in a dream-like fashion, scared stiff of seeing it up close. My legs were like jelly as I approached it. Somewhere along the journey Rosaleen had joined me. 'It's fabulous, just perfect for you,' she gushed. As I stretched out my hand to hold the dress I thought I would faint. It was the most perfect dress in the whole world. It was scarlet red, the perfect colour for Christmas. It had satin straps, a velvet bodice and then fell to the ground in layers of satin. It was even the right length. 'I have to try it on,' I whispered to Rosaleen. The next few minutes passed in a haze. The dress was perfect, but I couldn't get it, could I? I had already looked at the price tag on it. My mind started to work overtime, I knew that I couldn't let an opportunity like this pass me by. I would regret it for the rest of my life.

(female, 20)

Be that as it may, if you subscribe to the 'shopping is like sex' simile then it is impossible not to be struck by the broad parallels between the procreative and purchasing behaviours of males and females. Men, to put it crudely, adopt a 'wham bam, thank you mam' approach to shopping. They claim to know what they want; they expect to get it; they don't mess around; they are in and out as quickly as possible, if you'll pardon the expression; and rapidly work their way through one consumer conquest after another. What's more, they simply can't comprehend the female shopping psyche, which seems to involve examining what's on offer in every available outlet before settling on the preferred choice, the least worst option.

I can identify myself as an apathetic shopper, the type that likes to dash in and out, neither eating, browsing nor socialising in the effort to get the whole business over as quickly and as inexpensively as possible . . . Unfortunately my girlfriend's Number One leisure activity is shopping, so it follows that we shop 'til we (almost literally) drop in every fashion boutique, leather boutique, gift shop and jewellery store that the resort has to offer.

(male, 22)

It was then that I was marched down to Dolcis to look at shoes – for myself. I was told to pick a pair because that was what I was getting for Christmas. In two minutes I had fitted them on, asked for the match of it and Sarah had paid for them. Why can't women be the same? Why can't they walk into a shop and in 30 seconds make up their mind whether there is something they like or not? I suppose I'm not the only man to ever ask this.

(male, 21)

To begin with it wasn't too bad, we were going in and out of a few shops and I just followed behind her looking at the sales assistants who were quite nice, as she browsed among the displays, but the novelty began to wear off and I began to get fed-up. After a while . . . I noticed she had not many bags and I commented on this . . . to which she replied, saying that she liked such and such a skirt, etc., so let's go back to that shop again. I asked her why she didn't buy it in the first place and she answered, 'What if I had bought it and found something nicer later?' But she hadn't and everything she did like she didn't find anything nicer, so it all began again. 'Let's go back to this shop.' So once again I was getting trailed round women's shops . . . Why can't women shop as I do? I leave the house. I know exactly what I want and where to get it. I might see something else and buy it and then leave and go home. I've discussed this with my friends and they all feel the same. I guess I will never understand why women shop the way they do.

(male, 22)

Women, admittedly, are prone to occasional wild, reckless, impulsive, impassioned flings with simply irresistible products that make them go weak at the knees (and which may never be unwrapped or worn). Similarly, men's love 'em and leave 'em approach is more manifest in the breach than the observance, especially when 'shopping' is conveniently redefined as 'work' (books), as 'leisure' (CDs), as a 'hobby' (computer games) or – try not to laugh – an 'investment' (stamp collecting). Yet, on the basis of the introspective accounts, there do appear to be broad gender-related differences in consumer performance, the shopping act – call it what you will.

By the third store I was getting very impatient and agreed to meet her at the car in fifteen minutes. Having left the groceries in the car I decide to buy a pair of jeans. Entering the nearest store selling jeans I head straight for the Levi's rack. Wrangler jeans are reduced but for any street cred you need to wear Levi's. Any clothes shopping I ever do always follows the same pattern.

I know what I want and if they fit I buy them, no problem. The blue/black 508 jeans look good, size 34, yes, and also the charcoal grey. So, off for a quick try on. Why therefore do other people ponder the purchase so much? I enter the compartment and pull on the first pair. Good fit. Sold. Parting with £35 has never been easier.

(male, 21)

I have a problem with shoes, you see, or should I say a fetish. I've got shoes, shoes and more shoes. Shoes that I've bought just because I had to have them, nothing to wear them with, though. My favourite pair, black suede, Italian, very high heels. Bought on sale in here for a song, £15. Just had to have them. Mind you I've only worn them about twice, they might look good but when I get home my feet are killing me, felt I was walking on stilts all night. But, I had to have them.

(female, 43)

Shopping with men in particular is a challenge in itself. You always get the usual comments, knowing all too well that the majority of time what they say is completely different from what they mean. Familiar complaints include: 'I'm not going in there' ('it's a woman's shop, isn't it?'); 'We could make the next bus if we hurry up' ('I'm really fed up and I'm not hanging about for another hour for the next one'); 'That was the dress you tried on about two hours ago' ('why didn't you buy it the first time we were in here, it would have saved all this hassle'). The list goes on and on. They just don't understand, do they?

(female, 23)

This contrast in the shopping styles of the sexes (and sexual styles of the shoppers) is interesting in itself, but it really comes to a head, as it were, when opposite sexes shop together. Sharing each other's interests is purported to be one of the keys to a successful long-term relationship, or so they tell me, yet the essays suggest that, far from being a form of foreplay, shopping with a partner is fraught with danger. In fact, it is clear that the gender wars are frequently fought on the female terrain of the shop front. Some men expect sexual favours in return for going shopping, or try to make their girlfriends jealous by flirting with attractive sales assistants, whereas women exploit male shopaphobia to redress perceived intra-partnership power imbalances or, in keeping with the classic courtship schema, seek to test the extent of their lover's commitment.

My long-standing policy on the 'shopping issue' had been to avoid Cookstown town centre on Saturdays at all costs. It would appear, then, that my devious fiancée using her powers of persuasion (details of which I shall not go into for fear of lowering the tone of what will prove to be a ground-breaking piece of work – not!) had managed to corner me into it, for believe me, folks, shopping in Cookstown on the Saturday before Christmas is a fate worse than death and something to be endured either under sufferance (or with the prospect of favours of the bedroom variety to follow).

(male, 22)

I walked like a lap-dog to a shop called Paris, which as the name suggests sells women's clothing. As I stood there waiting for the girls, I began to feel awkward and to add to the embarrassment Emma started to take the mickey by asking what I thought about particular items of lingerie.

(male, 21)

Flanked by a protesting James, who is either on the verge of murder or exploding, I try to calm him down with those three soothing, tender words, 'Oh shut up!' Sensing another outburst, I dive into the shop, select and pay for the jacket and appear before James has realised I've gone! 'WHY COULDN'T YOU HAVE DONE THAT TWO HOURS AGO?' Here we go again, the usual rant, 'We could have been out of here in five minutes! When I go shopping I get what I want in one shop and go home – inside half an hour. You have to go into every shop and then back to the first one and pick the first thing you saw. We could have been home ages ago!' Are all men the same? Why is it they have to apply this macho, chauvinistic image to everything? Men are better at this. Men are better at that. We can do our shopping in five minutes!

(female, 23)

It seems, then, that women not only wear the trousers in shopping milieux, but they try on every available pair just to make sure their partners get the message, know their place, learn who's boss. Indeed, in extreme cases, the imbroglio of retailing-induced emotional trauma can lead to the temporary, or occasionally irretrievable, break down of relationships.

My boyfriend came into town with me that day, not to add an opinion, just to hold the money. It was in one leather jacket shop that I tried on a beautifully fitted, military-style jacket. I knew even before I put it on that it had far too many buttons and stripes on it for my liking. After all, I did not want people saluting me when I came into a room . . . I knew he was disappointed that our shopping trip had not come to an early end. 'Next stop, Top Shop,' I delighted in telling him, safe in the knowledge that he hated the place. I found it a challenge to get him inside this female frenzy of a clothes shop, instead of outside with the other, pitiful males. I triumphed that he could 'hack it', only on my account.

(female, 21)

On the way out of the automatic doors at the Tower Centre, Graham spies a sportswear store and decides he wants to have a look. 'Awe, come on in here a minute.' 'No, Graham, listen we're running out of time as it is without stopping to look at stupid stuff.' 'You never go anywhere I want to go, it's the same old story, we always have to go where you fucking want to go!' But as always he relents and we go straight out and down the street to Benetton.

(female, 21)

It was then that my missus finally blew. She couldn't take any more and decided to have a go at me. Class. Firstly, she gave me that 'bad eye' look, and I knew that, while I hadn't done anything wrong, that was clearly the problem for her; she viewed it as I just hadn't done anything. That was not the end of it, however. 'Get your hands out of your pockets and do something.' That was it. Blow town. Go anywhere, just as long as it's away from here.

(male, 21)

The intention of Graham and me going in here was to buy two scarves, one for me and one for his niece as a present. It ended up in a row. I believe that if you have to pay dear for a thing, you're entitled to take as long as you like in choosing it. Graham obviously has a different outlook on this. We'd picked up a scarf for the niece and I was still trying to decide what colour I wanted when the sales assistant came back to us for a second time to enquire if we needed any help, so Graham pointed out the blue scarf and she entered the amount in the till and held out a perfectly manicured hand for payment. He wasn't ready for this so quickly and after struggling to get his hands into the pockets of his jeans he gave her a crumpled and screwed up £20 note, which she took great precision in unfolding. I was raging, bloody seething. I wasn't ready and he just went on ahead and got served. So we walked out (well, I actually stumped on ahead) and along the street to the Fairhill Centre. He started to complain about the girl in Benetton, that she should have put the scarf in the bag first and then asked him for the money. I just thought, it'll harden you, won't it?

(female, 21)

Such acts of retailing-refracted revenge thus highlight the negative side of the sex 'n' shopping equation. Although many academic authorities have alluded to the supposed connection between shopping and sex, the unstated assumption is that the experience is entirely pleasurable, that the joy of sex and the joy of shopping are somehow congruent or homologous. There is, however, a sorrowful side to shopping and a sorrowful side to sex, as I can personally testify (though I'd prefer not to talk about it just now, if you don't mind).

Wonderful though many consuming encounters undoubtedly are – large, mixed-sex crowds of people in close proximity have inherent erotic potential – going shopping can and often does prove deeply unsatisfying. For every windfall from the ugly tree, whose very gargoylesque presence boosts one's self-esteem, there are several people much better looking, much better dressed and much better financially, physically or matrimonially off than ourselves. These beautiful people can be and are belittled, especially if they are 'mere' shop assistants, but they still make everyone else feel a fat, frumpy, frightful failure by invidious comparison.

We head on up towards Corn Market and into Propaganda, a shop which I am not terribly fond of. This is due to the fact that everyone who works here is kitted out, head to foot, in about £700 worth of designer gear. For some reason, when I am in their presence, I come over all inferior. I am not alone in this feeling, as I have conferred with my friends on this matter, who I also find experience 'Propaganda paranoia'.

(male, 22)

Unfortunately, in order to go to the next place which is called Acme it is necessary to walk through the centre of town which involves passing, or in my case 'attempting' to pass, other shops. We go into French Connection, just to see what we can't afford and walk out wondering if their newspaper advertisement for a shop assistant read, 'must be of Cosmo-model appearance, standard of education negotiable'.

(female, 22)

There was another couple in the queue who were in stark contrast. They looked very well-to-do, both about fifty years of age and obviously overly dressed up for mere Christmas shopping. The phrase, 'I am not worthy' springs to mind.

(male, 21)

As soon as you walk through the doors, the waft of perfumes and aftershaves hits you up the face. Right, to the testers. Behind the counter, all I can see is these girls with make-up and hair done to perfection. I hate them. Maybe I'm just jealous. I reach out to lift one of the testers and I hear a voice, 'Can I help you?' I abruptly answer, 'No thank you!' I hate that question, it really annoys me.

(female, 22)

In a similar vein, the multifariously mirrored retailing environment not only reflects well upon us, or so we like to think, it also shows off our grotesque bodies. Without doubt, the crucible of these cruel encounters with the 'ugly bloke' within is the changing cubicle, where harsh lighting, trick mirrors and inconvenient chinks in the curtains contrive to condemn all but the most egomaniacal to profound paroxysms of self-loathing (not that I've ever felt, or needed to feel, that way about myself).

Fortunately, most of the cubicles were empty and I had the opportunity to try several before finding one where the curtains aspired to cover more than 70% of the gap. A single hook was thoughtfully provided on which to hang my coat, jumper, jeans and the yet to be purchased suit. My own clothes were consigned to the floor. With a gap of about two inches either side of the curtains, I felt but failed to look like a Chippendale with stage fright.

(male, 22)

After walking around the store about five times, ensuring I didn't miss anything, nothing grabbed my attention. Feeling very depressed, I left the store with good intentions to start a diet in the morning so as to fit into the clothes most shops had to offer.

(female, 22)

List in hand, I struggled with my new purchase over to Dorothy Perkins against gale-force 8 winds and torrential rain. Two customers besides myself were in DP's. Caught a glimpse of myself in a mirror, you know one of those that are meant to make you look skinny so you buy the damn clothes?? My hair was really beginning to go curly, and after all the effort I'd put into it!!

(female, 23)

Feeling faint from my repulsive reflection in the window I began rummaging in my oversized handbag (which only contained a purse) for a handkerchief, to no avail. Damn! I desperately needed to blow my nose. My sniffing and snorting only adding to the attention I was already drawing to myself. I carefully adjusted my hair to prevent the trickling drips of water streaking my make-up, and it suddenly dawned on me that I wasn't quite sure what I was going to buy.

(female, 21)

Worse still, for women at least, is the communal variant of the changing room, which exposes their rolls of fat, unsightly cellulite and laddered tights to the adjacent supermodel, the entire shop, the whole world, all of whom are watching and won't stop giggling.

I selected my size and joined the long, winding queue that I presumed was snaking its way into the changing rooms. OH NO!, it was communal and I was wearing threadbare underwear and I hadn't shaved my legs. I had got this far, however, and I wasn't turning back now. I was sandwiched between a sylph-like blonde in silver hot-pants and a portly woman who smelt of something nasty.

(female, 22)

The things that sort of exasperate me about shopping include . . . changing rooms that are communal (who wants to see my horrible body?), are too small (I have acquired countless bruises while trying to demolish minuscule cubicles), have curtains that must have shrunk in the wash and I am convinced that the mirrors are different from the one in my bedroom, because I certainly look different in them.

(female, 20)

No sooner had I entered the changing room when I turned swiftly on my heels and walked out, handing the item to the assistant with a polite thanks but no thanks look on my face. The reason for this being the open-plan changing room. Sorry, but my cellulite is for my eyes only. I wouldn't like to subject anyone to the sight of my unclothed body. If I do, in a moment of madness, brave these changing rooms you can be sure that as I am admiring what I think is my own reflection in that 'little black number that would take you anywhere' it will suddenly hit me that it is not actually me but instead it is that supermodel like babe who happens to be trying on the same outfit somewhere behind me, at which point I will try to struggle back into my clothes without revealing any of my body, and run.

(female, 22)

For men, meanwhile, there is nothing but nothing more mortifying than standing outside the female changing area – unfailingly situated in the lingerie section – while their partners wrestle and ruminate inside. (Mind you, some of us manage to cope fairly well with the ordeal.)

I was left standing outside changing rooms by myself and strange women in their bare feet would come out from behind the curtains and look at me as if I was some sort of pervert. I thought I was the only person who would feel like this, but I met another man abandoned outside the changing cubicles and he had the same feelings as myself.

(male, 22)

I personally detest women's clothes shops, because Aideen sweeps through the store lifting items left, right and centre, then over to the changing rooms. 'You stay there, I will be out in a moment.' Now you're left standing outside the women's changing rooms, with women looking at you, as if to say, what's he doing here? You feel a complete berk, especially if she doesn't appear every now and again to reassure you.

(male, 22)

Going shopping with a member of the opposite sex is a real pain, as she (my girlfriend) tries one thing on, doesn't like it . . . tries 20 things on, doesn't like them, leaving me standing, waiting to give my 'expert opinion' – if I have one. The best thing about this is that I get a chance, when she is changing, to look at the lingerie section, fantasising what my girlfriend would look like in them, or Mariah Carey or even what Jim McDonald's wife, Liz, in *Coronation Street*, would look like in them.

(male, 21)

Sorry, I forgot, there is something worse than the knicker patrol but only for the congenitally homophobic. Shut that changing room door!

Suddenly, from the back of the collection point, two new assistants appeared. Well, my God, I'm not homophobic or anything, but these two were as queer as a bottle of chips and a six pound note rolled into one. Roderick and Miles were their names. FUCK! They looked like something out of a cabaret act or something! Something you would find in London's Soho, billed under something like 'Bongo-Boys'. However, in their bitchy way they settled the crowd down and actually got the right items to the right people . . . Roderick came over to me, not literally, to ask my name, to enquire about my order and how long I was waiting.
    'Excuse me, sir, would you tell me your name and how long you've been waiting?'

160

'McDaid and about 45 minutes,' I said in an uncomfortable and sarcastic manner.
'Oh, Oh!, that's not good enough. We'll have to hurry your order through.'
By this stage I was convinced of his sexual tendencies. The tipped blonde hair was the final straw. Arsebandit. I could hear him barking orders over the phone, round the back. Well, more purring the orders in his feminine way. Fruitcake. Miles turned and barked at Roderick which caused a bit of friction between them. Roderick then turned and apologised to Miles but Miles totally ignored him. Roderick was denied!

(male, 21)

Above and beyond putting one's pale, pustular and podgy physique on painful display, or indulging in unfailingly unflattering corporeal comparisons with countless svelte surrounding sexpots, it seems that consumer goods themselves can castrate, frustrate or emasculate the shopping experience. Just as they serve as symbolic stepping stones to a more alluring self, so too they draw disagreeable attention to the less beguiling side of ourselves. Clothes that don't fit, or are incorrectly sized, or incompatible with our colouring, or exaggerate our imperfections, or are just 'not me', are constantly encountered, to the abyssal misery of the consumers concerned.

Before I knew it I was once again in the fitting room. Several dresses later I came to the conclusion that a tub of Slimfast would be a much wiser purchase as I did not possess the traditional hour-glass figure so essential for the fashion design of the moment.

(female, 22)

I get into the queue for the changing room. Armed with the dress of my dreams. I find a cubicle, quickly undress myself and put on the dress. It is too tight. I can't believe that I have put on so much weight! Feeling really embarrassed and annoyed with myself I take the dress off again. As I am taking it off and hanging it up again I notice that the dress is actually a size 8, which had been placed on a size 10 hanger by mistake.

(female, 21)

'Blessed' with a tall, well-proportioned, size 14 figure, I am in that (un)enviable position of being considered outsized in 'normal' shops and only a little girl in outlets catering for the fuller figure . . . Shopping for clothes can be a very traumatic experience, especially if it coincides with a semi-depressed state. On occasion I have been known to sink to the floor in despair (restrictive garments allowing) wailing, 'I'm fat, I'm ugly, no-one loves me.' And all because the lady cannot fit into a garment that should really belong in the children's department. So I have come to two conclusions, either I am totally obese, the largest woman in the universe, and a completely different shape to boot, or else someone, somewhere is waging a war against females who still practise that age-old ritual, known as eating.

(female, 20)

From Miss Selfridge to Gap to Parks to Debenhams, you name it we went but did we purchase? No. All I experienced was hopping in and out of changing rooms, getting all hot and bothered with shop assistants telling you that everything looked lovely on you even though you were poured into the little black number or your spare tyre was bulging out over the waist of the trousers. Why do people do that? Are they on commission? I would never tell anyone that something looks lovely on them when you know deep down that she looks like fuck all in it. Left Castlecourt feeling fat and tired, thinking that's it, diet starts tomorrow.

(female, 22)

Almost as bad is merchandise that, if indulged in, only compounds the grotesque body problem (crisps, chocolate, cola, cigarettes, etc.) and which has to be resisted, albeit with difficulty. Indeed, certain sex-related or potentially sex-related goods can prove excruciatingly embarrassing, for men in particular, as can specific retail stores.

Every five or six weeks I have a terrible shopping experience, that is shopping for toiletries such as shampoo, deodorant (spray and stick), bubble bath, toothpaste, shaving foam, yellow Bic razors and, an odd time, moisturiser (don't tell anyone). I always feel that people are watching me. I don't look up in case they are. It is the same feeling I used to get when I was 16, trying to get into a niteclub. This is especially the case when purchasing moisturiser and, NO, I am not a sissy, I just have dry skin on my eyebrows. Shopping for toiletries is done quickly. I do not stand and ponder over one deodorant or another, sniffing here, spraying there. I lift the same items every time and go to the checkout with my hand over my mouth, constantly looking at my feet. I always become embarrassed with this. The counter assistant is bound to think that I am a real smelly so and so, needing all this deodorant.

(male, 21)

After leaving Next I walked up the escalator towards The Body Shop. When I was younger all the girls at school would buy from The Body Shop, so I don't like to be seen buying from there. Every time I pass The Body Shop I would buy a small container of White Musk Shower Gel. I love the smell of the shower gel and I have even got the guys in the rugby team into using it. It is now considered vital tackling gear and I don't mean rugby tackling. Generally, however, I hate shopping in chemists, especially Boots and especially for items like Vaseline and Deep Heat. Pharmacists don't seem to realise I use them for rugby purposes and hence give me funny looks.

(male, 20)

Tempting as it is to tell our essayists to pull themselves together – misconstrued though that might be – it is clear from the introspective accounts that consumer concupiscence cuts both ways. The shopping environment undoubtedly provides ample fodder for concocting romantic or erotic fantasies (e.g. travel brochures as a magic textual carpet to exotic sexual adventures in foreign

162

climes; when I wear this dress I'll look drop-dead gorgeous; if I buy my girl-friend this CD player will she reward me with a kiss, or two, or more?).

> As I turned to cross the floor to the other side of the shop I was immediately confronted by a pure white table, vibrant in its contrast with the mellow mood of the dark green shop. Upon it was a pyramid-shaped display of olde-worlde glass bottles, reflecting layers of light from the toned-down lighting of the shop, which enhanced the pure essence-like impression of the perfumes they contained. Sampling several, which ranged from the most sickening sweetness of lavender to the enriched poignancy of wild musk, it suddenly struck me that this was the essential element that was missing from my seduc-tress tactics. Finally dragging myself away from the inspired images of myself walking along a beach at sunset with deep reddish-brown shades of silk flow-ing with my movements – I ended up at the aromatherapy section. Alternatively inhaling calming and stimulating herbal scents, my equilibrium was re-established.
>
> (female, 22)

However, it can also inflame disagreeable or indeed nightmare scenarios, from being made to feel cheap under the baleful male gaze to fears of frenzied sexual assault in shopping centre car parks.

> Walking down the street we both spotted an off-licence, so we decided to get a 'carry-out' for that night. After entering the shop we were immediately stared at by two 'old' men. One was operating the cash register while the other stood at a door at the far end of the shop. I felt as if they were giving the impression that young girls shouldn't be drinking. A wave of guilt came over me . . . I don't think I can recall feeling so uncomfortable in a shop before. I was hoping it would be worth it later on that night.
>
> (female, 22)

> The car park reminded me of one of those American movies where a woman is approaching her car after a late night at work and is attacked by a psycho rapist. I got a shiver thinking how scary it would be to walk through it by myself late at night.
>
> (female, 21)

Likewise, the anthropomorphisation effect that is apparent at the yes-yes-yes end of the consuming spectrum is equally apparent at the not-tonight-dear-I've-got-a-headache end of the sex 'n' shopping scale. Stores are suspected of deliberately withholding their favours, or attempting to break off long and happy relation-ships, and desperately desired products successfully secrete themselves from view or pretend to be washing their hair that night. Similarly, the clichéd 'chat-up' lines of sales assistants are regarded as the equivalent of 'do you come here often?', 'what's a girl like you doing in a place like this?' or 'if I said you had a beautiful body would you hold it against me?'. Well, would you?

The manager came over and explained the situation and kept apologising, there was nothing he could do . . . I couldn't believe the way this worked out. I always thought Topshop was a reliable friend. But I have since forgiven them and continue to shop there.

(male, 22)

Now I don't know, but every time I am in the mood for shopping, I dash off to the nearest shop, cash in hand, only to find that there is nothing to buy. Maybe the shops don't want to sell to me.

(female, 20)

Our 'tour of duty' continues and while passing River Island I spot pinstriped trousers I have been hunting for what has seemed eternity. The race starts, into the shop, up the stairs (trying to avoid any manslaughter charges from killing someone if I lose them) find the rail, my size – where's my size?! Has some psychopath been one step ahead of me, intent on trying to drive me mad? Before I tear my hair out I need to compose myself and as politely as possible, considering my frame of mind, ask for assistance.

(male, 22)

While browsing in every store, I always hear an assistant approaching me. I think to myself, super, smashing, great, time to play the interested consumer. 'Can I help you?', they always ask. This statement gives me the shits. I wish someone would devise a new way for assistants to ask if they could help me. They are most likely thinking the same thing about me because of my answer, 'No, I am only looking.' Just as they are about to leave me I will go, 'Ah, do you see this boot, do you have it in a nine?' I have no intention of buying boots, I just love wasting their time because, after all, that is what they are there for. I try the boots on, walk around in them and then go back to the assistant, smile and say, 'Thank you, I will be back later.'

(male, 21)

Most significantly perhaps, the orgasmic ecstasy of finding the perfect product or gift is counterpointed by the agonising frustration, the heart-rending, tear-shedding, teeth-grinding, carpet-chewing, cold-showering, cat-kicking torment of failure.

Sinking my feet into the deep pile carpet I felt soothed by the gentle music. I walked to the ladieswear department and there it was, the dress of all dresses! A warm chiffon creation with layer upon layer of quality textile, flowing from a fitted satin bodice, soft to the touch and pleasing to the eye. Feeling euphoric, I sprinted to the first assistant that I could find and asked her to fetch my size. She apologetically informed me that 'them dresses are out of stock, love'. Gutted, I reluctantly returned the dress to its rail and meandered down the escalator to the Food Hall.

(female, 22)

After waiting patiently to cross at the traffic lights, I almost sprinted over and hailed the shop with adoration. Passing the fully glassed window that contained what looked like hundreds of shoes, my eyes for once could not see enough. I was almost pushing other so-called shoppers out of the way to determine whether or not the display contained the one and only thing I wanted. And there they were, gorgeously standing on a tall, almost regal platform, a pair of sleek, well cut, long, knee-length boots! My heart jumped, my stomach leapt and my eyes almost doubled in size. I bounced forward, almost knocking down a customer deeply engrossed in a pair of shoes. When I reached my desired destination, I ran my hands up and down their tailored physique. I lifted them gently off the platform, eased the zip down, slid off my sandal and sock, and placed my foot into my dream boot. They looked fabulous. I slowly began zipping them up, but alas they stopped just above my ankle. The fat (or as I prefer to call it – large calves) was destroying and obviating my chances of success. It was looking at me almost saying 'you haven't a hope in hell of getting this zip past me love' . . . I attempted to pull up the zips on a number of different styles, but it was useless. I seriously wanted to take a bacon slicer to my legs and cut half of it away. So again I left the shop empty-handed.

(female, 21)

I had made it to the front of the queue and was facing an overly attractive girl who was about twenty or twenty-one years of age. The wait was worthwhile, I thought. I gave her the docket that I had carefully filled out and she proceeded to type the information into her little computer. Standing with £40 in my hand I prepared to pay for the product. The following conversation took place:

'I'm sorry sir, but there does not appear to be any of those products in stock at the present moment.'

'You're kidding, aren't you?'

'I'm afraid not, but we can order you the product from another branch but it may not be here for Christmas. It is a Christmas present, isn't it?'

My initial thoughts of this girl being a goddess were ruined in a matter of seconds. This girl had suddenly turned from a romantically approachable girl into the wicked witch of the west. I followed the yellow brick road directly out of the store. The thought of nooses and razor blades clearly in my head.

(male, 21)

What's more, the sheer torture of failing to find what one's looking for – ill-defined though the intention often is – is reinforced by the evident success of surrounding shoppers, whose pregnant carrier bags are not only indicative of sated consuming passions but evidence that they have the wherewithal to acquire what our penurious essayists are denied.

I left the shop and slowly walked up to the front of Castlecourt, ready to leave. My feet were trailing behind me. I had lost the spring in my step. I could see everyone coming into Castlecourt with bags upon bags of shopping and there was I carrying nothing but the bag I left with.

(female, 20)

I eventually get to try the outfit on. It's lovely but I have to think realistically. I can't afford it. However tempting it may be I must put it back and get on with my real mission of the day, Christmas shopping. Depressed, I walk out of the store . . . I spend ages walking around Castlecourt dandering in and out of all the shops looking at all the very tempting merchandise. The temptation in Bay Trading and Dolcis is almost too much for me to handle. There were so many nice things. Christmas is a really colourful time of year and a happy time too, if you have loads of money.

(female, 21)

In these circumstances, some retailing inadequates, some sad gits of shopping, some cuckolds of consumption, some mackintosh wearers of marketing descend to petty acts of jealousy, hostility, spite, possessiveness and revenge. All of the negative emotions associated with human sexual relations are thus expended in the bordello of consumer behaviour. (Not that I would ever patronise that kind of amatorial establishment. Do you think they take plastic?)

A depressing problem that I have developed as an impulsive shopper is that I always buy items that lie well outside my income bracket. However, this does not prevent the purchase, otherwise my shopping day would be ultimately destroyed, knowing that I could have had it but now someone else will have an even better day than me.

(male, 21)

I went to get a seat. As I was waiting all I could think was how jealous my friend would be, because she has also admired them but only after I spied them first.

(female, 20)

As I stepped into the shop I felt all the familiar symptoms take a grip of me. I felt so panicky, there was so much to look at. My eyes darted everywhere as I tried to take everything in, all at once. I was petrified in case in the split second that it took me to scan the shop that I would have missed my dream dress and that someone else would have bought it. My heart sunk and leapt with exhilaration all at once.

(female, 20)

On my way to Laser I kept replaying the situation in Currys over and over in my mind. I would normally relate that sort of staff attitude to shoe shops and definitely did not expect to get harassed while shopping for a video recorder. As I was reaching Laser I was determined to buy a video from them to avoid having to go back to Currys. If they were going to treat me so badly then this is how I would punish them.

(female, 21)

Others, by contrast, luxuriate in self-indulgent forms of compensatory consumption. Sweets, for instance, seem to serve as a substitute for shopping, which as we all know is a substitute for sex. Are sweet-eating habits indicative of sexual proclivities, I sometimes wonder? I'm a Curly Wurly man myself – know what I'm saying? Weaned on gobstoppers and rhubarb rock, I was. By the way, if you so much as mention Fruit Pastilles, Fisherman's Friend, soft centres or melt in the mouth not the hand, my lawyers will be in touch. *Comprende?*

On seeing the thousands of people grocery shopping, I decided not to risk a trolley and took a basket instead. The one thing guaranteed to cheer me up when I got home would be a sticky dessert. I was dazzled by the selection and took about 5-10 mouth-watering minutes to eventually opt for the little sticky toffee puddings.

(female, 22)

When I am slightly depressed, when the world is blue and no-one loves me, my shopping trip nearly always involves a visit to the nearest café or confectionery outlet in search of that ultimate remedy – chocolate.

(female, 20)

I slipped or I tried to slip the sandal onto my right foot. It was virtually impossible. Did my foot expand overnight? I felt like Bigfoot. I knew the sandal was the correct size, so I forced it onto my foot. The length was perfect but unfortunately the width wasn't. The petite straps that went across the sandal didn't look quite so petite as they did before. They definitely didn't look elegant now. It looked like I was trying to squeeze my foot into a sandal that was two sizes too small for me. I suddenly got a sinking feeling in my stomach and my smile was gone. There was no point in trying the other sandal on and there was no point in getting a bigger size. With saddened eyes I looked up at the shop assistant and handed her back the sandals. She tried to cheer me up by pointing out other types of sandals but it was no good. My bubble had burst! All the excitement had disappeared. I just wanted to get out of the shop and go home and eat lots of chocolate fudge cake, as this is what comforts me whenever I get depressed.

(female, 20)

While we're on the subject of confectionery, it is striking that the introspective process transported many of the essayists back to their childhoods. Christmas shopping in particular seems (understandably) to call forth the inner child, as do encounters with mothers-to-be or indeed mothers *per se*. Obviously, at this late stage in the proceedings, we don't want to get wrapped up in shopping psychobabble – just lie back and tell me about your infantile trauma with the cuddly toy in the Early Learning Centre – but it seems that shopping with mother is the root cause of countless consumer psychoses. The complete lack of fathers in the introspective essays is no less significant, in my untutored opinion. Oedipus shops. Psychopaths R Us. Sigmund U Like. Lacan can.

Then like a vision from heaven I see it, hanging high on a rail. The glow from its warm colour engulfs me. I bound over to where the burnt orange suit is hanging and search like a madwoman for my size. Yes, it's here. Happy dayz, I want to shout out loud. I hug the suit close to me, like a child with a teddy that someone is trying to take away.

(female, 20)

I am the original lone shopper. I prefer to shop alone. This I blame on my childhood when my mother treated me as the daughter she never had, dragging me round endless clothes shops in search of the eternal bargain. Far from putting me off shopping, it actually encouraged me, although I now prefer to drag myself around at my own pace.

(male, 22)

I couldn't believe it, two pairs sitting in Topshop that I liked. In a tizzy due to childish excitement, I looked for the sales assistant to ask her for a size four. Yes, both pairs in a four. I bought a pair and walked out smiling from ear to ear. I'll have to go out tonight so I can wear my new red shoes. They'll look great with my short red cord skirt.

(female, 21)

I have always had an eye for good-looking staff as far back as I can remember (that is, around the age of 7 or 8, as this was the age I was first allowed to go to shop without my parents for sweets). The Beefers sweetie shop, which we called it, used to have a girl behind the counter called Fiona. At around the age of 10 or 11, me, my brother and my cousin used to go into this shop and ask for 10p or, pushing the boat out, 20p worth of sweets. We used to pick the jar or one of the jars from the top shelf – why you may ask? – because in order to reach for these sweets Fiona had to stand on a stool and we three used to stand and look at her nice behind and snigger like the stupid little schoolboys that we were. It got even more X-rated when these sweets were placed into paper bags, which she leaned forward to get at, with her low-cut top on. I have no need to tell you where we then looked. No need to wonder why I am on my third set of teeth since the age of 13!

(male, 21)

So, what are we supposed to make of all this stuff, apart of course from the crying need to strait-jacket the author or call his white-coated attendants, at least? Well, rather than try to get too serious and scholarly about it – justifying the methodology, defending the mode of exposition, summarising the 'findings', and so forth – let me just conclude by suggesting that the key outcome of this exercise concerns the nugatory side of consuming passion. The fact of the matter is that shopping, like sex, is often far from satisfactory. Not only is shopping physically frustrating, in so far as bodily imperfections are exposed to the harsh light of changing rooms and unbecoming inter-consumer comparisons, but it is metaphorically frustrating on account of unrequited love for must-have-can't-have merchandise. Anguish, bitterness, betrayal, pain, remorse, regret, despair, self-abasement – in fact, all of the symptoms of heartache – are on agonising display, though the torture comes in many different forms. Some men, for example, are prone to premature acquisition or buyer's droop – except when engrossed in their hobbies, pastimes and collectibles (those plastic blow-up dolls of consumer society) – whereas many women seem to be engaged on an impossible, all-consuming search for the perfect product, the marketing equivalent of Mr Right. Indeed, it is only a slight exaggeration to state that certain shopping expeditions are akin to chivalric quests of the romantic tradition, an unending pilgrimage towards the ultimately unattainable grail of true love.

Reluctant as I am to derail the passion wagon of consumption, or draw attention to the darkness in the tunnel of retailing love, the aversive side of sex 'n' shopping has great significance for Campbell's (1987) 'romantic ethic', his thesis that contemporary consumer behaviour is driven by heightened pre-experience expectations and post-purchase disappointments. This may well be true, but the introspective essays indicate that consumer dejection, dissatisfaction and disenchantment derive as much from the frustrations of *not* getting what they want as they do from the discontent that inevitably accompanies the attainment of our heart's desire. Failure, in fact, further stimulates consumer desire, heightens the anticipation and fuels the fantasy that, according to Campbell, eventually slams into the brick, all-too-brick wall of unromantic everyday reality. What's more, as Campbell's thesis is premised on the questionable assumption that consumption experiences are always anti-climactic, introducing a double negative dimension creates a conceptual space for the admittedly paradoxical possibility of customer satisfaction, even if this is short-lived. If, in addition, Douglas's (1997) antithetical stance on shopper behaviour – her eminently plausible thesis that consumers often don't know what they want but know what they don't want – is taken into account, then it can be contended, *contra* Campbell, that an apophatic ethic informs the spirit of postmodern consumption.

In this regard, of course, the apophatic ethic of shopper abjection is perfectly in keeping with the paradigmatic schema of romantic love. Romantic love, as Lystra (1989) observes, involves an ever-deepening, ever more intense cycle of interpersonal ecstasy and agony. As doubts, anxieties, petty jealousies and minor, albeit painful ordeals are overcome or obviated, mutual attraction and commitment are thereby augmented. Counterintuitive though this appears at first, romantic relationships are immeasurably strengthened by doubt, disappointment, despair and their associated, if undeniably tortuous, trials, tribulations and torments. Trials, tribulations and torments, let it be said, that are invariably intentionally imposed, if sometimes unconsciously, as tests of true love.

> The most paradoxical fact of courtship testing was that romantic love fed upon and thus gained strength from the anxiety cultivated by the tests themselves . . . When mutual interest existed, doubt and anxiety actually intensified romantic passion, perhaps because contemplating the end of a relationship through an

effective courtship test could force one to imagine life without the lover, thus pointing to his or her value and meaning. The power of courtship testing and especially the role of anxiety in strengthening romantic bonds should not be underestimated . . . doubt was a great sharpener and intensifier of the tender passions.

(Lystra 1989: 179–80)

The same, in my view, is true of consuming passions. To paraphrase Oscar Wilde: there is only one thing better than getting what you want and that is not getting what you want. What, then, has love got to do with it? Love is all, I say. All you need is love, to my mind at least. Love of money may be the root of all evil, but the money of love is the root of all marketing. Mint imperial anyone?

Note

1 Although he has discussed both romanticism and introspection at length, Holbrook (1993, 1996) never makes the basic point that introspection was one of the key traits of the romantic movement.

References

Brown, S. (1998a), *Postmodern Marketing Two: Telling Tales*, London: ITBP.
Brown, S. (1998b), 'The wind in the wallows: literary theory, autobiographical criticism and subjective personal introspection', in J.W. Alba and J.W. Hutchinson (eds), *Advances in Consumer Research, Vol. XXV*, Provo: Association for Consumer Research, in press.
Brown, S. and Reid, R. (1997), 'Shoppers on the verge of a nervous breakdown: chronicle, composition and confabulation in consumer research', in S. Brown and D. Turley (eds), *Consumer Research: Postcards from the Edge*, London: Routledge, 79–149.
Campbell, C. (1987), *The Romantic Ethic and the Spirit of Modern Consumerism*, Oxford: Blackwell.
Douglas, M. (1997), *Thought Styles: Critical Essays on Good Taste*, London: Sage.
Furst, L.R. (1969), *Romanticism in Perspective: A Comparative Study of Aspects of the Romantic Movements in England, France and Germany*, Basingstoke: Macmillan.
Gould, S.J. (1995) 'Researcher introspection as a method in consumer research: applications, issues and implications', *Journal of Consumer Research*, 21, March, 719–22.
Holbrook, M.B. (1993), 'Romanticism and sentimentality in consumer behaviour: a literary approach to the joys and sorrows of consumption', in M.B. Holbrook and E.C. Hirschman (eds), *The Semiotics of Consumption: Interpreting Symbolic Consumer Behaviour in Popular Culture and Works of Art*, Berlin: Mouton de Gruyter, 151–228.
Holbrook, M.B. (1996), 'Romanticism, introspection and the roots of experiential consumption: Morris the Epicurean', in R.W. Belk, N. Dholakia and A. Venkatesh (eds), *Consumption and Marketing: Macro Dimensions*, Cincinnati: South-Western, 20–82.
Levy, S.J. (1996), 'Stalking the Amphisbaena', *Journal of Consumer Research*, 23, December, 163–76.
Lyons, W.E. (1986), *The Disappearance of Introspection*, Cambridge, MA: MIT Press.

Lystra, K. (1989), *Searching the Heart: Women, Men and Romantic Love in Nineteenth-Century America*, New York: Oxford University Press.

Sherry, J.F. (1996), 'Review of *Consumption and Marketing: Macro Dimensions*', *Journal of Macromarketing*, 16(2), 107–8.

Simpson, D. (1995) *The Academic Postmodern and the Rule of Literature: A Report on Half-Knowledge*, Chicago: University of Chicago Press.

Veeser, H.A. (ed.) (1996) *Confessions of the Critics*, New York: Routledge.

Wallendorf, M. and Brucks, M. (1993) 'Introspection in consumer research: implementation and implications', *Journal of Consumer Research*, 20, December, 339–59.

9

ROMANCING THE UTOPIAN MARKETPLACE

Dallying with Bakhtin in the Powerscourt Townhouse Centre

Pauline Maclaran and Lorna Stevens

Introduction

In this chapter we adopt a 'stream-of-scholarly-consciousness' approach in order to evoke the romantic spirit of the utopian marketplace. In using the word 'romantic' we mean to suggest that rather than reflecting the external reality of the retail landscape of the Powerscourt Townhouse Centre we seek to describe the experiential and emotional response that it engenders in us. As we browse around the Powerscourt Townhouse Centre, a festival marketplace in Dublin, we use the concepts of Mikhail Bakhtin to light our way and highlight the utopian aspects of our experience. Our exploration becomes a spellbinding journey around a place which is pure theatre, pure entertainment; where players and spectators intermingle in a brilliant and dazzling fiesta; and where desires float freely in a perfect mixture of fantasy and reality. Sometimes it is the vibrancy and variety of the place, sometimes the fascination of the people and sometimes the lure of the products themselves that capture our collective imagination and send it soaring towards the dizzy heights of the Powerscourt atrium. Here in the heart of this theatre of dreams the utopian flame burns brightly, kindling our hopes and desires as we stroll in a postmodern haze of illusion and reality.

Dallying with Bakhtin

Mikhail Bakhtin, the supremely gifted Russian literary critic and cultural theorist (Brown et al. 1997), is described as the philosopher of discourse and human communications (Danow 1991). It is therefore particularly appropriate that his concepts should illuminate our understanding of the marketplace. After all, at the heart of the marketplace there is usually the 'buzz' of communications between buyers and sellers, the barter and banter over the exchanges taking place. Indeed, the significance of market exchange has always gone well beyond economic considerations. Mumford (1961), for example, has drawn our attention to the fact that even in Greek times the 'agora' was more than just a place for sale and exchange. The market square, this focus of community, this intersection of different cultures, has always been a liminal space where sacred and secular, mundane and exotic, local and global have mixed in an exciting and intoxicating cocktail (Goss 1993; Stallybrass and White 1986). Here is present the hustle and bustle of community, the possibility of chance meetings, the lure of the bargain, the discovery of a 'hidden gem', the exoticism of unusual fruits and spices, the babble of strange voices, the curiosity of unfamiliar bodies and new faces. Accordingly, then, many connotations of the strange, the unusual, of 'otherness', have gleamed through and beyond the market's more mundane transactions, and this is where the market's transformative, transgressive, and hence utopian, potential lies (Moylan 1986; Sargisson 1996).

Bakhtin (1968) recognised this essential quality of the market, its air of excitement and celebration, its promise of (good) fortunes, fun and fantasy; indeed, he was the first theorist to capture the market's spirit with the phrase 'the utopian marketplace'. He believed that the medieval marketplace provided an alternative to everyday life, a 'second life' for the townspeople. The marketplace with its frequent carnivals and performances, its festive atmosphere, readily created a place where the drudgeries and cares of life could be suspended, albeit temporarily; a place where a 'utopian realm of community, freedom, equality and abundance' could be entered.

Although in many respects our many modern retailing forms have now largely eclipsed the traditional market, its soul flourishes still in the utopian elements which remain undimmed. In fact, recent commentators on the shopping mall have noted that this is very much the case (Chaney 1990; Goss 1993; Kowinski 1985; Langman 1992). Like the carnivals and fairs of old, the mall's utopian environments still provide an alternative to normality; a space where everything is negotiable and anything is possible; where desires may be satisfied; where products or goods are transformed from simply satisfying wants to the communication of meaning.

There can be little doubt that, increasingly in our modern consumer society, shopping has become a spectator sport, a recreational pastime providing not only sensory but emotional stimulation (Campbell 1987). A shopping trip may be an exploration and adventure where the promise is in the journey rather than in the destination itself (Gabriel and Lang 1995). Browsing behaviour may both be an end in itself (Bloch et al. 1989) or an intrinsically pleasurable experience in its own right, with consumer goods holding out a promise of what might be, of endless possibilities to fulfil one's dreams and fantasies. In Debord's (1994) 'society of the spectacle' consumers are no longer perceived as rational problem solvers but rather as pleasure seekers who search for sensations through the experiential aspects of shopping (Bloch and Bruce 1984). Indeed, these multisensory aspects are central to hedonic consumption (Hirschman and Holbrook 1982). A purchase, therefore, may frequently be less important than the overall experience, with the desire for, rather than the actual purchase of goods, often serving as a bridge to displaced hopes and ideals (Belk 1996; McCracken 1988) and the joys of longing rivalling those of actual gratification (Campbell 1987).

The 'festival marketplace' is downtown's answer to the suburban mall (Maitland 1985) and indeed, in many ways it encapsulates the spirit of the traditional marketplace. Characterised by a historic and theatrical atmosphere, its very name recalls the marketplace so vividly described by Bakhtin, drawing as it does for its atmosphere on a historic setting. Here the emphasis is on an informal and relaxed style of shopping. There are few necessities to purchase; any goods that may be seen as a little out of the ordinary, including luxuries, are given precedence (Reekie 1993). Through entertainment and a profusion of eating areas a venue is created which attempts to offer the excitement and fun of the fairs of bygone eras. The festival marketplace is in many respects the epitome of theatre, a place where consumers may be simultaneously players and spectators. It is, therefore, considered to best illustrate the nature of recreational shopping, a majority of its visitors coming purely to browse and 'soak up' the experience (Maynard and Milligen 1995).

The voyage to utopia

In this chapter we would suggest that the experiential and emotional qualities of these visits are kindled by the utopian flame that burns brightly at the heart of such a marketplace; which like Abrams's (1953) lamp radiates around and within, casting an encircling, enhancing and all-embracing life-glow to the people and objects on which it casts its light. This is a flame which sparks our poetic imaginations into fashioning and projecting passion into a simple shopping experience, thereby hallowing the commonplace, what Wordsworth was moved to describe as 'the simple produce of the common day' (Bloom 1971).

We very much would agree with Hirschman and Holbrook (1992) who suggest that all consumer behaviour can be regarded as a text in search of interpretation and we bring our sensory and cultural responses to bear as an integral part of that interpretation. Consequently, we think it is appropriate that we use Mikhail Bakhtin's literary concepts, in this case specifically his concepts of *chronotope*, *carnivalesque*, *heteroglossia* and *polyphony*, to highlight this utopian propensity, as we go on our own exploration of a festival marketplace, the Powerscourt Townhouse Centre in Dublin.

During this quest we ourselves make use of a literary technique, stream-of-consciousness, to better capture the mood of the utopian marketplace and convey its essential spirit to our readers. Stream-of-consciousness is a technique which seeks to record the random flow of impressions through a character's mind (Peck and Coyle 1984). One of its best-known devotees was,

174

of course, James Joyce who used it in *Ulysses* (1922) to present, among other things, the complexity of a Dublin day. One of the principal points about this method is that it acknowledges the complexities and chaos of the human mind. This makes it a particularly fitting technique to use in conjunction with Bakhtinian thought which attempts to comprehend the complex human factors that make dialogue possible (Clark and Holquist 1984). Perhaps equally importantly, however, as self-confessed romantics, this technique also permits us to give free rein to the expression of our imaginations, thereby attaining what Frye has described as an expanded consciousness (Holbrook 1996: 33). Romanticism is all about the manifestion of innermost thoughts and the internal made external; it is about the overflow of expression that Lord Bryon so aptly described as the 'lava of the imagination' and Wordsworth referred to as the 'spontaneous overflow of powerful feelings' (see Abrams 1953). In recognition, therefore, of our blend of this expressive technique and Bakhtin's concepts we have called our approach 'stream-of-scholarly-consciousness' as we reach out and engage you, the reader, in our utopian dialogue.

The magic kingdom

Powerscourt Townhouse Centre is indeed magical. Like the fabulous Morean island of Utopia, it too is a serendipitous finding, just off Clarendon Street in Dublin city centre, which is like falling out of time into a more perfect world. This is the retail magic that Crawford (1992) refers to, where a spellbinding atmosphere presents another world, 'a utopia of consumption', both a no-place (ou-topia) and yet a place of happiness (eu-topia); a place where consumers are free to fantasise about what Belk et al (1996) have referred to as 'myself-that-could-be'. Here imaginative and imaginary desires are given precedence over material ones. It is the dream world referred to by Williams (1982) where consumers are an audience to be amused through entertainment and where arousal of 'free-floating desire' is as important as any purchase.

The Bakhtinian notion of *chronotope* can deepen our understanding of how Powerscourt achieves these utopian effects, this transposition to a better world of multiple possibilities, multiple shopping experiences. The concept of chronotope is the manner in which time and space are conceived by an author. It is the organising centre for the fundamental narrative events in a novel. Chronotope gives the meaning that shapes the narrative through the representation of events in certain ways; it provides a primary point from which scenes may unfold. Often, for example, normal laws of time and space may be suspended, transformed, broken or dissolved in accordance with the achievement of desired 'special effects' (cf. Brown 1998; Brown et al 1997).

Just as the classic travellers to those utopian lands portrayed by More (1516), Bellamy (1887) and Morris (1890) were temporally and spatially removed from the present, so too for the Powerscourt explorer time and space are distanced from the present. Powerscourt is like becoming cocooned in multiple

Figure 9.1 The front entrance

Figure 9.2 The front entrance hall

Figure 9.3 Nodding people, talking people

Figure 9.4 The stage and grand piano

time warps which are compellingly contradictory, delightfully disorientating. It conveys the impression, illustrated so lucidly by Eco (1986), of entering and leaving time in a spatio–temporal haze where the centuries are confused. As we enter the impressive portals of the Powerscourt Townhouse Centre, have we in fact gone back in time and are we in Lord Powerscourt's elegant Dublin residence built in 1774? As we falter for a moment in the original front hall with its regally severe Georgian lines, its black and white marbled floor and cold period fireplace, the family portrait bearing down on us says 'yes' (Figs 9.1, 9.2). However, a moment later, through the beckoning door on the far side of the hall, we're on the threshold of a dream. Like Alice we've passed through the looking glass into another time, another space, which is neither past nor present; a 'paraxial realm', the space behind the image where anything may happen (Jackson 1981). We enter a 'consumer wonderland' (Carter 1984), a space full of hope, at once a longing for the past and a promise for the future. Our eyes feast on the colourful and buzzing marketplace that has taken over the inner sanctum of the Powerscourt mansion. Our vision sweeps upwards to the lofty atrium, then round the white, wrought iron balustrades which enclose balconies ablaze with cafés, restaurants, signs, canopies, flowers, foliage and, of course, people, lots of them: talking people, nodding people, gesticulating people, watching people, people-watching-people (Fig. 9.3). This is a spectator's paradise. Are we in a Georgian courtyard (the architecture)? A piazza in Italy (*La Piazza*, the Italian restaurant)? A square in Holland (the Haagen Daz stall)? A diner in America (the *Whistle Stop Café*)? Or then again are we at a night at the opera? The grand piano on centre stage suggests we might be (Fig. 9.4). Yet the tall brass Victorian street lamps casting a gentle glow in the air around us suggest otherwise. Agnew's (1986) 'worlds apart', the marketplace and the theatre, with their long-standing metaphorical connections and symbiotic coexistence in medieval fairs and festivals (Davis 1991) are again drawn together; here in Powerscourt they merge into a single world apart.

The Land of Cockaigne

All our desires are here in abundance, in this utopian cornucopia of leisure shopping. Powerscourt creates a land of plenty in which to eat, drink and be merry, or then again, to simply pass through, browse and dream. This is the utopianism of 'The Land of Cockaigne', a popular poem about a mythical land where food and drink flow freely all year round; a poem that paints in words what Bruegel paints on canvas. It is Morton's (1969) 'topsy-turvy' Utopia of the Folk, full of what Bakhtin (1968) describes as 'popular laughter'. The concept of the *carnivalesque* is for Bakhtin a world-turned-upside-down where everyday norms are questioned and even ridiculed; where fools become wise and the sacred is profaned; where a poor man can become a king. Traditionally the carnival, literally 'a farewell to flesh', is a festival which is devoted to riotous amusement and revelry, a celebration of worldly pleasures to be followed by a period of abstinence. This joyous, inverted world existed, therefore, in opposition to the official, the serious, the ecclesiastical; in the carnival there is a wholesale transfer from the elevated, spiritual plane to the material and bodily reality of life, a fantasy of consumption (Hutcheon 1983). It also celebrates invention and human creativity and opens up liberating possibilities, freeing us from the constrictions of the 'humdrum' and educating our desires (Gardiner 1993). The carnival is an idiom of social experimentation where utopian fantasies are performed and collective desires for a better world are expressed (Bristol 1985).

The festival marketplace, then, offers an indulgence in worldly pleasures, a suspension of responsibilities, an opportunity for pleasures which we partake of in the knowledge that the real world of denial awaits us when we leave. We enter the festival marketplace, this utopia of consumer desires, and willingly suspend our disbelief as we are seduced by a myriad of pleasures, identities and choices. Like the nominally impossible utopia, the carnival provides a conceptual space in which to play with the imagination, and Powerscourt too provides a space where anything may happen, anything goes. It is a space within which to fantasise and dream away the dissatisfactions of everyday existence by inverting the normal order of things; by putting wrong to right and transforming ugliness into beauty. This festive air of excitement and anticipation is palpable as we gaze into shop windows which hint at potential transformations and (financial) transgressions. We feel the enticement of the electric blue wig in *Wigwam*; the pampering softness of the *Buttercup* beauty salon; the harmonious aura emanating from the *Colour-Me-Beautiful* stall. We marvel at the profusive displays of antiques and crafts; the sparkling opulence of *Joseph Appleby*, the diamond jeweller, and *Patrick Flood*, the goldsmith. We try to resist the extravagant lure of the many designer labels.

On centre stage the pianist sings 'Candle in the Wind'. The lingering melody weaves into the atmosphere. People pause to listen awhile. 'And it seems to me you lived your life, like a candle in the wind', drifts onwards and upwards floating into the atrium. In a fleeting, melancholy moment we pay our respects to Marilyn, goddess of desire. As we wander on, our eyes become captivated by the picture galleries on either side as we are drawn into faraway lands of golden sands and glistening white domes. Undoubtedly this shopping experience is about feelings, fantasy, and, yes, it is fun! It is indeed Hirschman and Holbrook's (1982) hedonic consumption. This, however, is a flame that will never die. This is the flame of desire where wanting rather than having produces the pleasure (Belk *et al.* 1996; Campbell 1987; McCracken 1988); this is Campbell's (1987) 'mentalistic hedonism'. It is also a utopian flame, for the essence of utopia is desire, desire for a different and better way of being (Levitas 1990); a flame which is perpetually fuelled by our fantasies as we consciously and unconsciously rearrange reality and our place in that reality (Geoghegan 1987).

Dream lover

One of Powerscourt's richest treasures is the kaleidoscopic palette that it offers browsing shoppers to inwardly sketch exciting and potential alternatives to our own everyday lives. Imagined pleasures are often more enjoyable than their real-isation and so the modern consumer becomes a 'dream artist' whose restless dissatisfaction with reality is the backcloth against which these fantasies are woven (Gabriel and Lang 1995). Utopian thinking is born from dissatisfaction, this strain between what is and what might be (Plattel 1972); it too pushes us forever onward in search of new and better possibilities, stretching the bound-aries of our illusions and continually stimulating fresh hopes and desires (Hunter and Hunter 1975).

An essential part of Powerscourt's utopian spectrum is the diverse choices of potential dream worlds it proffers to the consumer; a 'pick and mix' utopian selection, so to speak. To better illuminate the effectiveness of this rich diver-sity we can draw on Bakhtin's understanding of *heteroglossia*. This concept is used by Bakhtin to show that language is not an abstract or unified system as tra-ditional Saussurean linguistics suggests. Instead, it is always in a state of flux; meanings are never singular or uncontested but plural, debatable, contradictory and open to multiple interpretations as sites of perpetual struggle. Heteroglossia is the multiplicity of voices, the actual languages, which are spoken at any one time by speakers of a particular language. Social groups and classes, generations, men and women, professional groups, trades people or ethnic groups, all take their own particular meanings and connotations from words and phrases. In this way the concept of heteroglossia embraces subtleties in a language ranging from large dialectical differences to the slang of the year or the slogan of the hour (Dentith 1995). Bakhtin categorised authors, schools and genres accord-ing to whether they supported this struggle in language and allowed the various competing voices to interact with each other (the heteroglot novel), or whether they sought to conceal these differences and discords to one single voice (the monoglot novel) (Clark and Holquist 1984).

Like the heteroglot novel Powerscourt's environment revels in variety; it invites and even welcomes differences, diversities and, indeed, deviations from the norms of everyday shopping. Its two entrance points epitomise its het-eroglossian elements. The imposing, original Georgian entrance to Lord Powerscourt's residence, leading through the empty and deserted front hall, evokes our Anglo-Irish aristocratic ancestors long since vanquished and van-ished (Figs 9.1, 9.2). In stark contrast, the 'other', the original back entrance with its crude flagstones, is nowadays the more welcoming, an intriguingly narrow passage, through stalls teaming with flowers, fruit and jostling bodies which leads us to the 'people's marketplace', now victorious and vibrant (Fig. 9.5). Here many voices ring out; there are many parts for many players in the scenes that unfold before our eyes. High art (*Solomon Galleries*) and low art (*Blazing Salads*, the vegetarian restaurant's logo); urban (*Dublin's Fair City*

Figure 9.5 The other entrance

Sandwich Bar) and rural (*Ow Valley Farms, Co Wicklow*); professional (*Patrick Flood, Designer Goldsmith, Fellow of the Institute of Professional Goldsmiths*) and trade (*Keys-Cut-Here*); all are intermingled. Voices from the past (*Courtville Antiques*) and voices from the present (*Pzazz Hair Design*); voices from near (*Dublin Craft*) and voices from afar (*Chompy's Deli Restaurant*); all are intertwined. The black and white artistry of Giles Norman's photographic prints stands shoulder to shoulder with the multi-coloured Athena reproduction prints next door. We can search through the contemporary bric-à-brac in the nooks and crannies of the *Banana Tree* or gaze into the mists of Irish mythology at the *Handmade Irish & Celtic Jewellery Stand*, just opposite. It is here, with this eclectic mix of goods that the ancient and utopian spirit of the marketplace is once again recreated (Fig. 9.6).

All the world's a stage

Yet in Powerscourt there is very much a unity in this diversity and the many multifaceted sides produce a glorious and tantalising whole. In this festival marketplace it is the total experience that matters. This is an environment which

Figure 9.6 The Banana Tree

should not be fragmented or atomised into constituent and analysable elements for this is an environment where the whole is indeed greater than the sum of its parts. It is the overall quest in a place like this, the journey itself, which involves and engrosses the consumer together with its concomitant daydreaming, its mixture of fantasy and reality, which offers us something better into which to escape for a while. This, however, is not the prescribed and pre-determined extravaganza of a Disneyland, condemned by Marin (1984) as a 'degenerate utopia', reflecting only the values unique to American society; a place where the voice of its author/narrator (Walt Disney) shuts out other voices. No, Powerscourt is a place that has been conceived through the aesthetics of *polyphony*, a Bakhtinian concept closely linked to heteroglossia. Polyphony means that as well as many voices the narrator's voice is not dominant but only one among many. Its artistic goal is to simultaneously conceive the various contents of the world by means of several voices which do not fuse in one consciousness. Rather, they co-exist on different registers generating a dialogic dynamism between themselves (Malcuzynski 1983). Polyphony constitutes an ensemble of voices, each expressing different themes, yet harmoniously conceived as a totality; it includes others and allows difference; the voices of characters and that of the narrator engage in an unfinished dialogue.

Powerscourt is truly polyphonic. It is like a multi-melodic performance with many different individual voices harmonising within the same production. This is a 'heterotopia' to represent a postmodern vision of utopia, where community is based on the inclusion of differences, where different forms of talk are allowed to exist simultaneously and where heterogeneity does not inspire conflict (Siebers 1994). Here we have the voices of the 'Dubs' themselves, mingling with the 'culchis' in from the country, the Northerners down for a day's shopping and the more exotic voices of the many foreign tourists: Americans, Spanish, Germans, Italians, who gather together in Powerscourt. Here, also, there are no conspicuously contrived traffic flows, no carefully targeted anchor stores with 'perfect' layouts, no fantasies carved out in advance for us. Instead we have controlled chaos, organised disorganisation. Powerscourt is for the postmodern consumer whose self-identity is an ongoing consumption project continuously in flux and in flight from the status quo (McCracken 1987). In this environment we as consumers can choose and shift between a wide range of narratives and identities in a never-ending dialogue between the ideal selves portrayed through marketing images and the self-ideals to which we aspire. Whatever our guiding metaphor for consumption activities (Thompson et al. 1994), there is the thrill of endless possibilities and desires to be found by us and for us in Powerscourt. This is pure entertainment where utopian function is privileged over utopian format; where we are presented with what utopia would feel like rather than shown how it would be organised (Dyer 1977). We too can take the stage and step into the spotlights to become the star of our own show, as we create our own utopian visions and act out our fantasies and daydreams.

So we are at once both spectator and player in the changing vistas which surround us. See how now for a moment the inner courtyard of Powerscourt, with its tiered windows overlooking the movement of people below, recalls an innyard. The inn, the travellers' rest, was traditionally an oasis of calm within which to rest and play awhile.[1] Like Shakespeare's Globe, with its motto *Totus Mundus Agit Histrionem* ('all the world's a stage'), this is a world within a world, a stage upon which exchanges, interchanges, play and interplay occur. This is a dialogic world where 'we' as consumers create our own meanings which are never stable as they ripple on to the next word, the next sentence, the next pause, the next intake of breath. As we stroll around this shopping paradise our eyes flicker and we imagine a delightful Elizabethan spectacle occurring before us within the restrained symmetrical lines of the Georgian façade which frames it. Simultaneously we are onlookers in the galleries and players on the stage, observing the action unfolding from above, or participating in the consumer experiences on offer at ground level below. And, indeed, this may be reversed, as the galleries are themselves observed from below, as a multiplicity of scenes are enacted tier upon tier, layer upon layer, above us. The distinction between illusion and reality becomes increasingly blurred, the symbolic subverts the material, as we focus on consuming this exhilarating experience in Powerscourt, a truly postmodern utopian marketplace.

> For in and out, above, about, below
> 'Tis nothing but a magic shadow-show
> Play'd in a box whose Candle is the sun,
> Round which we phantom figures come and go.
> The Rubaiyat of Omar Khayyam

Note

1 With its windows facing into the entertainments on offer in the courtyard below, the galleried inn was the blueprint upon which early theatre was based (Burgess 1970).

References

Abrams, M.H. (1953), *The Mirror and the Lamp: Romantic Theory and the Critical Tradition*, Oxford: Oxford University Press.

Agnew, J.C. (1986), *Worlds Apart: The Market and the Theatre in Anglo-American Thought 1550–1750*, Cambridge: Cambridge University Press.

Bakhtin, M. (1968), *Rabelais and His World*, Cambridge, MA: MIT Press.

Belk, R.W. (1996), 'On aura, illusion, escape and hope in Apocalyptic consumption: the apotheosis of Las Vegas', in S. Brown, J. Bell and D.J. Carson (eds), *Marketing Apocalypse: Eschatology, Escapology and the Illusion of the End*, London: Routledge, 87–110.

Belk, R.W., Bilkent, G.G. and Askegaard, S. (1996), 'Metaphors of consumer desire', *Advances in Consumer Research*, 23, 368–73.

Bellamy, E. (1986 [1887]), *Looking Backward*, New York: Penguin.

Bloch, P.H. and Bruce, G.D. (1984), 'Product involvement as leisure behaviour', *Advances in Consumer Research*, 11, 197–202.

Bloch, P.H., Ridgway, N.M. and Sherrell, D.L. (1989), 'Extending the concept of shopping: an investigation of browsing activity', *Journal of the Academy of Marketing Science*, 17 (Winter), 13–21.

Bloom, H. (1971), *The Visionary Company: A Reading of English Romantic Poetry*, Ithaca: Cornell University Press.

Bristol, M.D. (1985), *Carnival and Theater: Plebian Culture and the Structure of Authority in Renaissance England*, New York: Routledge.

Brown, S. (1998), *Postmodern Marketing Two: Telling Tales*, London: ITBP.

Brown, S., Stevens, L. and Maclaran, P. (1997), 'Mucha do about nothing: literary theory, the Bakhtin Circle and postmodern marketing communications', *Proceedings of Three American Marketing Association Special Conferences*, Dublin, 12–15 June, 774–86.

Burgess, A. (1970), *Shakespeare*, London: Jonathan Cape.

Campbell, C. (1987), *The Romantic Ethic and the Spirit of Modern Consumerism*, Oxford: Basil Blackwell.

Carter, E. (1984), 'Alice in the consumer wonderland: West German case studies in gender and consumer culture', in A. McRobbie and M. Nava (eds), *Gender and Generation*, Basingstoke: Macmillan, 185–214.

Chaney, D. (1990), 'Dystopia in Gateshead: the Metrocentre as a cultural form', *Theory, Culture and Society*, 7(4), 49–68.

Clark, K. and Holquist, M. (1984), *Mikhail Bakhtin*, Cambridge, MA: Harvard University Press.

Crawford, M. (1992), 'The world in a shopping mall', in M. Sorkin (ed.), *Variations on a Theme Park*, New York: Hill and Wang, 3–30.

Danow, D.K. (1991), *The Thought of Mikhail Bakhtin*, London: Macmillan.

Davis, T.C. (1991), 'Theatrical antecedents of the mall that ate downtown', *Journal of Popular Culture*, 24(4), 1–15.

Debord, G. (1994), *Society of the Spectacle*, New York: Zone Books.

Dentith, S. (1995), *Bakhtinian Thought: An Introductory Reader*, London: Routledge.

Dyer, R. (1977), 'Entertainment and utopia', *Movie*, 24 (Spring), 2–13.

Eco, U. (1986), *Travels in Hyperreality*, London: Pan Books.

Gabriel, Y. and Lang, T. (1995), *The Unmanageable Consumer*, London: Sage.

Gardiner, M. (1993), 'Bakhtin's carnival: utopia as critique', *Utopian Studies*, 3(2), 21–50.

Geoghegan, V. (1987), 'Marxism and utopianism', in G. Beauchamp, K. Roemer and N.D. Smith (eds), *Utopian Studies*, Lanham, MD: University Press Of America, 37–51.

Goss, J. (1993), 'The "Magic of the Mall": an analysis of form, function, and meaning in the contemporary retail built environment', *Annals of the Association of American Geographers*, 83(1), 18–47.

Hirschman, E.C. and Holbrook, M.B. (1982), 'Hedonic consumption: emerging concepts, methods and propositions', *Journal of Marketing*, 46 (Summer), 92–101.

Hirschman, E.C. and Holbrook, M.B. (1992), *Postmodern Consumer Research: The Study of Consumption as Text*, Newbury Park, CA: Sage.

Holbrook, M.B. (1996), 'Romanticism, introspection, and the roots of experiential consumption: Morris the Epicurean', in R.W. Belk, N. Dholakia and A. Venkatesh (eds), *Consumption and Marketing: Macro Dimensions*, Cincinnati, Ohio: South-Western College Publishing, 20–82.

Hunter, D. and Hunter, H. (1975), 'Siddhartha and a Clockwork Orange: two images of man in contemporary literature and cinema', in P.E. Richter (ed.), *Utopia/Dystopia?*, Cambridge, MA: Schenkman Publishing, 125–42.

Hutcheon, L. (1983), 'The carnivalesque and contemporary narrative: popular culture and the erotic', *University of Ottowa Quarterly*, 53(1), 83–94.

Jackson, R. (1981), *Fantasy: The Literature of Subversion*, London: Routledge.

Kowinski, W.S. (1985), *The Malling of America*, New York: William Morrow & Co.

Langman, L. (1992), 'Neon cages: shopping for subjectivity', in R. Shields (ed.), *Lifestyle Shopping: The Subject of Consumption*, London: Routledge, 40–82.

Levitas, R. (1990), *The Concept of Utopia*, New York: Philip Allan.

McCracken, G. (1986), *Culture and Consumption*, Bloomington: Indiana University Press.

McCracken, G. (1987), 'Advertising: meaning or information?', in P.F. Anderson and M. Wallendorf (eds), *Advances in Consumer Research*, 14, Provo, UT: Association for Consumer Research, 121–4.

McCracken, G. (1988), *Culture and Consumption: New Approaches to the Symbolic Character of Consumer Goods and Activities*, Bloomington: Indiana University Press.

Maitland, B. (1985), *Shopping Malls: Planning and Design*, London: Construction Press.

Malcuzynski, M.P. (1983), 'Mikhail Bakhtin and contempory narrative theory', *University of Ottowa Quarterly*, 53(1), 51–65.

Marin, L. (1984), *Utopics: The Semiological Play of Textual Spaces*, trans. R.A. Vollrath, Atlantic Highlands, NJ: Humanities Press International.

Maynard, P. and Milligen, J. (1995), *Retail Leisure and Tourism: A Report Prepared by the English UK Tourist Board and Jones Lang Wootton*, London: Verby Print.

More, T. (1965 [1516]), *Utopia*, London: Penguin.

Morris, W. (1993 [1890]), *News From Nowhere and Other Writings*, London: Penguin.

Morton, A.L. (1969), *The English Utopia*, London: Lawrence and Wishart.

Moylan, T. (1986), *Demand the Impossible: Science Fiction and the Utopian Imagination*, New York: Methuen.

Mumford, L. (1961), *The City in History*, New York: Brace and World Inc.

Peck, J. and Coyle, M. (1984), *Literary Terms and Criticism*, Basingstoke: Macmillan.

Plattel, M.G. (1972), *Utopian and Critical Thinking*, Pittsburgh, PA: Duquesne University Press.

Reekie, G. (1992), 'Changes in the Adamless Eden: the spatial and sexual transformation of a Brisbane department store 1930–90', in R. Shields (ed.), *Lifestyle Shopping: The Subject of Consumption*, London: Routledge, 170–94.

Reekie, G. (1993,) *Temptations: Sex, Selling and the Department Store*, Perth: Allen and Unwin.

Sargisson, L. (1996), *Contemporary Feminist Utopianism*, London: Routledge.

Siebers, T. (1994), *Heterotopia: Postmodern Utopia and the Body Politic*, Michigan: The University of Michigan Press.

Stallybrass, P. and White, A. (1986), *The Politics and Poetics of Transgression*, Methuen, London.

Thompson, C.J., Pollio, H.R. and Locander, W.B. (1994), 'The spoken and the unspoken: a hermeneutic approach to understanding the cultural viewpoints that underlie consumers' expressed meanings', *Journal of Consumer Research*, 21 (December), 432–52.

Williams, R. (1982), *Dream Worlds: Mass Consumption in Late Nineteenth-Century France*, Berkeley, CA: University of California Press.

10

IN SEARCH OF THE LOST AURA

The object in the age of marketing romanticism

Benoît Heilbrunn

Comment des choses se jettent-elles en avant dans une masse sensorielle continue?
(Pascal Quignard, *Petits Traités*, I, XII, 'Le mot de l'objet')

To design is to transform prose into poetry.
(Paul Rand, *Design, Form and Chaos*, 1993)

Introduction

In his 'The work of art in the age of mechanical reproduction', Walter Benjamin (1936) shows how art objects have lost part of their original meaning and authenticity due to their ever increasing reproduction and diffusion. The reproduction of art objects goes together with the loss of authenticity, uniqueness and distinctiveness which considerably reduces their propensity to surprise, fascinate and thus to illuminate. What Benjamin said about art objects in 1935 seems to apply exactly to today's everyday objects and especially to products, brands and discourses created and diffused by marketers. Due to an extreme process of standardisation, these so-called objects seem to have lost their meaning, that is, their authenticity. The aim of this chapter is to suggest some conditions under which marketing could romanticise our dull everyday lives surrounded by undifferentiated products and discourses. The analysis is mainly based on the concept of 'aura', as developed by Walter Benjamin. The conditions under which aesthetic and functional properties of objects may be reconciled, so as to create 'auratic objects', are fixed. The parallel drawn between art objects and marketed objects thus accounts for the possibility for marketers to rethink and redesign 'illuminating' objects.

Duchamp, du signe, du sens

In 1917, the French artist Marcel Duchamp created a scandal by exhibiting at a famous exhibition in New York a public urinal, which was to become the very first *ready made* object. Duchamp's artistic gesture intended to show that manufactured objects such as bicycle wheels, dustbins or chairs could arbitrarily be promoted as works of art and thus be exhibited in musems and exhibitions, depending on the discretionary power of the artist (Thevoz 1980). This historical artistic posture is very significant as regards the status of the work of art in contemporary society. Duchamp's aim was to question the difference which had been made since the Renaissance between the craftsman and the artist. This social mythification of the artist responded to a diffused and collective aspiration which corresponded to the gradual deChristianisation of Western societies who transferred their religious fervour to art. Museums have replaced places of pilgrimage and now represent, for the tourist industry, much more than a cultural alibi: a cultural tribute, a sacred legitimisation (ibid.: 148). Duchamp therefore aimed at a substantial and self-deconstructive activity by promoting standardised objects as artistic. This blurring of genres together with a deconstruction of symbolic hierarchies illustrate the shift of art into industry, thereby leading to a collapse of the boundaries between art and everydaylife. The correlated expansion of the role of art within consumer culture led to the famous 'aestheticisation' of everyday life promulgated by Featherstone (1991) and others (e.g. Morace 1990). This movement has been said to be one characteristic of the postmodern condition (Lyotard 1979). Be it modern, postmodern, over-modern (!) or even none of those, the American philosopher John Dewey had already pointed out the fact that art is not something special but a significant part of everyday experience and that real understanding of life is synonymous with aesthetic enjoyment. The aesthetic dimension has gained importance within the area of mass consumption, which means that visual and sensory aspects have gained an increasing importance in terms of consumer preference and choice for many products: clothes, cars, kitchen appliances, etc. The consumer has shifted from *homo economicus* to *homo aestheticus* (Ferry 1990) in the sense that sensory and aesthetic dimensions have gained much more importance in consumer's choice than they used to. Together with this, our time is based on the concept of reproducibility which goes together with the concepts of authenticity, authority and originality. There seems to be a loss of meaning in consumer objects mainly due to the conjunction of two factors: (1) a societal move from craftsmanship to industrialisation which leads to the serialisation of objects, and (2) a marketing approach based on the design of objects which respond most closely to consumer needs and therefore exclude a surprise effect.

The problem we want to raise here may thus be summarised as follows: how to reconcile the necessary standardisation of objects which is intrinsically linked to the consumer society and the need for objects which are still able to communicate an aesthetic dimension even though they are widely reproduced and copied?

The object in the age of reproducibility

First, it is necessary to go back to the dilemma posed by industrialisation and the necessity of reproducing identically any object across time and space. As Benjamin remarked in 1931, the object has lost in contemporary society the status of originality and of unicity. In his article 'The work of art in the age of mechanical reproduction' (1936), Benjamin interprets two kinds of art: auratic and mechanical. Traditional art, he argues, possessed an aura of authenticity which surrounded the original – non-mechanically reproducible – work, endowing it with qualities of 'uniqueness', 'distance', and 'otherness'. These auratic qualities of the original, humanly crafted work of art elicited a meditative response from the onlooker which enabled him or her to transcend time and to perceive the beauty of the work of art as a quasi-eternal moment of completion. Benjamin traces this auratic dimension of art back to its magico-cultic origins in primitive history (Kearney 1994: 164). He invokes the theological idea of a collective psyche (*anima mundi*) which could generate recurring archetypal images and thereby transcend the limits of normal time. He further identifies these auratic images with Goethe's *Urphänomene* (eternal forms that recur through history), Baudelaire's *correspondances* (an aesthetic conflation of spiritual and material meaning) and Leibniz's *monads* (the idea that each autonomous consciousness somehow precontains the totality of experience within itself in crystallised form) (Kearney 1994: 164). The distinction made by Benjamin between handcrafted and technological art is expressed in two different kinds of experience: 'auratic' *Erfahrung* or integrated narrative experience and technological *Erlebnis* or atomised, fragmented experience. *Erlebnis* exemplifies the loss of the sense of traditional wisdom and communal narrative. Thus, the rise of radio and electronic media spells the death of linear, narrative coherence by promoting a form of dislocated information and simulation which communicates in isolated sensory moments – in 'shock of novelty', as Benjamin described it – subversive of the auratic qualities of contemplative distance and uniqueness (Kearney 1994: 164-5). Whereas *Erfahrung* provides an experience of the beautiful in which the ritual value of art appears through an authentic aura of the work of art which depends on its being embedded in the fabric of sacred tradition, the technologically reproduced work demands an immediate accessibility:

> The social bases of the contemporary decay of the aura . . . rests on two circumstances, both of which are related to the increasing significance of the masses in contemporary life. Namely, the desire of contemporary masses to bring things 'closer' spatially and humanly, which is just as ardent as their bent toward overcoming the uniqueness of every reality by accepting its reproduction. Unmistakably, reproduction as offered by picture magazines and newsreels differs from the image seen by the unarmed eye. Uniqueness and

permanence are as closely linked in the latter as are transitoriness and reproducibility in the former . . . The adjustment of reality to the masses and of the masses to reality is a process of unlimited scope, as much for thinking as for perception.

(Benjamin, 1936: 216–17)

Mechanical reproduction emancipates the work of art from its traditional dependency on 'authentic originality', and excludes no one from the art of communication. Dispensing with the idea of a single 'original', the photographic print or film reel – any number of which can exist – makes cultural experience available to anyone who wishes to participate:

> The technique of reproduction detaches the reproduced object from the domain of tradition. By making many reproductions it substitutes plurality of copies for a unique experience. And in permitting the reproduction to meet the beholder or listener in his own particular situation, it reactivates the object reproduced. These two processes lead to a tremendous shattering of tradition which is the obverse of the contemporary crisis and renewal of mankind.
>
> (ibid.: 215)

Owing to the serialisation process, the unicity of objects is seriously jeopardised and the value of authenticity (*Echtheit*) is virtually destroyed. But what is in fact the main difference between the original work of art and its multiple reproductions? What is changed according to Benjamin is not the original *per se* but the relationship between the public and the original work of art. He calls this difference, 'aura', a sort of halo which infuses the work of art, a kind of immaterial atmosphere which provides the original with a character of originality. A work of art is always created at a particular moment, in a particular place, in a unique manner, and this unicity explains in some way the mystery surrounding ancient works of art which can be found in cultural places, churches and other sanctuaries. They seem to keep the secret of their past splendour and the effect they may have produced on the ones who contemplated them. Benjamin reminds us that, historically, art is linked to ritual and magical practices that our civilisation seems to have forgotten. Any tradition is based on the transmissibility of authenticity; the aura of a work of art, and the function of the rite are precisely to help this transmission of an old heritage (Jimenez 1997: 360). Modern reproduction techniques no longer need this traditional mediation: they act according to speed and simultaneity. They are not concerned with an aura which they can neither preserve nor communicate. Our era thus seems to be solely concerned with the functions of reproduction, exchange, exhibition and transaction. The progressive decline of the concept of aura means that works of art lose their cultural value and are attributed an exchange value which makes them as negotiable as any other consumer goods.

The brand's dilemma

Brands are very interesting in this perspective because they at the same time glorify and annihilate the concept of authenticity, being based on a paradoxical combination of contradictory functions. The first role of brands goes together with a psychology of simplification in the sense that brands play a labelling function which reassures consumers by assuming a homogeneity of quality and consistency over time and space. A brand indicates that the endorsed product or service is identical wherever and whenever it is bought. The brand first acts as a label of authenticity which proves that the product meets all requirements and expectations and therefore eludes any surprise. The psychological and economic power of brands is based on an ability to reproduce *ad infinitum* a consumer experience. This ability of the brand to duplicate an experience in some way explains most loyalty patterns. On the one hand, the brand reassures consumers because they know who manufactures the product, where it comes from, etc. Herein lies the main paradox of brands in the sense that the brand plays the role of a sign which guarantees the origin and authenticity of the offer through a possibility of duplication, whereas authenticity originally supposes unicity and the impossibility of any duplication. The brand reduces the distance and originality, and cancels any possible surprises, pleasant or not. On the other hand, a brand does not boil down to an authenticating function. Together with a simplifying function, the brand plays a complexifying function, in the sense that it has to surprise consumers and to create emotional value. Consumption cannot be reduced to functional expectations because it also includes emotional and existential benefits which sometimes even exceed utilitarian expectations, as illustrated by Hirschman and Holbrook (1982). As emotions and affects *a priori* exclude standardisation, it is necessary for brands to innovate, that is to de-standardise, to surprise, that is, to break codes and rules. The brand has to innovate in order to inject value on the market and it thus needs to surprise consumers with new products, images, messages, shapes, colours, etc. The paradoxical role of the brand, as related to the concept of authenticity, may therefore be summarised in the following manner: a brand must erase all surprise (reassurance function) by reducing to the utmost the distance between consumers and the product (distance is here considered as both a physical distance and a psychological distance), and it must simultaneously create the greatest possible distance between consumers and products (innovative function) so that consumers are surprised. The paradox of the brand is that it must at the same time create and abolish distance. We would now like to tackle this 'distance dilemma' by showing that marketers may still be able to create 'auratic' objects.

A marketing versus an aesthetic credo

To assert that marketing is able to create enjoyable or aesthetic objects might seem at first glance contradictory to marketers' main mission and philosophy.

The standard approach to marketing assumes that marketers should research the needs of their target markets and design products accordingly. Here is for instance the way a product is defined in a now very standard textbook: 'a product is anything that a firm offers to satisfy the needs or wants of consumers' (Doyle 1994: 34). The current ideology is that a company is successful in so far as it meets the current and potential needs of customers more effectively than its competitors. The marketer is therefore not concerned with the expression of aesthetic beliefs, but with the understanding of consumer expectations. Marketing is thus by its very nature built on an 'ideology of reception' (it is necessary to identify customers' expectations) and not on an 'ideology of expression'.

Moreover, value is not conceived as something which stands out from the manufactured product, but rather appears as constructed through a sequential process. This value creation process is very often decoded, analysed and implemented through a temporal process (as illustrated for instance in the concept of value chain) in which the value of goods is collectively co-constructed, co-accepted and co-digested. In this perspective, value is essentially grasped as a programmed differential process (to be 'valuable' means more or less to be 'different'), which in fact often leads to a lack of creativity, inventivity and imagination. This credo is for instance expressed in one of the few 'customer value basics' identified by Naumann: 'customer value expectations are formed relative to competitive offerings' (Naumann 1995: 24).

The concept of differentiation which has infused marketing practices is in this perspective very interesting, because to be different always means more or less to differ, to be different from other beings; it is as if any object could not emerge *per se* and could only exist in a differential network, through a series of relationships of oppositions and resemblances with other objects. In this perspective there seems to exist no seminal object, but only a series of differences (*simulacra*, as Baudrillard would say) which are promoted to capture value on the market. This approach to value which is nothing less than praise of a kind of anti-chaos order necessarily raises the following question: has marketing really lost (or just never had!) a capacity to illuminate? This issue appears all the more problematic when one compares the marketing credo with the aesthetic credo. The latter is more or less based on the expression of a subjectivity through various forms and senses, which explains why the modern conception of art is very strongly linked to the notion of subjectivity. An art object is above all something which was made by an artist and which expresses a kind of interior voice. This assumption does not imply that the meaning of the work of art only lies in an expressive gesture: the status and meaning assigned to a work of art also largely depend on its reception, i.e. the social, economic, cultural and intellectual conditions under which the work of art is received (Jauss 1978). This brief comparison sets out the question regarding the ability of marketers to design objects which can be enjoyed for themselves and not only because they meet consumers' needs. The issue we want to address now is whether marketing and aesthetics are really incompatible.

The need to romanticise everyday objects

The penetration of science and technique into our daily environment has eliminated most technical barriers to the production of objects. New forms and functions can now be used, thus enlarging the field of possibilities and the creative abilities of designers. An increasingly competitive environment has increased the use of new technical and creative possibilities in design. The conjunction of these two factors has led to three major challenges related to the status of objects in contemporary society:

1   Consumer objects have experienced a crucial disjunction between matter and form. Matter – which is always considered the solid, stable, inert counterpart of ideas – has, thanks to huge technological progress, become pliable and capable of being moulded into any possible form (Manzini 1995: 222). New forms and functions are now possible. This phenomenon, often related to a dissemination of worthless products, leads to an impoverishment of sensory experience, of superficiality and of loss of relations with objects. It is for instance possible to consider that at the beginning of the nineteenth century, a four-person family of average income was surrounded by 150 to 200 objects at most, including crockery and clothes. Nowadays, a similar family would have about 2,500 to 3,000 objects (Branzi 1988), including electrical appliances and decorative objects. A person is said to come into daily contact with approximately 20,000 products. Design has an essential role in giving meaning to objects, doing so by the shapes, colours and materials of the object. As Lorenz reminds us, 'in a world where many new products are similar in function, components and even performance, a product's design – its shape, its look, and above all its image – can make all the difference'. The role of designers is to semantise, that is, to differentiate the product, in other words to make consumers love the product in the sense that love was defined by George Bernard Shaw as 'a gross exaggeration of the difference between one person and everybody else'.
2   Consumers are immersed in an uncontrolled number of signs and confronted with the phenomenon of semiotic pollution. Designers have to invent products and design signs that can survive in a consumption and societal environment saturated with products and signs.
3   The reproducibility of objects inevitably leads to the fading of meaning of most everyday objects which have just become mere commodities and have thus lost their substance.

Design and the re-enchantment of experience

Design infuses every object in the consumer world and gives form to immaterial processes such as goods, services, etc. In a culture of 'doing', it becomes essential to determine why and for whom things are designed and produced. Giorgio Vasari (1511–74), an Italian painter and architect, author of the famous *Lives of the Painters, Sculptors and Architects*, was one of the first artists to attempt a definition of painting through the concept of design. Drawing (*disegno*), he writes, means the art of outlining figures by means of appropriate curves. In most marketing textbooks the concept of 'design' is either completely ignored, or fallaciously presented as a mere dimension of the product. The meaning of design is nevertheless much more profound. As an English word, 'design', which appeared in 1588 as a modern derivative of the Latin *designare*, means to mark or point out, delineate, contrive. 'Design' also come from the French *désigner*, to indicate or designate, and can be defined as planning for action or miniature action. In a broad sense, Simon defines design in the following manner: everyone designs who devises a course of action aiming at changing existing situations into preferred ones (Simon 1969: 55). It is interesting to note that the French word 'design' has two antecedents which cast light on its meaning; design is related to both *dessein* (project, invention of a plan of action, constructive forethought) and *dessin* (drawing). Design thus means both to plan out in systematic, usually graphic, form and to create or contrive for a particular effect or purpose.

Design can also be understood as the manipulation of content through form and vice versa. Even though content is the raw material of design, form, in turn is the reorganisation of content, in the sense that 'to form' is to fix visual relationships in a given space. Therefore design is much more than simply to assemble, to order, or even to edit: 'it is to add value and meaning, to illuminate, to clarify, to modify, to dignify, to dramatize, to persuade, and perhaps even to amuse. To design is to transform prose into poetry' (Rand 1993: 3).

Design activity is part a Promethean activity which consists in the production of both material and immaterial artefacts from which we build our everyday environment (Manzini 1995). The designer's role is to make the world habitable in both utilitarian and existential terms. The increasing importance of design for consumers is related to the growing importance of images in contemporary culture which become a persuasive means of motivating people to express themselves. The social exchange of goods is essentially a symbolic process which enables people to communicate through the medium of objects. With consumer society, objects lose their material and functional status by their integration into sign systems. Consuming is defined by Baudrillard as the organisation of material substance into signifying substance: 'to become an object of consumption the object must become a sign' (Baudrillard 1968: 277). Products have meaning not solely as objects, but also as elements of a vast sign system, through a process of semantisation. Consumers thus invest products and brands with personal and emotional values. There are basically two kinds of values associated with objects: utilitarian values and existential values. An object is seen as essentially utilitarian when it is perceived by the user as mainly serving particular functions (electrical goods, furniture, kitchen appliances, etc.). The effectiveness with which objects fulfil these functions plays a large part in their evaluation, and much consumer behaviour is directed at searching for information about such effectiveness. The role of design is to convey an impression of effectiveness, solidity, through appropriate features, colours, and materials. Objects may also have existential connotations in the sense that they are designed and marketed to convey such connotations as emotional value, importance to the individual, etc. The design of products and signs necessarily has to take into consideration the various types of existential values related to the consumption of objects. These might include such values as social values (the product design might indicate that the user belongs to a given social category), emotional values (the product design has to arouse feelings and affective states), and epistemic values (the ability of the product to arouse curiosity and to provide novelty). The latter refers to the necessity for consumers to live new experiences through the use of products which provide innovative combinations of shape, materials, colours, etc. The importance of these existential values in the choice of products and brands, and therefore in the way consumers perceive the design of products, is also related to hedonic consumption which has become a new paradigm of consumption. Hirschman and Holbrook (1982) have identified the main characteristics of this hedonic consumption process, that is, first, emotional desires prevail over utilitarian motivations in the choice of products and services, and second, consumers may project on to a product a subjective meaning which exceeds by far the real attributes this product may actually possess. The consumption of products does not thus refer any longer to an act of destruction effected by the consumer, but rather as an experience in which the priority is given to affective factors.

Broadly speaking, the designer is a 'modest demiurge . . . who takes charge of the daily environmental pattern in a hedonistic context where the measure of his action is the quality of life' (Moles 1989: 129). The work of a designer classically fulfils a series of functions, which have been identified by Moles (ibid.: 122–3). These functions are:

1   *Information*: the design of a product indicates what the product is and who the manufacturer is (i.e. who does what), where the product originates from, what is the product's reason for being, how much the product costs, etc.
2   *Propaganda*: the product design urges the consumer to use the product in such and such ways, and/or under such and such conditions.
3   *Consonance* of consumers with their goals and expectations: product design as well as advertising can play an *a posteriori* role, after the purchase, of strengthening consumers in their choices in relation to their images of what has value.
4   *Social consciousness*: product design often connotes signs of belonging to a given social class or socio-economic category.

These functions broadly fall into two main categories of functions which are semantic and aesthetic. Any object always embodies both a denotative message and a connotative message. Denotation refers to the fact that the object conveys information about its functions, what it stands for (semantic function), whereas connotation refers to an aesthetic dimension which conveys a subjective impression and emotion about the product (aesthetic function). Thus the tasks of the product designer are to understand what are the main expectations (functional and existential) of consumers towards the products and to design products accordingly. In other words, the designer's role is to design shapes and to use materials which schematise, strengthen and activate the desired and appropriate dimensions (solidity, resistance) valued by the target customers, given the fact that this functional dimension of the product is always accompanied by an aesthetic message.

From *exophoria* to euphory

It is widely accepted that the shape of an object more or less follows its function. The shape of objects indicates the possible use(s) of the object (what the object stands for), hence for instance the work on ergonomy. This conception of the object as a tool is very utilitarian because it considers an object's value as linked to its functional utility. The shape of the object indicates its use but also adds an unescapable aesthetic dimension (there is no innocent shape!) which may contribute to the redefinition of the object. In some way the shape of an object may by far overlap its function. There is a degree of freedom which gives the designer the opportunity to disconnect (sometimes quite radically) form and function. Let's consider for example the lemon squeezer designed by Philippe Starck and which looks like a rocket, or other cooking utensils manufactured by the Italian company Alessi. These objects propose totally new approaches to such familiar objects such as bottle openers, kettles, pepper mills. By breaking the usual codes of representation, the designer opens the object to a plurality of meanings which contribute to resemantise the objects beyond their functional purpose. Thus the design of any object implies two dimensions: first, an *endophoric* dimension which guarantees that the object belongs to a certain class and organises the invariable elements and, second, an *exophoric* dimension which allows for radical formal innovation in the object category (Polinoro 1989: 69). So all the stylisation attempts at formal codifications, which do not entail the iconic convention establishing that a given object belongs to a certain category, can be said to be endophoric; on the contrary, all the iconic hybridation processes and all the attempts to resemantise objects can be said to be exophoric. On the one hand, the endophoric axis limits, crystallises and adjusts; on the other hand, the exophoric axis invents, diffuses and disorientates. The first axis makes the object recognisable and has a reassurance function, whereas the second axis destructures the object and responds to new expectations. Let us consider for instance the kettle designed by Michael Graves for Alessi: this object is very strongly exophoric because of its very cone shape which destabilises the idea of a kettle, but also because of the little bird sitting on the spout which conveys the idea of lightness and defies the geometrical rigidity of the object. Looking at the kettle for the first time, one is disorientated by an object which seriously questions its identity as a kettle and searches for a new identity outside the functional aspect (Polinoro 1989: 70).

The open object and the consumer as a reader

The exophoric work on the object leads us to question the identity of the object, that is its potential belonging to a given *a priori* category. In other words, by playing with the exophoric dimension, the designer does nothing less than break the endophoric codes so as to open the object to new interpretations. The aesthetic code is in fact the result of a dialectic between the conventional code and the innovative message (Eco 1968; Nöth 1990: 427-8). By their innovative character, aesthetic messages infringe the rules of their genre and thus negate the code. But at the same time, the new message creates a new aesthetic code: 'every work [of art] upsets the code but at the same time strengthens it, too . . . by violating it, the work completes and transforms the code' (Eco 1968). Thus Eco describes this innovative process as one of over-coding, i.e. the creation of new rules on the basis of pre-established ones. Aesthetic overcoding generates a kind of semiotic 'surplus' on the level both of content and of form. By this surplus of expression and of content, the object becomes open to multiple interpretations. The essential feature of codes and messages is, according to Eco, openness. Because of its ambiguity and the plurality of cultural subcodes, the aesthetic message has the character of an 'empty form', into which the recipient inserts meanings. The interpreter 'tries to accept the challenge posed by this open message and to fill the invisible form by his or her own codes' (ibid.: 165). An object is always more than what it was originally designed for. It might even be recoded by consumers using a code different from the one used by the creator.

There is thus no single meaning assigned to an object but, on the contrary, a plurality of meanings. An object is different from a tool in the sense that it does not necessarily boil down to a mere utilitarian function. It might be embedded within an aesthetic dimension which gives it value beyond its functional purpose, and might even sometimes totally eradicate its semantic function. The meaning of an object is not a fixed property imposed by the designer but results from a kind of negotiation between the designer/producer and the consumer/reader. This issue was addressed by Arthur Danto in his book entitled *The Transfiguration of the Commonplace*, in which he tries to explain why the facsimilés of Brillo boxes exposed by Andy Warhol in 1964 may be perceived as works of art whereas one can find almost identical objects in any supermarket:

> There was a certain sense of unfairness felt at the time when Warhol piled the Stable Gallery full of his Brillo boxes; for the commonplace Brillo container

was actually *designed* by an artist, an Abstract Expressionist driven by need into commercial art; and the question was why Warhol's boxes should have been worth $200 when that man's products were not worth a dime . . . In part, the answer to the question has to be historical. Not everything is possible at every time, as Heinrich Wölflin has written, meaning that certain artworks simply could not be inserted as artworks into certain periods of art history, though it is possible that objects identical to artworks could have been made at that period.

(Danto 1982: 44)

The other part of the answer lies in the concept of interpretation. Danto contends that if there is no aesthetic difference between the commodity and the copy made (on purpose) identical by the artist, only interpretation helps to understand this 'transfiguration' of a banal object into a work of art. Even though this approach is in many respects contestable, its main interest lies in the fact that Danto points out the importance of interpretation, i.e. the reception of the work of art, whereas most aesthetic theories usually focus on either the production of the work of art or transcendent criteria which are imposed to the spectator. The point we want to make is the fact that in some way the aesthetic status of the object lies in the viewer's eye as well as in the designer's gesture.

Walter Benjamin's 'aura' and the re-illumination of objects

Some objects may through their design redefine their original function and create an aesthetic experience which may sometimes be an emotional shock. In other words, some objects even though they are only objects may have a real aura. First, what is etymologically the notion of *aura*? Aura was first used as a medical term given by the Ancients to indicate a particular state of the body preceding either epilepsy (*aura epileptica*) or hysteria (*aura hysteria*). Aura is thus originally linked to a violent physiological experience. That is why the auratic experience differs from the experience of the beautiful. Burke (1990) made the distinction between the sublime and the beautiful in the following manner: the sublime is not only linked to aesthetic enjoyment but is also linked to a mixture of pleasure and pain. The satisfaction derived from the experience of the sublime results from an association of imagination and reason, but this particular feeling goes together with a sensation of danger, of something which seems horrible and terrible. The experience of the sublime arouses a physiological reaction. This type of reaction one might have in front of auratic objects such as the kettle previously mentioned. Aura is hence linked to a kind of transfiguration and it also means a breath or a sort of halo which envelops or stands out from a person and can only be perceived by initiated persons. In mythology the aura was used to describe some sorts of Sylphs, i.e. subtle and aerial divinities which used to frolic with the Zephyrs. In artistic terminology, aura is used to manifest what stands out from a character and serves to underline its exceptionality. The concept of aura was widely developed by Walter Benjamin in a text on the 'history of photography' (1931) and in the previously mentioned text 'The work of art in the age of mechanical reproduction' (1936). 'Aura' is defined by Benjamin as 'a unique phenomenon of a distance however close it may be' (*ein einmalige Erscheinung einer Ferne, so nah sie sein mag*). These objects designed through a marketing process have an 'aura' because they remain unapproachable and distant however close they may be. This is consistent with the etymology of the word object, *ob-jectum*, that is, something which stands in front of us with an evident resistance, something which remains exterior to us, with a definite property of strangeness and otherness (Sartre 1943). Auratic objects are able to create proximity to and distance from the viewer. Proximity because they may be used in everyday life and be appropriated by users; distance because they question their identity as functional objects and may be considered as open aesthetic objects which provide a multiplicity of potential meanings. They do not show exactly and instantly who they are, and what they are designed for. Even though they are highly visible, such objects remain in a zone of invisibility. Their power goes beyond visibility, like a sixth sense, and this contributes to the creation of a sort of double distance between the object and the viewer. This distance is what creates an aesthetic and emotional shock, the shock being for Burke what distinguishes an experience of the beautiful from an experience of the sublime. The idea of shock is fully consistent with the original medical meaning of the concept of aura which is a set of symptoms which precedes and in some way announces an epileptic crisis.

Such objects are thus much more than beautiful objects, in the sense that they offer a new perception of the world. By being auratic, an object is enjoyed *per se* independently from its functional purpose; it does nothing less than project the viewer into a new world. The object is in this case nothing like a representation of consumers' expectations and desires. It does not resemble or imitate anything except itself. The object is not an object in the world but a real 'breakthrough' in the world which lets us perceive another world (Grimaldi 1983). Through the vision of the object, another world appears. Therefore the aesthetic perception of the object is a metaphysical experience of strangeness and otherness. But through this strangeness appears a new vision of the world. The object remains inaccessible, unattainable and this inaccessibility is exactly what makes us view the world differently, with much more intensity, through a kind a glorification of our everyday experience.

Conclusion: proposals for a little philosophy of the toothbrush

Let us conclude this brief analysis with an object which illustrates the possibility of daily objects becoming auratic thanks to creative and ingenious designers. This object is a toothbrush designed by Philippe Starck for the French brand Fluocaril. The object is first presented in a semi-opaque packaging which plays very well with both visibility and invisibility, presence and distance. The object has all the recognisable features of a toothbrush, and still, it seems to look like something other than a toothbrush, a kind of old pen, for instance. Moreover, apart from its obvious aesthetic qualities, this toothbrush appears to be made of two parts: a brush and a stand. The stand is symbolically very important because it means that this object has gained autonomy, a physical autonomy in the sense that it does not have to be hung up, laid down or even hidden. The toothbrush might exist *per se*, standing on its stand and thus become a decorative object. Hence, through a resemantisation process, the object is viewed differently and it makes us see the world differently: in a sense it has gained some aura . . .

References

Baudrillard, J. (1968), *Le système des objets*, Paris: Gallimard.
Benjamin, W. (1972–89 [1931]), 'Kleine Geschichte der Photographie', *Gesammelte Schriften*, Rolf Tiedeman, Hermann Schweppenhäuser *et al.* (eds), Frankfurt/Main, Suhrkamp, Vol. II, 1, 368–85; French translation in *Etudes Photographiques*, 1, November (1996), 7–39.
Benjamin, W. (1972–89 [1936]), 'Das Kunstwerk im Zeitalter seiner technischen Reproduzierbarkeit', *Gesammelte Schriften*, Frankfurt Suhrkamp, Vol. I, 2, 471–508; translated as 'The work of art in the age of mechanical reproduction', in *Illuminations*, Hammersmith, London: Fontana Press, (1992), 211–44.
Benjamin, W. (1979), *Correspondance*, edited by G. Scholem and T.W. Adorno and translated into French by G. Petitdemange, Paris: Aubier, 2 vols.
Benjamin, W. (1997), *Sur l'art et la photographie*, Paris: Editions Carrés.
Bowie, A. (1990), *Aesthetics and Subjectivity from Kant to Nietzsche*, Manchester: Manchester University Press.
Branzi, A. (1988), *Pomeriggi alla media industria*, Milan: Idea Books.
Bucci, A. (1992), *L'impresa guidata dalle idee*, Milan: Domus Academy Press.
Buchanan, R. and Margolin, V. (eds) (1995), *Discovering Design: Explorations in Design Studies*, Chicago: the University of Chicago Press.
Burke, E. (1990 [1757 and 1759]), *A Philosophical Enquiry into the Origin of our Ideas of the Sublime and the Beautiful*, Oxford: Oxford University Press.
Courtine, J.-F et al. (1988), *Du Sublime*, Paris: Belin.
Crozier, R. (1994), *Manufactured Pleasures: Psychological Responses to Design*, Manchester: Manchester University Press.
Dagognet, F. (1985), *Rematérialiser, Matières et matérialisme*, Paris: Vrin.
Dagognet, F. (1989), *Eloge de l'objet. Pour une philosophie de la marchandise*, Paris: Vrin.
Danto, A. (1982), *The Transfiguration of the Commonplace: A Philosophy of Art*, Cambridge, MA: Harvard University Press.
Deroche-Gurcel, L. (1997), *Simmel et la modernité*, Paris: PUF.
Derrida, J. (1978), *La vérité en peinture*, Paris: Flammarion.
Didi-Huberman, G. (1992), *Ce que nous voyons, ce qui nous regarde*, Paris: Editions de Minuit.
Doyle, P. (1994), *Marketing Management and Strategy*, Hemel-Hempstead: Prentice-Hall.
Eco, U. (1962), *Opera Arte*, Milan: Bompiani.
Eco, U. (1968), *La struttura assente*, Milan: Bompiani.

Featherstone, M. (1991), *Consumer Culture and Postmodernism*, London: Sage.

Ferry, L. (1990), *Homo Aestheticus. L'invention du goût à l'âge démocratique*, Paris, Grasset.

Floch, J.-M. (1988), 'The contribution of structural semiotics to the design of a hyper-market', *International Journal of Research in Marketing*, 4, 233–52.

Francastel, P. (1956), *Art et technique aux XIXème et XXème siècle*, Paris: Èditions de Minuit.

Grimaldi, N. (1983), *L'art ou la feinte passion. Essai sur l'expérience esthétique*, Paris: PUF.

Hirschman, E.C. and Holbrook, M.B. (1982), 'Hedonic consumption: emerging concepts, methods and propositions', *Journal of Marketing*, 46 (Summer), 92–101.

Holbrook, M.B. and Hirschman, E.C. (1982), 'The experiential aspects of consumption: consumer fantasies, feelings and fun', *Journal of Consumer Research*, 9 (September), 132–40.

Hottois, G. (1997), *De la Renaissance à la Postmodernité. Une histoire de la philosophie moderne et contemporaine*, Brussels: De Boeck Université.

Jauss, H.R. (1978), *Pour une esthétique de la réception*, Paris: Gallimard.

Jimenez, M. (1997), *Qu'est-ce que l'esthétique?*, Paris: Gallimard.

Kearney, R. (1994), *Modern Movements in European Philosophy*, 2nd edn, Manchester: Manchester University Press.

Lyotard, J.-F. (1979), *La Condition postmoderne. Rapport sur le savoir*, Paris: Editions de Minuit; published in English, 1984, *The Postmodern Condition: A Report on Knowledge*, Manchester: Manchester University Press.

Manzini, E. (1995), 'Prometheus of the everyday. The ecology of the artificial and the designer's responsibility', *Design Issues*, 9(1) (Fall), 5–20; reproduced in R. Buchanan and V. Margolin (eds), op. cit., 1995, 219–43.

Margolin, V. (ed.)(1989), *Design Discourse: History – Theory – Criticism*, Chicago: The University of Chicago Press.

Millet, C. (1997), *L'art contemporain*, Paris: Dominos, Flammarion.

Moles, A. (1989), 'The legibility of the world: a project of graphic design', *Design Issues: History, Theory, Criticism*, 3(1), 43–53; reprinted in V. Margolin (ed.), op. cit., 1989, 119–29.

Morace, F. (1990), *Controtendenze: una nuova cultura del consumo*, Milan: Domus Academy.

Naumann, E. (1995), *Creating Customer Value. The Path to Competitive Advantage*, Cincinnati: International Thomson Publishing.

Nöth, W. (1990), *Handbook of Semiotics*, Bloomington: Indiana University Press.

Polinoro, L. (ed.) (1989), *L'officina Alessi/L'atelier Alessi*, Crusinello, F.A.O.

Rand, P. (1993), *Design, Form and Chaos*, New Haven and London: Yale University Press.

Rochlitz, R. (1992), *Le désenchantement de l'art. La philosophie de Walter Benjamin*, Paris: Gallimard.

Saint Girons, B. (1993), *Fiat Lux. Une philosophie du sublime*, Paris: Quai Voltaire.

Sartre, J.-P. (1943), *Being and Nothingness: A Phenomenological Essay on Ontology*, New York: Philosophical Library.

Simon, H. (1969), 'The science of design: creating the artificial', in *The Sciences of the Artificial*, Cambridge, MA: MIT Press, 55–6.

Steiner, G. (1989), *Real Presences. Is There Anything in What We Say?*, London: Faber and Faber.

Thevoz, M. (1980), 'Art et société', in C. Delacampagne and R. Maggiori (eds), *Philosopher*, Vol. 2, Paris: Fayard/Presses Pocket, 147–53.

Van Raaij, F. (1993), 'Postmodern consumption', *Journal of Economic Psychology*, 14(3), 541–63.

11

ADVERTISING ILLUMINATION

Romantic roots of postmodern promises

Paul Power and Barbara B. Stern

Postmodernism's liberatory potential cannot yet be achieved. The reason for this delay is the growing influence of the market – which is a modern institution.

(Firat and Venkatesh 1995: 245)

while the marketing literature is nothing if not voluminous, it has to be said that the essential enchantment of the marketplace still eludes us.

(Brown 1997: 2)

We propose that the 'essential enchantment' of the marketplace is still elusive because the current era is an age of transition, a time when modernism and postmodernism coexist, albeit uneasily. Many postmodern advertisements eschew informational appeals – the mainstay of the modern advertising tradition – in favour of imagery, endowing mundane products with magical, mystical, and otherwordly qualities. None the less, products related to information technology – computers, for example – epitomise the triumph of science, logic, and rationality. They also epitomise the commoditisation of technical products, and advertising aims at preventing them from 'looking like the interchangeable commodities they really are' (Manes 1997: F-7).

This can be done by providing technical information about features, often even when the features are of 'dubious value', such as backlit buttons and massive speakers. It can also be done by using imagery that associates the product with fun, fantasy, or feelings – bypassing a rational appeal to focus on a romantic one.

This rational–romantic tension pervades postmodern culture, which draws from romantic roots to mount its critique of the Enlightenment, the critique of the cultural principles characteristic of modern society that trace their legacy to the eighteenth century (Cahoone 1996). When advertisements present both information and imagery, this tension is actualised by the juxtaposition of the cardinal tenets of modernism (faith in reason, universal truth, and scientific knowledge) with those of postmodernism (acceptance of the irrational, toler-ance of divergence, and scepticism about science).

Advertisements for products associated with information technology are especially convoluted, for electronic communication is itself both mysterious and explainable. Even though the origin of products that enable electronic communication was made possible by scientific endeavours, the diffusion and adoption of these products challenge beliefs about the self that underlie the rationalist tradition. One such belief is the assumption of fixed identity and a stable self, characteristic of the modern (and pre-deconstructive) condition. In contrast, under postmodern conditions, persons exist in a state of continuous construction and reconstruction (Gergen 1991: 6–7). At present – a millennial moment – both modern and postmodern concepts intertwine in advertisements aimed at persuading consumers to purchase information technology products. Despite the fact that these products (Borgmann 1984) are at the 'heart of the postmodern market culture' (Firat and Venkatesh 1995: 251; Sherry 1987), they have not yet penetrated the mass market to the extent that they are present in every home.

Market overview: the electronic community

Let us begin with an overview of the market for information technology, just now poised to penetrate the mass market. Growth has been rapid, with the World Wide Web attracting 150,000 new users per month (Pitkow and Recker 1994) and now totalling over 35 million users worldwide (Weber 1996). In terms of diffusion theory, Internet usage has expanded beyond the innovative segment of computer adepts to the group of early adopters, who precede the mainstream majority in adoption of innovations. According to Nielsen Media Research (1996), whereas 23 per cent of the innovators – long-time users whose usage pre-dates August 1995 – identified themselves as 'computer pro-fessionals', only 11 per cent of newcomers do so. The 'newcomers' represent a 1990s' phenomenon, for although 70 per cent of the long-timers have used a computer for five or more years, only 59 per cent of the newcomers began using computers before 1990. In addition, access to the Internet is not neces-sarily a function of computer ownership, for whereas 88 per cent of long-timers own a computer, only 72 per cent of newcomers do.

Demographic differences among the long-timers versus the newcomers are legion. As usage has spread from a small niche market to a broader population segment, users have become a more diverse group. For example, whereas 67 per cent of long-timers are male, only 60 per cent of newcomers are. Further, although 56 per cent of long-timers are highly educated (college degree), only 39 per cent of newcomers fall into this category. And, although 27 per cent of long-timers are affluent (households with incomes of over $80,000), only 17 per cent of newcomers are. Thus, Internet use is expanding beyond the primarily male, highly educated, affluent innovators and beginning to make inroads into the early adopter segment, which is becoming more female, less highly educated, and less affluent. Note that although the female segment is increasing, it is not yet fully tapped. The diffusion of product use from a small group of sophisticates to a larger and more mainstream segment is facilitated by advertising, perhaps the most important means of influencing the majority market.

The purpose of this chapter is to present a detailed examination of one such advertisement to demonstrate the tension between romantically rooted postmodern themes and rationally driven informative data. It uses literary analysis to identify five postmodern themes and trace the mystical elements derived from romanticism and then presents a deconstructive reading to describe the clash between romantic (postmodern) imagery and rationalist (modern) information.

The justification for a close reading of a single exemplar (Stern 1996) is twofold. First, it makes general postmodern themes (Firat and Venkatesh 1995) specific by presenting evidence of the themes' history, attributes, and functions. A view through the literary lens allows insight into the debt that these themes owe to the romantic tradition and their difference from modern themes that dominate informational advertisements. Second, it makes the generalisation that advertising is a 'communication arena in which human reality is mediated' (Mick and Buhl 1992: 317) specific by focusing on the mediation process. This focus reveals the process of constructing and reconstructing reality by means of close investigation of a single product-specific text. That is, the analysis moves from the general to the specific to demonstrate the way that 'postmodern themes' and 'mediated reality' work in a real-world exemplar.

Close reading: postmodern themes and romantic roots

The exemplar is a two-page print advertisement for a Sony personal computer that appeared in computer and lifestyle magazines as part of a $15 million campaign in Fall 1996 to launch the firm's new PC (see Figure 11.1). The target market was identified as current PC owners, and the campaign was designed to persuade them to trade up (Johnson 1996). Although the advertisement did not mention price, we comparison-shopped for computers and found the Sony PC to be in the same $2,500 to $3,000 price range as other popular brands such as Dell and Compaq. However, whereas most of those brands use informational advertisements that emphasise features, price, and/or service, the Sony advertisement takes another tack. It includes both informational and evocative elements, but does so via an unusual physical layout that reverses the central/peripheral binary commonly found in advertisements for high-tech products. In this exemplar, the information is peripheral and the imagery is central. The picture and copy take up the entire horizontal two-page spread, displacing technical information about the computer by relegating it to a subordinate and lateral position.

Beginning with the evocative elements, note that the largest part of the

Figure 11.1 Advertisement for Sony PC

picture is a fantasy scene (two androgynous individuals occupy a desolate land-scape and gaze in wonder at discarded technical artefacts such as an old-fashioned computer monitor and keyboard, an oscilloscope, and a rabbit-ears television antenna). Even the product picture and name ('pc by sony') are smaller than the scene, and although placed in an eyecatching position (upper left corner), most of the headline area is empty space between the picture/name and the brand name ('SONY', in the upper right corner).

The copy, below the PC in the picture, continues the evocative appeal, for the copy is a four-line poem, in free verse (our numbering):

1   the future will become vivid
2   spreadsheets will crumble before creativity
3   information will marry entertainment
4   they will have many children

The trademark Intel Pentium logo appears in the lower right corner, and the Sony phone number and web site Universal Resource Locator (URL) are in the lower left. In contrast to the dominant picture and its accompanying poem, a narrow vertical sidebar contains a list of product features and technical infor-mation. It is important to emphasise that the sidebar can only be read if the reader turns the entire magazine sideways, for it is a half-inch strip placed along the left side of the left page that reads from left to right, rather than from top to bottom. Thus, the placement of the informational part of the message makes it awkward to access, unlike the picture and poem, which are easy to see and read. That is, rather than emphasising features (see Resnick and Stern 1977) as an informational message would, the advertisement aims at a more transforma-tional representation to convey 'the experience of using (consuming) the advertised brand' in a manner not typically associated with the brand experience (Puto and Wells 1984: 638).

Because the technical information is in a subordinate position, the advertise-ment requires doubly effortful reading – the reader must first expend mental energy to decode the romantic allusiveness and must then expend physical energy to access the information. To decode the romantic/postmodern themes, we use Stern's method of textual analysis originally found in literary criticism (1988a, 1988b, 1989a, 1989b, 1991). Stern (1988a) introduced the idea of advertising as literary text, and Scott (1994) emphasised the importance of visual elements to the rhetorical goal. In our exemplar, literary analysis is justi-fied by the nature of the copy – it is a poem. To examine it in detail, let us begin by considering the five postmodern themes identified by Firat and Venkatesh (1995).

1 Hyperreality

The first line of the poem – 'the future will become vivid' – announces the 'hyper' and 'hyped' theme of a vision of intensified reality 'more' real than real life could ever be. The picture and text work together to mediate reality (Mick and Buhl 1992) by reconfiguring it as a futuristic 'revelation, to the regenerate eye, of a new Heaven and earth' (Abrams 1971: 426). The new world is made vivid by the light emanating from the Sony PC. This vision stems from the romantic preoccupation with the moment of ecstasy, a staple of poetry from Wordsworth to the 'Beats'. Recall that this group of 1950s' poets (Jack Kerouac, Allen Ginsberg, Lawrence Ferlinghetti and others) considered 'beat' the diminutive of 'beatific', an ecstatic state of altered reality induced by mystical religious experiences and/or mind-bending substances (hallucinogens, marijuana, alcohol, and so forth).

No matter how induced, the ecstatic moment of illumination is marked by the perceiver's feeling of temporal discontinuity – linear time seems to be attenuated, foreshortened, stopped, or completely gone. The foundation of intensely experienced reality is a disregard for the constraints of time and space, which mire people in the here and now. The advertisement depicts an illuminated Moment (Brown 1997) in which time is not a progressive flow but, rather, a static instant. It does so by showing the conflation of past (landscape artefacts), present (product), and future (central figures) captured in the beam of light coming from the PC. Linearity is replaced by destabilisation of chronological reality to represent an epiphany of 'charismatic revelation in the commonplace or trivial object' (Abrams 1971: 385). The Sony PC is the 'commonplace' object that serves as an agent of revelation by illuminating the dead past. The ground-level collection of discarded objects symbolises the domain of earthly reality (Mick and Buhl 1992) mediated or reconstructed by the Sony monitor's light shining down from a higher (heavenly) region.

The illuminated Moment (Abrams 1971; Brown 1997) is a neo-romantic construct, part of the cultural system that contextualises the advertisement (Sherry 1987). It was first popularised by the early romantics, and it has taken on new life in the twentieth century in absurdist drama (Esslin 1969) and Cubist art (Janson 1962). Visual and literary art represent these moments to demonstrate the influence of subjective time, which often fixates on the ideal past (as in nostalgia) or the equally ideal but not-yet realised future. In the advertisement, Sony's 'technologies of simulation' provide the power for the light cone, which represents the superior future shining down on the rubble of the past.

The futuristic human figures embody the theme of hyperreality. They are harlequins, a class of characters whose ambiguity projects so many conflicting meanings that they can be interpreted according to any previous construction or reconstructed in a new way (Bauman 1993). They give physical form to Rimbaud's 'credo of disordering, of derangement, of mixture' (Brown 1997:

13), itself a characteristic of the nineteenth-century French romanticised harlequin (as opposed to the more buffoonish English counterpart) (Welsford 1961). Harlequins have long been associated with cultural reinvention, for although they originated as clowns in ancient drama, over the centuries they have come to exemplify shape-shifting powers and mutability (Welsford 1961). The costumes of the figures in the Sony advertisement reflect the Renaissance influence, notably that of actors in the Italian *commedia dell-arte*, identifiable by their motley patches, shaved heads, and masked faces. The figures also wear motley garb (bodysuits with multicolored triangular patterning), have closely cropped sleeked-back hair, and sport oversized eyeglasses that reveal/conceal just as do masks. Their huge eyes (like those of Picasso's characters in *Les Demoiselles d'Avignon*, see Janson 1962), reveal puzzlement and wonder as they discover the landscape of concealed and half-buried objects – 'abused and broken remnants of other people's lives' (Hamilton 1970: 387).

Their eyeglasses, like Derrida's 'blinds' (Kamuf 1991), both reveal and conceal their eyes – windows on the soul. The glasses reflect the monitor screen's illumination, which directs attention to the contrast between old modernist products and the new offering. In this way, a spiritual moment of illumination – the instant at which the glories of the new PC burst in on the consumer's mind – is given physical form by a spotlight. This acts as visible signification of a 'revolution in seeing', one which enables a perceiver to see a familiar object anew (Abrams 1971: 411). What happens is that the 'manifold magic kingdoms of hyperreal estate' (Brown 1997: 11) become one of 'surreal estate' when the computer's rays highlight the modernist wasteland.

2 Fragmentation

In this wasteland, every object is cut off 'from its context in the ordinary world and in common experience' (Abrams 1971: 419). The theme of fragmentation is visibilised by the collection of objects 'disconnected and disjointed in their representation from each other, their origins and history, and contexts' (Firat 1991). It serves as a postmodern manifestation of the romantic yearning for 'a long, immense, and calculated disordering of all [the] senses' (Rimbaud 1963: 268). In marketing terms, fragmentation disrupts mundane reality by defamiliarising ordinary objects so that they appear less mundane. In so far as computers are commodity products differentiated, when at all, by 'features of dubious value' (Manes 1997: F-7) 'the advertisement emphasizes fantasy rather than features and uses temporal, spatial, and social disjunctures to convey the special style of the Sony brand (Meyrowitz 1985).

The triple repetition of the brand trademark – the mysterious inscription 'VAIO' – demonstrates the separation of signs and signifiers that is an aspect of spatial disjuncture. It appears on the pedestal holding the Sony monitor, on the upper portion of the speaker tower, and on the upper part of the blonde figure's arm. The trademark functions as a detachable consumption sign that broadly references style and fashion rather than as a label that merely indicates legal ownership of a trademark (Firat and Venkatesh 1995). VAIO associates style with products and people. It is an emblem of the computer's stylishness (squared-off lines, clean edges, bright colours) as well as of the harlequins' fashionableness (eyeglass frames, skin-tight apparel, footgear, make-up). Visual reiteration of the first copy line's promise ('vivid future') is provided by the background colours (orange and blue) against which VAIO stands out on the monitor screen and the characters' clothing.

The use of a brand identifier to erase a distinction between the human and the product domain reflects mechanistic consumption, a condition in which people's actions are 'necessitated and imposed by the natures of the products they use' (Firat 1991: 72). Multiple appearances of VAIO attached to humans and objects alike categorise all things as fragmentable – able to be broken down into parts and moved, rearranged, and reclassified at will (Firat and Venkatesh 1995). In the romantic tradition, the power to fragment came from the poet-composer – the 'seer' (Rimbaud's label) who recreated the parts/whole dynamic to achieve 'gnosis – the revelation of absolute novelty' (Abrams 1971: 417). Hegel's metaphor compares the fragmenting process to a 'gradual crumbling' away of the old world order prefatory to the illuminated Moment when 'lightning, all at once reveals the edifice of the new world' (Hegel 1977 [1807]: 380). The advertisement implies that a Sony product empowers this new world, with the triple repetition of VAIO serving as the electronic trinity that (re)integrates all things in one.

3 Decentred subject

Reintegration follows fragmentation and is signified by the androgynous new humans in the guise of harlequins. Their sexual mutability reflects decentred identity, a notable characteristic of the postmodern individual (Gergen 1991) who engages with the hyperreal Internet culture. Cyberspace is so anonymous that people can shift sexual identity at will, for 'the self is multiple, fluid, and constituted in interaction with machine connections; it is made and transformed by language; sexual congress is an exchange of signifiers; and understanding follows from navigation and tinkering rather than analysis' (Turkle 1995: 15).

The postmodern theme of decentred individuals is made visible in the advertisement by means of the androgynous figures, whose philosophical lineage is traceable to Paracelsus (see Brown 1997) and earlier esoteric writers in the mystical tradition. The androgyne is the ideal prelapsarian human, one 'who reunites the two sexes into the unitary form they had exhibited before their separation' after the fall of Lucifer (Abrams 1971: 160). Prior to Lucifer's expulsion from Heaven (ibid.: 160), unfallen beings possessed the attributes of both sexes and were Godlike, complete in themselves.

The romantics were especially attracted to the myth of primal innocence, viewed as an ideal state destroyed by the sexual division of humans into male and female. Although this myth was central to the mystical view of the universe, it was discredited by Newtonian science. However, Coleridge and later romantics (Abrams 1971) revived it, praising androgyny as a return to innocence. To the romantics, androgynes epitomised the ideal of unfallen humanity in a state of primal innocence, for they perfectly unified the formerly (and sinfully) divided forces of maleness/femaleness, spirituality/materiality, and mind/body.

Even though the advertisement's harlequins are androgynes situated in the future world rather than the past one, they retain the characteristics that define decentredness. Far from having fixed identities, harlequins are sexually fluid, temperamentally mutable, perpetually in the process of 'newing and improving' themselves. Historically the harlequin is 'wholly a creature of make-believe, without background' (Welsford 1961: 309) and, as such, a perennially open character not tied to a specific context, shape, or sex. The advertisement, like many postmodern texts, uses sexual terms to depict decentredness, for the figures show both male and female consumption affinities. That is, they wear lipstick, nail polish, and rings with large stones, yet also sport mannish hairdos and unisex costumes. The blonde appears to be somewhat more feminine (the shadows on her midsection suggest the outline of breasts), and the brunette appears more masculine. However, each could be male, female, or both, for they resemble those harlequins in French theatrical fantasies who appeared as half-male/half-female and shifted from one sex to the other (ibid.). Gender-bending is postmodernised in the advertising fantasy, an allusion to the indeterminate sexual community of electronic intercourse (Turkle 1995).

The concomitant of androgyny that has made it so appealing to postmodernists is the deprivileging of patriarchal authority that occurs when masculinity and femininity are co-equal. The advertisement implies sexual equality (rather than hierarchy) in that it does not establish masculinity as an indicator of superiority (Goffman 1979). Note that whereas the figure on the right is the more apparently female one, she is also larger, more upright, and more detached from her surroundings than the one on the left. That is, although her appearance is more female, she occupies a position more usually taken by male advertising figures. The implication is that discarding gender fixity frees individuals from hierarchical sex roles and the patriarchal assumption of male dominance (Heller 1993). In marketing terms, the implication of female dominance may be an aspect of a targeting campaign aimed at a minority segment – women consumers of computers.

4 Reversal of production / consumption

This implication is strengthened in line 2 of the copy ('spreadsheets will crumble before creativity'), which empowers the feminine side of human nature – playful, creative, and nurturant. The line makes explicit the devaluation of modernist ideas about work as superior to play by claiming the superiority of creative activities. Derogation of business productivity (Hickey and Orta 1990) underlies the metaphoric use of 'crumble', reminiscent of Hegel's prediction that the old world will break apart so that the new one can be revealed. In the advertisement, Sony's computer is positioned as a transformational power capable of turning an instrument of production (information manipulation) into one of consumption (experiential entertainment). The recategorisation of creativity as an aspect of consumption rather than of production is a phenomenon peculiar to the postmodern era, a time when consumption has 'become the means of self-realisation, self-identification' (Firat 1991: 72), and self-expression.

However, a marketing rationale for claiming creativity as a product benefit lies in its association with Sony's competitive advantage in the electronics market. The firm is known principally as a manufacturer of entertainment-oriented electronics rather than as a manufacturer of computers, and the emphasis on the PC as an experiential tool references the firm's competitive advantage in its customary domain. In this way, an association is set up between the Sony computer and fantasy/fun rather than information processing/work, for unlike IBM, Dell, or Apple, Sony's image is not that of a leader in information technology. By reversing the importance of work/fun and the role of the computer in enhancing creativity rather than productivity, the advertisement reconfigures the product such that the Sony image becomes an advantage.

5 Juxtaposition of opposites: sex and space

Product reconfiguration is taken further in lines 3 and 4 ('information will marry entertainment/they will have many children') by means of the marriage metaphor, the most striking instance of the postmodern habit of juxtaposing 'anything with anything else' (Firat and Venkatesh 1995: 255). The metaphor mixes machines and humans in its anthropomorphisation of the product. By endowing a computer with sexual powers – procreation is the metaphoric ground – the concept of reproduction is transferred from the animate world to the inanimate one, extending the abstract opposites in line 2 (work/play) to the sexual domain. When the abstractions are recast as gender differences, work = information = masculinity, and creativity = entertainment = femininity. The merger of opposites results in hybrid offspring that break down category barriers such as male/female, text/border, future/past, production/consumption, and subject/object. Humanising the Sony computer endows it with sexual qualities and establishes it as the locus of childbearing – a mechanical womb.

The boundary-less state calls for a deconstructive reading, especially since Derrida used words such as

> conception, formation, gestation, and labor . . . with a glance toward the operations of childbearing – but also with a glance toward those who . . . turn their

211

eyes away when faced by the as yet unnamable which is proclaiming itself and which can do so, as is necessary whenever a birth is in the offing, only under the species of the nonspecies, in the formless, mute, infant, and terrifying form of monstrosity.

(1993 [1966])

The merging of sexual identity and the poetic marriage of opposites itself juxtaposes the terrifying yet exciting aspects of creation.

In so far as juxtapositions are a condition of the postmodern world, the expectation of a clear and comprehensible outcome no longer obtains. Whereas the modernist New Critics presumed eventual clarification of ambiguous pairings and the structuralists presumed eventual reconciliation of binaries, post-structuralists accept disjuncture, inconsistency, and irreconcilable opposites. Derrida (1993 [1966]) is the most outspoken champion of irreconcilability (Stern 1996). Despite the controversial relationship between deconstruction and romanticism (see Graff 1980; Norris 1983; Scholes 1974), Berman's genealogy is pertinent: 'Deconstruction in America has, in effect, continued on the path into romanticism along which we followed the New Critics; it has attained the point where all language is like poetry, specifically romantic poetry' (1988: 278). Looked at this way, juxtapositions reaffirm inevitable conflicts, unstable meanings, and confusions, and advertising is the holy writ that reveals Rimbaud's 'credo of disordering' (Brown 1997: 13).

This credo guides spatial and temporal domains in addition to the sexual one. In the advertisement, the spatial layout confounds informational and evocative appeals. Indeed, the layout can be interpreted as a parody of informational messages, for it makes the pictorial fantasy central and the product features marginal (Stern 1996). This disrupts the expected peripheral and central functions of borders and text in this product category by marginalising information and highlighting imagery. The placement of fact and fantasy in positions opposite from the usual ones forces the information-oriented consumer to engage in physical effort by turning the magazine sideways. In addition, figure and ground (the picture's sterile landscape versus the poem's praise of fertility) compete for the background/foreground position. In sum, the Sony advertisement mediates reality – or, more accurately, hyperreality – via themes of juxtaposition, fragmentation, intensification, reversal, and destabilization (Stern 1996). Although the bundle of themes is considered 'postmodern', it is actually a reworking of ideas popularised by the romantics, who themselves discovered the basic materials in early Christian mysticism.

Conclusion: between two worlds?

Production is the dominant scheme of the industrial era; simulation is the reigning scheme of the current phase that is controlled by the code (Baudrillard 1994: 83). The co-existence of overlapped production and simulation in popular culture is expressed in the question: Is advertising a modern institution in a postmodern world? Baudrillard (1994) summarises the dilemma of overlap in a time of transition – our millennial era. He frames it as tension between 'simulacra that are productive, productivist, founded on energy, force, its materialization by the machine and in the whole system of production' versus 'simulacra of simulation, founded on information, the model, [and] the cybernetic game' (ibid.: 121). Tension extends to advertising, where the information-driven model – the dominant modernist paradigm – rubs up against the imagery-driven model of the postmodernists. Our exemplar contains both, with the romantic and mystical message more dominant than the feature-driven sidebar. However, we do not know whether consumers will be more persuaded by pictures and a poem than by product features. The consumer targeted by Sony may or may not find fantasy appealing, for as Firat and Vankatesh (1995) point out, an aspect of hyperreality is the inclination or willingness among members of the culture to realise, construct, and live the simulation (ibid.: 252). In this regard, we suggest that the Sony advertisement may demand too much by being too hyperreal and too fragmented. The difficulty in accessing product feature information puts the advertisement at odds with itself in a way that may be interesting to some consumers, but confusing to others. As Stewart and Ward (1994) remind us, there is no subtlety in advertisers' interest in advancing the norms and practices of the modern consumer society. The challenge that faces a contemporary marketer is to get its message heard above the noise of advertising clutter and media fragmentation.

References

Abrams, M.H. (1971), *Natural Supernaturalism: Tradition and Revolution in Romantic Literature*, New York: W.W. Norton.

Baudrillard, J. (1994), *Simulation and Simulacra*, Ann Arbor: University of Michigan Press.

Bauman, Z. (1993), 'Postmodernity, or living with ambivalence', in J. Natoli and L. Hutcheon (eds), *A Postmodern Reader*, Albany, NY: State University of New York Press, 9–24.

Berman, A. (1988), *From the New Criticism to Deconstruction: The Reception of Structuralism and Post-structuralism*, Urbana: University of Illinois Press.

Borgmann, A. (1984), *Technology and the Character of Contemporary Life: A Philosophical Inquiry*, Chicago: University of Chicago Press.

Brown, S. (1997), 'Tore down à la Rimbaud: the 4 Bs of marketing illuminations', in S. Brown, A.M. Doherty, and B. Clarke (eds),*Proceedings of the Marketing Illuminations Spectacular*, Belfast: University of Ulster, 1–15.

Cahoone, L. (1996), *From Modernism to Postmodernism: An Anthology*, Cambridge, MA: Blackwell Publishers, Inc.

Derrida, J. (1993 [1996]), 'Structure, sign, and play in the discourse on the human sciences', in J. Natoli and L. Hutcheon (eds), *A Postmodern Reader*, Albany, NY: State University of New York, 223–42.

Esslin, M. (1969), *The Theatre of the Absurd*, Garden City, NY: Anchor Books.

Firat, A.F. (1991), 'The consumer in postmodernity', *Advances in Consumer Research*, 18, 70–6.

Firat, A.F. and Venkatesh, A. (1995), 'Liberatory postmodernism and the reenchantment of consumption', *Journal of Consumer Research*, 22, 239–67.

Gergen, K.J. (1991), *The Saturated Self: Dilemmas of Identity in Contemporary Life*, New York: Basic Books.

Goffman, E. (1979), *Gender Advertisements*, Cambridge, MA: Harvard University Press.

Graff, G. (1980), 'Deconstruction as dogma', *Georgia Review*, 34, 404–42.

Hamilton, G.H. (1970), *19th and 20th Century Art*, Englewood Cliffs, NJ: Prentice-Hall.

Hegel, G.W.F. (1977 [1807]), *Phenomenology of the Spirit*, trans. A.V. Miller, Oxford: Clarendon Press.

Heller, A. (1993), 'Existentialism, alienation, postmodernism: cultural movements as vehicles of change in the patterns of everyday life', in J. Natoli and L. Hutcheon (eds), *A Postmodern Reader*, Albany, NY: State University of New York Press, 497–509.

Hickey, L. and Orta, I.V. (1990), 'Old infomation and presupposition in advertising language', *International Journal of Advertising*, 9, 189–96.

Janson, H.W. (1962), *History of Art*, Englewood Cliffs, NJ: Prentice-Hall.

Johnson, B. (1996), 'Sony to spend $15 mil behind home PC intro', *Advertising Age*, 24 June [On-line]. Available: http://adage.com/ns-search/news_and_feat.

Kamuf, P. (ed.) (1991), *A Derrida Reader: Between the Blinds*, New York: Columbia University Press.

Manes, S. (1997), 'In picking a computer, speed is not of the essence', *The New York Times*, (9 December), F-7.

Meyrowitz, J. (1985), *No Sense of Place: The Impact of Electronic Media on Social Behavior*, New York: Oxford University Press.

Mick, D.G. and Buhl, C. (1992), 'A meaning-based model of advertising experiences', *Journal of Consumer Research*, 19, 317–38.

Nielsen Media Research (1996), 'CommerceNet/Nielsen Internet Demographics Recontact Study March/April 1996 Executive Summary' [On-line]. Available: http://www.nielsenmedia.com/commercenet/exec.

Norris, C. (1983), *The Deconstructive Turn*, New York: Methuen.

Pitkow, J.E. and Recker, M.M. (1994), 'Results from the first World-Wide Web user survey. GVUs WWW User Surveys' [On-line]. Available: http://www.cc.gatech.edu/gvu/user_surveys/.

Puto, C. and Wells, W.D. (1984), 'Informational and transformational advertising: the differential effects of time', *Advances in Consumer Research*, XI: 638–43.

Resnick, A. and Stern, B.L. (1977), 'Analysis of information content in television advertising', *Journal of Marketing*, 41, 50–3.

Rimbaud, A. (1963), *Œuvres Complètes*, R. de Reneville and J. Monquet (eds), Paris: Pléiade.

Scholes, R. (1974), *Structuralism in Literature*, New Haven, CT: Yale University Press.

Scott, L. (1994), 'The bridge from text to mind: adapting reader-response theory to consumer research', *Journal of Consumer Research*, 21, 461–80.

Sherry, J.F. (1987), 'Advertising as a cultural system', in J. Umiker-Sebeok (ed.), *Marketing and Semiotics: New Directions in the Study of Signs for Sale*, Berlin: Mouton de Gruyter.

Stern, B. (1988a), 'How does an ad mean? Language and services advertising', *Journal of Advertising*, 17, 3–14.

Stern, B. (1988b), 'Medieval allegory: roots of advertising strategy for the mass market', *Journal of Marketing*, 52, 84–94.

Stern, B. (1988c), 'Figurative language in services advertising: the nature and uses of imagery', *Advances in Consumer Research*, 15, 185–90.

Stern, B. (1989a), 'Literary explication: a methodology for consumer research', in E.C. Hirschman (ed.), *Interpretive Consumer Research*, Provo, UT: Association for Consumer Research, 48–59.

Stern, B. (1989b), 'Literary criticism and consumer research: overview and illustrative analysis', *Journal of Consumer Research*, 16, 322–34.

Stern, B. (1991), 'Detailed image analysis: poetic methodology for advertising research', *International Journal of Advertising*, 10, 161–80.

Stern, B. (1994), 'Classical and vignette television advertising dramas: structural models, formal analysis, and consumer effects', *Journal of Consumer Research*, 19, 601–15.

Stern, B. (1996), 'Deconstructive strategy and consumer research: concepts and illustrative exemplar', *Journal of Consumer Research*, 23 (September), 136–47.

Stewart, D.W. and Ward, S. (1994), 'Media effects on advertising,' in J. Bryant and D. Zillmann (eds), *Media Effects: Advances in Theory and Research*, Hillsdale, NJ: Lawrence Erlbaum Associates, 315–63.

Turkle, S. (1995), *Life on the Screen: Identity in the Age of the Internet*, New York: Simon & Schuster.

Weber, T.E. (1996), 'Who uses the Internet?', *Wall Street Journal*, 9 December, R6.

Welsford, E. (1961), *The Fool: His Social and Literary History*, Garden City, NY: Anchor Books.

12

FAR-FLUNG ROMANCE

The love affair between researchers, SMEs and
their internationalisation process

Andrew McAuley

Prologue

Romance, for me, began and often ended standing beside a designated meeting point, usually a radiator, in my school. These were the castellated towers in my emerging journey into the fabled landscape of love where maidens fair, and not so fair, could be wooed. If one was lucky the maiden could be beguiled into a date which preferably consisted of a visit to the back row of the local cinema while the silver screen flickered.

On one famous occasion my quest for love seemed well within reach. The hottest new girl in town said 'yes' to a date at the cinema on Saturday night. The film was an Elvis concert but that was of incidental importance as the real entertainment was to take place in the proverbial 'back row of the movies'. Alas, this quest was to remain outwith my grasp as the Irish Republican Army blew the cinema to smithereens late on the Friday night. Peace may yet come to Ireland in my lifetime but some things will take longer to forgive!

Introduction: the quest outlined

It is said that one's reach must exceed one's grasp or else what's a dream for? In seeking the seemingly unattainable we have a reason to go on. We create for ourselves a quest which is just satisfying enough to motivate the chase to continue in the often vain hope that in a blinding moment of revelation all will fall into place and the building blocks of our mind's desire will somehow fit and contentment will reign. Somehow I think this is a genetic trick to keep us pursuing the nigh impossible while in reality we are being tormented and the gods simply kill us for their sport. There is no ultimate solution to the quest. There is no answer providing unity. There is only the (re)search.

The study of the internationalisation process of small and medium-sized enterprises (SMEs) has many apparent parallels with this. Much effort has been put into attempting to find a comprehensive definition of what internationalisation is, as well as into finding ways of conceptualising the process. So far there is no broad agreement on the first issue and little on the second. In addition, the literature offers little which would be of value to the SME owner looking for a route map to the land of international success.

The argument put forward here is that progress in this sub-discipline of marketing, namely, the study of SME internationalisation and more broadly international marketing, has been hindered by the methodologies adopted. In addition, the way we structure and present our knowledge to ourselves and the world at large too often fails to excite. All this has constrained the development of new ways of looking at the world resulting in similar studies being undertaken time after time which have added little to the collective whole. Thus, this particular sub-topic within marketing has not benefited from the same intellectual debate and creative thinking as, for example, consumer behaviour has experienced. The relative sterility of the research has left the topic seemingly exhausted and very much in the doldrums.

However, all is not doom and gloom; signs of life have been detected on the margins of the SME internationalisation literature. As this chapter illustrates, the romantic metaphor can provide a framework for interpreting what has gone before and what might come in the future. The quest for greater clarity in our knowledge of SME internationalisation remains, as yet, unfulfilled. An adventurous journey awaits brave knights willing to advance into this landscape littered with the failures of previous campaigns. Later in this discussion the potential contribution of a romantic interpretation will be assessed more fully but first let us rouse the dragon from its lair.

Rousing the dragon

Somewhere at the back of my mind is a quotation about seeing through a glass darkly. Originally I thought it might have been by Yeats or MacNeice but, to my surprise, it turned out to be St Paul in a letter to the Corinthians: 'For now we see through a glass, darkly; but then face to face: now I know in part; but then I shall know as I am known' (1 *Corinthians* 13:12). This seems to reflect the promise of research to lead to the fabled kingdom of knowledge. Methodology is the pivot around which research revolves. As long as we keep the faith and follow recognised methodological frameworks then methodology offers the path to everlasting glory and a place in category one journal heaven. However, I worry that we have created a dragon that blinds us from seeing the world as it really is, blasting us as it does with its fiery tongue if we dare to stray.

In truth, I would like to slay that dragon and pillage its den in search of the mysteries it currently guards. Too often its seems we are held in check by methodologies we have created for ourselves. Confined in our academic towers like the Lady of Shalott only able to view the world via a reflection in a mirror. Is it not time to gaze out on Camelot and engage the world directly and on a

217

more personal level? Let the mirror be cracked from side to side so that we can deal with the curse we have brought upon ourselves.

The process of change in a discipline can often be very slow with occasional rapid bursts of activity. Often these changes are dependent on some thinkers deciding not to be bound by certain 'obvious' methodological rules, or because they unwittingly broke them. The Copernican Revolution, the rise of modern atomism and the wave theory of light all owe their origins to this process. Between such events there is always a danger that a discipline becomes too set in its ways. Maybe I'm just biased but the management disciplines seem awfully dry when compared to some of the creative talent seen in the world of art. Look how Miro and Picasso came along and revolutionised the representation of the human face and figure. Consider the vibrant colours of Van Gogh and Gauguin as a means to understanding our world. All these artists found a unique way of expressing their view of the world. Van Gogh in his many letters to Theo graphically expressed his vision, for example he regarded the cypress trees as black marks in a sun-filled landscape: 'it is one of the most interesting black tones, and I can't think of any other tone that was as difficult to capture. One has to see the cypresses here against the blue, or more correctly in the blue' (Roskill 1963).

The ability to take what we see and represent it in its individual context – '*in the blue*'- is the essence of our project. These artists and their work provide, for me, a metaphor for the richness of different ways of expressing oneself as routes to understanding. Having said that, there is no implication that the route should be linear – that would be a far too simple view of our world. The only principle that does not inhibit progress is, as Feyerabend (1975) has said, 'anything goes'. Thus, the ongoing search for methodological rigour is perhaps a distraction from what the central focus should be: namely, the journey itself and its outcomes.

Within this context our obsession with methodological issues appears a little over-rated. Americans appear to be even more obsessed than those of us on the edge of Europe but, rumour has it, our 'mainland' European colleagues are more concerned with what they are trying to achieve rather than the methods they use to get there. Perhaps there is hope, but first let us look more closely at SMEs and internationalisation.

Slaying the dragon

Dragons often have many heads and in this discussion two heads will be dealt with. The first is the theoretical attempts which have been used to conceptualise SME internationalisation. The second issue to be discussed will look at how we represent our knowledge for consumption.

The trials and tribulations of SMEs and internationalisation

The internationalisation process of SMEs is a complicated but often necessary process for many firms in small domestic markets. Much of the literature has traditionally concentrated on the activities of the large multinational enterprises. It is fair to say that, to some extent, the issue of internationalisation as it relates to smaller firms has been relatively neglected. This is not to suggest that research on small firms in international markets is lacking. There has indeed been much produced on the general theme of small firm export behaviour, including the role of exports in small firm growth and the performance characteristics of exporters; but the underlying processes and patterns of small firm internationalisation have yet to be fully addressed.

Further, it is with some angst that McAuley (1995) noted that there is little research in this area which would be of use to the SME owner. Even allowing for the division between pure and applied research, one could have hoped for a better outcome after over thirty years of research into the broader theme of exporting. Many of the studies appear to be 'more of the same' offering few concrete outcomes with x, y and z being important determinants of exporting one week and a, b and c being the key influences the following week. It is also possible to bemoan the fact that there is little reapplication of existing methodologies to test previous findings, nor are there many attempts at longitudinal work. International cross-cultural studies are also in short supply.

To date, in the literature the process of internationalisation has been captured in various ways by three dominant schools of thought, namely, Foreign Direct Investment (FDI) theory, the stages models of internationalisation, and the Network perspective on internationalisation. Of these, FDI theory and the stage models have received the greatest attention in the general literature, while interest in the network perspective is more recent. In all three schools of research, most of the literature (both conceptual and empirical) is in the context of larger, multinational, manufacturing companies.

A review of the literature by Coviello and McAuley (1995) suggested that no definitive picture could be drawn of what internationalisation involves and how the process occurs for the smaller firm. It can be argued that part of the reason for this is the fact that most empirical approaches have been reductionist rather than holistic and expansionary in their efforts. It is only recently that efforts have been made to examine the internationalisation process across more than one school of research. It is apparent that while these schools of thought have been treated as being distinct they are in fact inter-related. Evidence of this can be seen in Aharoni's (1966) finding that FDI reflected a staged managerial learning process. More recently, Bodur and Madsen (1993) highlighted the overlap between FDI and the network perspective, while Bell (1995) and Coviello and Munro (1997) have identified the influence of networks on the stages approach to internationalisation.

This evidence suggests that while each school of thought can provide a partial understanding of the internationalisation process as it affects the smaller firm, it may be that a fuller explanation would be achieved from the integration of these approaches. Second, studies of internationalisation have suffered from being cross-sectional and based on one point in time, thus providing limited depth regarding the longitudinal process of internationalisation. Third, few studies employ more than one method of data collection. Most rely on aggregated quantitative data rather than qualitative sector specific data. Fourth, few studies make any attempt to cross cultural boundaries which is ironic given the nature of internationalisation. Finally, there is little guidance available in the literature to assist managers in their jobs.

Internationalisation has come to remind me of the old story of the blind people and the elephant. When asked to describe it, one person, grabbing its tail said 'Why, it's thin and rather long and feathery at the end.' Another clasping a foot said 'No, it's solid and round like a tree'; a third, feeling the tusk, disagreed, comparing it more to a pointed spear. So it is with internationalisation: we see a dragon with many heads depending on our approach and methods used. It should not be surprising then that no commonly accepted definition exists on the scope of the internationalisation concept. This is confirmed by Whitelock and Munday (1993) and McAuley (1995). This is partly due to the diffuse nature of much of the research conducted in this area which has involved many disciplines, theoretical models and units of analysis. If ever a definition is to be acknowledged, then it must, of necessity, be holistic.

To be fair, some reflective articles do exist but they are often few and far between and appear as 'voices crying in the wilderness'. Welch and Luostarinen (1988) offer a useful analysis of internationalisation as a concept. Others (Anderson 1993; Johanson and Vahlne 1990, 1992; Melin 1992) have attempted to review the subject and prescribe their own panacea: for example Aaby and Slater (1989) have called for better research design and longitudinal studies and this can only be endorsed. However, other authors, for example Miesenbock (1988), faced with a lack of progress, fall back on the call for greater sophistication of our techniques and statistical analysis. It is just possible that this is the wrong direction to go in. Rather than throwing ever more powerful computer programs and fancy mathematical algorithms (after thirty odd years of such attempts to 'explain' exporting) at the problem, perhaps the best route forward is to do something relatively simple for a change.

The structure and presentation of our knowledge

The second area of concern within SME internationalisation and more generally in marketing is the presentation of our knowledge. Perhaps I worry too much, and here I may be speaking 'tongue in cheek', but who decided that knowledge/meaning must be contained within the confines of 3–4,000 words? Who decided that two publications a year in so-called top journals constitutes a sensible way to gauge the pursuit of knowledge? Who decided that the size of the OHP screen would structure our presentations? As one of my students said recently at a class presentation: 'I had to make it very simple so as it could fit in the computer.'

I worry about the words we use, the ways we choose to present our work. The narrowness of our audience; Narcissus would be proud, don't we look lovely? There is still too much emphasis on the use of the academic article as the key measure of our output. Researchers should also be encouraged to seek a wider audience, for example via journalists. Then we will have to accept a trade-off between accuracy and the greater coverage achieved by the medium. The increasing possibilities of electronic publishing on the Internet, in time, will also revolutionise the way we disseminate our work with the added advantage of immediate feedback.

Why can't we write more freely? Why have we adopted this pseudo-scientific approach to the presentation of our research in some vain search for credibility? Take the enormous impact of Fergal Keane's *Letter to Daniel* (Keane 1996) or the poem 'Do Not Stand At My Grave And Weep', by an unknown writer, which was found in a soldier's belongings after he was killed in Northern Ireland (BBC 1996). The latter had an enormous impact on listeners when it was first broadcast on the BBC in 1995. Where is the equivalent impact of writing in marketing? Can we not write to communicate with a wider audience in a more direct way? What is to stop us from moving beyond the proverbial 'ivory tower?' Where is the poetry in marketing? Where is the writing in marketing? Where is marketing?

We need to find better forms of expression and borrow, where possible, from other disciplines; for example, a little book by Hildick (1968) identifies thirteen types of narrative. Just think what fun we could have in marketing if we used some of the narrative types suggested as a means to aid our communication. Basic story situations as suggested by Hildick (1968) are:

1 It happened to him
2 Here and now
3 Listen while I tell you
4 As I sit here at my desk
5 Opening another bottle, he continued
6 All-dialogue
7 The spotlight and the flourish (in the form of a play)
8 One or two routine questions (catechetical)
9 Dear lovelace (epistolary)
10 Dear me (in the form of a diary)
11 The orderly scrapbook (documentary)
12 The disorderly mind (stream of consciousness)
13 The string of pearls (series of first-person narratives in third-person frameworks)

It would be so liberating to see more of these forms being used in marketing. It is depressing to think that the basic structure of the traditional academic article could remain unchanged at the tail end of the next millennium. We should free ourselves from the tyranny of its structure and the constraints it places on our use of language. Its structure does little more than to suppress the creative communication skills of people in the discipline.

In pursuit of better writing the basic concern of the romantics can provide an inspiration. Day (1996) uses the definition from *The Oxford Companion to English Literature* to launch his discussion of romanticism: 'Emotionally it expressed an extreme assertion of the self and the value of individual experience . . . together with the sense of the infinite and the transcendental . . . The stylistic keynote of romanticism is intensity, and its watchword is "Imagination".' If only this were our central rallying cry in our (re)search for marketing. Let us consider the romantic offering further.

The romantic offering

Part of the attraction of the romantics was their role in the dislocation and disintegration of much literary skill and knowledge that previously had been orderly, systematic, and hallowed by tradition. Kroeber (1960) has suggested that the romantic era was one of reconstruction and re-formation. Like other eras that had gone before it was based on the rejection of many ideas and techniques that had, to previous generations, been regarded as the very essence of civilised behaviour and thought. This upheaval goes too far for some including Guerard (1942) who see parallels in the romantic link to the French Revolution and the rise of fascism in Europe in the 1930s. However, Abrams (1953) views romanticism more kindly as an insistence of individual values against the growing pressures towards conformity. While new ways of viewing the world may bring with them an awkwardness due to their unfamiliarity, any such awkwardness is not the harbinger of a fatal flaw but, rather, is a sign of life. Without periods of re-orientation no art or academic discipline can avoid stiffening into sterile rigidity and repetitiveness.

While such change can bring with it its own dissatisfaction and the lyrics of some of the romantic poets do appear half-logical, nevertheless they did help us to move away from the idea that any poem should be fully comprehensible on first reading. Instead this gave way to the notion that a good poem at first reading should be mysterious and provocative of deeper study. Poetry underwent a metamorphosis from being a predominantly rational method of discourse to a predominantly supra-rational method.

The romantics were, in a very real sense, aware of the importance of a holistic approach to the world. To them good and evil, innocence and experience, sensual passion and spiritual passion were definite, irreducible components out of whose interactions the process of human experience arose. Once these elements have been isolated, analysis cannot be carried any further, and it becomes the poets' task to synthesise. Thus, in Coleridge's view, opposite or discordant qualities including intellect with emotion, thought with object and the idea with the image had to be reconciled through synthesis (Bloom 1970). This view was in stark contrast to the attempts by Newton to produce mathematical formulae to reduce events, for example the flight of a cannon ball to a static formula. Newton's calculus appears to measure a curve by dividing it into infinitesimally small segments. For artists like Blake, a line is a complete and indivisible unity, explicable only in terms of the totality of its entire movement.

Those taking part in a period of change can be ridiculed by their contemporaries. Consider the treatment of the Impressionists and how the term 'refusenik' was turned around to become a badge of honour. Such movements are not entirely free from earlier periods of artistic tradition although they primarily strive towards something new which is more personal and more intense in expression. The paintings created by the Impressionists do not attempt to convey a conception of experience as being objectively apprehendable as, say, Claude Lorraine would have done. Instead, they offer the opportunity to step inside the painter's vision. The energy source of the painting is subjective and creative and cannot be written down; we must enter into the vision of the painter if we are to understand.

There are many threads within the romantic movement which can be adapted to our (re)search. Holbrook (1995) provides an overview to the variety of interpretations of romanticism. Themes which appear time and again include imaginative, creative, personal, intuitive, emotional and chaotic. Latching onto Holbrook's approach to consumer behaviour which is subjective, personal and introspective and translating that into the SME internationalisation process, we emerge with an approach which bases itself on the experience of the process as lived through by the individuals involved. Thus, we have a link between the approach and concerns of the romantics and an approach to (re)search which, as we shall see in the next section, is more developed in consumer research than in SME internationalisation.

Reading the entrails

There are signs of life in parts of the literature but less so in the SME literature than in consumer behaviour. Holbrook (1995) traces the history and evolution of consumer research from the 1960s–90s. In the 1960s he characterises it as being neopositivistic managerially relevant studies of decisions to purchase goods and services. By the 1990s it is a more inviting, pluralistic and all-embracing doctrine, namely, 'Scientific and Humanistic Marketing and Consumer Research Includes Neopositivistic and Interpretive Managerially Relevant and Intrinsically Motivated Studies of Decisions to Buy Goods and Services and of Experiences in the Consumption of Artwork and Entertainment'. Many authors have contributed to the undermining of neopositivist consumer research since the early 1980s (Anderson 1983; Deshpande 1983; Hirschman 1986, 1989; Peter and Olson 1983) and in doing so have moved the debate into the postmodern context. Hirschman and Holbrook (1992) provide a useful critique of the philosophies influencing the methods used in consumer research and, in the end, call for a greater tolerance between researchers.

As the philosophical underpinnings have shifted, so too has the means of communication. In his approach Holbrook has moved away from the formal academic writing style which he states can be described as 'the bland, the impersonal, the remote, and the colorless militantly on parade'. Instead he pleads for an infusion of imagination and offers a style based on the liberal arts which seeks to use words which will find some resonance in human lives. This resonance will only be found if the approach taken to understanding consumption is subjective, personal and introspective.

In the study of SMEs and their internationalisation process there has been little debate centred on methodological approaches. There exists a broad divide between the quantitative and qualitative approaches. We have the large sample number-crunchers, on the one hand, and the in-depth interview brigade, complete with the focus group rapid deployment force, on the other hand, and where has it got us? Given the volume and vitality of the work in consumer behaviour, the opportunity for cross-over is evident. Beneath the broad quantitative–qualitative divide there are some researchers who are exploring new ways of dealing with the world and a number merit recognition. These researchers are often using the 'tell me about . . .' approach so as to allow the respondent to describe their activities in their own words, for example Anderson (1997), Ennis and Ali (1997), Jack and Bower (1997).

In my own work I have recently fallen back on a childlike simple approach to the complexities of the world which we try to understand. The crux of this methodological shift is simple: 'Tell me a story'. In many cultures the storytelling method has had a powerful influence on the transmission of knowledge between the generations. Work by Caulkins (1988) provided an insight into how an anthropological framework could be used as a basis for research on the social structure and culture of small business. Hopkinson (1997) has used narrative to good effect in the study of conflict in a distribution channel. It has been suggested by other authors that narrative has a role to play in economics and the physical sciences as well as, more obviously, in psychoanalysis (Nash 1990; Sarbin 1986). Other disciplines have also used this method to focus their enquiry; for example, one method of historical enquiry (adapted from Harris 1971) follows four points:

1   primary concern is with the particular;
2   explanation may take into account the thoughts of relevant individuals;
3   explanation may use general laws;
4   explanation relies heavily on the reflective judgement of individuals.

This very much reflects my approach in some recent work on the internation-alisation process in small companies within the Scottish arts and crafts sector which is discussed in the next section.

The internationalisation process in Scottish craft businesses

In working with these companies it becomes apparent that a holistic approach is necessary to advance the understanding of these micro businesses, otherwise only a partial picture would be achieved. Thus, having the story of the company related by the individuals involved is the key way of achieving understanding. The growth of a company can be related as much to the internal personal (psychological) development of the entrepreneur as it can be to the external 'visible' development of the company.

This method also reveals the relevance of the theories of internationalisation discussed earlier to these companies. For example, one company was founded in 1993 and is located near Stirling. The founder is a textile designer who pro-duces fashion and furnishing accessories. Her entry into the export markets occurred after a contact, one of the judges at her final degree show, who liked her work showed it to knitwear designers she knew in Germany, Holland and Ireland. These designers also liked her work and the first export orders followed. Since then she has also exported to Japan. This clearly illustrates the value of networks and the fact that the move was unplanned by the entrepreneur herself.

By contrast, another example, a weaving company, illustrates the importance of networks but this time being used in a more formally planned way. This company was founded in the far north of Scotland in 1991 and is involved in the production of fashion accessories. The key influence here on their export-ing activity was that a previous company had existed from 1986–90. Crucially, the international networks developed by the designer associated with the orig-inal company were maintained by the new company as part of their business strategy. This planned use of networks paved the way for the international suc-cess and the company now has agents in France, Italy, Japan and the USA. Indeed, all of the company's turnover has traditionally come from export mar-kets. It is only since 1995 that the domestic market has been given serious marketing consideration.

What, then, is the relevance of these examples to the theories of interna-tionalisation? Well, these companies do not adhere to any incremental model of internationalisation. They do not concentrate on the domestic market, neither do they develop markets in psychologically close countries, nor is internation-alisation characterised by a steady, logical, controlled sequential process. As for foreign direct investment theory, these firms are really too small to contemplate such a notion in the foreseeable future. Of the three key theories of interna-tionalisation only network theory has any relevance to the behaviour of these companies.

Many of the companies in this study were 'born international' in that they exported during their first year of operation. These companies exhibit similar characteristics to previous studies of 'born internationals' but at the same time they are different. This can partly be seen by looking at the definitions used by Oviatt and McDougall (1994). They speak of an international new venture as 'a business organisation that, from inception, seeks to derive significant competitive advantage from the use of resources and the sale of outputs in multiple countries'. In addition, these businesses are described as having an international vision, an innovative product or service which is marketed via a strong network and tightly managed organisation focused on international sales growth.

While elements of the above descriptions apply, for example having an innovative product and making use of networks, there is much less emphasis within the craft businesses on the planned, systematic and targeted growth of sales in export markets. This apparent unplanned nature of the beginnings of exporting by two-thirds of the companies echoes some of the early literature on exporting behaviour (Hunt *et al.* 1967; Simmonds and Smith 1968) of the late 1960s. In that literature, an unplanned responsive approach to overseas business was often held as being the very epitome of bad practice. On the other hand, having talked to these entrepreneurs, one begins to have some sympathy for the approach. An opportunity arises and they take it. Is there anything wrong with that? After all we must give them some credit for being entrepreneurial in running their small business! It is more likely that our models in to which we try to squeeze them lack the flexibility to cope with the dynamism of the world in which they operate and we observe.

This, of course, begs the question: is it possible to build a more holistic model which helps to explain the internationalisation process of the companies and the key influences upon it? The richness of the material gained from the interviews with the entrepreneurs provides a good starting point for this process. From the interviews certain features begin to repeat themselves across the businesses. For example, the importance of having a unique product which helps to develop a market niche; having a good design which the entrepreneur is willing to adapt for the export market; being interested in the customer and developing a relationship over time. Clearly, the personality of the entrepreneur also greatly influences the activities of the business. These people are not afraid to give something a go. They will take a risk without having full information and are prepared to use the expertise of others, for example freight forwarders, to get an export order organised.

Figure 12.1 attempts to synthesise those influences on the 'born internationals' which encourage them to take advantage of the opportunity to internationalise their business. These have been grouped into four sets of attributes. Moving from the top left of the diagram clockwise the first set of attributes are 'Product' related. Design has a key influence on the success of the product while the customer's perception of the Scottish image is important as discussed in the country of origin literature. Other product-related features which the entrepreneurs highlight are quality, price and delivery.

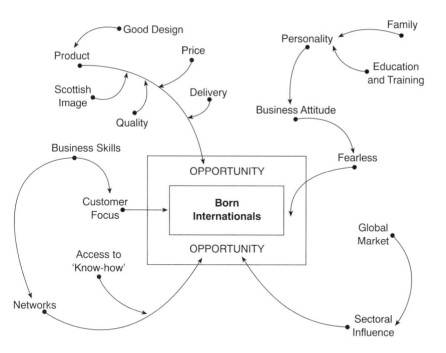

Figure 12.1 Key infuences on 'born' internationals

The second set are 'Personal and Psychological' related. Within this group of factors the family background of the entrepreneurs and their education and training play an important role in shaping them. One respondent remembers the entrepreneurial activities of her mother in shaping her view of being in business and what it involves.

Moving to the bottom right of Figure 12.1 and the third set of attributes which are 'Industry' related, it appears that for some of the firms, particularly those in the fashion, jewellery and publishing industries, being part of a global industry does exert a strong influence on their international behaviour.

The final set of attributes are 'Cognitive' related. The key influences which emerge here are related to business skills including having a customer focus and making good use of networks. In addition, it is important that the entrepreneurs know where to seek 'know-how' once the individual's own skills have been surpassed.

While Figure 12.1 seeks to display the key influences, as revealed from the stories told by the respondents, it is recognised that other factors may be at play and the links between the groupings will be more complex than this two-dimensional representation. However, this study has shown that an approach which deals with individuals and attempts to reconcile influences through

227

synthesis while developing a holistic overview is a rich vein of enquiry. Such an approach is essential if we are ever to unravel the love affair between researchers, SMEs and their internationalisation process.

Conclusion: sacking the lair

This discussion began by outlining the problems encountered on our quest for knowledge of the internationalisation process of SMEs. If only we can slay the multi-headed dragon of methodology and representation then we can sack the lair and open up ourselves to the possibility of alternative routes to understanding. An understanding of the world is the major goal of all academic disciplines, not just scientific disciplines. The same goal is shared by religion, the arts and philosophy. For all the understanding sought is associated with the perception of an underlying order and unity in the chaotic world of experience. It may well be that the order is a myth but still we search for whatever is there. It is up to us to discover what we can.

The SME internationalisation process is out there and is happening all the time. Our quest is to unwrap the present. There is an excitement about achieving any insight, an experience which can be emotional and comparable to that experienced by the religious mystic, the poet, the drunk and the insane. We need to be less bound by the conventions of methodologies, more willing to adopt the Woolworths' approach to 'pic'n'mix', our methods adopting the 'anything goes' principle and by doing so allowing for the possibility of progress. Despite the despair there are, at times, glimpses of hope with some people being brave enough to buck the trend and tell it like it is. The basis of this approach, particularly in relation to smaller firms and their internationalisation process, is essentially story-telling, less formal than the case study, but more akin to anthropological approaches. This ethnographic approach, while popular particularly with younger researchers, still finds resistance from reactionary reviewers. Time itself will solve this problem but we all could do more to help create the spirit of tolerance spoken of by Hirschman and Holbrook (1992). There is no one way up the mountain; we need a multiplicity of approaches woven together if we are to shine some light on the world and make some sense of it. There is hope but there is an on-going need to re-evaluate this game we play with methodologies.

In terms of the study of SMEs and their internationalisation process, the examples drawn from the study of Scottish crafts businesses have attempted to show both the inadequacy of traditional methodologies and mainstream theories of internationalisation. We are seeing a mainly unplanned entry into export markets; 'no reason, it has just come,' as one respondent said. These companies challenge our search for a robust and elegant 'one theory fits all' scenario and if we distil the material to the individual level we begin to see the crucial influences on their internationalisation activities.

It could be argued that our study of SMEs and their internationalisation process has eluded the reductive aims of the positivist school. To borrow from Keats, the goblin has not been driven from the hearth, and the rainbow has not been robbed of its mystery. Just as the romantics led a renewal and re-orientation in their art so too is there a need for such a movement in the study of SME internationalisation to avoid the area falling into sterile rigidity and repetitiveness. Much remains to be done and thankfully the romance of the quest is not dead. It is of course a cliché to say that romance is not dead but it is no less true despite its overuse. We discover it in our daily lives and often it is at its best in small or hidden things. To borrow from Keats again: the melodies we hear are sweet, but those unheard are sweeter. It is this transcendental quality to which marketers should aspire. Perhaps we try but capture it only in ham-fisted language – sell the sizzle not the sausage. It is possible to find new ways of using language and it is possible to paint internationalisation, for example the new British Airways tail designs.

Caspar David Friedrich, regarded by many as the quintessential romantic artist, created spectacular landscapes notable for their powerful evocation of supernatural and elemental forces. Vast pinnacles plunge to unseen depths while mists flood the valleys between; broken trees lie rotting across caverns and maybe, just maybe, lead to a new path on the journey through our imagined world. For me, on my personal journey, the marketing landscape is no different. I respond to the whole, to pattern, overlook difference and seek diversity. Organisation can be too constrictive. Material is best dealt with randomly, intuitively to allow new patterns of meaning to emerge. It is possible to see symbolism in many things; these should be read in many ways. Categories are only temporary, a stage on the journey to be created and recreated as events occur. It is important to adapt and to seek differences where others see uniformity. In this marketing landscape it is possible to be dynamic and flexible without being totally chaotic. Like filter feeders we progress by continuously seeking and processing, reacting to each new (re)search experience by integrating them into the whole. In other words:

> The art I create
> The poetry I write
> The music I love
> Are all connected
> Each
> Part of the crisis
> That is me.

It is perhaps true to say that the romantics replaced the idea of art as imitation with the idea of art as creation. It still maintained links with past literatures and traditions, exploiting them where appropriate and, in so doing, mirroring the contemporary (re)search in marketing for dynamic and often joyously eclectic lamps to light our many worlds. It should be remembered that there is no idea, however ancient and absurd, that is not capable of improving our knowledge.

All that is needed is an openness to change, an attitude of mind which challenges the chauvinism which resists alternatives to the status quo.

Epilogue

Sands of Knowledge

Footsteps in the sand
Unseen Traveller
Walking on
Whose gentle mark
The wind erodes
Follow quickly
Before the path
Slowly fades
Step upon step
Takes you closer
But no nearer
To the Traveller
The sands lead on
And on.
Behind
Another Traveller
Sees fresh marks
And follows.

References

Aaby, N.E. and Slater, S.F. (1989), 'Management influences on export performance: a review of the empirical literature 1978–1988', *International Marketing Review*, 6(4), 7–26.

Abrams, M.H. (1953), *The Mirror and the Lamp: Romantic Theory and the Critical Tradition*, New York: Oxford University Press.

Aharoni, Y. (1966), *The Foreign Investment Decision Process*, Graduate School of Business Administration, Boston: Harvard University Press.

Anderson, A.R. (1997), 'Entrepreneurial marketing patterns in a rural environment', paper presented at the AM/AMA/UIC Symposium on the Marketing Entrepreneurship Interface, Dublin, January.

Anderson, O. (1993), 'On the internationalisation process of firms: a critical analysis', *Journal of International Business Studies*, 24(2), 209–31.

Anderson, P.F. (1983), 'Marketing, scientific progress, and scientific method', *Journal of Marketing*, 47 (Fall), 18–31.

BBC (1996), *The Nation's Favourite Poems*, London: BBC Books.

Bell, J. (1995), 'The internationalisation of small computer software firms – a further challenge to "stage" theories', *European Journal of Marketing*, 29(8), 60–75.

Bloom, H. (ed.) (1970), *Romanticism and Consciousness: Essays in Criticism*, New York: Norton and Company.

Bodur, M. and Madsen, T.K. (1993), 'Danish foreign direct investments in Turkey', *European Business Review*, 93(5), 28–43.

Caulkins, D. (1988), 'Networks and narratives: an anthropological perspective for small business research', SEF Occasional Paper Series 01/88, University of Stirling: Scottish Enterprise Foundation.

Coviello, N.E. and McAuley, A. (1995), 'Internationalisation and the entrepreneurial firm: what do we really know?', paper presented to the UIC/AMA Symposium on the Marketing Entrepreneurship Interface, Washington, DC, August.

Coviello, N.E. and Munro, H.J. (1997), 'Network relationships in the internationalisation process of small software firms', *International Business Review*, 6(4), 361–86.

Day, A. (1996), *Romanticism*, London: Routledge.

Deshpande, R. (1983), 'Paradigms lost: on theory and method in research in marketing', *Journal of Marketing*, 47 (Fall), 101–10.

Ennis, S. and Ali, M. (1997), 'Opportunities and obstacles to small business development in a developing economy: the case of Multan in Pakistan', paper presented to the AM/AMA/UIC Symposium on the Marketing Entrepreneurship Interface, Dublin, January.

Feyerabend, P. (1975), *Against Method: Outline of an Anarchistic Theory of Knowledge*, London: Verso.

Guerard, A. (1942), *The France of Tomorrow*, Cambridge, MA: Harvard University Press.

Harris, R.C. (1971), 'Theory and synthesis in historical geography', *The Canadian Geographer*, 15, 157–72.

Hildick, W. (1968), *Thirteen Types of Narrative*, London: Macmillan.

Hirschman, E.C. (1986), 'Humanistic inquiry in marketing research: philosophy, method, and criteria', *Journal of Marketing Research*, 23 (August), 237–49.

Hirschman, E.C. (ed.) (1989), *Interpretive Consumer Research*, Provo, UT: Association for Consumer Research.

Hirschman, E.C. and Holbrook, M.B. (1992), *Postmodern Consumer Research: The Study of Consumption as Text*, London: Sage.

Holbrook, M.B. (1995), *Consumer Research: Introspective Essays on the Study of Consumption*, London: Sage.

Hopkinson, G. (1997), 'The Emperor's new clothes (or not) as the case may be', in S. Brown, A.M. Doherty and B. Clarke (eds) *Proceedings of the Marketing Illuminations Spectacular*, Belfast: University of Ulster, 155–66.

Hunt, H.G., Froggatt, J.D. and Hovell, P.J. (1967), 'The management of export marketing in engineering industries', *British Journal of Marketing*, (Spring), 10–24.

Jack, S.L. and Bower, D.J. (1997), 'Entrepreneurship in the periphery: some examples from Scotland', paper presented to the AM/AMA/UIC Symposium on the Marketing Entrepreneurship Interface, Dublin, January.

Johanson, J. and Vahlne, J.-E. (1990), 'The mechanism of internationalisation', *International Marketing Review*, 7(4), 11–24.

Johanson, J. and Vahlne, J.-E. (1992), 'Management of foreign market entry', *Scandinavian International Business Review*, 1(3), 9–27.

Keane, F. (1996), *Letter to Daniel: Dispatches from the Heart*, London: Penguin.

Kroeber, K. (1960), *Romantic Narrative Art*, Madison: The University of Wisconsin Press.

McAuley, A. (1995), 'An assessment of research into the internationalisation process', in G.E. Hills *et al.* (eds), *Research at the Marketing/Entrepreneurship Interface*, Chicago: University of Illinois Press, 331–42.

Melin, L. (1992), 'Internationalisation as a strategy process', *Strategic Management Journal*, 13, 99–118.

Miesenbock, K.J. (1988), 'Small businesses and exporting: a literature review', *International Small Business Journal*, 6(2), 42–61.

Nash, C. (1990), *Narrative in Culture*, London: Routledge.

Oviatt, B.M. and McDougall, P.P. (1994), 'Towards a theory of international new ventures', *Journal of International Business Studies*, 25(1), 45–64.

Peter, J.P. and Olson, J.C. (1983), 'Is science marketing?', *Journal of Marketing*, 47 (Fall), 111–25.

Roskill, M. (1963), *The Letters of Vincent van Gogh*, London: Collins.

Sarbin, T. (ed.) (1986), *Narrative Psychology: The Storied Nature of Human Conduct*, New York: Praegar.

Simmonds, K. and Smith, H. (1968), 'The first export order: a marketing innovation', *British Journal of Marketing*, (Summer), 93–100.

Welch, L.S. and Luostarinen, R. (1988), 'Internationalisation: evolution of a concept', *Journal of General Management*, 14(2), 34–55.

Whitelock, J. and Munday, P. (1993), 'Internationalisation of the firm: two cases on the explosives industry', *Journal of International Marketing*, 1(4), 19–30.

13

MAGICAL ROMANCE

Commercial rafting adventures

Eric J. Arnould, Linda L. Price and Cele Otnes

Magic and fantasy are everywhere. Ghanaian Ak'uaba dolls have become a popular talisman for childless North American baby boomers who still hope for a child (Worthington 1997). Halloween is in vogue as an adult holiday (Santino 1994). Television shows such as the *X-Files* (Kozinets 1996) and *Buffy the Vampire Slayer* are wildly popular. Extreme leisure experiences that offer personal transformation have experienced dramatic growth in participation (Caudron 1992). *Life* magazine reports that 48 per cent of Americans believe in astrology. In a 1984 National Opinion Research Council study 67 per cent of respondents said that they had experienced extrasensory perception, while an earlier survey found that 35 per cent of respondents felt very close to some powerful, external spiritual force (Blum and Golitzin 1991; Miller 1997). Fifteen different African-derived medical and magical systems thrive in the New World, including Haitian-inspired Hoodoo and Conjure, and Cuban-inspired Santeria in the USA. Umbanda, an Afro-Brazilian religion, is estimated to reach 30 million largely white, middle-class followers primarily in Brazil (Voeks 1997: 2). Successful entrepreneurs like Anita Roddick of the Body Shop and Richard Branson of the Virgin Empire consult specialists in the Chinese art of *feng shui* or luck management (McSherry 1996). What is this resurgence of magic and fantasy all about?

Purpose

This chapter explores the evocation of magic in a leisure services context, commercial white water river rafting. We argue that magical fantasy is a discursive practice enmeshed in and engendered by the marketing age. And we represent magical fantasy as an embodied, multisensory, empowering response to the problematics of postmodernity.

Given the historical triumph of the modernist scientific approach to marketing theory with all its attendant and thorough-going utilitarianism (Brown 1997), it is not surprising that fantasy, feelings and fun remained beyond the pale of academic marketing until the mid-1980s (Holbrook and Hirschman 1982). Despite compelling evocations of the sacred (Belk *et al.* 1989) and ritual dimensions of some consumer behaviours (Rook 1985), precious little exploration of magical consumption experiences is to be found in marketing research (Arnould and Price 1993; Belk 1991, 1996; McCreery 1995b; Otnes 1995). Following Coleridge, we suggest that magic has an unduly neglected truth value for understanding imaginative, expressive acts (Taylor 1979), in this case, certain consumption experiences.

What is magic?

Magic, science, and religion are overlapping modes of human activity (Malinowski 1954; Tambiah 1990). Social theorists argue that religion was the dominant practice in Western intellectual life before the Enlightenment. Many thinkers also agree that science and utilitarian rationality have dominated modes of thought and action since the beginning of the seventeenth century (Thomas 1971). But now the projects of utilitarian science and economics increasingly fail to compel (Lyotard 1984). The resurgence of national and religious fundamentalisms and the proliferation of cults as discursive practices are evidence of the retreat of utilitarian rationality from ordinary social life. Magical fantasy too is enjoying a renaissance.

Magical fantasy can be seen as a creative and aesthetic reaction to the inadequacies of the world (Stoller 1989, 1995). In pre-industrial cultures, recourse to magic has long been a strategic way of resolving intractable social problems, and when effective, magic and magical fantasy can create a change of state in human actors (Bettelheim 1977; Malinowski 1954). In a search for new grounds of meaning and in reaction against the perceived dehumanisation of utilitarian thought and economic practice, magical ideas and language were re-introduced into Western thought by the romantic movement of the late eighteenth century (Abrams 1953, 1971; Kroeber 1988; Taylor 1979). We detect a resurgence of magical fantasy in the context of commercial white water river rafting and speculate that consumers increasingly desire leisure experiences that enact romantic, magical fantasy.

Magical fantasy concerns itself with the relationship between human beings and the natural world. The idea of magical space is vividly evident in Leenhardt's study of Melanesian landscapes. For Melanesians, the landscape mediates between the invisible and visible worlds, it is an area of 'lived myth'. The life of each group is guarded by its totems and ancestors immanent in the landscape; ultimately, participation in ritual in specific places enacts the relation between man [sic] and/or the transcendent (Tambiah 1990: 106). Similarly, romantic magical 'fantasy seeks to develop a vision of the world in which humans cohabit with nonhumans' (Kroeber 1988: 23). 'Indeed, one of the most prominent features of English romantic thought is the belief', not unlike that ascribed to Leenhardt's Melanesians and other pre-industrial peoples, 'that the universe is a living unity which could be known through the imagination' (Piper 1962: 3).

Most anthropologists would agree that central to traditional magical practice is the activation of certain indefinable 'latent virtues' in the immaterial world. This activation may be thought of as 'an exploratory procedure through which the human actor learns about the world and acquires knowledge that can subsequently be put to use' to achieve certain ends or reach certain destinations (Brown 1986: 168). Similarly, romantic 'fantasy originates in the possibility of an authentic otherness' (Kroeber 1988: 3). Levi-Bruhl (1973) asserted that the magical experience is touched by a characteristic emotion, the sentiment of the presence and action of an invisible power and contact with a reality other than the reality given by everyday circumstances. This framing puts the matter in a manner consistent with romantic views of the power of the imagination. Indeed, for Wordsworth, 'the Spirit makes its life known through the Forms [taken by nature], and the whole doctrine [of the world soul] rests on an emotional, and perhaps mystical response to them' (Piper 1962: 78).

While practical, magic clearly is unlike Western science in its reliance on the immaterial. In many magical systems, latent virtues and invisible powers take the form of spirits of various kinds, but this is not essential. For example, in romantic fantasy, the fantasist 'is guided by a desire for what does not exist unless he brings it into being' (Kroeber 1988: 61). However, the linking of persons and these immanent powers to achieve certain ends is essential to all magic including magical fantasy. The linkage of persons and immanent powers resonates through romantic fantasies like Keats's 'La Belle Dame Sans Merci' or Coleridge's 'Rime of the Ancient Mariner' as well as in contemporary magic-oriented television programmes and practices such as *feng shui* mentioned above.

Magic in pre-industrial societies consists of ritual acts that are directed towards concrete or practical ends; magic has material consequences. Unlike the objects of religious devotions, then, when properly evoked, magical forces must act. At a minimum, we would restate Malinowski's (1954) hypothesis that magic ritualises people's optimism, and enhances their faith in the victory of hope over fear. Similarly, from Keats to García Marquez, romantic fantasy is

> an attempt to overcome the sense of man's alienation from the world by healing the cleavage between subject and object, between the vital purposeful, value-full world of private experience, and the dead postulated world to re-animate the dead universe of the materialists.
>
> (Abrams 1953: 65)

'Romantic fantasy is a protest against the violence of enlightened, rationalised, Voltairean society that makes superstitions one of its principal victims' (Kroeber 1988: 6).

Magic, according to Stanley Tambiah, serves to restructure and integrate the minds and emotions of the actors (1968: 202). Thus, magicians engage in acts that are not merely instrumental but also expressive; magic aims both to do and to say something. In Michael Taussig's evocative phrasing, 'magical beliefs . . . are poetic echoes of the cadences that guide the innermost course of the world' (1989: 15). Magic, like romantic fantasy, takes language, symbols, and intelligibility to their outermost limits to alter man's fate. Unlike rationalistic Cartesian science then, magical thinking and action are straightforwardly rhetorical, based on metaphor and simile. And unlike scientific thought, magical praxis willingly mixes practical motives with emotional and aesthetic ones (Horton 1993). Similarly, 'the most powerful impulse within romantic fantasy is its efforts to regain the [hopeful] viewpoint of the superstitious' in an effort to restore balance to the world (Kroeber 1988: 6).

Building on consensus in the ethnological literature and intriguing parallels with romantic fantasy, we propose that river magic depends for its effects on the interaction of three elements: the condition of the performer, a rite and a verbal formula. We next turn to a discussion of these elements of river magic. Elsewhere we explore the parallels between river magic and pre-industrial magical systems (Arnould et al. 1997). Here we overview the elements of magic but concentrate on juxtaposing romantic theory and data drawn from our river rafting research.[1]

The condition of the performer

As in romantic fantasy, contact with a reality other than the reality of everyday circumstances marks the experience of magic. In this case that something is often termed 'nature', and is manifested in the ever-changing character of the river environment, and the transcendent qualities often attributed to wilderness in American social thought, as in romantic thought in the 1790s (Arnould et al. 1998; Piper 1962). Sorcerers and other participants in magical rites typically enter into dangerous situations, contact with unseen forces being inherently dangerous. In river rafting, danger is materialised in the river itself, a natural force that opens the door to experience. One guide says:

> I mean it breaks down . . . I mean, people sort of have their roles defined, right? And, so, then they go out into this overwhelmingly beautiful place, and a dangerous place. Basically running the rivers that we run or being in any of these places, a lot of times you're doing some stuff that's dangerous. And so, that sort of redefines them – who they are, where they're at. That, in and of itself, opens up a door.
>
> (interview river guide, swm20s)

The transformation effected on the trip comes about as participants engage in novel experiences that challenge them perceptually, physically, emotionally, and socially.

For magic to be effective, people have to be in the right state of mind to experience transcendent powers. 'A romantic poet,' like Keats or Coleridge, 'undertaking fantasy of necessity must put himself in a state of mind in which he can believe he thinks what he says. In a disenchanted world he must enchant himself' (Kroeber 1988: 39) as the poets do in 'La Belle Dame Sans Merci' or 'Kubla Khan'. Similarly, in the context of river rafting both clients and river guides must be ready. For clients, this readiness is often expressed in advance of a rafting trip as a form of romantic longing for otherness, nature, and escape from civilisation and its discontents. Comments excerpted in Table 13.1 from open-ended questions included in a pre-trip survey conducted in 1991 illustrate this readiness. Guides often phrase readiness as 'respect' for natural forces. The

Table 13.1 Romantic longing for otherness

I want the river and surroundings to be . . .	The key feelings and experiences I want are . . .
Clean, with no signs of civilisation, other than ourselves, to be intruding on the pristine environment.	Sense of isolation, serenity, transport back in time to when the sediments of the canyons were first being deposited, when a river started to carve the canyons.
Natural, clean, wild.	To be in the great outdoors and to go back to nature.
Beautiful to observe and refreshing to spend time in.	Next to nature, far away from anything I'm familiar with.
Breath-taking, away from civilisation, peaceful.	Being in an unspoiled environment, enjoying the scenic beauty.
Clean, undisturbed by commercial ventures.	Satisfaction, accomplishment, relaxation.
Clean, unpopulated, wilderness, rapids yet pools to recover in.	Awe and excitement.
Remote and challenging.	Totally different from our other vacations.
Peaceful, hopefully as few people as possible.	Taking in the surroundings and being apart from civilisation.
Unspoiled wilderness.	The thrill of successfully making it through a rapid right side up. The awe of enjoying God's creation.
Natural and unpolluted.	Solitude, humility and nature, and adventure.

following verbatim quote from an interview conducted in 1995 captures some river guides' views of respect. Note the references to immaterial forces:

> The way I put it, you've got to give the river gods or we call her Ma River sometimes. You've got to give it *respect* at all times, cause when you're not respecting her is when she's going to spank ya, she's gonna reach out and grab ya and cause havoc with ya. But if you give her respect all the time I feel that you are . . . you're going to be all right. And, I mean, that's kind of the knock-on-wood, you know, not gonna flip [the raft].
>
> (interview, river guide, swm20s)

Consistent with romantic views of nature's immanent power, rafters sometimes articulate magical power as something that sometimes inheres in nature and sometimes it inheres in people. These two ideas similarly cohabit in Coleridge's 'The Ancient Mariner' where nature is sometimes represented as 'made up of living intelligent forces, seen sometimes as parts of a divine mind . . . working to fulfill divine purpose' (Piper 1962: 86–7). But in this poem Coleridge also wrote of the imagination as a powerful moral force also capable of working on the environment to produce transformations on the actor. The two views are reflected in our data. The former view is captured in the following interview excerpts. Here magic inheres in nature:

> The power of the river, the power of the rocks, I mean, there's a lot of strength in them all, and that power overwhelms a lot of people as well.
>
> (interview, river guide, swm20s)

> as soon as you push off that beach, at the put-in where you start your river trip, it's magical. It really is. That's where the river magic comes in. It's like you go through this door, and you close it when it goes behind ya . . . you're in that magical environment out there in the wilderness that just sucks you in, and it just absorbs ya. And, you get absorbed in it, and you just don't think about anything else but what's around you and what's going on. And, sometimes, you're not even thinking about that, it's just that you're gone, you know? You're just out there . . . I can just sit there and look around, you know? And, look at the sky and the clouds going by, and the big canyon walls.
>
> (interview, river guide, mwm40s)

A student wrote something similar in a classroom exercise elicited years earlier: 'On the opposite pole the tranquility, that feeling of being an intimate part of the pristine canyon environment; complete and perfect contentment.' The latter view is expressed in the following interview excerpt. Here the possibility of transformation inheres in the human imagination:

> I don't really know how to explain it. It's something that needs to be experienced, where you're out in the canyons and you're kinda one with what's around you and, um, it feels like that's sorta where the human condition

belongs. People really shine when they get out there, for the most part. It really seems to bring out the best in all kinds of different people. Putting them in a natural state. Like getting them 'back to nature'.

(interview, river guide, swf)

Another guide reinforces the idea enunciated by the romantic poets 200 years ago that people have in them a real power of transformation:

People probably have the power inside them to really become more influenced, more appreciative of nature. But I think that people who are out here all the time, the guides, they're running around the river and know all these little details, an area that people are going through to try to steer people in the right direction.

(interview, river guide, swm30s)

Finally, another guide's commentary combines both views, that magic is 'a power unleashed from the depth of a "mind possessed," particularly in wild circumstances where men tap the powers hidden in nature as well as in themselves' (Taylor 1979: 25):

I think it's very natural. It's a chance to really get out and, people are, its perfect, people are ready for it, they're ready to pee right off the boat, they're ready to kiss the wall, they're ready to sorta reach out and grab (I: 'your arm gestures look like you're embracing?). Yeah, how often do you get a chance to hug, kiss this gigantic rock that's so much bigger than you are . . . And I think it's embracing nature. It's, and fate you know, Warm Springs [rapid], it's right down, you know you're looking right down the throat of Warm Springs, you can't really see it. But I think in your mind, people are looking down the throat of Warm Springs, that's you know an extremely powerful force of nature right down there.

(interview, river guide, swm30s)

Rites and formulae (which we discuss next) entail the multisensory re-enactment of cultural memories recognised and comprehended through the body of the performer. As such, rites and formulae seize the imagination of the performer and help to channel and express the magical potential that inheres in nature and the participants.

A rite

In pre-industrial societies, magical manipulations consist in part of ritualised, frequently mimetic, acts directed toward concrete or practical ends. Thus, traditional magical rites involve rule-governed, routinised, symbolic activity. River rafting is organised as a rite completed over several days that effects emotional contact with higher forces. The rite is orchestrated over a number of days on which there is a characteristic unfolding of emotions thought by participants to be energising, natural, true, and unique. Day one of the trip evokes a lot of emotional arousal characterised by anxiety, confusion, and exhilaration that guides attribute to initial contact with the unknown. Guides describe day two as about opening up, going through the door, tuning down a couple of notches, and emotional letdown. Characteristic emotions include relaxation and happiness. Days three and four are the emotional heart of the experience of a five-day rafting trip. The greatest release of temporality occurs; people are caught up in 'river time'. Participants experience aesthetic pleasure, affection, warmth and flow. 'Everybody's dirty and grunged out and they don't care' (swm20s). On the final day of the trip, rafting experiences are inscribed on the everyday life to which people return. A 'silent float' helps some digest their experiences. Others re-tell their experiences, beginning the transformation of experience into personal narrative memories mixed with the fund of myths and legends evoked in the wilderness. Here the power of metaphor and analogy to restructure the minds and emotions of the actors comes most strongly into play.

Schieffelin (1985: 709) observes 'magical performances are effective by socially constructing a situation in which the participants experience symbolic meanings as part of the process of what they are already doing'. One guide speaks of the creation of this routinised process as a modality for magical experience:

> You try to get into a pattern or habit or routine, so to speak, with life. Life becomes very simple then – you know, wake up, have breakfast, get on the river, have lunch back on the river – it's kind of neat . . . you kind of overcome the . . . self-induced expectations and life becomes more routine and you have more time to appreciate everything around you for the actual experiences. Trying to make it as mindless as possible and when I make it mindless and stop thinking about it, I think then I have time to appreciate a lot of subtleties around you. You become more perceptive.
>
> (interview, river guide, mwm30s)

Guides' comments illustrate the notion that routine activity can animate the power inherent in nature and enable participants to experience symbolic meanings. For example:

> they realize they're not beating the rapids, the rapids are working with them, and they're working with the rapids. And, I think, they start seeing more of a harmony with it. Sort of understand that it . . . almost has a spirit to it; itself, and it almost gets real, sort of animated, in and of itself. Sort of personalised. So it changes from what they first see it as to what they see it as when they leave.
>
> (interview, river guide, swm20s)

Magical rites have a dual structure. Apropos magic in pre-industrial contexts, Tambiah remarks that:

a puzzle is posed by magic by virtue of its dual structure. On the one hand, it seems to imitate the logic of technical/technological action that seeks to transform nature or the world of natural things and manifestations. On the other hand, its structure is also transparently rhetorical and performative. The now puzzling duality of magic will disappear only when we succeed in embedding magic in a more ample theory of human life in which the path of ritual action is seen as an indispensable mode for man anywhere and everywhere of relating to and participating in the life of the world.

(Tambiah 1990: 82–3)

This duality is frequently in evidence in river rafting data. For example, one guide juxtaposed the work and imaginative fascination characteristic of rafting when he stated:

The first day's hard work and orientation and day two is like big waves and everybody kind of gets this big feel of the waves. Then on day three you're off on beautiful, beautiful canyons . . . [People] really tune down a couple of notches into a slower mode.

(interview, river guide, swm20s)

Responses to a single survey question also reflect the dual structure of the rafting experience, one that is both practical and performative. Some participant comments excerpted in Table 13.2 seem to emphasise skill building experiences, others transcendent and transforming experiences.

When effective, magical rites unleash primal emotions. Thus 'for Coleridge, nature was symbolical . . . its appearances were designed to impress the mind of man and to bring him to know God', the most primal of forces (Piper 1962: 79). Participation in symbolically charged rites may bring people into imaginative contact with such higher forces. When properly prepared people and natural phenomena are in a relation of contiguity; rites help translate that relation into one of existential immediacy and shared affinities. An excerpt from an interview provides one instance of this link between persons and the magical vitality of the natural world (Taylor 1979). It reflects one river guide's belief in the possibility of rafting to reassert a romantic mystical link between people and nature:

that's a really neat place, it's so . . . It's a 3,200 foot cliff wall there and that's just kind of an overwhelming feeling, looking up at that wall and huge waves splashing up and stuff upstream. And the roar of the river going by it. That's a magical spot.

(interview river guide, swm20s)

An excerpt from participant observation field notes captures another instance of emotional contact between people and natural symbols:

we're sort of looking up at the little . . . at the breast of the little, tiny nestling that was up there. And, I think people did crane their necks for it and, I think,

Table 13.2 Skill-building and transformative themes

An especially meaningful thing I learned about myself was . . .	
Technical, skill-building	*Transcendent, transformative*
002 I could guide a ducky boat	001 my personality varies when I'm isolated . . .
011 I wasn't afraid after almost kissing a rock the first day out	018 I was at peace with me
	009 that I'm strong, in many ways – and that it's not something you lose . . .
014 that I'm okay and with a little encouragement and confidence I can do a lot of things	027 to always be me – it's a lot easier to get to know others who know the real you
017 my leadership capabilities and areas of improvement	
	028 I can do almost anything I put my mind to
031 that I can survive without the basic technology	029 I truly do have feelings towards preservation/easy to lose sight in city
032 I can do anything I set my mind to	
034 I can KAYAK!	012 I can enjoy/respect nature
035 I actually want to learn how to kayak now – it was a blast!	030 I'm at total peace with self and life here
046 even though I'm 'older' and its been decades since I've 'roughed' it like this, I was up to . . . the challenges	031 I also learned that nature is the most beautiful thing
	037 that I doubt myself more than I should
050 it rekindled my fondness of the white water and the challenges it presented	038 that I love nature more than I could have imagined and that it is my base in life
	040 I prefer quiet appreciation of the environment
	047 one night . . . the whole group bonded . . .

that when [a guide] remarked that one of the kayakers sort of called out to another one, 'Hey, we're pulling off to look at a cactus wren', with some kind of a look on his face, as if it was a kind of a silly thing to do. And, [the guide] said, 'Well, there's no more important things to do here.'

(6/95 participant observation notes)

Rites take participants to a timeless place where the transformation of contiguity into affinity becomes possible. In the river rafting context, artefactual remains of the Fremont peoples who inhabited the Southwest a thousand years ago, and then mysteriously disappeared, are emblematic of this timelessness:

> I go up there and you can see the people's fingerprints in the mud on the granary. You can still see that there, and it's been there for over a thousand years probably. And, it's just this real special place that you just get this . . . it's more of a spiritual thing than a physical thing for me. It's like you just sit there on this ledge, you know a 100 feet of river, and you can just feel the energy from those people that were there before, you know?
>
> (interview, river guide, mwm40s)

Guides and many customers interpret their experiences in terms of an essentially romantic reading of emotional experience, as an unleashing of inherent potentials. The emotional power of the rite is illustrated by comments at a trip's end. For some, the silent float provides an opportunity to meld with nature:

> And, uh, we had a half-hour quiet rowing on our boat that stretched to an hour. During which time we just listened and, uh, [the guide] even wrote some in his journal. He announced that afterwards it was perhaps the best hour he'd spent on a trip. Watched a heron fly along, up against the hillside during this time. It was wonderful. I was just listening to the birds, and the air, and the water, the sounds of a natural symphony. Wonderful. Watching the water, glinting and running off the sandstone blocks way up above us as they emerge up out of Whirlpool Canyon.
>
> (6/95 participant observation notes)

Others encounter the ability of magical experience to transcend the boundaries of social status and role and create an experience of communitas (Turner 1969):

> One of the most telling moments on the float down from lunch to the take out – I was sitting in the oar boat with D, looking downstream in A's oar boat – and I was watching Ely, the pediatric surgeon, bailing out the boat. So, here's a pediatric surgeon bailing out the boat of a 22 year old, kind of a spacey river guide, and as I remarked to D, 'Look at that, isn't that something?' He says, 'Yes, it's beautiful. Out here things like that don't matter.'
>
> (6/95 participant observation notes)

Others tell stories that juxtapose the fear and ecstasy that characterise magical experience:

> Pilot Jim said the worst . . . the moment of fear . . . his worst – it was a moment of fear – when he wasn't able to roll out of the trouble at Little Joe [rapid], and the best was a moment of absolute quiet under Echo Rock where

he and Al were just sitting. And he said as Al said at the time, 'These are the moments that you treasure.'

(6/95 participant observation notes)

Some participants find on the last day that they have been transformed, and begin to try to reintegrate their experiences with the return to normal life that lies ahead:

Cause once you get off of Split Mountain, I mean, it kind of . . . it's just work. You know, unloading the boats, getting 'em rolled up, getting 'em on the trailer, all that type stuff, it's just work, and mostly customers are just standing around there thinking about 'Oh, wow, we're going back – we're going to go out and do this – or I've got a plane to catch.'

(interview, river guide, mwm40s)

I think . . . I remember somebody on my last trip saying, uh, you know, I'm gonna go back to work and all those things it seemed like they were, you know, things that were stressing me out aren't gonna be stressing me out any-more. You kinda . . . you keep that feeling with you. Keep that feeling of . . . it just kinda keeps things in perspective a little bit. Things that we let disturb us so much in our lives that really aren't that . . . problems.

(interview, river guide, swf 20s)

When unleashed, primal emotions can produce magical transformations. River guides speak often of the way rafters experience the magical power in the wilderness:

It's so much bigger and stronger than you that it really does start to become this god for, for people that are there all the time.

(interview, river guide, swm30s)

And people want to maybe want to believe in something extra out there . . . something extra, super extra . . . the force behind the river.

(interview, river guide, swm30s)

the person coming away from the river kind of feeling a little bit of tran-scending force or changing force through their river trip. I think a lot of that comes from a kind of instructor's attitude towards it.

(interview, river guide, wm30s)

In sum, contact with transcendent forces becomes possible when people and natural phenomena are placed in a relation of contiguity. It occurs when through a state of heightened emotion and creative energy, they translate that relation into one of existential immediacy and shared affinities. Participation in the rite enacts the relation between men and women and the immanent or tran-scendent that, in romantic conceptions, inheres in nature.

244

A formula

Romantic interest in magical fantasy focused more on the performative dimensions than the practical 'by seeking to uncover magic possibilities, especially in the processes of linguistic articulation' (Taylor 1979: 29). The manipulation of poetic symbols was central to this task. Indeed:

> the magician's power to transform inert things with his words becomes the model for the [romantic] poet's nonmimetic fabling, and magic comes to describe the enchanted world created by the imagination, as opposed to the artifice and convention and mimesis supposed to be typical of neoclassical art.
>
> (Taylor 1979: 29)

Romantic poets were much interested in spells primarily because of their metrical properties. 'Hypnotic sound, heavy-handed and repetitive, approaches nonsense and pulverises meaning . . . As poems to be chanted, spells emphasize words as sounds more than words as meanings, intended to reach us . . . at some level below reasoned discourse' (ibid.: 58). While poetry is not much in evidence on rafting trips, hypnotic sound is. And guides frequently evoke the sound of water to account for the transformative qualities of the rafting experience, for example:

> I think there's magic in moving water. Just the sound, the look, the feel of it . . . You get on it, and it moves you to a certain spot and then you get off it and you hear it all night long. You wake up in the morning and the first thing you hear is the river, the last thing that you hear when you go to bed is the river, and all night long it's going and all day long it's just going. That's why I think it's hypnotizing.
>
> (interview, river guide, mwm30s)

By combining rich and vivid imagery with limited and formulaic language, magicians create a metaphorical order that conforms to their meaningful aspirations (McCreery 1995a; Rosaldo 1975). Adherence to the sequencing has metaphorical significance that moves participants around in metaphorical space. The combination of formalised speech with multisensory imagery brings to life a return to established social or cosmological patterns. Ritual language, as recognised by romantic poets, is a mechanism by which metaphors work. Its formality subtly compels those who accept its use to accept its message as well. Some of the guides seemed to recognise this truth, for example:

> I think the instructors are the ones that can give the students a mind set that this is a magical place, this is a place that you can be somebody that you may never have been before, and you can learn something from it that you can't learn anywhere else.
>
> (interview, river guide, mwm40s)

'Like the magical universe the poetic one is full of participations, sympathies, and transformations' (Taylor 1979: 49). Thus when guides reframe experience for customers in terms of their mystical understandings, customers are invited to share the guides' metaphorical space:

> on this last trip I was walking along and I saw this beautiful flower. I said 'Oh, man, look at this really beautiful flower.' And the person that was standing right next to me said 'It's a weed.' And I said, 'It may be a weed, but that's still a really beautiful flower.' And the guy sort of stepped back and thought 'Yeah, I guess it is.' And, that right there was, I think, a step for him in seeing beauty in things that he doesn't typically see beauty in. Sort of redefined it.
>
> (interview, river guide, swm20s)

From Coleridge, the romantic movement took the 'notion that men are super-natural' – an idea that 'extends to their having power through passionate language to transform the nature from which they are separating themselves' (Taylor 1979: 65). One guide evokes the power to move nature:

> *Interviewer*: Can you talk about some other ways appeasing the river gods is talked about?
>
> *Guide*: They're really silly ways, I mean, really silly things, but like if it's really windy, you don't talk about it, you don't say the W word and, hopefully, if you don't talk about it, it'll go . . . you just don't mention it . . . and if it's . . . even if it's calm you never say the W word cause it will tend to . . .
>
> (interview, river guide, mwf 30s)

Another guide evokes the power both to move and to animate nature:

> *Guide*: I don't think I've ever met a single river guide that hasn't said 'River Gods please be good to me today.' Even some of the cockiest, most arro-gant, and some of the best guides . . . you know, they go kiss the water. I mean, it's just a . . . it is so powerful in there . . .
>
> *Interviewer*: They just want to be sure?
>
> *Guide*: And the river can just . . . it has a mind of its own . . . it can do so many . . . throw a boil up here . . . the waves can break right when you hit it and, I don't know, is it just the randomness of nature or is there some-thing to it, you know? I don't know.
>
> *Interviewer*: So people are better able to get a hold of that when they're on the river?
>
> *Guide*: I think so, I think they – yeah. Just sort of stop seeing the river as this just thing and start seeing it as alive, as almost a thinking being, I don't know. And, I think, that's why you see them doing that – that's sort of what we do. I don't think I'll ever run that rapid without kissing Tiger Wall.

Sometimes customers too begin to assume the power to change nature through poetic language as when rafters transformed Paul Simon's song *Kodachrome* into a chant designed to compel the sun to appear:

> So just before lunch, when everyone was standing around enjoying the warm sun, a cloud came over the sun. In response, Al and Mike and Michael and Patsy and that crowd, initiated the sun song . . . Paul Simon's *Kodachrome*. We began . . . first began singing on the bus, on the way to the put-in. After we sang, the cloud went away, and people remarked, 'See, the sun's out again.' And, someone else remarked, 'Yeah, you know, this is how religions get started.' Someone said to keep singing.
>
> (6/95 participant observation notes)

One river guide commented on this phenomena:

> *Interviewer*: Do clients seem to get into it?
> *Guide*: Uh-huh. Some do, yeah, some continue to add to stories and make up stories of their own or add to the jokes. Like 'Don't do this or the river god's going to . . .'
> *Interviewer*: Okay, so, they, sort of like, get into the playfulness of it?
> *Guide*: Yeah. But I think there is the playful nature of it, and then there's something that a lot of people feel that goes much deeper than that.

Magical speech also evokes cultural myths (Stoller 1995). The speech may in some sense form sentiments so elemental that they are body-felt, re-enacting fragments of cultural memories. In telling and retelling these stories, 'metaphors become symbols, they begin to perform more strictly magical feats, becoming the thing they signify and at the same time remaining themselves' (Taylor 1979: 55). For example:

> *Guide*: I really think I could see me being that person. I could see me, you know, getting on the horse, and going and rounding up, and checking the cattle, and making sure the fences are okay, and doing the 7 day drive to Sunnyside to get the cattle out, you know? I could see me doing that stuff, you know? So, I guess, maybe that's what it is.
> *Interviewer*: Okay, that kind of a connection.
> *Guide*: And, it's almost like living my life through this person, and it's real, because he was there and actually did it. It's not like watching a movie or something that's like, 'Oh, well, I want to be a cowboy,' you know? It's like these are words from somebody that was a cowboy. You know, this is real, and I'm standing on the ground where that person actually was raised and did these things.

We wonder whether the Odin evoked in the following excerpt could be a faint cultural echo of Odin in Thomas Gray's magical poem 'The Descent of Odin', that sought to link magic hidden within the depths of nature with the magic which the poet-magician desires to impose upon this nature (Taylor 1979: 24):

247

Well, you know, I tell the stories about Odin, the river god, and the Seventh Rock [it's always loose], and kissing the Tiger Wall, and those are all kind of fun superstitions but, for me, there really is a lot of spiritual connection between myself and who I am, and the rivers, and the environment out there that I have chosen to live in . . . I think there is a deeper connection there for a lot of people.

(interview, river guide, swf 30s)

Discussion

Magic is virtually a taboo subject in post-Enlightenment Western scholarship, including marketing. Magic has long been viewed as the antithesis of science. Similar to phenomena like fun, fantasy (Holbrook and Hirschman 1982), flow (Csikszentmihalyi 1990), charisma, and love (Belk and Coon 1993), the existential reality of magical experience evades utilitarian definition and scientific verification or replication. Perhaps because magical practices do not operate in terms easily accessible to Western prose conventions and Cartesian rationality (Stoller 1989; Stoller and Olkes 1987; Turner *et al.* 1992), even cultural anthropology features relatively few ethnographies of magical practice (e.g. Brown 1986; Fortune 1963; Malinowski 1935). In addition, magic sometimes stands in opposition to the social order. Magicians and witches are sometimes viewed as anti-social entities; magicians earn their knowledge through sometimes covert personal trials; by definition, practising magicians deviate from normative behaviour (Evans-Pritchard 1975).

Many of these characteristics of magic led the romantic poets to a celebration of magic and magical fantasy. Romantic fantasy was a celebration of the magical in societies for which magic had become 'benighted superstition' (Kroeber 1988: 1). Romantic poetic fantasy in the work of Coleridge, Thomas Gray, William Collins, Shelley, and even some works of Wordsworth was a response to the modern condition of rationalised civilisation, of 'culture deprived of enchantment. It sought to uncover magical possibilities especially in the processes of linguistic articulation and narrative' (Kroeber 1988: 29). The romantic poets sought a way to revitalise the 'material and mechanical universe' of Descartes and Hobbes through a melding of language, imagination, and the power inherent in nature (Abrams 1953: 65). The romantic poets thought that:

> If they could demonstrate that nature responded to songs and spells, they could disprove materialistic views of nature . . . They could prove not only they but nature herself had depths and mysterious sources of energy that the proponents of Hume and Voltaire scoffed at. If they could show that the depth and forces respond to incantations by virtue of a sympathy that exists between the spirits of nature and the spirit in man, they could banish the arguments of rationalists.
>
> (Taylor 1979: 14)

Indeed, for Shelley, 'the omnipotence of mind over matter' could be found. Indeed, 'it is in the rhythmical words of the poets that the internal and external energies converge, energies that are by turns political, scientific, and spiritual' (Taylor 1979: 191). Yet we know that the romantic movement declined with Keats and Byron, doomed by its excessive faith in the power of words, and its ideals have fallen from fashion.

Since the second half of the eighteenth century, dominant scientific and political practices equate social progress with broader modern utilitarian projects that include the bureaucratisation of professions and the rationalisation of production and consumption, which are in turn linked to the spread of technology and industrialisation. The industrial economy is linked to the project of rationalisation indirectly, through what Durkheim called 'organic solidarity'. Because modern society is integrated through the reciprocal dependency founded in the technical division of labour and marketplace exchange, Durkheim and other scholars of modernity argued that modern society does not require adherence to fantastical magical beliefs to hold together. Enshrined in orthodox economics, operations research, and structural functionalist social science is the belief that rational ideas can prevail (O'Keefe 1982).

But what happens should organic solidarity fail? Writing after the decline of romanticism, Durkheim called for a state-sponsored cult of reason and individualism to prevent this, a cult whose functions have been served by economics and related fields. However, popular belief in the rationalising project of modernity may have been shaken by dire changes in social structure: extreme occupational specialisation, economic uncertainty, globalisation of markets for capital, labour, and cultural productions, the withdrawal of social safety nets, and heightened anomie and alienation amongst the poor. The problems of postmodernity thus include: bureaucratisation of social life, loss of agency, fragmentation, and technological change without the meta-narrative of progress, and breakdown of other modern master narratives (Featherstone 1990, 1995; Firat and Venkatesh 1995; Lyotard 1984). Still science has so usurped the role of traditional cosmology that our view of the universe is no longer somatocentric. That is, for many westerners, the universe is no longer responsive to the human condition, and it is no longer inhabited by a hidden but efficacious divinity (Laughlin 1993). As Mary Douglas puts it, the imponderable forces in our world are represented not by spiritual beings immanent in the natural landscape but 'by forms to complete in triplicate, parking meters, inexorable laws. [Our] cosmos is dominated by [consumption] objects of which [we] and [our] fellow humans are victims' (1973: 61).

Postmodern theorists argue for a breakdown in certain master narratives, cultural pre-understandings, or Castoriadis's 'radical imaginary'. It may be the increasing redundancy of people in production, and the reduction of their social role to that of mere consumers, and the resultant retreat of individuals from the democratic process and the responsibilities of citizenship that contribute to postmodern anomie. Certain global tendencies mark more the growth of religious and quasi-religious cults, of resurgent mythic nationalisms, and manufactured ethnicity, than the triumph of secular reason (Costa and Bamossy 1995; Featherstone 1990, 1995).

But where does this imaginary lie? Not merely in words as the romantic poets believed. Some anthropologists argue that it lies in part, in the embodied rituals that trigger cultural memory and myth, and inscribe bodies and selves in a cultural tradition (Bell 1992; Stoller 1995). Hence, part of the dramatic growth in new festivals, rituals, public ceremonials (Kuglemass 1994; Santino 1994) and even cults in recent years may signal a nostalgic, magical attempt to reinvent, and reinscribe bodies and persons in vivid, body-felt cultural traditions. Similarly, the special attraction of ritualised wilderness adventures lies both in their experiential dimensions and also in essentially romantic mythic representations of nature (Arnould *et al.* 1998; Celsi *et al.* 1993; Kaplan and Kaplan 1989). It may be therefore, that if 'the world becomes strange to the mass because they have withdrawn from the rational processes of society (or because they have been edged out of active participation in them) they may start to behave magically just to cope' (O'Keefe 1982: 463).

Our study of river magic suggests that two hundred years after the romantic movement briefly flowered, magic and enchantment have not been driven from culture by the utilitarian logic of the market. We feel that magic will enjoy a resurgence in postmodernity. The spirit that drove the romantic movement seems alive in the phenomena cited at the outset of the chapter, in the resurgence of festivals and the florescence of activities like river rafting. What links these practices to the romantic movement is the same. 'To establish that man shares his own life with nature was to reanimate the dead world of the materialists, and . . . to tie man back into his milieu' (Abrams 1953: 65). Rafting experiences are even consistent with the then revolutionary, now magical-seeming late eighteenth-century pantheistic philosophy of nature adopted by the romantic poets. This philosophy envisioned: 'an independent life and sensibility in every organized form of being, even those apparently inanimate [that] opened the way for the possibility . . . of a moral relationship between man and natural objects' (Piper 1962: 72).

Magic and magical fantasy, such as that experienced by river rafters, help us to imagine how language and experience can create meaning, how they might determine, not merely refer to, the nature of lived reality. Magical fantasy

> allows us . . . to reassert our human power to overcome the strength of human creations which function to dehumanise us by confining us within reified structures of our own making. Fantasy is an enabling mode because it recovers for us a necessary sense that there is something other than ourselves for us to wonder at together.
>
> (Kroeber 1988: 139)

The resurgence of magic presents both threats and opportunities to marketing practice. The undeniable growth of experiential consumption among well-off consumers may signal a sea-change from a mimetic to an expressive consumption mode, just as romanticism signalled a change from a mimetic to an expressive mode of artistic production (Taylor 1979: 17). While romanticism no longer dominates artistic production, neither is mimesis a prominent precept. Similarly, as others have suggested (Brown 1995; Firat and Venkatesh 1995) we may be entering a long period in which expressive consumption dominates. Marketers who can respond to consumers' desire for expressivity may thrive.

Magic also threatens because magical practice opposes the techno-rationalistic logic that rules marketing practice. In part because of its anti-social character, magic eludes easy control. And imaginative magical outcomes are not easily manipulated. Advertisers and other marketers often use the language of magic and ritual (McCreery 1995b; Otnes and Scott 1996) without really understanding the elements (condition of the performer, rite, and formula) that make magical experience possible. Marketers can provide rites, formulae, ritual artefacts and vivid imagery to evoke cultural memory. But while magic can be marketed, embodied magical experience cannot be so easily created. And the desire for magical experience is not fully satisfied by fraudulent appropriations, e.g. 'the magic of Disney'. For magic to succeed, actors must actively lend their bodies to the process, both creatively and aesthetically, rather than as passive consumers (Stoller 1995). Ultimately, even if marketers deploy magic strategically, marketers may discover that the irrationality and explosive vitality of magical systems limit their ability to appropriate magical cultural forms and meanings.

Note

1 Three primary sources of data collected in 1995 on river rafting are employed – depth interviews with fifteen experienced river guides based in eastern Utah, ten days of participant observation white water river rafting on the Yampa River in Dinosaur National Monument, and post-trip surveys with 50 plus customers of 5-day raft trips. These data were supplemented with results of about one hundred surveys conducted with rafting participants in 1991 and participant observation data collected on several rafting trips the same year. Our interpretations are also based partly on essays about river rafting composed as a classroom exercise with several dozen students. This data is supplemented with a dozen student interviews on magical experience. The chapter also draws on interview data with consumers focused on the transformative aspects of ordinary products, as well as on analyses of consumer product advertisements.

References

Abrams, M.H. (1953), *The Mirror and the Lamp: Romantic Theory and the Critical Tradition*, New York: Oxford University Press.

Abrams, M.H. (1971), *Natural Supernaturalism: Tradition and Revolution in Romantic Literature*, New York: W.W. Norton & Co.

Arnould, E.J. and Price, L.L. (1993), 'River magic: extraordinary experience and the extended service encounter', *Journal of Consumer Research*, 20(1), 24–46.

Arnould, E.J., Price, L.L. and Otnes, C. (1997), 'Making consumption magic', working paper, Tampa, FL: University of South Florida.

Arnould, E.J., Price, L.L. and Tierney, P. (1998), 'The wilderness servicescape', in J.F. Sherry, Jr. (ed.), *Servicescapes: The Concept of Place in Contemporary Marketing*, Lincolnwood, IL: NTC Publications.

Belk, R.W. (1991), 'The ineluctable mysteries of possessions', in F. Rudmin (ed.), *To Have Possessions: A Handbook of Ownership and Property*, special issue of *Journal of Social Behavior and Personality*, 6(6), 14–55.

Belk, R.W. (1996), 'On aura, illusion, escape and hope in apocalyptic consumption: the apotheosis of La Vegas', in S. Brown *et al.* (eds), *Marketing Apocalypse*, London: Routledge, 87–107.

Belk, R.W. and Coon, G.S. (1993), 'Gift giving as agapic love: an alternative to the exchange paradigm based on dating experiences', *Journal of Consumer Research* 20(3), 393–417.

Belk, R.W., Wallendorf, M. and Sherry, J.F., Jr. (1989), 'The sacred and profane in consumer behavior: theodicy on the Odyssey', *Journal of Consumer Research* 16(1), 1–38.

Bell, C. (1992), *Ritual Theory, Ritual Practice*, Oxford: Oxford University Press.

Bettelheim, B. (1977), *The Uses of Enchantment: The Meaning and Importance of Fairy Tales*, New York: Vintage Books.

Blum, R. and Golitzin, A. (1991), *The Sacred Athlete: On the Mystical Experience and Dionysios, Its Westernworld Fountainhead*, Lanham, MD: University Press of America.

Brown, M.F. (1986), *Tsewa's Gift: Magic and Meaning in an Amazonian Society*, Washington, DC: Smithsonian Institution Press.

Brown, S. (1995), *Postmodern Marketing*, London: Routledge.

Brown, S. (1997), 'Marketing science in a postmodern world: introduction to the special issue', *European Journal of Marketing* 31(3/4), 167–82.

Caudron, S. (1992), 'Thrill-seekers proliferate', *Industry Week* 16 November, 27–34.

Celsi, R.L., Rose, R.L. and Leigh, T.W. (1993), 'An exploration of high-risk leisure consumption through skydiving', *Journal of Consumer Research* 20(1), 1–23.

Costa, J.A. and Bamossy, G.J. (eds) (1995), *Marketing in a Multicultural World: Ethnicity, Nationalism and Cultural Identity*, Newbury Park, CA: Sage Publications.

Csikszentmihalyi, M. (1990), *Flow: The Psychology of Optimal Experience*, New York: Harper & Row.

Douglas, M.O. (1973), *Natural Symbols*, New York: Random House.

Evans-Pritchard, E.E. (1975 [1937]), *Witchcraft, Magic and Oracles Among the Azande*, Oxford: Clarendon Press.

Featherstone, M. (ed.) (1990), *Global Culture*, London: Sage Publications.

Featherstone, M. (1995), *Undoing Culture*, London: Sage Publications.

Firat, A.F. and Venkatesh, A. (1995), 'Liberatory postmodernism and the reenchantment of consumption', *Journal of Consumer Research* 22(3), 239–67.

Fortune, R. (1963 [1932]), *Sorcerers of Dobu*, New York: E.P. Dutton.

Hartig, T., Mang, M. and Evans, G.W. (1991), 'Restorative effects of natural environment experiences', *Environment and Behavior*, 23 (January), 3–26.

Holbrook, M.B. and Hirschman, E.C. (1982), 'The experiential aspects of consumption: consumer fantasies, feelings, and fun', *Journal of Consumer Research*, 9(2), 132–40.

Horton, R. (1993), *Patterns of Thought in Africa and the West*, Cambridge: Cambridge University Press.

Kaplan, R. and Kaplan, S. (1989), *The Experience of Nature: A Psychological Perspective*, Cambridge: Cambridge University Press.

Kozinets, R.V. (1996), "'I want to believe:" An ethnography of the "Xphiles" subculture of consumption', paper presented at the Association for Consumer Research Conference, Tucson, AZ, October.

Kroeber, K. (1988), *Romantic Fantasy and Science Fiction*, New Haven: Yale University Press.

Kuglemass, J. (1994), 'Wishes come true: designing the Greenwich Village Halloween parade', in J. Santino (ed.), *Halloween and Other Festivals of Life and Death*, Knoxville, TN: University of Tennessee Press.

Laughlin, C.D. (1993), 'Revealing the hidden: the epiphanic dimension of games and sport', *Journal of Ritual Studies* 7 (Winter), 85–104.

Leenhardt, M. (1982), *Do Kamo: Person and Myth in the Melanesian World*, J. Clifford (ed.), Berkeley: University of California Press.

Levi-Bruhl, L. (1973 [1949]), *Notebooks on Primitive Mentality*, Oxford: Blackwell.

Levi-Strauss, C. (1987 [1950]), *Introduction to the Work of Marcel Mauss*, trans. F. Baker, London: Routledge & Kegan Paul.

Lyotard, J.-F. (1984 [1979]), *The Postmodern Condition: A Report on Knowledge*, trans. G. Bennington and B. Massumi, Manchester: Manchester University Press.

McCreery, J.L. (1995a), 'Negotiating with demons: the uses of magical language', *American Ethnologist* 22 (February), 144–64.

McCreery, J.L. (1995b), 'Magic, Malinowski, and advertising: on choosing metaphors', in J.F. Sherry, Jr. (ed.), *Contemporary Marketing and Consumer Behavior*, Thousand Oaks, CA: Sage Publications.

McSherry, M. (1996), 'Parallel lines', *Horizons* October–November, 8–9.

Maffesoli, M. (1996), *The Contemplation of the World*, trans. S. Emanuel, Minneapolis: University of Minnesota Press.

Malinowski, B. (1935), *Coral Gardens and Their Magic*, 2 vols, New York: American Book Co.

Malinowski, B. (1954), *Magic, Science and Religion and Other Essays*, New York: Doubleday Anchor Books.

Mick, D.G. and Fournier, S. (1995), 'Technological products in everyday life: ownership, meaning, and satisfaction', Report No. 95–104, Cambridge, MA: Marketing Science Institute.

Miller, K. (1997), 'Star Struck!', *Life* July, 38–52.

O'Keefe, D.L. (1982), *Stolen Lighting: The Social Theory of Magic*, New York: Continuum.

Otnes, C. (1995), 'The transformative power of products', paper presented at the Association for Consumer Research Conference, Minneapolis, MN, October.

Otnes, C. and Lowrey, T.M. (1993), 'Til debt do us part: the selection and meaning of artifacts in the American wedding', in L. McAlister and M. Rothschild (eds), *Advances in Consumer Research*, 20, Provo, UT: Association for Consumer Research.

Otnes, C. and Scott, L.M. (1996), 'Something old, something new: exploring the interaction between ritual and advertising', *Journal of Advertising* 25 (Spring), 33–50.

Piper, H.W. (1962), *The Active Universe: Pantheism and the Concept of Imagination in the English Romantic Poets*, London: The Athlone Press.

Rook, D. (1985), 'The ritual dimension of consumer behavior', *Journal of Consumer Research,* 12(3), 251–64.

Rosaldo, M. (1975), 'It's all uphill: the creative metaphors of Ilongot magical spells', in M. Sanchez and B.G. Blount (eds), *Sociocultural Dimensions of Language Use*, New York: Academic Press.

Santino, J. (ed.) (1994), *Halloween and Other Festivals of Life and Death*, Knoxville, TN: University of Tennessee Press.

Schieffelin, E.L. (1985), 'Performance and the cultural construction of reality', *American Ethnologist* 12 (November), 707–24.

Schouten, J. and McAlexander, J.H. (1995), 'Subcultures of consumption: an ethnography of the new bikers', *Journal of Consumer Research*, 22 (1), 43–61.

Stoller, P. (1989), *The Taste of Ethnographic Things*, Philadelphia: University of Pennsylvania Press.

Stoller, P. (1995), *Embodying Colonial Memories*, New York: Routledge.

Stoller, P. and Olkes, C. (1987), *In Sorcery's Shadow: A Memoir of Apprenticeship Among the Songhay of Niger*, Chicago: University of Chicago Press.

Tambiah, S.J. (1968), 'the magical power of words', *Man* n.s., 3, 175–208.

Tambiah, S.J. (1990), *Magic, Science, Religion, and the Scope of Rationality*, Cambridge: Cambridge University Press.

Taussig, M.F. (1989), *The Devil and Commodity Fetishism in South America*, Chapel Hill: University of North Carolina Press.

Taylor, A. (1979), *Magic and English Romanticism*, Athens: University of Georgia Press.

Thomas, K. (1971), *Religion and the Decline of Magic*, New York: Scribners.

Turner, E., with Blodgett, W., Kahona, S. and Benwa, W. (1992), *Experiencing Ritual: A New Interpretation of African Healing*, Philadelphia: University of Pennsylvania Press.

Turner, V. (1969), *The Ritual Process*, Chicago: Aldine.

Voeks, R.A. (1997), *Sacred Leaves of Candomblé*, Austin: University of Texas Press.

Williamson, J. (1978), *Decoding Advertisements: Ideology and Meaning in Advertising*, London: Marion Boyers.

Worthington, C. (1997), 'Of dolls, karma and the pursuit of motherhood', *The New York Times* 30 November, 45.

14

THE UNBEARABLE LIGHTNESS OF MARKETING

A neo-romantic, counter-revolutionary recapitulation

Stephen Brown

> The idea of eternal return is a mysterious one, and Nietzsche has often perplexed other philosophers with it; to think that everything recurs as we once experienced it, and that the recurrence itself recurs ad infinitum! What does this mad myth signify?
>
> (Kundera 1984: 3)

The pretentious 'introductory' part

According to Milan Kundera (1984), the 'mad myth' of eternal return has heinous implications for the history of humankind, irrespective of its truth value. If events, as Nietzsche posits, are condemned to occur again and again in perpetuity, then they are endowed with much greater significance than they are under the 'traditional' regime of linear, Western, Judaeo-Christian time. Whereas it is possible to come to terms with the horrors of, say, Auschwitz, Hiroshima or the Somme, knowing that they were once-and-for-all occurrences and thus never likely to be repeated, the prospect of the perpetual reappearance of such iniquities places an impossible burden upon contemporary decision takers, since their actions will inevitably come back to haunt them for ever and ever. Amen.

The same crushing weight is also apparent at the less elevated, albeit equally meaningful, level of everyday human existence. If, as Kundera avers, everything we do is certain to recur – in all its excruciating detail – then our daily actions, activities, ambitions and aspirations suddenly assume a much greater degree of significance than they 'ordinarily' do. Like the apocryphal butterflies of chaos theory, the metaphorical flapping of our existential wings may give rise to behavioural tornadoes on the other side of the globe. So pregnant are the possible implications of our everyday actions that we may be frozen into a state of perpetual inactivity, fearful of the eternal consequences of our mundane but potentially ruinous behaviours. Eternal recurrence, in effect, makes the present tense.

Fascinating though such speculations are, the fact of the matter is that events occur but once, as every sensible person knows. No matter how much we would like to go back and repair our past mistakes, misjudgements and misdemeanours, or revel in fleeting moments of minor personal triumph, the past is indubitably the past. It cannot recur. Indeed, as our behaviours, however idiotic or bizarre, are guaranteed to fade into ultimate nothingness, our daily existence is less fraught, less momentous, less burdensome under linear time than under Nietzsche's eternal return of the same.

For Kundera, however, this very 'lightness of being' – this sense of existential freedom, of ephemerality, of relief – is itself intolerable, since it demands a greater degree of creativity, of innovativeness, of risk-taking, of achievement than most of us are comfortable with or are capable of attaining. Hence, the significance of insignificance, the consequences of inconsequentiality, the very weightlessness of life, weigh heavily upon us. We are resigned to, and entrapped by, the unbearable lightness of being.

The 'let's-see-what-we-can-make-of-this-stuff' part

If history, unlike historians, does not repeat itself, then only the most millenarian of marketing Muggletonians would surmise that the *fin* of our *fin de siècle* is a rerun of the romantic revolution of the late eighteenth century. It is, I grant you, hard not to see parallels between the storming of the Bastille in 1789 and the latter-day fall of the Berlin Wall, which was not only timed to perfection – give or take a few months – but was followed, like its prodigious predecessor, by the presumptuous if short-lived assumption that a new world order of peace, love and understanding had magically materialised. However, for the purposes of discussion and in an admittedly contrived attempt to bring this book to a semi-coherent conclusion,[1] it may be worthwhile conceding the concept, the notion, the possibility, of eternal recurrence – but just this once! Nietzsche, remember, was merely recycling much recycled concepts of cyclical time – forerunners include Vico, Polybius and Heraclitus (see Brown 1995a; Campion 1994; Trompf 1979) – which were part of the magical, mystical, illuminist tradition referred to in an earlier chapter (not, to repeat, that I'm one to repeat myself, or rework old ideas, or rehash prior publications, or recycle cycles of papers of papers on cycles, or anything that smacks of reiteration, recapitulation, resuscitation . . .).

This concluding chapter, then, concludes with a conclusion about conclusions; precedes that with a call to resurrect the carnivalesque spirit of one emblematic pre-modern marketer; the scene for which is set by a light regurgitation of the main lessons arising from the present volume; and which is prefixed in turn by an examination of the perceived parallels between romanticism and postmodernism (well, somebody's gotta deal with that one before it's too late). All these are heralded by a summary execution of an executive summary which pretentiously reverses the order of events in order to eventuate the reversal of the reader–writer relationship. Postmodern readers, remember, are made not found, though some readers are made to founder more than others. (Did you imagine for a moment that this was going to be a conventional closing chapter? Please! Some of us have pseudo-intellectual reputations to preserve.)

The 'eternal return of the paean' part

Just as it is possible to identify analogues between the falls of the Bastille and the Berlin Wall, so too the intellectual turmoil that swirled in the slipstream of liberty, equality and fraternity is replicated by our own revolution in thought, which labours under the augean label 'postmodern'. Certainly, the congruence between romanticism and postmodernism is nothing if not striking (Livingston 1998; Readings and Schaber 1993; Tarnas 1991). Perhaps the most obvious parallel is the basic fact that would-be summarisers of the latter often resort to the self-same list of adjectives as prospective explicants of the former – intuitive, creative, spontaneous, insouciant, iconoclastic, imaginative, etc. – and these are contrasted in turn with the purportedly distinguishing features of postmodernism's intellectual predecessor, that which its prefix prefixes (i.e. the rational, logical, ordered, controlled character of modernism). Consider, for example, the following undeniably orotund passage, which with the substitution of neoclassicist for modernist and romantic for postmodernist could just as easily have been written about the earlier movement:

> Postmodernists offer ambiguity where modernists offered certainty, they seek complexity where their predecessors sought simplification, they find disorder where their forebears found order, they see a glass that is half-empty instead of half-full and they challenge convention by refusing to accept the accepted. Postmodernists espouse individuality as opposed to universality, advocate plurality instead of consensus, place heterogeneity above homogeneity, emphasise dissent rather than conformity and champion difference where modernists stressed similarity. In short, they replace the traditional modernist emphasis on reason, objectivity and control with unreason, subjectivity and emancipation, with paradox, uncertainty and instability, with a rationale that rejects rationality.
>
> (Brown 1995b: 166)

Analogous inventories of antitheses notwithstanding, another remarkable similarity between romanticism and postmodernism is their sheer incoherence. Now, this is not to say that they cannot be comprehended, though that has indeed been said. Porter and Teich's (1988: 4) frank admission that 'there is something intrinsically and astonishingly complex about romanticism' has been echoed by countless commentators on the postmodern condition. As the late, great and far from unforthcoming Ernest Gellner memorably announced,

> Postmodernism is a contemporary movement. It is strong and fashionable. Over and above this, it is not altogether clear what the devil it is. In fact, clarity is not conspicuous among its marked attributes. It not only generally fails to practice it but also on occasion actually repudiates it . . . there appear to be no 39 postmodernist Articles of Faith, no postmodernist manifesto, which one could consult so as to assure oneself that one has identified its ideas properly.
>
> (1992: 22–3)

Incoherence has its place, as readers of my, er, *œuvre* will readily testify, but it seems to me that the principal reason for the air of confusion that surrounds both -isms is due to their sheer catholicism, their infinite variety, their astonishing plurivalence and pervasiveness. Like romanticism, postmodernism commenced in the aesthetic sphere but has since spread out into almost every nook and cranny of the contemporary socio-cultural matrix (e.g. Anderson 1995; Appignanesi and Garratt 1995; Ward 1997). Postmodern films, music, buildings, plays, television programmes, clothes, cuisines, gardens, holidays, religions, politicians, comedians, families, bodies, diseases, and so on are literally two an Ecu these days. The shelves of our libraries and bookshops are sagging under the weight of texts with 'postmodern', or one of its copious cognates, in the title. And, the A to Z of academic disciplines – from accountancy to zoology – has been infiltrated, some would say stiffed, by the intellectual body snatchers of postmodernity. The inevitable upshot is that 'postmodern' is rapidly coming to refer to just about anything and everything, as was the case with 'romantic', albeit its very omnipresence is deeply ironic since postmodernism is opposed to universal, totalising or nomothetic modes of thought and, *à la* romanticism, places great store by difference, diversity, singularity, specificacy, locality and suchlike.

Of course, once everything becomes 'postmodern' (or 'romantic' or whatever), then the term has lost its power to discriminate and rapidly becomes meaningless. Just as romanticism had been reduced to a vogue expression by 1830 – apparently, it was being applied to Parisian tailors, milliners, pastrycooks, doctors and apothecaries, as well as pulp fiction, decorative knick-knacks and *objets d'art* (Honour 1981: 55) – so too postmodernism has become exasperatingly ubiquitous, a late twentieth-century synonym for 'vague', 'baffling', 'trendy', 'pretentious' or 'pseudo-intellectual'. It is, in fact, the *dernier-cri* of pseudo-intellectualism, as a pseudo-intellectual once aptly put it (Brown 1998a: 258). In these circumstances, it is little wonder that those individuals whose names are most closely associated with the postmodern movement (Derrida, Baudrillard, Foucault, Rorty, Feyerabend, etc.) have publicly detached themselves from the label, though in this respect they are merely repeating the disassociative actions of their romantic forerunners such as Hugo, Goethe, Byron, de Vigny and Delacroix (Cranston 1994). Granted, the latter group's objection to being dubbed romantic was itself a characteristically romantic expression of the characteristically romantic emphasis on individuality and uniqueness – rebelling against romanticism is very much in keeping with the rebelliousness of romanticism – but it also reflected an understandable reluctance to be categorised, to be pigeonholed, to be aligned with any school, coterie, movement or 'association of mediocrities', as Delacroix charmingly put it. According to one prominent authority, however, this resistance to categorisation is again entirely compatible with the antinomian romantic/postmodern spirit:

> whilst each new generation of romantics establish their credentials by denying that they are indeed romantics . . . the analyst has had to accept the emotional truth of such claims whilst repudiating their literal meaning, thus recognising that continuity in rebellion which is the romantic tradition.
>
> (Campbell 1987: 219)

The 'time for a new section' part

Naturally, I hesitate to generalise about two movements that abhor generalisations, yet our present postmodern effluvium is, by any reckoning, astonishingly similar to the romantic efflorescence of the late eighteenth century. The 'PoMo' signifier, for example, has innumerable signifieds and if not exactly free-floating, it certainly levitates from time to time (or Levittates in the case of postmodern marketing). There is a complete lack of consensus over what it is or isn't, or whether it is in fact an 'it'. The most cogent definitions of the phenomenon come from opponents, agnostics and the unconverted (Callinicos 1989; Harvey 1989; Rosenau 1992). And, if truth be told, the buccaneering air of transgression, of subversiveness, of impertinence, of rebelliousness that once accompanied postmodern thought appears to be rapidly disappearing as it settles into the well-upholstered armchair of academic orthodoxy (Callinicos 1995). In these respects, of course, it is once again akin to its formidable forerunner. Romanticism, as we observed in Chapter 1, proved all but indefinable; it served as the orthodoxy against which subsequent expressions of aesthetic dissent could rail and by far the most influential assessments of the movement were posited in the early years of the present century by antagonists like Irving Babbitt, T.E. Hulme and T.S. Eliot (much of the ensuing debate, indeed, has been devoted to defending, not simply defining, the romantic propensity, though it remains to be seen if the post-postmodern skirmishes will be waged on the same territory).

There is, however, more to the postmodernism/romanticism comparison than sheer pervasiveness, definitional difficulties and the radical–reactionary trajectory that characterises movements, fashions and ideologies generally (Garner 1996). Both represent an attempt to break down the barriers between high art and low. Thus *Lyrical Ballads* deliberately embraced the modalities of commonfolk and treated degraded subject matters (the poor, the oppressed, abandoned children, etc.) with the reverence normally reserved for the elevated biblical, mythical and aristocratic themes addressed by neoclassicists. Postmodernism, likewise, examines *déclassé* cultural forms – comic books, glossy magazines, hairstyles, soccer, heavy metal, soap operas, shopping – with the seriousness traditionally accorded to 'proper' culture. The language employed by PoRo populists, admittedly, has been sufficiently high falutin' to attract derision and ridicule – in *Don Juan*, for example, Byron challenges Coleridge, his fellow romantic revolutionary, to 'explain his explanation' and the syntactic excesses of postmodernists are routinely condemned – as has their inordinate fondness for abstract theorising. Nevertheless, a de-differentiating tendency is common to both.

Equally equivalent is the romantic/postmodern antipathy to Science (with a capital S). It is no exaggeration to state that Newton, Locke and the mechanistic Enlightenment worldview, which underpinned the neoclassical ethos of propriety, rationality and reason, was reviled by the romantics (Berlin 1981, 1991). The narrow pragmatism of the Newtonian paradigm had, in effect, 'clipped an angel's wings'. It only served to disenchant the world, to rob it of its mysteries and magnificence, to reduce everything and everyone to machines, automatons, the inhuman. In a Newtonian universe, everything was knowable and predestined, nothing was left to chance, determinism was all, base utilitarianism our fate. The romantics, to be sure, were proselytising at the outset of the Industrial Revolution, and the inestimable benefits of science and technology have only really made themselves manifest in the last 200 years. Yet, William Blake's heartfelt plea, 'May God us keep/From single vision and Newton's sleep!', continues to strike a chord with many postmodernists. While few would deny that Western science has brought untold benefits, for those in the developed world at least, it has done so at enormous environmental, economic, social and political cost (Brown 1996). The limits of science are as apparent to contemporary romantics as they were to their prodigious precursors. Indeed, there is ample evidence of an emerging 'postmodern' approach to science (chaos, complexity, Gaia, etc.), which is again reminiscent of 'natural philosophy', its remarkably successful romantic forerunner (Hobsbawm 1973).

Another astonishing similarity between the great revolts of the late eighteenth and late twentieth centuries is their fixation with the nature and characteristics of the Self. Hard though it is to believe, our colloquial or commonplace conception of the Self as a stable, autonomous, unified, free-thinking individual, with feelings, needs, desires, emotions and, not least, 'personality', dates from the romantic period (Gergen 1991; Lyons 1978). Prior to that, people tended to be regarded – and regarded themselves – as exemplars of more general categories, most notably members of a religious denomination, class, profession, extended family and the like. Even the soul did not belong to a specific sinner, since it was created by God and situated in mortal flesh for a fleeting period. However, thanks to the romantics' obsession with what Coleridge termed 'the infinite I AM' (that is, their desire to uncover the authentic self and express its emanations freely and creatively, without recourse to accepted patterns or fixed conventions), a whole new conception of human subjectivity started to emerge (Bygrave 1986; Furst 1969; Lystra 1989). This romantic sense of the Self, as passionate, profound, purposeful and moved by mysterious powers that surged beneath the surface veneer of consciousness, is still very prevalent, albeit refracted through modernist sensibilities which regarded reason, logic, objectivity, systematicity and facticity as central to human nature – Freud notwithstanding. Although this modernist 'man as machine' metaphor is also alive and well, it is being superseded by the mutable, multiphrenic, fragmented, nomadic, negotiable, pick'n'mix selves/identities/lifestyles/roles of the post-modern condition (Gergen 1991).

The fluidity of the postmodern self and the abyssal depths of its romantic predecessor resonate, to some extent, with one of the key tropes of both movements. *Movement.* Despite the competing claims of 'text', 'cyborg', 'seduction' and so on, the postmodern landscape is striated with similes of mobility: travel, circulation, restlessness, nomadism, migrancy, tourism, vagabonds, border crossings, postcards and the like (see Belk 1997; Brown and Turley 1997; Kaplan 1996). The same is true of the romantic period, the artworks of which were suffused with wanderers, vagrants, pilgrims, travellers, troubadours, mariners, minstrels, outlaws, outcasts, excursionists and solitary journeys into the inner self or, indeed, times past (e.g. Coleridge's 'Rime of the Ancient Mariner', Keats's 'Endymion', Byron's 'Manfred' and *Childe Harold's Pilgrimage*, Caspar David Friedrich's celebrated painting *The Wanderer Above the Mists*). Bloom (1970), remember, regards romanticism *per se* as the quest romance internalised; that is to say, a renaissance of the Renaissance romance tradition, but transposed from an external search, albeit in a mythical or otherworldly setting, to an internal quest for the grail of self-knowledge and personal salvation (see also Abrams 1971; Elam 1992; Frye 1963).[2] Be that as it may, an overwhelming sense of disturbance, agitation, crisis, fitfulness, change and Becoming (as opposed to Being) is shared by romanticism and postmodernism alike.

Just as movement is a characteristic metaphor of PoRo, so too their defining mode of expression is *ironic* (Behler 1990; Hutcheon 1994; Rose 1993). Irony, admittedly, long pre-dates the romantic period – Plato's dialogues and *eiron*, the stock 'dissembling' figure of Ancient Greek comedy, are two prominent antecedents – as do its copious satirical siblings (parody, sarcasm, invective, persiflage and the like). What's more, irony was much prized during the neoclassical era and, indeed, central to the analytical apparatus of the modernist New Critics (Childers and Hentzi 1995; Gray 1992). However, it reached new heights of sophistication during the romantic epoch and, so prevalent is irony nowadays, that postmodernism has been described as 'the philosophy of inverted commas' (Scruton 1994: 504). Thus, the Schlegels coined the term 'romantic irony' to describe a mode of writing where the author builds up the illusion of reality only to subvert it by revealing that it is, in fact, the work of an author

(Byron's *Don Juan* and Sterne's pre-romantic *Tristram Shandy* are classics of the genre). The intrusion of author figures, self-reflexive asides and frame-breaking devices are also commonplace in postmodern novels 'about novelists experiencing difficulty writing novels' (Watkins 1991: 21). In this respect, however, postmodern ironists like Auster, Eco, Calvino, Stoppard, Letterman and Partridge (plus their academic avatars – Derrida, de Man, Rorty and Baudrillard) are merely rearticulating what Tieck, Chamisso, Hoffman and many other exponents of the German *Märchen* tradition attempted approximately 200 years ago.[3]

Ironically enough, the parallels between romanticism and postmodernism do not end with irony. One thinks, for instance, of both movements' extensive antecedents, their fondness for the fragment, their concern with issues of exoticism and the Other, their retrospective/holistic/organicist inclinations, and so on. Indeed, if we concede that they are part and parcel of the same anti-Enlightenment impulse, which periodically comes to prominence only to slacken and subsequently lose its grip on the collective consciousness, then the homologous nature of romanticism and postmodernism is only to be expected (Tarnas 1991). There is a danger, however, of over-emphasising the analogues, of falling into the trap of what Wellek and Warren (1963: 119) term 'positive analogy'; in other words, a tendency to over-emphasise the similarities between different periods and to downplay the differences. The sheer heterogeneity of the romantic and postmodern conditions is sufficient to ensure that those determined to find parallels will find them, whereas those predisposed to identifying differences will discover them too. This 'negative analogy' is perhaps most marked in the closely related 'dichotomisation' issue; our propensity to emphasise the differences between romanticism/neoclassicism, on the one hand, and postmodernism/modernism on the other. Such Jeckyll/Hyde-style dichotomies, needless to say, are never as clear-cut as they are made out to be. Just as it is possible to identify neoclassic romanticism and romantic neoclassicism, so too modern postmodernists and postmodern modernists are readily observable. For Lyotard, in fact, postmodernism is, and always has been, the contemporary avant-garde, that which lies 'beyond' what is currently acceptable or expected. Hence his celebrated, if ostensibly oxymoronic, statement, 'A work can become modern only if it is first postmodern. Postmodernism thus understood is not modernism at its end but in the nascent state, and this state is constant' (Lyotard 1984: 79).

The 'show me the marketing' part

Despite these caveats, it is important not to downplay the fact that revolutionary changes undoubtedly took place at the end of the eighteenth century, that equally revolutionary events are unfolding during the present *fin de siècle*, and that there are concordances between the two. From our own perspective, perhaps the most significant of these are: first, that both romanticism and postmodernism commenced in the cultural sphere, involved a valorisation of aesthetics and comprised a reaction to the profound social and political turmoil of the times (Simpson 1993; Talmon 1979; Wu 1997). Thus, the American and French Revolutions comprised the breeding ground of romanto-genesis, while the counter-cultural strain of the 1960s/1970s cusp, coupled with the latter-day collapse of the Communist bloc, did likewise for the postmodern parturition (Jencks 1989; Bertens 1995). Second, both movements were characterised by an all-pervasive mood of melancholia, apprehension, abjection, anxiety and despair, albeit leavened by a shaft of ironic, mordant, self-deprecatory wit (Clay 1981; Cranston 1994). This 'sense of an ending' – apocalypse, calamity, crisis, transition and profound change – was common to both, as was the paradoxical ethos of exhilaration in the face of extinction, the thanatic thrill of impending obliteration, the strange mixture of terror and hope that informs the apocalyptic mind set (Abrams 1971; Brown *et al.* 1996; Shaffer 1995). Third, and of particular relevance to our present marketing concerns, is that periods of intense chiliastic expectation are often associated with times of profound economic-cum-technological change and the disturbing, dispossessing, dislocating, redistributive disruptions that invariably follow in their wake (Cohn 1970; Kumar 1995). Just as romanticism is often regarded as a protest against the dehumanising effects of the Industrial Revolution, so too postmodernism is often treated as the superstructural nutri-grain bun around the B(a)SE burger of late capitalism, even though an inferno of consumption is the profoundly ironic outcome (Jameson 1991; Rosenau 1992).

In point of fact, postmodernism's somewhat paradoxical relationship with the marketplace is no less striking that than of romanticism, referred to in Chapter 1. Not only have many postmodern artists turned to the commercial sphere for inspiration (Warhol, Morley, Madonna), or cut their aesthetic teeth in marketised domains like advertising (Ridley Scott, Salman Rushdie), but one of the key measures of 'success' in the postmodern artworld is bottom-line performance in the market – tickets sold, prices achieved, people attracted, etc. Postmodern museums, let's be honest, are like shopping malls *manqué*, or are franchised like friendly neighbourhood fast food operations (e.g. the McGuggenheim in Bilbao), and shopping malls now look like museums, except that there's no entry charge. Carrier bags, posters and promotional paraphernalia are regularly displayed in art galleries and few would deny that the prices charged by, say, Kostabi or Koons have more to do with the signature – the brand name – than the mass-manufactured or, as often as not, sub-contracted artwork itself.

For many commentators, in truth, marketing- and consumption-related phenomena comprise the acme of postmodernism. Eagleton (1996: 133), to cite but one prominent academic authority, observes that 'many a business executive is a spontaneous postmodernist'. Yet marketing scholarship is anything but postmodern – tell you what, let's call it *neo-romanticism* – in tenor. Our journals are repositories of 'modern' marketing science – how does *neo-neoclassicism* grab you? – though a few neo-romantic rumbles have been heard on the distant horizon, a condition perhaps of our highly charged, crisis-ridden, *fin de siècle* intellectual climate. As Thompson notes in Chapter 4, these postmodern/neo-romantic researchers remain firmly on the margins of the discipline, partly through necessity, partly through choice and partly, one suspects, because of the inability or unwillingness of the centre to attend to their utterances.

The 'once more with feeling' part

Heteroglot though these voices crying in the neo-romantic wilderness undoubtedly are, the present volume has sought to bring a judicious selection of them together for your enlightenment and edification. What is more, by presenting them in a format familiar to the marketing mainstream – the generic textual mould beloved by the Big-Fat-Books-About-Marketing brigade – it is hoped that *Romancing the Market* will appeal to, rather than appal, the academic marketing masses. Open minds, warm welcomes, abundant bunting and a frazzled fatted calf are possibly too much to hope for in these sadly schismatic scholarly times – though we make a mean Bar-B-Q sauce – but, before we go our separate ways, it might be worthwhile reminding ourselves of a few key points arising from the foregoing chapters.

The first of these is that there's more than one way to skin a cat (and, Heaven only knows, Morris Holbrook has tried). Marketing's neo-neoclassical mind set is *not* the only way of looking at commercial milieux. The romantic, illuminist, counter-Enlightenment tradition described in the chapters by Brown, Power and Stern and Arnould *et al.*, goes back just as far – further, in fact. It is different from, not inferior to, perspectives predicated upon Enlightenment values, and postmodernism is merely the most recent of its many reincarnations. To dismiss neo-romantic marketing as a passing fad, an aberration, a temporary artefact of our discipline's mid-life crisis, is to peremptorily abandon a very long established, para-primordial, possibly innate worldview. To intimate that it is an irrelevance or indeed irrational is to ignore the importance of irrelevance and irrationality, as Jantzen and Østergaard cogently showed in Chapter 7. To suggest that it is a retrograde, backward or (surely not) degenerate step is to subscribe to the discredited Western myth of inexorable human and scientific progress. To believe that rigour, reason, rationality and rectitude are the be-all and end-all of marketing scholarship is short-sighted to the point of – well – myopia. Never forget that there are more things in heaven and earth, Theodore, than are dreamt of in your marketing philosophy.

A second point pertains to the sources and methods employed by marketing's neo-romantic fellowship. Following Rorty's (1989) recommendations that we look to imaginative literary genres like ethnography, journalism, comic books and docudramas for postmodern inspiration, our league of gentlepersons is moved by music (Brown), poetry (Holbrook), fine art (McAuley), novellas

(Belk), movies (Thompson), fashion designers (Heilbrunn), deconstructionists (Power and Stern) and, not least, the inner self (Maclaran and Stevens). It must be emphasised that these do not represent second-hand or substandard sources of 'evidence', as some mainstream marketers may mistakenly surmise, nor are they any less 'pure', 'natural' or 'elemental' than *real* empirical data. If anything, the reverse is true. The romantics maintained – and many commentators continue to maintain – that creative artists are better able to articulate the nature of the human condition than any number of well-meaning, washed-in-the-blood-of-the-scientific-method marketing researchers with their clipboards, show-cards, multicoloured pens and ersatz rapport-building patter. Granted, not everyone accepts the undeniably romantic contention that poetic insights are, or ought to be, privileged in the epistemological scheme of things, but at the very least it behooves us to acknowledge that while aesthetically refracted sources and methods are undeniably 'mediated', so too are questionnaires, interview transcripts, scanner data and the like. Let's not fall for the metaphysics of marketing presence, folks.

Another issue relates to the ostensible 'crisis of representation' that has plagued many other disciplines and is beginning to appear on the academic marketing agenda (see Stern 1998). This revolves around the growing belief that established methods of representing or depicting marketplace phenomena are no longer up to the task. The 'standard' scholarly paper (pick a journal, any journal), structured in the 'standard' scholarly sequence (introduction, problem, method, hypotheses, results, discussion, conclusion), containing the 'standard' scholarly concepts, models and frameworks (life is a boxes and arrows diagram), using the 'standard' styles of scholarly expression (third person, past tense, prosaic prose), just doesn't seem capable of capturing the world 'out there', everyday neo-romantic reality, the postmodern marketing condition. As McAuley expostulates in Chapter 12 (220–1)

> who decided that knowledge/meaning must be contained within the confines of 3–4,000 words? Who decided that two publications a year in so-called top journals constitutes a sensible way to gauge the pursuit of knowledge? Who decided that the size of the OHP screen would structure our presentations?

The response to this state of affairs has been twofold. On the one hand, new forms of representation are being espoused and experimented with by marketing academics. In the present volume, Holbrook has made the case for stereoscopic photographs, though other possibilities include video, radio, cartoons, music and the Internet. On the other hand, established modes of scholarly discourse are being supplemented by much more expressive/lyrical/poetic styles of writing. These neo-romantic modalities are epitomised by Maclaran and Stevens's stream-of-scholarly-consciousness, Thompson's show-me-the-logocentrism and Arnould *et al*'s powerful evocation of the evocative power of magic (though I suppose my own admittedly amateurish scribblings in

Chapter 8 might just qualify – at a pinch, I grant you, and only because I'm a good friend of the editors).

Of course, the basic problem with alternative forms of representation is that they raise two other very important issues concerning legitimisation and relevance. Legitimisation refers to the fact that new modes of discourse cannot be judged by established criteria of assessment – validity, reliability, objectivity, truth, etc. Well, they can and are judged by such standards but, given the manifest inappropriateness of such standards, new literary forms are certain to come up short, 'failure' is inevitable, a foregone conclusion, a racing certainty. The corollary, then, is what criteria *should* be applied to alternative approaches? What constitutes 'good' work in, say, stereoscopy or stream-of-scholarly-consciousness? The answers to these questions do not feature *in* the present book, though they are likely to be features *of* it. That is to say, it is the reviewers and the academic community as a whole – using whatever undefined criteria they employ – who will pass judgement on the legitimacy of *Romancing the Market* and decide whether or not the present text passes muster.

Even if this book is dismissed out of hand by all and sundry, that does not necessarily mean they are right or correct in their assessment. It merely means that they are in a position of sufficient power to make their opinions heard, attended to and 'count'. (If anybody detects a whiff of getting one's retaliation in first about this disingenuous argument, you're just the sort of person who should be prevented from reviewing *Romancing the Market*. Neo-romantic sympathisers only need apply.) Many, however, might quite reasonably wonder what it's all about, what's the point of this type of text, what possible *relevance* it has to marketing as a whole. To my mind, these types of question are of paramount importance, though this is possibly not the place to address them in detail (wriggle, wriggle). However, the issue of 'relevance' was alluded to in a number of chapters – Wensley's and McAuley's, most notably – and several of the contributors have elsewhere expounded on this particularly thorny topic.

It seems to me that there are at least two sides to this question, which for convenience we can term *purpose* and *produce*. First, what is the purpose of what we do as academics? Apart from pedagogic considerations, is it our job to 'assist' marketing practitioners, as Wensley and McAuley seem to think, or to undertake 'pure' research for its own sake, as Belk (1995) and Holbrook (1995) have heretofore indicated (see Brownlie and Saren 1997)? Second, what kind of academic 'produce' should we be producing? Do we stick with the neo-neo-classical stuff that has – hmmm – served us so well in the past, and occupies approximately 90 per cent of the space in our journals, or opt for the kinds of kite-flying neo-romanticism contained in many of the chapters herein? Horses for courses, of course, is the obvious answer to both. Some academics are pragmatists, others are purists, some are model-builders and others aren't. But the basic problem is that practitioner-orientated pragmatism is privileged over pure scholarship within our discipline, as is the 'standard' scholarly product over blue-sky buffoonery. Yet the evidence clearly indicates that practitioners are not impressed with extant academic output (Brown 1998b). It follows, then, that the 'Midwestern empiricists' cannot continue to wrap themselves in the flag of relevance, albeit their neo-neoclassical endeavours can continue to be justified as pure research. Conversely, is the work of the neo-romantics completely irrelevant to practitioners? Yes it is, but only if relevance is narrowly defined as a matrix, a model, an algorithm, a framework or, God help us, one of those blank pages (sorry, 'worksheets') that you often find in practitioner-orientated texts. But *not* if relevance means helping practitioners think about the nature of marketing. Indeed, the ultimate irony is that 'pure' postmodern research (that is, research conducted by academics in non-business disciplines) is literally full of references to marketing managers, strategies, advertising campaigns and the contemporary marketing condition.

Important though these political concerns are – not least because our definition of what marketing 'is' has serious implications for the careers of those academics who don't accept the accepted definition – they boil down to what I have elsewhere grandiosely termed, *l'esprit du marketing* (Brown 1997). To my mind, marketing is essentially romantic in spirit. Magic is its *métier*. Imagination, inspiration, insurrection, incantation, instauration and illumination its watchwords. Marketing, to put it in a nutshell, is a bit raffish, a bit rambunctious, a bit of a lovable rogue. When asked, for example, how he managed to make his *pawnshop* so signally and consistently successful, the manager of what must surely rank as one of the hardest of hard marketing stations, recounted the following morality tale:

> The majority of people who pawned items redeemed them. But one item was consistently left behind: Polaroid cameras. I think the reason was that the film for the camera was expensive. People bought the cameras for the instant gratification, but dropped them for the cost. It took creative salesmanship to move those cameras. We invested in a few rolls of Polaroid film and always kept at least one camera loaded. If a customer was considering buying a Polaroid or even just looking at one, we had this little drama. Pretending that we didn't know the camera was loaded, we demonstrated how simple it was to work and we *accidentally* took a picture of the customer. Sixty seconds later, when the picture was done, so was the sale.
>
> One lesson here is the power of demonstration, but more important is the power of magic. People love to be amazed, and creating magic has become a key tool in the marketing process. Sometimes the magic is technological, like the electronic scanners at supermarkets or the grocery cards that credit a customer for all the coupons being offered. Or it can be about service, like the kind offered by a furniture superstore when it rains: teenagers with umbrellas run out to the cars to escort customers into the store.
>
> We looked for the magic every day in the products we sold, or we created magic in the way we sold them. It was just another day in the pawnshop.
>
> (Rossin 1997: 12)

In my opinion, the fundamental problem with the marketing philosophy, as it is presently constituted, is that it assumes marketing practice must be whiter than white, that marketers must adore and abase themselves before their customers, that the uncouth side of commercial life is not 'proper' marketing as such and ought to be extirpated. Not so, I say. It should be built upon and celebrated. There's absolutely nothing wrong with being cheap and cheerful, or a little bit vulgar (as the romantic poets maintained in their time and as post-modernists maintain today). Marketing hails from the wrong side of the academic tracks and there's no need to be ashamed of it or pretend we're something we're not. Lest there is any misunderstanding, however, let me emphasise that I am not for a moment suggesting marketers should rip their customers off, except in so far as the rip-off is compensated by an intangible feelgood (or even feelbad) factor. Marketing is magic, marketing is fun, marketing is amazing, but we seem to have forgotten the fact. Certainly, there is very little magic, fun or amazement in the academic marketing literature. It's time for a change, I say, a change for the worse. In our neo-romantic, topsy-turvy world, remember, bad is good, worse is better, worst is best . . .

The 'humbuggery' part

Clearly, my romantic desire to re-manticise marketing, to reinstate its inherent magic, to re-illuminate marketing letters, is bound to be dismissed by the scholarly mainstream as an illusion at best or hallucination at worst. It might even earn me the coveted 'Walter Mitty of Marketing' label, for good measure. A role model is called for, I'm sure you agree. Time to unleash the fourth B of marketing illuminations alluded to in an earlier note (you do read the notes, don't you?). The person I'm thinking of dates from the romantic period, was a contemporary of Freddy eternal recurrence Nietzsche, and he was not only one of the first but one of the best marketing men of all time. I'm referring to P.T. Barnum (1810–91). That's right, Phineas Taylor Barnum, the greatest-show-on-earth Barnum, the one-born-every-minute Barnum, the never-give-a-sucker-an-even-break Barnum, the roll-up-roll-up-see-the-bearded-lady Barnum, the 'sun of the amusement world' Barnum, 'from which all lesser luminaries borrow light' (Kunhardt et al. 1995: 253). Entrepreneur, impresario, museum curator, three-ring circus inventor and freakshow facto-tum, Barnum was a chiseller, charlatan, chancer, cheat, coxcomb, cozener and con-artist supreme. He was also a marketing practitioner nonpareil. Barnum believed in ripping people off, but he did so in such an enjoyable, entertain-ing and endearing way that consumers flocked to have their hard-earned money misappropriated. A satisfied dissatisfied customer, surely, is the epitome, the Everest, the Evander Holyfield of marketing achievement (Harris 1973; Saxon 1989).

Consider, for instance, the Joice Heth hoax. She was the purported 161-year-old 'nanny' of George Washington, no less, who was exhibited around the country to huge crowds, keen to hear tales of the founding father's childhood,

268

only to be exposed as a mere 80-year-old fake. Then there was the Fiji Mermaid stunt of 1842, which comprised the tail of a fish and the body of an orang-utan (Barnum wrote anonymous letters to the newspapers 'denouncing' it as a fix, thereby attracting even more punters determined to check for themselves). Then there was the 'free' buffalo hunt in Hoboken, New Jersey, where Barnum negotiated a secret cut from the Hudson River ferry operators, massive crowds of New Yorkers made the trip, and, needless to say, the four forlorn buffaloes failed to stampede on cue. Then there was the celebrated 'white' elephant episode of 1882. Disappointed with the colour of his expensive acquisition, the great man gave it a couple of clandestine coats of Dulux Brilliant White (and when informed that the 'white' elephant of a rival circus had died, Barnum famously retorted 'It was dyed already'). And then, of course, there was the sublime Jumbo the Giant Elephant soap opera. He purchased the prodigious pachyderm from the Royal Zoological Gardens in London; engineered an enormous public outcry about its imminent departure to the Colonies (newspaper campaigns, protest songs, parliamentary debates, pleading letters from the royal family, etc.); brilliantly exploited the recalcitrant beast's refusal to enter its beautifully appointed transporter cabinet ('Let him lie there for a week if he wants to,' Barnum wired, 'it's the best advertisement in the world'); organised a 'victory parade' through the streets of New York from the docks to Madison Square Garden (where Barnum's circus was just about to open, conveniently enough); and not only made a fortune from Jumbo memorabilia but recouped his entire investment within three weeks of the gala opening night (the word 'jumbo' also entered common parlance at this point).

Above and beyond his staggering marketing skills, Barnum was a superb public speaker. He used to go on huge speaking tours of America and Europe. So successful were they, that he paid off his massive personal debts – incurred by ill-advised property speculation – on the strength of his oratorical abilities alone. And you'll never guess what he talked about. Got it in one. The principles of marketing. Granted, his keynote speeches were entitled 'The Art of Making Money' and, naturally, 'The Art of Losing Money', but they were about what we today would call marketing management. This was in the 1850s, 1860s and 1870s, remember, long before there were marketing courses, degrees, textbooks and the like. These Principles of Barnumarketing included (it's bullet-point time, boys and girls, keep your heads down):

- Drive ahead.
- Don't spare the steam.
- Select the right location.
- Make all the noise possible.
- Be systematic.
- Keep down the expenses.
- Don't get above your business.
- Use lots of light.

His golden rule of golden rules, however, was that there are 'various trades and occupations which need only notoriety to ensure success, always provided that when customers are once attracted they never fail to get their money's worth'. . . 'The Mermaid, Joice Heth etc were used by me as skyrockets or advertisements to draw attraction to the Museum,' he explained. 'I don't believe in duping the public, but I believe in first *attracting* and then pleasing them' (Kunhardt *et al.* 1995: 47).

Indeed, it doesn't take a great deal of textual Barnumesquery to demonstrate that the great man was a proto-neo-romantic marketer. If, as argued earlier, PoRo consists of pervasiveness, definitional difficulties, a radical–reactionary trajectory, high and low combined, anti-science inclinations, incessant movement and an ironic outlook, then Barnum fits the bill on all counts.[4] He was nothing if not ubiquitous, possibly the most famous man of his time. Aside from Ulysses S. Grant's celebrated statement that he 'was the best known man in the world', letters addressed to 'Barnum, America' reached their destination as a matter of course. He was impossible to pin down or define. Was Barnum a showman, museum curator, philanthropist, impresario, orator, property developer, best-selling author, newspaperman, bankrupt, con-man, collector (of stereoscopic photographs!) or mere marketing man extraordinaire? He started as a classic rebel, prankster and self-styled 'Prince of Humbugs' – reviled by polite society – yet ended his life lauded by princes and presidents alike and hailed as one of the greatest men of the nineteenth century. Barnum's *New York Times* obituary was even printed in advance so that the man himself could peruse and comment on it. He successfully straddled high and low culture, not simply by means of his 'museum', which was conveniently situated equidistant from the Bowery slums and high society New York, nor on account of the fact that he effectively rescued the theatre for families and upper-class audiences (Barnum's shows were spotlessly clean and wholesome, whereas the theatre was then regarded as sordid and sinful), but *contra* the servile style of commercial discourse that then prevailed, he wrote his advertisements, newspaper articles, books and general gallimaufry in vivid vernacular language.

What is more, although he was a great enthusiast for, and exploiter of, new technology – railroads, electric light, telegraph, etc. – Barnum had little time for the dry and dusty side of science, as his carnivalesque 'museum' and peripatetic circuses readily testified (albeit the circus was not billed as such but as a 'Grand Traveling Museum, Menagerie, Caravan and Hippodrome').[5] Movement, indeed, was a constant feature of Barnum's existence, from his days as an itinerant impresario with Jenny 'the-Swedish-nightingale' Lind and General Tom Thumb (two years touring the capitals of Europe), to his last incandescent, intercontinental huzzah, the 1889-90 'Greatest Show on Earth' in London's Olympia Auditorium. Irony, parody and playfulness, furthermore, were an integral part of Barnum's larger than life character. Despite his strict Calvinist upbringing (shades of Campbell), he was a prankster without peer. To cite but a single example, when the Joice Heth hoax was discovered during her autopsy, Barnum convinced the proprietor of the *New York Herald*, one of the most august newspapers of the time, that the 161-year-old was not only alive and well, but playing to packed houses in Boston. The proprietor fell for the bait, published a spurious 'Heth Lives!' story and, when the prank was duly revealed, became a national laughing stock. Barnum then and there realised that, 'The truth, the whole truth, and nothing but the truth was not a necessity. In fact, whenever there was a whiff of doubt about the authenticity of what the public crowded to see, so much the better' (Kunhardt *et al.* 1995: 20).

The real significance of P.T. Barnum, however, lies not in his superlative, if hitherto unacknowledged, contributions to the practice and theory of marketing (he could tell as well as show); nor the stupendous financial success achieved on the back of his commercial humbuggery (he was one of the richest men in America); nor his solid grounding in the marketing system (a grocery store-keeper to start, he also worked as a wholesaler, publican, auctioneer, lottery agent, advertising copywriter and, believe it or not, mousetrap salesman); nor his lifelong interest in the occult (he denounced the quackery of mediums, psychics and clairvoyants yet exhibited all sorts of 'supernatural sights', 'spiritual manifestations', 'black art triumphs' and 'matchless works of magic'); nor, to repeat, the fact that he was adored by his customers even as he shamelessly ripped them off. *The real lesson, rather, resides in the neoclassical side of this great marketing romantic.* This neoclassical side was called Bailey, James A. Bailey. Bailey was the organiser, the arranger, the fixer, the efficiency expert behind the scenes, whereas Barnum was the marketing magician. The pinnacle of their joint endeavour, the above mentioned 'Greatest Show' in London, illustrates this perfectly:

> The logistics for the journey were staggering – it would take a small fleet to cross the Atlantic with a menagerie, carfuls of equipment and gear, bandwagons, an enormous herd of horses, Roman chariots, costumes galore, eight tons of posters and ads, and 1,240 performers. But that was Bailey's job, exactly the kind of complex management he was skilled at. It was Bailey's task to construct slings that would lift elephants and camels aboard, to measure every cage and wagon so all would fit snugly, to dream up the idea of freezing the meat for all the flesh-eating animals. It was the job of Bailey's 79-year-old, white-haired partner to make sure that for three months a man named Barnum was on the tip of every last Britisher's tongue.
>
> (Kunhardt *et al.* 1995: 337)

I think I can speak for every contributor to this book when I say that it is not our intention to suggest that academic marketing should dispense with its neoclassical side and replace it with romanticism. Attractive though that counter-revolutionary possibility undeniably is – not least when the mainstream denounces postmodernists as chimerical pseudo-intellectuals (now you know where flattery gets you) – it is necessary to acknowledge that

271

neoclassicism has and will continue to have its place in the great marketing scheme of things. To my mind, the basic problem with marketing scholarship is that there is too much Bailey and not enough Barnum. It should be Barnum & Bailey, remember, not Bailey & Barnum and, after approximately 100 years of academic endeavour, it's about time we got them in the right order.

The 'unbearable lightness of marketing' part

Conclusions, as every author knows, are awkward beasts, a bit like Jumbo the recumbent elephant. The rapidly diminishing pile of rectos informs the reader that the end is nigh, the twist in the tale is imminent, the who-dun-it is about to be revealed. Expectations are raised, the entire text is on the line, the writer's do or die time has arrived. Will it be a happy, sad, ironic, outrageous, unexpected or unreliable ending? Will it be an open ending (stopping in the middle of a conversation à la Henry James's *The Ambassadors*), an ambiguous ending (John Fowles' *The French Lieutenant's Woman*), an ending about endings (David Lodge's *Changing Places*) or an ending about beginnings (James Joyce's *Finnegans Wake*)? The beginning of the end is nigh.

To be sure, such denouement dilemmas rarely trouble the neo-neoclassicists of the marketing academy, since it's simply a matter of recapitulating the overall argument and noting that – all together now – further research is necessary. Neo-romantic marketing types aren't so lucky, though we could of course resort to reflecting on the 'further research is necessary' cliché or even indulge in metatextual reflections on textual reflections on the 'further research is necessary' cliché (though it goes without saying that further research on this metatextual issue is necessary). These finishing frustrations are reinforced when we're dealing with the conclusion of a concluding chapter which concludes with a conclusion about conclusions . . .

As you've probably gathered, I desperately need a get out of jail free card and, fortunately, Freddy eternal recurrence Nietzsche is ever ready to lend a hand. The essential question, then, is if I had to write this conclusion all over again would I start with a conclusion about conclusions? No. What I would do instead is restate the eternal recurrence thesis and ruminate on the unbearable lightness of marketing. But, as everyone knows, events do not recur and hence we're struck with this inconclusive conclusion, left floundering in an aporia of endings, the terminal building of terminations. Or are we?

Let's try again. Few would deny that marketing has proved to be an extraordinarily successful academic discipline. As we are repeatedly informed, it emerged from the rib of economics at the turn of the present century; reinvented itself in the middle-to-late 1950s thanks to Drucker, Levitt, Keith, McKitterick, McCarthy and manifold other exponents of total customer orientation; and, despite the disenchanted demurral of diverse dyspeptics, delinquents and drop-outs, it seems set fair for an even more illustrious future of conceptual achievement and cerebral renown. Certainly, copious commentators on the state of late twentieth-century marketing scholarship concur that just as its past is glorious, so too its future is bright (e.g. Kerin 1996; Lehmann and Jocz 1997; Malhotra 1996). Provided, of course, we all stick together, embrace the relationship marketing paradigm (what else is there?) and 'refuse to be distracted by the siren voices of postmodern promiscuity, importuned by the sodomites of post-structuralism or seduced by any analogous whores of intellectual Babylon' (Brown 1996: 253).

If, however, we had to do it all over again – or were condemned to do it again by the eternal return of the academic same – would we pursue managerial relevance rather than pure scholarship?; aspire to the dizzy heights of (pseudo)scientific status?; broaden the marketing concept into domains where it is manifestly unwarranted?; develop asinine, emotionless, reductionist frameworks of consumer and buyer behaviour?; or champion organisation-wide espousal of the marketing philosophy at the cost of de-layered and re-engineered marketing departments? Would we continue to consort with economists?; embrace model-builders with a passion?; or dally with the charlatans of strategy (who have, so we're told, consistently stolen all of marketing's conceptual clothes)? Would we simper before the macho my-hard-disk-is-bigger-than-yours men of statistical callisthenics, mathematical manipulation and (if only it were true) pumping irony? Would we prostrate ourselves at the feet of the paradigm shifters of relationship marketing, even though it is little more than a rehash of the original marketing concept? And, most fundamentally of all, would we continue to embrace our ever-onward, ever-upward, higher and higher, shoulders of giants, more is good, things can only get better, progressivist ideology of the absurd? Marketing, don't you know, is the best a man can get. Well, that's what the textbooks tell us . . .

The beauty of modern marketing, of course, is that we are not condemned to do it all over again. Thanks to the prevalence of the linear, progressive model of time, our errors of omission and commission are behind us; we can put away our childish things; and revel in the lightness of marketing being. After all, 'the absolute absence of a burden causes man to be lighter than air, to soar into the heights, take leave of the earth and his earthly being, and become only half real, his movements as free as they are insignificant (Kundera 1984: 5). Thus, we can be creative, be innovative, be different, be radical, be original – unless, admittedly, our current belief in linear time is also due to recur at some yet to be determined point(s) in the future.

But, even if we are correct about non-recurrence, how can we cope with the crushing burden of lightness? How creative should we be? How much innovation can we accommodate? Does difference really make a difference? When does radical become reactionary? What's so original about originality? Will, in our unfettered postmodern world, the discipline bounce up like a compressed spring now that the shackles of modern marketing are dissolved or has the field been squashed flat by the oppressive weight of our 'distinguished' past? And, does anyone really care anyway?

Regardless of how well we deal with Kundera's (1984: 6) 'most mysterious, most ambiguous of all' dilemmas, the unbearable lightness of marketing is ultimately liberatory. By raising the very prospect of doing it all over again and drawing attention to the sheer pervasiveness of the progressivist model of marketing time, it suggests that alternative possibilities are available to us. By drawing upon the creative, spontaneous, imaginative ethos of the romantics, this book has sought to highlight some of these methodological, epistemological, representational and indeed inspirational options. Not every contributor, admittedly, sees things the same way but we all share a desire to change the marketing script, to free the marketing spirit, to light a candle for the future of marketing. Let's set sail on the marketing love-boat, let's tie the marketing love-knot, let's send a marketing love-letter. After all, as the old advertising byline for Mills and Boon reminds us, 'you can't have too much romance'.

No, that's not a very good ending either. Let's give it another shot. I know, we'll finish with the dying words of Goethe, one of the greatest thinkers of all time, possessor of the largest vocabulary ever recorded (estimated 50,000 words, more than twice Shakespeare's) and, thanks to *Werther* and *Faust*,[6] perhaps the principal progenitor of the romantic movement. His final utterance, appropriately enough, was 'Mehr Licht' (more light), though the precise meaning of this expression remains moot. Did he mean, 'Open the curtains, a tad'? Was he referring, as the psychoanalyst Otto Rank avers, to the first glimpse of daylight on emerging from the womb? Or, was he speaking about the light of insight, inspiration, imagination, illuminism and romance? 'Mehr Licht', indeed.

The 'notes' part

1 To paraphrase a military titan of the romantic era, Routledge Expects!

2 'The hero of the internalised quest is the poet himself, the antagonists of quest are everything in the self that blocks imaginative work, and the fulfilness is never the poem itself but the poem beyond that is made possible by the apocalypse of the imagination' (Bloom 1970: 19).

3 'In Tieck's plays there is a deliberate attempt to confound the imaginary and the real: characters in the play (or in a play within the play) criticise the play, complain about the plot, and about the equipment of the theatre; members of the audience expostulate and demand that the illusion, on which all drama rests, be preserved; they are in turn answered sharply by the play's characters from the stage, to the bewilderment of the real audience; at times musical keys and dynamic tempi engage in dialogues with each other' (Berlin 1991: 233).

4 Some of the more observant among you may have noticed that I've overlooked romanticism's emphasis on the Self. (By the way, if you have and are scouring this note for a proper explanation, you really ought to get out more.) Actually this is an intriguing one. While it could be argued that Barnum reinvented himself – brilliantly, it has to be said – on many occasions, his real forte lay in reinventing the selves of his employees. The most extravagant biographies were concocted for his collection of 'freaks' – giants, dwarves, missing links, fat boys, living skeletons, Circassian beauties and the like.

5 Barnum was officially recognised by the Smithsonian as a 'distinguished promoter of the

natural sciences', though 'unlike the scientist, Barnum could never let evidence speak for itself. He liked to dress it up, give it a spin all his own' (Kunhardt et al 1995: ix).

6 Numerous historical figures have been posited as the prototype of Faust, but one of the strongest contenders is our old friend Paracelsus (see Pachter 1961).

The 'references' part

Abrams, M.H. (1971), *Natural Supernaturalism: Tradition and Revolution in Romantic Literature*, New York: W.W. Norton.

Anderson, W.T. (1995), *The Fontana Postmodernism Reader*, London: HarperCollins.

Appignanesi, R. and Garratt, C. (1995), *Postmodernism for Beginners*, Cambridge: Icon.

Behler, E. (1990), *Irony and the Discourse of Modernity*, Seattle: University of Washington Press.

Belk, R.W. (1995), 'Studies in the new consumer behaviour', in D. Miller (ed.), *Acknowledging Consumption: A Review of New Studies*, London: Routledge, 58–95.

Belk, R.W. (1997), 'Been there, done that, bought the souvenirs: of journeys and boundary crossings', in S. Brown and D. Turley (eds), *Consumer Research: Postcards from the Edge*, London: Routledge, 22–45.

Berlin, I. (1981), 'The counter-Enlightenment', in I. Berlin, *Against the Current: Essays in the History of Ideas*, Oxford: Clarendon, 1–24.

Berlin, I. (1991), 'The apotheosis of the romantic will: the revolt against the myth of an ideal world', in I. Berlin (ed.), *The Crooked Timber of Humanity: Chapters in the History of Ideas*, London: Collins, 207–37.

Bertens, H. (1995), *The Idea of the Postmodern*, London: Routledge.

Bloom, H. (1970), 'The internalisation of quest romance', in H. Bloom, *The Ringers in the Tower: Studies in Romantic Tradition*, Chicago: University of Chicago Press, 12–35.

Brown, S. (1995a), 'Postmodernism, the wheel of retailing and will to power', *International Review of Retail, Distribution and Consumer Research*, 5(3), 287–310.

Brown, S. (1995b), *Postmodern Marketing*, London: Routledge.

Brown, S. (1995c), 'Christaller knew my father: recycling central place theory', *Journal of Macromarketing*, 15 (Spring), 60–73.

Brown, S. (1996), 'Art or science?: fifty years of marketing debate', *Journal of Marketing Management*, 12(4), 243–67.

Brown, S. (1997), 'The end of the illusion: millennial madness, *fin de siècle* fever and postmodern marketing apocalypse', *Marketing Insights* (Internet journal).

Brown, S. (1998a), 'The unbearable lightness of marketing: a neo-romantic, counter-revolutionary recapitulation', in S. Brown, A.M. Doherty and B. Clarke (eds), *Romancing the Market*, London: Routledge, 255–7.

Brown, S. (1998b), *Postmodern Marketing Two: Telling Tales*, London: ITBP.

Brown, S., Bell, J. and Carson, D.J. (1996), 'Apocaholics anonymous: looking back on the end of marketing', in S. Brown, J. Bell and D.J. Carson, *Marketing Apocalypse: Eschatology, Escapology and the Illusion of the End*, London: Routledge, 1–20.

Brown, S. and Turley, D. (1997), 'Travelling in trope: postcards from the edge of consumer research', in S. Brown and D. Turley (eds), *Consumer Research: Postcards from the Edge*, London: Routledge, 1–21.

Brownlie, D. and Saren, M. (1997), 'Beyond the one-dimensional marketing manager: the discourse of theory, practice and relevance', *International Journal of Research in Marketing*, 14(2), 147–61.

Bygrave, S. (1986), *Coleridge and the Self: Romantic Egotism*, Basingstoke: Macmillan.

Callinicos, A. (1989), *Against Postmodernism: A Marxist Critique*, Cambridge: Polity.

Callinicos, A. (1995), 'Postmodernism as normal science', *British Journal of Sociology*, 46 (December), 134–9.

Campbell, C. (1987), *The Romantic Ethic and the Spirit of Modern Consumerism*, Oxford: Blackwell.

Campion, N. (1994), *The Great Year: Astrology, Millenarianism and History in the Western Tradition*, Harmondsworth: Arkana.

Childers, J. and Hentzi, G. (1995), 'Irony', in J. Childers and G. Hentzi (eds), *The Columbia Dictionary of Modern Literary and Cultural Criticism*, New York: Columbia University Press, 160–1.

Clay, J. (1981 [1980]), *Romanticism*, trans. D. Wheeler and C. Owen, Oxford: Phaidon.

Cohn, N. (1970), *The Pursuit of the Millennium*, London: Pimlico.

Cranston, M. (1994), *The Romantic Movement*, Oxford: Blackwell.

Eagleton, T. (1996), *The Illusions of Postmodernism*, Oxford: Blackwell.

Elam, D. (1992), *Romancing the Postmodern*, London: Routledge.

Frye, N. (ed.) (1963), *Romanticism Reconsidered*, New York: Columbia University Press.

Furst, L.R. (1969), *Romanticism in Perspective: A Comparative Study of Aspects of the Romantic Movements in England, France and Germany*, Basingstoke: Macmillan.

Garner, R. (1996), *Contemporary Movements and Ideologies*, New York: McGraw-Hill.

Gellner, E. (1992), *Postmodernism, Reason and Religion*, London: Routledge.

Gergen, K.J. (1991), *The Saturated Self: Dilemmas of Identity in Contemporary Life*, New York: Basic Books.

Giddens, A. (1990), *The Consequences of Modernity*, Cambridge: Polity.

Gray, M. (1992), 'Irony', in M. Gray (ed.), *A Dictionary of Literary Terms*, Harlow: Longman, 153-4.

Grenz, S.J. (1996), *A Primer on Postmodernism*, Grand Rapids: Eerdmans.

Harris, N. (1973), *Humbug: The Art of P.T. Barnum*, New York: Little, Brown and Co.

Harvey, D. (1989), *The Condition of Postmodernity*, Oxford: Blackwell.

Hobsbawm, E. (1973), *The Age of Revolution: Europe 1789–1848*, London: Abacus.

Holbrook, M.B. (1995), *Consumer Research: Introspective Essays on the Study of Consumption*, Thousand Oaks, CA: Sage.

Honour, H. (1981), *Romanticism*, London: Allen Lane.

Hutcheon, L. (1994), *Irony's Edge: The Theory and Politics of Irony*, London: Routledge.

Jameson, F. (1991), *Postmodernism, or, The Cultural Logic of Late Capitalism*, London: Verso.

Jencks, C. (1989), *What is Postmodernism?*, London: Academy Editions.

Kaplan, C. (1996), *Questions of Travel: Postmodern Discourses of Displacement*, Durham, NC: Duke University Press.

Kerin, R.A. (1996), 'In pursuit of an ideal: the editorial and literary history of the *Journal of Marketing*', *Journal of Marketing*, 60(1), 1–13.

Kumar, K. (1995), 'Apocalypse, millennium and utopia today', in M. Bull (ed.), *Apocalypse Theory and the Ends of the World*, Oxford: Blackwell, 200–24.

Kundera, M. (1984), *The Unbearable Lightness of Being*, trans. M.H. Heim, New York: HarperCollins.

Kunhardt, P.B., Kunhardt, P.B. Jnr, and Kunhardt, P.W. (1995), *P.T. Barnum: America's Greatest Showman*, New York: Knopf.

Lehmann, D.R. and Jocz, K.E. (eds) (1997), *Reflections on the Futures of Marketing: Practice and Education*, Cambridge: Marketing Science Institute.

Livingston, I. (1998), *Arrow of Chaos: Romanticism and Postmodernity*, Minneapolis: University of Minnesota Press.

Lyons, J.O. (1978), *The Invention of the Self*, Carbondale: Southern Illinois University Press.

Lyotard, J-F. (1984 [1979]), *The Postmodern Condition: A Report on Knowledge*, trans. G. Bennington and B. Massumi, Manchester: Manchester University Press.

Lystra, K. (1989), *Searching the Heart: Women, Men and Romantic Love in Nineteenth-Century America*, New York: Oxford University Press.

Malhotra, N.K. (1996), 'The impact of the Academy of Marketing Science on marketing scholarship: an analysis of the research published in *JAMS*', *Journal of the Academy of Marketing Science*, 24(4), 291–8.

Pachter, H.M. (1961), *Paracelsus: Magic into Science*, New York: Collier Books.

Porter, R. and Teich, M. (eds) (1988), *Romanticism in National Context*, Cambridge: Cambridge University Press.

Readings, B. and Schaber, B. (eds) (1993), *Postmodernism Across the Ages: Essays for a Postmodernity That Wasn't Born Yesterday*, Syracuse: Syracuse University Press.

Rorty, R. (1989), *Contingency, Irony and Solidarity*, Cambridge: Cambridge University Press.

Rose, M.A. (1993), *Parody: Ancient, Modern and Post-modern*, Cambridge: Cambridge University Press.

Rosenau, P.M. (1992), *Post-modernism and the Social Sciences: Insights, Inroads and Intrusions*, Princeton, NJ: Princeton University Press.

Rossin, J.E. (1997), 'At the pawnshop: lessons in creativity', *New York Times*, Sunday 13 April, 3, 12.

Saxon, A.H. (1989), *P.T. Barnum: The Legend and the Man*, New York: Columbia University Press.

Scruton, R. (1994), *Modern Philosophy: An Introduction and Survey*, London: Sinclair-Stevenson.

Shaffer, E. (1995), 'Secular apocalypse: prophets and apocalyptics at the end of the eighteenth century', in M. Bull (ed.), *Apocalypse Theory and the Ends of the World*, Oxford: Blackwell, 137-58.

Simpson, D. (1993), *Romanticism, Nationalism and the Revolt Against Theory*, Chicago: University of Chicago Press.

Simpson, D. (1995), *The Academic Postmodern and the Rule of Literature: A Report on Half-Knowledge*, Chicago: University of Chicago Press.

Stern, B.B. (ed.) (1998), *Representing Consumers: Voices, Views and Visions*, London: Routledge.

Talmon, J.L. (1979), *Romanticism and Revolt: Europe 1815–1848*, New York: Norton.

Tarnas, R. (1991), *The Passion of the Western Mind*, London: Pimlico.

Trompf, G.W. (1979), *The Idea of Historical Recurrence in Western Thought: From Antiquity to the Reformation*, Berkeley: University of California Press.

Ward, G. (1997), *Teach Yourself Postmodernism*, London: Hodder and Stoughton.

Watkins, A. (1991), 'Mr Heseltine may get his secret wish', *The Observer*, Sunday 20 October, 21.

Wellek, R. and Warren, A. (1963), *Theory of Literature*, San Diego: Harcourt Brace.

Wu, D. (1997), 'Introduction', in D. Wu (ed.), *Romanticism: An Anthology*, Oxford: Blackwell, xxx–xxxviii.

INDEX

279